# Street Vendors in the Global Urban Economy

# Street Vendors in the Global Urban Economy

Editor
## Sharit K. Bhowmik

Routledge
Taylor & Francis Group

LONDON AND NEW YORK

First published 2010 by Routledge

2 Park Square, Milton Park, Abingdon, Oxfordshire OX14 4RN
52 Vanderbilt Avenue, New York, NY 10017

*Routledge is an imprint of the Taylor & Francis Group, an informa business*

First issued in paperback 2019

Transferred to Digital Printing 2010

*Typeset by*
Star Compugraphics Private Limited
D–156, Second Floor
Sector 7, Noida 201 301

British Library Cataloguing-in-Publication Data
A catalogue record of this book is available from the British Library

ISBN: 978-0-415-55372-8 (hbk)
ISBN: 978-0-367-17647-1 (pbk)

# Contents

*Sally Roever*

# List of Tables

# List of Maps

# Foreword

Renana Jhabvala

This is an important book because it speaks for the urban poor, bringing us the lives that are usually hidden, papered over by commercial interests and advertising gloss. It shows us that the poor are a reality in every city, that they contribute to the economy and growth of the city, that they add vitality and life to the city, that city managers do grapple with their issues. Most of all, it points us towards plans and policies which can ensure that cities become inclusive and more equitable.

Cities are growing rapidly in most parts of the world as people migrate in search of a better life. This growth creates intense competition for the resources of the city and increasing inequalities between those who contribute to the growth of the city through their labour, and those who benefit from the city's links with the global economy. The term 'World Class Cities' has caught the imagination of city managers, and there is a sense of pride in becoming 'world class'. But what does a world class city really mean to these city managers and the vocal city dwellers who promote it?

The idea of a world class city in developing countries today is really a city of the rich, of high-rise buildings, global companies, multi-lane highways, luxury hotels. It is an imagined city where the poor do not exist, they have been transformed (miraculously) into a middle class, or they have been evicted. The reality is of course very different; cities are built by the labour and the hard work of the poor as much as by the finance of the rich, and in most cities in developing countries the 'world class' people remain a small minority, while the poor and the middle classes form the majority, struggling for existence in an often harsh environment.

In most developing countries, the image tends to be promoted as the reality. Except for an occasional *Slumdog Millionaire* the lives of the urban poor are effaced from statistics, from the media, from research, and from the consciousness of those who make or influence city policy. Even where the poor are obvious and visible, such as the thousands of street vendors on the roads and markets in every city, their existence is denied with phrases such as, 'these are transients and will disappear soon', or 'they have no right to be there', or they are 'obstructions to traffic'. As Caroline Skinner in her chapter in this book, 'Street Trading Trends in Africa: A Critical Review', points out:

> This is connected to the focus in urban studies, policy and practise on 'world class' cities. Beaverstock, Taylor and Smith's work (2002) is a classic text in this literature. They establish a roster of world cities. . . . As Robinson (2002: 563) outlines, the notion of 'world' or 'global' cities has the effect of 'dropping most cities in the world from vision'. The position and functioning of cities in the world economy thus becomes the dominant factor in urban economic development planning. The implicit economic development policy prescriptions are that international investment should be pursued above all else. Informal activities, like street vending, in this paradigm, are seen as undesirable and their contribution to local economies is not recognised.

I have been associated with the struggles of street vendors ever since I joined the Self Employed Women's Association (SEWA) in 1977. Women street vendors were some of SEWA's first members more than 35 years ago in Ahmedabad, and led by Ela Bhatt (see Bhat 2006), the founder of SEWA, we struggled for many years with the municipal officials and with the police until we realised that the problems were much deeper than an uncooperative municipality and hostile policemen.[1] We realised that the municipal laws did not have any space for street vendors at all, and that the police laws required that they be 'cleared away'; no matter what actions we took, the street vendors were always going to be 'illegal'. We realised that the rallies we took out, the dharnas we held, the negotiations we entered into, would make police actions less brutal for a while, or would save the street vendors their space till the next official in the municipality was appointed, or the next board was elected. The solutions were short term. We also realised that it benefited many to keep street vendors illegal; police and municipality officials could collect bribes and let street vending go on at their discretion, and politicians could get votes as long as vendors remained insecure and dependent on the local politician to negotiate settlements with the authorities. No one was really interested in making the street vendors legal.

Since it was a question of legality, we approached the courts, and in 1984 we got a historical judgement from the Supreme Court of India. After that we went to the Gujarat High Court for various areas in urban Gujarat and from that time on, approached the courts regularly. The relief and solutions from the courts were somewhat longer term, but limited in scope and did not last beyond a few years. So we kept struggling on, feeling that for all our efforts, we were running in place. However, after neoliberal economics gained ascendency and liberalisation policies were implemented in India, we found that the situation had changed. We were no longer running in place, we were being pushed backward. As cities began to aspire to become 'world class', as the national agenda became growth of Gross Domestic Product rather than poverty removal, the eviction drives against street vendors became more extensive and longer lasting. We realised that new, higher-level solutions were required. We needed new policies and new laws, and we needed them at national, rather than local levels. The Self Employed Women's Association could not do this alone, nor could any other street vendors' association; we needed to get together.

In 1998 SEWA called a meeting of street vendor associations from all over the country and the National Alliance of Street Vendors of India was born. The Self Employed Women's Association also approached the National Ministry of Urban Development and organised a joint conference with the ministry on street vending in 2001, after which the minister announced that a National Policy on Street Vendors would be announced and set up a task force to formulate this policy. The policy was finally announced in 2004 and has been the basis for vendors' struggles subsequently.

In the 1990s there was the growing phenomenon of globalisation and in many ways this also affected street vendors as cities in developing countries began to see themselves as part of the global economy. They began to model themselves on London and New York, and later on Singapore and Shanghai, and the idea of the 'World Class City' gathered momentum. The Self Employed Women's Association realised that just as it is necessary to bring together street vendors at the national level, so also it is necessary to bring them together at the international level. In 1995, Ela Bhatt organised an international meeting of street vendors at Bellagio in Italy which gave rise to the Bellagio Declaration for Street Vendors, and in 2002 the International Alliance of Street Vendors—StreetNet International—was born.

The issue of street vendors is primarily one of popular perceptions. Street vendors view themselves as small business people serving the larger community by providing them essential goods. The richer city dwellers and the city managers view them as 'nuisances', as 'obstructions to traffic', and having no place in the ideal world class city. Unfortunately, the anti–street vendor perceptions get full play in the media while hardly anyone promotes the more positive view, so that the negative view becomes the popular perception.

The street vendors need champions who will promote a positive view of them as hard working poor entrepreneurs, contributing to the economy and serving the consumer by bringing commodities to their door step at reasonable prices. One such champion is Sharit Bhowmik, a respected academic who, all his life, has consistently been writing on issues of the poor and the informal workers. In 2000 he completed a research on street vendors in India, the first of its kind and the main resource for the National Policy on Street Vendors, as well as subsequent court cases (Bhowmik 2000). Women in Informal Employment: Globalizing and Organizing (WIEGO) was formed in 1997 as a network of researchers, activists and policy makers to highlight the issues of women in the informal economy at the international level. It supported the formation of StreetNet and also set up a research and policy section on 'Urban Policies' which promoted research-based urban planning for street vendors. This book has emerged from studies sponsored by WIEGO in different parts of the developing world.

The combined efforts of these 'champions' of street vendors have led to new perceptions internationally. First is the issue of visibility. Although street vendors are perhaps the most visible on the streets and in the markets, they become invisible when it comes to statistics. In most statistical systems street vendors are never mentioned and when national or local policies, programmes or plans are made they are ignored. One of the reasons is when statisticians collect data on workers, they do not distinguish between workers in factories, workers in establishments, workers in fields, workers in homes, and workers in the streets. Most official surveys treat workers as 'employees' who work in an employer's factory under his supervision. Alternatively, they assume a worker is self-employed and owns his own establishment. The self-employed worker using the street as her place of business is not distinguished.

Women in Informal Employment: Globalizing and Organizing realised that the official statistics do not have 'place of work' as a category while collecting data and so cannot give the policy makers, or the users of statistics, data on many types of workers such as street vendors or home-based workers. After efforts by WIEGO and SEWA the Government of India first included the category 'place of work' in its five-yearly massive National Sample Survey in 1999–2000. At the international level, the International Labour Organisation (ILO) has recommended the inclusion of 'place of work' as a category and subsequently, many countries have adopted it.

Another important contribution of the champions and supporters of informal workers has been to *define* street vendor as a separate category. Until the study by Sharit Bhowmik on Indian cities in 2000, street vendors had always been seen as part of the informal sector, along with shoe-shine boys, construction workers, domestic servants, and many others. However, putting together all these types of informal workers in one category blurred their separate issues and problems, and led to confusion on actions. The issues of domestic workers, who worked in others' houses, for example, were very different from those of street vendors, who worked in public spaces.

A definition of who should be covered was painstakingly built up in consultation with the vendors. Should those selling in markets be included, or only those selling in streets? How about if they were selling from a spot belonging to a private person? Should ambient vendors be included? How about those who had a permanent structure? At the end of a long consultative process a definition emerged which was later adopted by the National Policy.

A street vendor is broadly defined as a person who offers goods for sale to the public without having a permanent built up structure but with a temporary static structure or mobile stall (or headload). Street vendors may be stationary by occupying space on the pavements or other public/private areas, or may be mobile in the sense that they move from place to place carrying their wares on push carts or in cycles or baskets on their heads, or may sell their wares in moving trains, bus, etc. In this policy document, the term urban vendor is inclusive of both traders and service providers, stationary as well as mobile vendors and incorporates all other local/region specific terms used to describe them, such as, hawker, pheriwalla, rehri-patri walla, footpath dukandars, sidewalk traders, etc. (NCEUS 2006)

A similar consultation process was required to 'name' the street vendor. Should they be called hawkers? Or market traders? Or just vendors? Finally, the term street vendor was adopted by all, and has also been accepted internationally.

The importance of this book is that it takes a step towards giving an identity to these disregarded workers invisible in the World Class City paradigm. And having given them an identity it moves towards integrating them into the city and towards giving them a formal space, both physically as well as in policy and planning. As we have seen, giving them a name, a definition, and a place in the statistical system are essential steps. Equally essential is their own voice.

Policies are usually formed keeping in view the needs of a multiplicity of stakeholders. However, in order for a policy to be fair, the policy makers must be able to hear the voice of all the stakeholders. Unfortunately, the voice of some stakeholders is loud and clear, of others is whispered, and some, such as street vendors, are not heard at all. Partly because the street vendors are not well-organised, and partly because there is no forum in which they can speak to policy makers.

In every city of the world, there is always *some* organising among street vendors. However, these organisations are usually small, confining themselves to a particular street or a particular market. Furthermore, many of these organisations are sporadic, coming together in times of crisis and breaking up under the force of entrepreneurial competition. In many countries these organisations are controlled by small mafias who pay off the local authorities. An interesting aspect of this book is showing the variety of types and sizes of organisation that exist world-wide.

The types of organisations that exist depend considerably on the existing political framework in the country, with democratic regimes allowing more expression than authoritarian ones. In some countries there is a tradition of market organisations ruled by a 'head' and in a few cases by a 'queen'. However, these organisations are rapidly weakening and the political clout of the street vendors at the city level remains very low. In this era of globalisation, where voices not heard are swept aside, the function of an organisation like StreetNet at the international level and its affiliates like the National Alliance of Street Vendors of India (NASVI) at the national level is becoming crucial. The function of these new international and national organisations is to bring together the disparate and scattered groups of street vendors and give them a common interest in being part of a larger organisation. At the same time, they need to be active at the national or international levels, bringing the issues of street vendors to the fore.

Voice is not only the ability to get together, to form organisations, and to articulate issues, but also requires a forum for representation of these issues. In most cities, street vendors do not have a forum where they can negotiate their physical space or their space in the planning and policy process. In cities, physical space is a scarce resource, and in order to get a foothold, to negotiate for one's bit of space in the city, it is necessary to enter the negotiating process. This means that the street vendors need a presence in the political process as well as in the planning process, which at this time hardly exists. It is a struggle that street vendors and their 'champions' are still to embark on.

The studies in this volume confirm the fact that street vendors can only become a regular part of the city when there are clear regulatory frameworks in place at the city level. This requires that city authorities recognise the need to include street vendors into city policy. It requires clear rules for where, when and how many street vendors can be accommodated. It also requires clear-cut guidelines for street vendors to apply for space and transparent and fair criteria for choosing among applicants. In some Indian cities this has been turned into a farce, by having clear rules but for such a small number of street vendors that it makes no difference at all. For example, in Ahmedabad, with nearly 100,000 existing street vendors, the city authorities made elaborate rules for issuing 247 licences. The National Policy for Urban Street Vendors addresses this problem by stating that the number of vendors to be accommodated should be 2 per cent of the urban population, based on authentic surveys.

The questions of representation and regulatory frameworks go hand in hand. Regulatory frameworks drawn up without the voice and representation of the street vendors are likely to be unrealistic and meet opposition from the vendors. Also, implementing a regulatory framework requires the cooperation of the street vendors (an undisciplined lot, at the best of times!) and hence a great deal of acceptability. On the other hand, the city authorities often throw up their hands on the question of representation saying that of the many small existing organisations it is not clear who represents the street vendors. They say that they would like to deal with a few representative organisations, but how can they know who is representative?

An issue that is rarely addressed by city authorities or by street vendor organisations themselves, is: What should be the character of a representative organisation of street vendors? This has been discussed at some length in StreetNet and various national alliances, and the consensus seems to be that the organisations should be membership-based organisations of street vendors, that they should be democratic in their structure, that they should have a transparent and accountable financial system and that they should have a track record in working for the benefit of the street vendors.

And while addressing the issue of Voice it is also important to look at the voice of women vendors. Our experience in SEWA shows that women vendors are treated like a lower caste in the vendor community. There are earning hierarchies among street vendors. Ambient vendors earn less than those with a fixed spot; vendors with baskets are able to store less than those with carts; vendors selling perishables like vegetables earn less than vendors selling goods like clothes, who earn less than those selling 'modern' items like electronics. The studies in this volume show that in every country women are always at the lower end of the earning scale, with cheaper goods, less capital and worse selling spots.

Worse, generally, the organisations of street vendors do not particularly like women. The Self Employed Women's Association is an all-women's trade union, but we find that the other street vendors' associations rarely have women in their leadership; in fact, they work hard to even deny the existence of women vendors! This also has been one of the tasks of the new organisations like StreetNet et al.; to induce the existing vendor associations to recognise the importance of women street vendors and include them in their leadership. Both StreetNet and NASVI have reservations for women in their executive committees, and also have special programmes for women's leadership.

Organisations of street vendors and their supporters like WIEGO have taken up the difficult task of challenging the concept of world class cities which exclude them. StreetNet has called it the campaign for 'World Class Cities for All'. The first campaign is around high profile sports events. According to StreetNet (see www.streetnet.org.za):

It has become a boringly predictable reality that, when a country prepares to host a high-profile international event, the country and its local government authorities prepare to create 'World Class Cities' of a particular type, i.e. 'World Class Cities' which:

- will attract foreign investment,
- have modern up-to-date infrastructure,
- have no visible signs of urban decay,
- have smooth traffic flows,
- have no visible poor people or social problems.

Street vendors' organisations are usually a good barometer of these plans, as they start to notice plans for their eviction some time in advance of the main events. . . . The eviction of street vendors is usually accompanied by 'slum clearance' programmes in terms of which the poorest members of the population also lose their homes . . . which means that such people lose both their homes and their livelihoods at the same time, leaving little for them to fall back upon as their survival strategy.

StreetNet asks that cities formally adopt an inclusive concept of 'World Class Cities for All' with the participation of street vendors and other groups of the (urban) poor. This inclusive concept should ensure that no individual or group of street vendors shall be unduly disadvantaged by any urban improvement or urban renewal initiatives. Authorities should undertake to engage in participatory consultative processes with any persons or interest groups who may be affected in any substantive or material manner by any aspect of urban improvement or urban renewal initiatives, and establish multi-stakeholder negotiating forums in each city to ensure inclusive non-sectarian negotiation and consultation processes. Street vendors should be directly represented by their own elected representatives, with due regard to the representation of women (in the proportions in which they are found on the streets) and vendors with disabilities.

This book makes an important contribution to developing the concept of World Class Cities for All. It brings together evidence from around the world about all aspects of the lives of street vendors and their relationship to the city, leaving no doubt that they are deeply embedded in the urban economic and cultural ethos. It makes a compelling argument for a new concept of inclusive and nurturing cities.

## Note

1. The Self Employed Women's Association is a trade union of poor women workers in India, whose membership today is over one million women. Of these, a sizeable number of urban members are street vendors.

## References

Bhat, Ela. 2006. *We Are Poor But So Many*, New Delhi: Oxford University Press.

Bhowmik, Sharit K. 2000. 'Hawkers in the Urban Informal Sector: A Study of Street Vending in Seven Cities', prepared for National Alliance of Street Vendors of India (NASVI), available at www.nasvi.org and www.streetnet.org.za.

NCEUS (National Commission on Enterprises in the Unorganised Sector). 2006. 'National Policy for Urban Street Vendors', available at www.nceus.gov.in.

# Preface and Acknowledgements

The idea for this book originated while I was associated with the Urban Policies Programme (UPP) of Women in Informal Economy: Organising and Globalising (WIEGO). UPP worked in close collaboration with StreetNet, an international federation of street vendors' organisations and other national federations such as the National Alliance of Street Vendors of India (NASVI), the Korean Street Vendors Federation, etc. In order to assess the kind of research that was being done on street vending, WIEGO commissioned three research reviews from three continents — Asia, Africa and Latin America (these are included in this volume). The reviews showed that street vendors, though perhaps the most conspicuous of all informal workers, hardly ever attracted any scholarly attention. One could find only one or two major studies in some countries, while in several others no study of street vending seems to have been attempted. This is rather unfortunate because research can bring to fore the various issues and problems that surround street vending; it is important from the perspective of policy formulation as well as for advocacy. The present volume was conceived keeping in mind these concerns.

The volume tries to assess the contribution made by street vendors to the urban economy as well as the problems they face in conducting their business. In the era of globalisation, world class cities and shopping malls, we continue to find the city's pavements crowded with such vendors, selling an impossible array of goods that could perhaps give upmarket malls a run for their money. Globalisation has no doubt brought wealth to a few, but, just as surely, it has brought a great deal of hardship and suffering to the urban working poor. Street vendors cater primarily to these sections of the urban population, and though they are despised by supporters of world class cities they will remain part of the city for as long as the working poor need their services.

The contributors to this volume have tried to contend with these issues in an objective and non-partisan manner. The lone trade unionist, Dr Sanjay Kumar of the Self-Employed Women's Association (SEWA), was training to be an academic but found being an activist much more fulfilling and therefore switched over. We hope that this collection of articles will prompt other scholars and researchers also to take part in the study of informal employment and economy. I will not dwell on this subject any further, lest I repeat what has been discussed in the Introduction.

It is a collective effort of the contributors and the editor that has made this book possible. Editing the volume was a pleasure, especially because of the enthusiasm shown by the contributors towards its publication. I thank them all for their support. As mentioned above, WIEGO played a major role in the formative stages of the book. It is fitting indeed that Renana Jhabvala, National Co-ordinator of SEWA and Chairperson of WIEGO, should write the Foreword. I thank Renana for taking time from her very busy schedule to do so. Arbind Singh, Co-ordinator of NASVI, was a constant source of support that went a long way in my attempt to edit the volume. I am extremely grateful to Padma Prakash, former Associate Editor of *Economic and Political Weekly* and currently editor of *eSocial Sciences*, for going through the manuscript and editing it before it was sent to the publisher. I must also thank the editorial team at Routledge for doing an excellent job. Thank you Omita Goyal, Samira Junaid and Jaya Dalal for your combined efforts in bringing out this volume. Finally, I thank Indira Gartenberg, Reasearch Officer at the School of Management and Labour Studies, TISS, for all her help in preparing this manuscript.

# 1

# Introduction

Sharit K. Bhowmik

This is a collection of studies on street vendors. This section of the employed is perhaps the most visible in the urban informal economy. In fact, some may feel that they are too visible and their overbearing presence on the streets becomes a menace for commuters, especially for those using the pavements. The civic authorities in most metropolitan cities all over the world treat these 'intruders' on public property as a nuisance. The urban elites view them as eyesores that blotch the urban scenario. On the other hand, for the urban poor, especially the working poor, street vendors are a boon to their existence. These street traders provide cheap food, clothes and other items for their daily use. They are also easy to access as street vendors conduct their business in convenient places in the city where a large number of commuters pass. We have tried to assess the pros and cons of street vending in this volume. Though the focus is on India, as the largest number of chapters is from there, the study covers cities in other countries as well. We have tried our best to provide a global view on street vending. There are, however, some important issues that need to be clarified in order to get a holistic understanding of the situation. The following sections deal with these.

## Informal Economy

While discussing street vendors one has to delve into the nature of the informal economy. This was popularly known earlier as the informal sector as opposed to the formal sector and is called the unorganised sector in India. It includes all economic units and workers who are not a part of the regulated economic activities and protected employment relations (Chen 2004: 1). The concept of the informal sector was not popular till the 1970s, though this sector existed even then. For the industrially developed countries of Europe and North America, formal employment was the norm, especially in the U.S. after the Great Depression of 1929 and the post-World War II reforms in Europe. This type of employment entitles a degree of permanency to the job and the worker is entitled to retirement benefits after s/he retires from work. Workers who were not engaged in formal employment were proportionately small in number and did not merit any interest.

This idea of permanent employment being predominant in the economy was also echoed by developing countries in Asia and Africa. Though most workers in these countries were engaged in informal employment, their governments chose not to highlight their problems because employment in these countries was overwhelmingly in the agrarian sector. Modernisation of agriculture and industrialisation would surely change the situation as it had happened in developed countries.

It was only in the early 1970s that the notion of the informal sector gained currency. At that time the International Labour Organisation (ILO) was carrying out some major studies on the labour market in some of the countries on the African continent. One of the researchers was Keith Hart (1973), an anthropologist, who was studying the situation in Accra in Ghana in 1971. He found that quite unlike the organised markets in England, where he came from, there were workers who came to the city from their villages in the vicinity to offer their services as day labourers. These people would assemble at certain places in the cities and wait for possible employers to hire their services. He also found that there were sharp differences in retailing in England and these countries. In the developed countries, food grains and vegetables were available in stand-ardised packets that were sold in departmental or grocery stores. In Accra, villagers would come to the cities and sell their wares to the public at large. These were not standardised goods that were weighed and neatly packed. Instead, the street vendors who sold vegetables or food grains did so in open baskets. These were weighed in front of the customers who wanted to buy these goods. On the whole, the scenario appeared quite chaotic. There were workers who worked as day labourers and whose employers had no responsibility towards them, except for paying them their daily wage. The retail trade was equally unorganised with individual sellers rather than organised retail outlets. For lack of any other word to describe these activities, Hart labelled them as the informal sector, as compared to the formal sector.

Hart also found that there were four basic features of the informal sector that proved useful for employment in developing countries. These were:

- *Low levels of skill*: Most of the jobs in the informal economy are labour intensive, involving low levels of technology. The skills required from workers are rudimentary. Developing countries have large reserves of untrained, unskilled workers who have little or no education. These people cannot hope to find work in the formal economy as they do not have the skills needed for specialised jobs in the formal sector. Hence, they find employment in the informal economy. This sector, therefore, absorbs the surplus labour in the economy.
- *Easy entry*: Because of the low skill requirements, entry to the informal sector is comparatively easy. For example, it is easier for a person with low skills and little capital to take to street vending instead of starting a venture in the formal economy such as a grocery store.
- *Low-paid employment*: Wages of workers in the informal economy are low because of the low levels of skills of the workers. Moreover, easy entry in this sector is precisely because of low wages offered to the less skilled workers.
- *Largely immigrant workforce*: The labour employed in informal employment does not consist of local people and they are mainly immigrants. Hart presumes that migrants mainly possess low skills and that is why they can find work only in this sector. This feature is not necessarily correct because one finds a large number of local people who are engaged in this sector, especially in developing countries.

The Employment Mission of the ILO (1972) had noted that the traditional economic sector not only persisted along with modern enterprises, but it had expanded. The mission chose to use the term informal sector (coined by Hart a year earlier) rather than traditional sector. This sector included small-scale and unregistered economic activities.

Both Hart and the ILO believed that the informal sector was a transitory sector. It would disappear when these countries developed. The formal sector would expand and absorb the informal sector. In other words, day labourers or workers in unregistered small factories would be absorbed as formal sector workers and street vendors would possibly be absorbed into the organised retail sector as these countries develop and expand their formal sector. Hence, the ILO believed that these two sectors were independent of each other and the informal sector would disappear or reduce considerably as the formal sector expanded. This approach is known as the dualist approach and it is regarded as outdated considering the developments in the economy in recent years. In fact, we find that far from disappearing, this sector has grown tremendously in all countries, even in the developed ones.

It would be foolish to throw out the entire concept of a dualistic approach. These studies were important because they brought to light some important aspects of the informal economy, especially its potential for providing employment. In developing countries the informal economy was able to absorb surplus and untrained labour. However, it was by and large a concept that was not able to effectively understand changes in the economy, and why, despite development, this sector continues to expand. This, in fact, brings us to the other approach to studying the informal economy, namely the structuralist theory.

This theory was developed by Manuel Castells, Alejandro Portes and Lauren Benton in late 1989 though the issue was raised by Caroline Moser in her study in *World Development* in 1978 (Moser 1978). Portes and Castell argue that far from being independent of each other, the formal and informal sectors are related to each other. The enterprises in the formal sector use the informal sector for manufacturing components as costs are much lower. The informal sector enterprises are not subject to the laws that regulate production in the formal sector. The formal economy thus finds the informal economy a useful means for increasing its profits. At the same time the informal economy depends on the formal sector for its sustenance. The structuralists thus stress on the fact that there is a close, symbiotic relationship between the two sectors. This is to a large extent true as we can see low-paid, sweated labour in the informal sector being used to provide inputs to the formal sector. Small-scale industries are engaged in manufacture of parts that are used as inputs in the manufacture of goods produced in the formal sector. The automobile industry depends on a number of small manufacturers who supply the different components for making the vehicle. Similarly, we find that manufacturers in the developed economies outsource their production to the developing countries because manufacturing in the informal sector in these countries is much cheaper than in the developed countries.

The third theoretical approach is of the legalists. This approach was developed by Hernando de Sotto, a Peruvian economist who gained considerable fame because of his contribution to the understanding of the informal economy and urban poverty. The legalist theory states that the informal sector comprises small operatives who work outside the formal economy because they find the legal procedures too cumbersome to follow. These operators prefer to operate informally because the government procedures for giving them formal recognition are long-winded, complicated and difficult for them to understand. Hence, these people are not willing offenders. They try to circumvent the rules because they find them too complicated and time-consuming.

This theory perhaps explains best why street vendors prefer to engage in the informal economy. In most cases, as shown by the studies in this volume, street vendors can become legal operatives if they obtain licenses for plying their trade. This process, if allowed, is a cumbersome process. It would appear that the concerned authorities are only too keen to make the process of licensing so complicated that it becomes almost impossible for the semi-literate street vendor to comprehend what the forms contain. It is even more complicated to fill in the forms. Most street vendors do not have the capacity to do so. In fact, it is ironic that most governments try to simplify procedures for conducting large-scale business in the formal sector but they continue to make issues more complicated for the small operators.

After discussing the informal economy let us now deal with street vendors. Who are these people? What do they do? Why are they in the informal economy? We will deal with these questions in the next few sections.

## Who are Street Vendors?

This collection deals with street vendors and their role in the urban economy. Street vendors have been in existence since ancient times. In all civilisations, ancient and medieval, one reads accounts of travelling merchants who sold their wares in towns by going from house to house. There were also markets that were held at certain intervals—weekly, monthly, etc. Vendors would set up their stalls in these markets. They carried out their trade like any other merchants or shopkeepers. The main difference was that while shopkeepers and other merchants had fixed places to carry out their business, street vendors, as their name suggests, had no permanent places for their trade. They plied their trade on either the pavements in order to attract customers who were mainly pedestrians, or they moved from place to place carrying their goods on carts. Those who could not afford carts carried their wares in baskets on their heads. Others tied two baskets on either side of a bamboo pole which they would carry on their shoulders. In fact, one can still find street vendors in many of the poorer Asian countries carrying their wares in a similar fashion.

Street vendors are thus of two types, namely, those who squat in public places such as pavements, parks or other such places, and those that are mobile as they move from place to place in search of customers. The common feature in both cases is that the places for conducting business are not permanent. Hawkers that occupy public spaces may conduct their business from that spot for years but they do not have legal claims to that space. They can be evicted by the local authorities at any time. This sets them apart from shopkeepers and others as these people occupy space that is legally theirs and as such they have permanency of tenure.

Another major difference between street vendors/hawkers and shop-keepers is that they approach the likely customers whereas customers go to shops to buy their goods. In this sense, vendors are more customer-friendly than shopkeepers. This point was noted in a major decision of the Supreme Court of India (the apex court in the country) in the case of a street vendor, Sodhan Singh, a garment seller who operated from a pavement in New Delhi, the capital of India, along with other hawkers. The police and the municipal staff would frequently evict them and would confiscate their goods. The hawkers would be beaten up if they resisted.

Sodhan Singh contacted a lawyer who was willing to file a Public Interest Litigation (PIL) in the Supreme Court. The question raised was that harassment of these hawkers resulted in the violation of their fundamental right (Clause 19[1g] of the Constitution of India) to carry out trade as a part of their livelihood. The case ran for three years but after this the Supreme Court gave a landmark judgement. The main extract is given here:

> If properly regulated according to the exigency of the circumstances, the small traders on the side walks can considerably add to the comfort and convenience of the general public, by making available ordinary articles of everyday use for a comparatively lesser price. An ordinary person, not very affluent, while hurrying towards his home after a day's work can pick up these articles without going out of his way to find a regular market. The right to carry on trade or business mentioned in Article 19(1)g of the Constitution, on street pavements, if properly regulated cannot be denied on the ground that the streets are meant exclusively for passing or re-passing and no other use.

The above extract from the Supreme Court judgement is significant because it emphasises several important aspects of street vending and the use of public space. The judgement notes the positive role of street vendors in providing essential commodities to common people at affordable prices and at convenient places. Moreover, the judgement notes that street vending, if regulated, cannot be denied merely on the grounds that pavements are meant exclusively for pedestrians. The most important aspect is that street vendors are exercising their constitutional right to carry out trade or business, hence the practice should be regulated properly and not abolished.

In modern times we find that street vendors are rarely treated with the same measure of dignity and tolerance. They are targeted by municipalities and the police in urban areas as illegal traders; the urban middle class complains constantly about how these vendors make urban life a living hell as they block pavements, create traffic problems and also engage in anti-social activities. (Though more often than not, the same representatives of the middle class prefer to buy goods from street vendors as these are cheaper even though the quality is as good as those in the overpriced departmental stores and shopping malls.)

For most street vendors, trading from the pavements is full of uncertainties. They are constantly harassed by the authorities. The local bodies conduct eviction drives to clear the pavements of these encroachers and in most cases confiscate their goods. A municipal raid is like a cat-and-mouse game with municipal workers chasing street vendors away while these people try to run and hide from these marauders. Confiscation of their goods entails heavy fines for recovery. In most cases it means that the vendor has to take a loan from private sources (at exorbitant interest rates) to either recover whatever remains of his confiscated goods or to restart his business. Besides these sudden raids, street vendors normally have to regularly bribe the authorities in order to carry out their business on the street. All this means that a substantive income from street vending is spent on greasing the palms of unscrupulous authorities or private money lenders. In fact, in most cases street vendors have to survive in a hostile environment though they are service providers.

## Why Street Vending?

In most cities in the world the urban poor survive by working in the informal economy. This trend is prominent in developing countries. Poverty and the lack of gainful employment in rural areas and in smaller towns drive large numbers of people to the cities for work and livelihood. These people generally possess low skills and too low a level of education for the better paid jobs in the organised sector. Besides, permanent protected jobs in the organised sector are shrinking. Even those with requisite skills are unable to find proper employment. For these people, work in the informal sector is the only means of survival. This has led to a rapid growth of the informal sector in most large cities. For the urban poor, hawking is one of the means of earning a livelihood, as it requires minor financial input and the skills involved are low.

A large section of street vendors in urban areas are those with low skills and who have migrated to the larger cities from rural areas or small towns in search of employment. These people take to street vending when they do not find other means of livelihood. Though the income in this profession is low, the investment too is low and the people do not require special skills or training. Hence, for these men and women, street vending is the easiest way of earning their livelihood.

There is also another section of the urban population that has taken to street vending. These people, or their spouses, were once engaged in better paid jobs in the formal employment sector. Deindustrialisation in cities in many of the developing countries has created job losses in formal employment. This trend is very evident in cities in India and some of the Latin American countries. Many of the displaced, or their spouses, have become street vendors in order to eke out a living. Over the past few decades there has been a substantial increase in the number of hawkers in the major cities around the world.

So street vendors are those people who do not have employment or those who have lost their stable jobs. They try to overcome their problems by pooling their meagre resources and starting their own enterprises. They do not take to stealing or crime nor do they beg for a living. All they want is to live a life of dignity. However, the authorities in most cases do not let them live in peace. The studies in this volume show that in almost all countries one of the obsessions of street vendors and their organisations is of trying to negotiate with the authorities for space to run their business.

## Street Vending and Public Space

Before we move further let us examine what is meant by urban public space and what it means for the working poor. In a broad sense urban public space includes areas that are used for public activities. It can be defined as all physical spaces and social relations that use that space within the non-private realm of the city. Hence, urban public space includes pavements, parks, beaches, vacant spaces, etc. In developing countries urban public space becomes a valuable resource for the urban working poor for their livelihood as well as their living.

## *Control of Urban Public Space*

Who occupies urban public space? On the one side we have the working poor who use pavements for their work. The most prominent in developing countries are street vendors who can be found everywhere in the city. Another group are the casual workers who sell their labour every day. These people assemble on certain street corners where some of them are picked up for work by either labour contractors or employers. These workers include construction labour, carpenters, plumbers, painters among others. In both cases the people are regarded as illegal encroachers on public land.

Control over public space by the state and/or the civic authority is seen as control over the people, especially the working poor. Alison Brown (2006: 24), in her interesting exploration on public space, points out that the fascist government of Benito Mussolini in Italy (1922–43) was one of the first to recognise the importance of dominating public space. His government strictly regulated the use of public space and encroachers (in almost all cases the poor) were removed with brute force. The approach of the state is to treat the working poor as illegal encroachers so that the local authorities can exert total control over them. These activities undoubtedly make the working poor feel that activities relating to their livelihood are illegal and they rarely challenge the authority of the bureaucracy in a collective manner.

The civic authorities can show laxity in encroachment on public space where necessary. For example, housing societies of the middle and upper middle classes frequently encroach on public space by usurping land around their residences. Shops and restaurants also encroach on public space by building extensions onto the pavements. In most such cases the civic authorities ignore the intrusions or at the most frown on these activities but take no concrete action to remove the encroachers.

In the case of the urban working poor, the civic authorities are only too keen to evict them whenever there are complaints. When street vendors and slums are evicted the civic authorities make sure that their livelihood and their houses are destroyed. Raids conducted by the authorities to evict street vendors are similar to the carnage carried out by an invading army. The staff confiscate their goods and break their stalls. All this is done without recourse to any legal procedure. Most studies included in this volume show that the vendor is not provided with a list of goods confiscated. When the police raid the residences of suspected criminals and confiscate incriminating goods or documents they make a list of these. This is known as the seizure list and it is given to the person whose goods are confiscated. The civic authorities do not believe in such legalities when it comes to evicting street vendors. Similarly, while evicting slum dwellers they destroy their huts and whatever little movable assets they possess. Bulldozers, earth movers and cranes are used to destroy the residences of the poor.

## *Perceptions of Urban Public Spaces*

Though urban public space is a fact in the sense that we know what it is and the land records of the civic authorities will have accurate records on it, the perception of urban public space differs between communities. For the wealthy, public spaces such as parks, pavements and beaches are places for recreation. Pavements should not be encroached by pavement dwellers or street vendors because these may come in the way of their morning walks. Beaches should be clean because the wealthier sections want to relax on the sands and enjoy the sea breeze. Similarly, public parks are often taken over (adopted) by local residents' associations and are beautified and converted to jogging parks that are no longer accessible to the city's working poor. These examples are ways in which public spaces are usurped and converted to private space. The authorities play an active role in these processes because they encourage such 'adoptions' of public space.

For the working poor public spaces have different connotations. For street vendors wide pavements would mean places where they could earn their livelihood and provide for their families. For the poorer sections pavements are places where they can buy their daily needs from the street vendors who sell low-priced goods and food. For the urban poor, pavements and other public spaces could be places where they could reside as they cannot afford other housing.

Similarly, for the poorer sections, public spaces like beaches or parks are places for relaxation and recreation where they can also feast on low-cost food offered by street vendors. However, their behaviour and their clothes are vastly different from that of the upper classes who think that public spaces are their exclusive right. The municipal authorities too seem to second this approach as they actively help in excluding the poor from public places.

The main issue regarding the use of public space by the poor occurs mainly because there are no clear guidelines regarding the control of public space. The lack of clarity on the legal aspects of street vending creates the confusion on the use of public space. In most cases we find that there are no clear rules regulating street vending. The obvious fact is that street vendors operate only in public spaces. The use of this space, in legal terms, becomes important for regulating street vending. In most cases we find that allotting space on pavements to street vendors eases a lot of problems. It is possible to regulate them and also ensure that they do not transgress the legal boundaries framed by the appropriate authorities. This is exactly what the judgement of the Supreme Court of India was aiming at when it stated that if properly regulated street vendors could be an asset for the not too well-off shopper. On the other hand, vagueness in the legal framework gives rise to insecurity among street vendors as it allows a free hand to rent-seeking by the concerned authorities. We can see this happening in a number of studies in this volume—Mumbai, Delhi, Phnom Pen, Sao Paulo, and Caracas.

Besides the vagueness in the legal angle, another important issue is which authority actually controls public space. One would assume that urban public space is controlled by the concerned municipal authority. This is easier said than done. In many cases we can find conflicting claims between local government and the local municipal authority. In some cases, India being the most prominent, there are other authorities, besides the municipal authority, that have claims on public space. In Mumbai, whenever the Municipal Corporation tries to lay its claims on public space, there are a number of other authorities such as the Mumbai Metropolitan Region Development Authority, set up by the state government, the Port Trust of India that claims that it owns one-third of the land in the city, and finally the police that claim to have the authority to evict any person from the streets if they expose goods for sale.

In Delhi, there are a number of authorities that claim sole control over space. Negotiating with them can take almost a lifetime. At times these conflicting claims by different authorities can go in favour of street vendors, as in Caracas. Grande Boulevard is in the centre of the city and is a prize place for street vending. The vendors can exist because of conflicting claims on the space by two municipal authorities—each claiming that it has control over that public space (see Rincon in this volume). On the other hand, the multiple authorities that exist in Delhi have caused a lot of grief to street vendors of the Sunday Market. After this market was evicted from the precincts of the historic Red Fort, they were promised an alternative place. However, they had to run from pillar to post for over three years to find a suitable place that did not have counter claims by another authority (see the case study on Delhi).

## *Gender and Public Space*

Another important dimension of public space is gender. In most of the studies in this volume one can find that women are invariably given the inferior places for vending. This occurs even in countries where women form a majority in street vending. We find this trend more prominent in countries of South East Asia (Bangkok, Phnom Pen, Ho Chi Minh City, etc.). In Vietnam we find that mobile vendors are invariably women. They carry their wares in baskets that are slung at two ends of a bamboo pole. The woman carries this heavy burden on her shoulders and moves from house to house to sell her wares. Male vendors occupy spaces on the pavement and they sell more.

In the South Asian countries too where women usually form the minority in street vending, they are relegated to spaces that are inferior. The chapter on Asia has many such examples. In Patna in India, women vendors prefer to carry their wares on their heads and go from house to house to sell them. The males occupy the pavements and they seldom permit women to be amidst them. In case a woman is bold enough to squat on the pavement, she is frequently harassed sexually by the males till she leaves. Kyoko, while dealing with Cambodia in this volume, finds that women are permitted on the pavements by the male vendors provided they earn less than the males. Women whose earnings match those of the men are seen as a threat.

In most of these countries women prefer to occupy areas that are their preserves. These spaces are more often than not places that do not attract many clients. In Mumbai, women vendors sell smaller quantities of goods than the males. In fact, the study on India shows that in almost all cities, women vendors earn less than their male counterparts. This is partly because these women are poor and they are unable to invest much in their business. However, the more important reason is that they have to divide their time between housework and business whereas men can spend all their time in their business. Kyoko's study on Cambodia finds that street vending for women is an extension of their homes. They frequently bring their children along so that they can do their business and look after their children at the same time. In most cases they end up doing neither of the tasks well.

The status of women vendors in Asian countries invariably reflects the inferior status of women in these countries. Women are treated as socially inferior to males in these countries. This in turn is reflected in their economic life. There are cases where women have been able to compete with men and have in fact surpassed them. These are individual efforts and can be treated as exceptions rather than the rule. However, if women can organise themselves into trade unions and work as a collective they can achieve better results. The case of the Self Employed Women's Association (SEWA) shows that this is possible.

The Self Employed Women's Association is one of the largest trade unions in India and it organises women in the informal economy. Its base is in Ahmedabad but it also exists in other parts of the country. In this volume we have two examples of how SEWA has encouraged women vendors to increase their earnings. In fact, Ahmedabad is the only city in India where women earn as much as men. The union has played an important role in relocating street vendors in Delhi. Ironically, its efforts have benefited male vendors as well as they too get the benefits of the struggles of the women vendors in regularising public space for street vending (see the case of the Sunday Market in Delhi). Thanks to SEWA's efforts in highlighting the plight of women vendors, the National Policy for Urban Street Vendors in India has directed that women vendors should be allocated 30 per cent of the space for street vending.

## Natural Markets

In every urban area, especially in developing countries, there are areas where trade in the basic necessities of everyday life is conducted. If there are no permanent shops that help in such transactions, there will be street vendors who undertake these activities. For example, railway stations and bus terminuses attract large numbers of people who are in transition. In the mornings there are people who are rushing to catch trains or buses to their places of work. In the evenings these centres are places where the same people return, tired after a day's work. These people may not have the inclination or the energy to travel further to a regular market or departmental store to purchase some essential items such as food, clothes or household utensils before returning home. Instead, if they find vendors on the pavements outside these places, they will be much relieved. This service is not only convenient but it is also cost effective in many ways. The prices offered by street vendors are lower than those of regular shops. The purchaser does not have to make an extra trip to the nearest market for buying the goods s/he needs. This saves the cost of that trip and the time involved.

We can find similar clusters of street vendors in other places, such as public hospitals that attract patients from the poorer sections. They come from different places in the city or, in the case of district hospitals or speciality hospitals (for TB, cancer, etc.), from outside the city.

Their relatives and friends who visit them need food and drink. The patients too may need fruits or toiletries. Street vendors provide these services. In other public places such as parks and beaches, street vendors sell snacks, toys, balloons, etc., that are eagerly bought by people visiting such places.

Such places are known as natural markets. These are places where street vendors have the natural propensity to assemble because the customers find it convenient to purchase from them. Hence, whether one likes it or not, street vendors will assemble at such places not because they like to be there but because their services are needed by the public. The main problem in such cases is that more often than not, the local authorities, namely, police and municipal authorities, try to prevent street vendors from using such places for their trade. The studies from Asian and African countries show how vendors are forcefully evicted from these places through raids. The vendors on their part try to buy peace, literally. In other words, they bribe the authorities by parting with a substantial part of their daily earnings. There are several instances where the underworld becomes the messiah of street vendors by coming to their defence (Dhaka, Mumbai, Patna). Their motives are far from altruistic. They do this in order to extract money from the street vendors, a part of which is given to the authorities to keep them away. In such cases, if the vendors refuse to pay the goons, they face threats of eviction or of being beaten up by them.

This discussion on natural markets gives rise to two issues. First, if such markets help the public by serving their needs they should be protected and regulated by the authorities, instead of being regarded as encroachers. In the present state of affairs one can see that public places such as those in the vicinity of railway stations, bus terminuses, parks, gardens, beaches, etc., can become crowded because of the clustering of vendors who are competing with each other to sell their wares. The buyers too stop to inspect the goods for sale thereby blocking the thoroughfare. This increases the chaos at these places. Other commuters or visitors who want to use the passage are inconvenienced. These people may feel that by encroaching on public places street vendors are blocking their right to move freely. In fact, the positive and negative attitudes could be held by the same person at different times. While returning home from office the person may find street vendors at the railway station or bus terminus where s/he alights a boon as s/he need not make another trip to purchase goods needed for the house. However, on another day if the same person is in a hurry to return home without buying anything, s/he may find street vendors that block the passage a nuisance.

The second issue is that this form of illegality of operation by vendors in natural markets makes them victims of unscrupulous officers and their rent-seeking or targets of the underworld. The chapter on Sao Paulo shows how the vendors there manage to stay on the street through this network of rent-seeking. Both issues make street vendors vulnerable to evictions resulting in loss of livelihood.

In such cases one would expect the concerned authorities to try and regularise street vending as they provide services to a large section of the urban population. This can be done only if the needs of the street vendors and the customers are taken into account. This means that space must be provided to these natural markets so that others are not harassed. But this rarely happens because most urban plans do not make provisions for natural markets. These plans demarcate space for educational institutions, parks and gardens, public services like hospitals, bus terminuses, etc., but rarely for markets where street vendors can ply their business. If this was done, much of the congestion could be reduced, besides having convenient services for the public. Ironically, one can find such markets in Western European countries where street vendors are few in number though developing countries which have far greater numbers of street vendors do not seem to be concerned about this.

## Why this Book?

The initiative for bringing out this book was taken by the Women in Informal Employment: Organising and Globalising (WIEGO). I was for some time working on WIEGO's Urban Policies Programme which dealt with studies on street vendors and was also trying to build a bridge between trade unions and member-based organisations of street vendors and the academia. This programme worked closely with StreetNet, the international union of street vendors.

I realised that though the informal economy and informal employment have grown tremendously during the past few decades, there were few studies on this part of the economy. Street vendors form a major part of the informal economy because of their large numbers. They are also the most visible section in the informal economy. Yet, there are hardly any significant studies on street vendors. This was further confirmed when I did a survey on street vendors in Asia. I could find only one or two significant studies in each of the countries that were covered. I had to rely on newspaper reports in most cases to supplement the meagre data I could gather. I could not find any significant study in some Asian countries, especially those to the west of India like Pakistan, Iran, Egypt, Afghanistan,

Iraq, etc. These countries have fairly large numbers of street vendors but very little is known about them. I found that the reviews on Latin America and Africa faced similar problems.

This book tries to collate some of the significant studies on street vending in different countries so that we can get an insight into street vending as well as the problems faced by street vendors (and whether there are commonalities between the continents). The chapters included in this collection are from the three continents—Asia, Africa and Latin America. There are views of research on street vending in each of the continents and there are two chapters on cities in two countries each of Asia and Latin America, respectively. These are Bangkok (Thailand) and Phnom Penh (Cambodia) from Asia and Caracas (Venezuala) and Sao Paulo (Brazil) from Latin America. There are more chapters on India because there seem to be more studies on street vendors in this country. Even so, there is much more to be done in terms of research.

The chapters in this collection all deal with problems faced by street vendors as workers in the informal economy. They cover diverse economies such as the comparatively better-off economies of Latin America and the poorer countries of Asia. There does not seem to be any connection or comparison with a country like Brazil that claims first-world status with the battered, war-torn economy of Cambodia. What could there be in common between the poor street vendors of India who earn less than two U.S. dollars a day and who cart their wares on hand carts or other forms of cheap transport because they cannot afford anything else, and the street vendors of Peru or Korea who can drive down to their places of work in their cars and enjoy a fairly decent level of living?

Having lived with Korean street vendors in Seoul on two occasions I can contrast the differences between the stark living conditions of vendors in India who live in cramped quarters in slums with no basic amenities such as toilets or drinking water, with those of street vendors in Seoul. Street vendors in Phnom Penh live in worse conditions than their counterparts in Mumbai. There are no jobs and street vending is a major source of sustenance for the poor. Their income is further depressed because of rent-seeking by the officials. We find that civil servants in the country are not paid living wages and they prey on the poor to supplement their resources. This is a typical case of the poor exploiting the poor. Vendors in Latin America, especially those in Brazil, Columbia and Caracas, enjoy fairly decent living by the standards of their respective countries. What could be common between these vendors and their counterparts in African countries?

Despite the differences, there are similarities that connect street vendors all over the world. Street vending forms an important component of the urban informal sector. Though they may not be the largest component of the informal economy, they are the most visible. One can find street vendors in any city of the world, in developing countries as well as the developed countries. Cities in all countries of the developed world—Amsterdam, Berlin, Lisbon, New York, London, Paris, Athens, and Rome, to name a few—have street vendors. Why do they exist? The simple answer to this is that they perform functions that are needed by the population. If the people did not want to purchase from street vendors, they would never exist. In fact, we find that street vendors fill in a vital gap in the retailing chain.

This is the positive side of street vending. Many of the cities in the developed world have liberal policies towards street vendors. They have weekly markets where vendors can participate, and in some cases vendors can be allowed in some areas in the city. These vendors lend colour to the city's markets and they also promote tourism. The story is different in the developing countries in Asia, Africa and Latin America. Most street vendors are found in every city as they cater mainly to the needs of the urban poor. At the same time almost all municipal bodies are hostile to street vendors. They are harassed and face constant eviction. In most countries of Asia, Africa and Latin America, despite the level of living, vendors face constant harassment from the municipal officials and the police. In fact, we find that the poorer countries in Asia and Africa such as Kenya, Zimbabwe, Cambodia, and Vietnam are most oppressive on the urban poor in general and street vendors in particular. In other countries too there is a great deal of animosity for street vendors. Hence, we find this to be a common factor for street vendors in all parts of the world.

At the same time it would be incorrect to assume that street vendors are always victimised. We do have some good practices in some of the countries as the studies or the reviews show. These are few in number but they are there. There are three countries in Asia—Philippines, Singapore and India—that have national policies for street vendors. In two of these countries they exist only in name though Singapore tries to implement its policy for the good of vendors. Malaysia also has a positive approach, as well as Thailand. The South Asian Association for Regional Cooperation (SAARC) countries and those of Indo-China are perhaps the most severe against street vendors. These are poor countries and street vendors are those who try to overcome their poverty by their own limited capital. They perform a service to the urban poor that enables them to get essential supplies at cheap rates (especially food and clothing). Yet the governments of these poor countries are oppressive towards street vendors. Other countries too are not supporters of street vending but their actions may not be as severe as these countries. The following chapters in the book unfold the problems of street vendors. We have tried our best to be comprehensive in our approach but we do realise that there could be some cases that have been overlooked. We sincerely hope that this volume helps in clearing the different misconceptions about street vendors.

## Chapterisation

This book tries to examine the working and living conditions of street vendors in different cities of the world. The focus is, however, on India and Asia. We have tried to provide an overview of street vending in three continents of the South. The second chapter deals with street vendors in Asia. It tries to provide a macro view of different street vendors in this continent and their contrasts. Chapters 3 to 7 deal with specific cities in Asia. These provide the micro views on street vending in these cities. We have included a study by a young architect on street vending in Vadodra. This chapter is different from the others as it does not deal with the working conditions of street vendors but it shows how existing street vendors can be adjusted on the pavements with minor changes in the plans. This chapter is an adaptation of the author's dissertation to Centre for Environmental Planning and Technology (CEPT) University, Ahmedabad, and it had won her the gold medal for the best dissertation of that year. Chapter 9 discusses the situation in Africa. This chapter is a review of research on street vending in the continent. Chapter 10 is a review of research on street vending in Latin America whereas the next two chapters present studies on two Latin American cities, namely, Caracas and Sao Paulo. The last chapter provides an insight into the various strategies adopted by unions to get the Indian government to agree to a national policy for street vendors. This is an important study on advocacy and I think it holds true for most countries in the developing world. This is why we have not bunched it with the chapters on India.

## References

Brown, Alison (ed.). 2006. *Contested Space: Street Trading, Public Space and Livelihoods in Developing Cities*, Warwickshire: Intermediate Technology Publications Ltd.

Castells, Manuel and Alejandro Portes. 1989. 'The World Underneath: The Origins, Dynamics and Effects of the Informal Economy', in Alejandro Portes,

Manuel Castells and Lauren Benton (eds), *The Informal Economy: Studies in Advanced and Less Advanced/Developing Countries*, Baltimore: Johns Hopkins University Press.

Chen, Martha Alter. 2004. 'Rethinking the Informal Economy: Linkages with the Formal Economy and Formal Regulatory Environment'. Paper prepared for Presentation at EGDI-WIDER Conference, 'Unleashing Human Potential: Linking the Informal and Formal Sectors', 17–18 September 2004, Helsinki, Finland (also available at www.wiego.org).

Chen, Martha Alter, Joann Vanek and Marilyn Carr. 2004. *Mainstreaming Informal Employment and Gender in Poverty Reduction: A Handbook for Policy-Makers and Other Stakeholders*, London: Commonwealth Secretariat.

de Soto, Hernando. 1989. *The Other Path: The Economic Answer to Terrorism*, New York: Harper and Collins.

Hart, Kieth. 1973. 'Informal Income Opportunities and Urban Employment in Ghana', *Journal of Modern African Studies*, 11(1): 61–89.

Moser, Caroline. 1978. 'Informal Sector or Petty Commodity Production: Dualism or Independence in Urban Development', *World Development*, 6.

Portes, Alejandro, Manuel Castells and Lauren Benton (eds). 1989. *The Informal Economy: Studies in Advanced and Less Advanced/Developing Countries*, Baltimore: Johns Hopkins University Press.

# 2

# Street Vendors in Asia: Survey of Research

Sharit K. Bhowmik

This chapter examines the research literature on street vendors in Asia with the aim of assessing the magnitude of street vending in different countries and the composition of the vendors. Further, it collates information on the extent of unionisation of the vendors and other organisations, such as non-governmental organisations (NGOs), self-help organisations (SHOs), advocacy groups, etc., that work for their welfare. The data is based mainly on secondary sources.

## Introduction

The steady increase of the labour force in the informal sector in the last two decades can be traced back to two main factors: the rural–urban pull factor and reduced employment opportunities in the formal sector. Lack of gainful employment coupled with poverty in rural areas has pushed people out of their villages into the cities in search of a better existence. These migrants do not possess the skills or the education to enable them to find better paid, secure employment in the formal sector and they have to settle for work in the informal sector. There is another section of the population in Asian countries who are forced to join the informal sector. These are workers who were employed in the formal sector. They lost their jobs because of closures, downsizing or mergers in the industries they worked in and in order to survive they or their family members had to seek low-paid work in the informal sector.

The first category, namely the low-skilled rural migrants, exists in all countries of Asia but they are more prevalent in the poorer countries such as Bangladesh, Nepal, Cambodia, and Vietnam. These countries did not have a strong industrial base and in the past too, the urban workforce was engaged mainly in the informal sector. The second category, namely those working earlier in the formal sector, exists in countries such as Philippines, South Korea, Thailand, Malaysia, Indonesia, and countries that had large industries. The closure of several of these industries due to a variety of reasons—outsourcing of work to the informal sector, mergers of some of the corporations, downsizing of the production units, etc.—has resulted in large-scale unemployment in these countries. In most cases, the informal sector has absorbed this labour force. In fact, even manufacturing units have grown faster in the informal sector than those in the formal sector. For example, in India, the total workforce in the formal sector is around 30 million whereas the small-scale industries provide employment to 18 million workers. Around half of those employed in the formal sector are in white-collar jobs. Hence, clearly, workers in the small-scale sector out-number blue-collar workers in the formal sector.

Activities in the informal sector can be categorised as self-employed or casual (non-permanent) labour. A major section of those in the self-employed category work as street vendors. The rise in the number of street vendors is largely due to the lack of employment in other sectors, and it is also directly linked to the expansion of the informal sector in these countries.

A street vendor is broadly defined as a person who offers goods for sale to the public at large, without having a permanent built-up structure from which to sell. Street vendors may be stationary in the sense that they occupy space on the pavements or other public/private spaces or, they may be mobile in the sense that move from place to place by carrying their wares on push carts or in baskets on their heads. In this chapter, the term 'street vendor' includes stationary as well as mobile vendors and it incorporates all other local/region-specific terms used to describe them. In this study, the terms 'street vendor' and 'hawker' have the same meaning and have often been used interchangeably. There is substantial increase in the number of street vendors in major Asian cities. In India, estimates show that street vendors constitute approximately 2 per cent of the population of a metropolis. The total number of street vendors in the country is estimated at around 10 million. This number is likely to increase even further.

However, street vending survives not merely because it is an important source of employment but also because of the services it provides to the urban population. For the urban poor, street vendors provide goods, including food, at low prices. Hence, we find that one section of the urban poor, namely, street vendors, subsidises the existence of the other sections of the urban poor. Middle-income groups too benefit from street vending because of the affordable prices offered. These aspects are unfortunately ignored by the urban local bodies (ULBs) and the police because more often than not, street vending is considered an illegal activity and street vendors are treated as criminals. In fact, the studies and reports quoted in this study show that in almost all the Asian countries, street vendors have no legal status to conduct their business and they are constantly harassed by the authorities. In the following sections we shall discuss the status of street vendors based on reports and studies conducted in the different countries.

## Methodology and Data Collection

The first step in data collection was trying to identify the existing studies. I had come across a few studies while participating in seminars. I wrote to these people and asked them if they had any further contacts with other researchers. Unfortunately, this yielded hardly any results. The few researchers who had studied street vending were unable to put me in touch with others, because there is hardly any academic research conducted on this issue. I could get some leads but in most cases I got no response from them.

The next step was to contact the trade unions and NGOs working for street vendors. The National Alliance of Street Vendors of India (NASVI) had organised a conference on street vendors in Asia for StreetNet in 2002. I had not attended that conference but I got the list of participants from NASVI. This was a fairly impressive list and I tried contacting the organisations in the various countries, but here too I wasn't very successful. Though many of the unions had email addresses, they did not respond to my repeated emails and I was unable to establish direct contact with them. I was able to make contact with only some research institutes and NGOs in some countries. My main source of information were websites, from where I was able to access some documents and studies. The local newspaper reports contained information on the activities of street vendors and the attitudes of the authorities (government, police and ULBs).

After exploring all the possible sources, one can only conclude that although street vending is expanding rapidly, there is hardly any significant accessible research on this issue. There is an urgent need to encourage more research on this important segment of the urban informal sector.

In the following sections we shall summarise the data we have on the different countries. In the concluding section, we shall attempt to synthesise the studies along with information discussed in the earlier sections, with a view to comparing the situation in these countries. An attempt will be made to delineate the areas for further research.

## Country Studies

### Bangladesh

The number of street vendors in Bangladesh is large. Dhaka, the capital of Bangladesh, is also its largest city. According to the Dhaka City Corporation there are around 90,000 street vendors in the city (*New Age Metro* 2003). They operate mainly in the Motijheel, Baitul Mukarram, Gulistan, Shahbagh, and New Market areas. Street vending is considered an illegal trade and street vendors face constant harassment from the authorities. The vendors have to pay a sizeable part of their income as bribes in order to keep plying their trade. According to one report, vendors in the New Market area pay Tk. 200,000 a month to a gang that shares the collection with the law-enforcement agency (ibid.). Each vendor in this area pays around Tk. 200 a month to run his/her business. In other areas such as Baitul Mukarram, GPO and Purana Paltan, vendors pay the police Tk. 5 daily to avoid harassment. According to the Bangladeshi delegates who had attended the 2002 Asian Regional Workshop in Bodh Gaya, India, the street vendors of Bangladesh were more vulnerable than those in the neighbouring countries due to poverty, lack of space for vending and lack of awareness about their rights (NASVI 2002).

There is, however, a fair level of unionisation among street vendors, with several unions working among them. The most important is the Bangladesh Hawkers' Federation as it is linked to the trade union federation of the (then) ruling Bangladesh National Party. The federation has been negotiating with the government for a policy on street vendors. The first step in this direction is of forging alliances with other trade unions of street vendors so that a national alliance emerges. This can in turn pressurise the government to take up the issue of a national policy for street vendors. However, till such a consensus emerges, the street vendors in Bangladesh will continue to be regarded as illegal traders and will continue to be harassed by the authorities.

Political parties in Bangladesh continue to offer vocal support to street vendors, without doing anything concrete to improve their insecurity. For example, a news item in a popular daily in Dhaka carried the headline: 'Huda assures hawkers to protect their rights' (*The Bangladesh Observer* 2003). The report noted that while addressing a rally organised by the Bangladesh Hawkers' Federation at Dhaka, the communications minister, Barrister Nazmul Huda, assured hawkers that he would provide them all support to protect their rights and continue their profession in the city and that the government was 'pledge-bound' to protect the human rights of the citizens. Following up these statements was an attack on the opposition accusing them of wanting to disrupt the development efforts of the ruling party. The minister encouraged 'the people' (meaning the hawkers) to ensure that the opposition was not voted into power. Clearly, the minister simply used the issue of the hawkers as a political peg to castigate the opposition and pat his own back.

This approach is not unique to Bangladesh alone. In most countries where the number of street vendors is large, the ruling parties mobilise them for their political purposes. Because their livelihoods are insecure, vendors tend to flock to one party or the other for protection. These parties use street vendors for their political gains, and the vendors themselves do not get any tangible benefits from these alliances.

## Food Vendors

Food vendors are an important feature of Bangladeshi cities. A social welfare and cultural officer in the Dhaka City Corporation, Qazi Saif Uddin Ahmad (2000) notes that the street food industry provides employment to women and migrants with low educational background. The prices of street food are low and the urban poor benefit from this. Day labourers, rickshaw pullers, migrants from rural areas and the homeless depend on street food vendors for their nutrition. However, because of poor hygiene people often fall ill after eating street food and become victims of water-borne diseases.

Ahmad feels that there must be cooperation between the municipalities and the police for proper management of street food vending. He suggests that municipalities can formulate rules and regulations for the management of street food vending, but they need to be enforced by the police. How far this is feasible is anyone's guess. The experience in India is that such rules only help increase rent-seeking among corrupt officials but not in improving hygiene.

A study conducted by the Intermediate Technology Development Group on food vendors in Bangladesh and Sri Lanka notes that as street vendors are in the informal sector there is no systematic documentation of their numbers (Tedd et al. 1999). Observations indicate that there are a substantive number of food vendors in the urban areas. Their ages range between 25 to 60 years with a majority being in the age group 30–40 years. This study recorded the employment history of food vendors and found that their previous involvement in several urban-based, irregular and low-paid activities requiring hard manual labour pushed them into the street food business. These vendors do not always make much profit and tend to move from one place to another in search of better markets. The contribution of women to this trade is significant. Though women do not constitute a major section of food vendors in Dhaka, the male vendors depend on the women in their household for preparing the items for sale.

The study notes that street food effectively meets the requirements of a large section of the economically active urban population. But vendors are frequently victimised by the formal institutions such as the police, public health institutions, local government authorities, etc. They are also denied institutional credit facilities that could help in increasing their income. They have to rely exclusively on social networks for running their business.

## India

The number of street vendors in major Indian cities has increased sharply during the past few years. It is now estimated that around 2.5 per cent of the urban population are engaged in this occupation. The total number of street vendors in India is around 10 million. Their numbers have increased after the liberalisation policy of 1991. A fairly high proportion of vendors were once workers in the formal sector and have taken to street vending after they lost their jobs. This proportion is relatively higher in cities like Kolkata (50 per cent), Mumbai and Ahmedabad (30 per cent) which were once centres of industry but have seen large-scale closures in the past decade or two. Several large factories and establishments have closed down due to rationalisation and their workers have lost their secure jobs. As in other countries, for these people street vending is one of the ways of eking out an existence.

Studies on street vendors/hawkers are few and are focused mainly on some cities. Early studies on street vendors were conducted by the Self Employed Women's Association (SEWA) which is currently the largest trade union in Gujarat with branches in several other states. A study by SEWA in Ahmedabad notes that half the laid off textile workers in Ahmedabad have taken to street vending. The other vendors are mainly migrants from rural areas or from small towns who came to these cities to find employment and couldn't find regular jobs and have taken to street vending. The Self Employed Women's Association's research studies on street vendors in Ahmedabad have been used to highlight the plight of street vendors for the benefit of the government and the general public.

In 2000, the National Alliance of Street Vendors in India organised a study on hawkers in seven cities—Mumbai, Kolkata, Bangalore, Bhubaneswar, Patna, Ahmedabad, and Imphal (Bhowmik 2000). This could be taken as one of the more comprehensive studies on street vending. The NASVI study included an assessment of municipal and police laws, an examination of the use of public space in the city's plans and a study of consumers. Two more studies were conducted on street vendors in Mumbai, besides the one by NASVI. In 1998, the Brihanmumbai Municipal Corporation (BMC) commissioned the Tata Institute of Social Sciences (TISS) and Youth for Unity and Voluntary Action (YUVA) to conduct a census of hawkers on municipal lands (Sharma 1998). In 2001, SNDT Women's University, in collaboration with the International Labour Organisation (ILO) conducted a study on street vendors (SNDT Women's University and ILO 1999). Both studies contain a lot of useful information on the socio-economic conditions of these vendors.

An interesting aspect of these studies is that they all find common features among street vendors. Their earnings vary between Rs 50 to Rs 80 per day. Women earn between Rs 40 and Rs 60 per day. They work under gruelling conditions for long hours and are frequently harassed by the municipal authorities and the police. The NASVI study found that around 20 per cent of their earnings are taken as rent by the authorities. In Mumbai the annual collection of rent is around Rs 4 billion. A study by Manushi in Delhi (mentioned later) estimated the figure in Delhi to be Rs 5 billion. The SNDT-ILO study on Mumbai found that around 85 per cent of the street vendors complained of stress-related diseases—migraine, hyper-acidity, hyper-tension and high blood pressure.

The Manushi study in Delhi showed the stark reality of the vendors' lives and the nature of their exploitation and harassment by the authorities (*The Hindu* 2001). This study prompted the prime minister to write to the lt. governor of the Union Territory of Delhi to change the administration's oppressive policies on street vendors. The prime minister's office also issued a concept note on this subject which contained important guidelines.

In Delhi, town planners Geetam Tiwari and Dinesh Mohan (2000) have made significant contributions to the research on the use of pavement and road space and pollution control with regard to street vending.[7] They have shown that having street vendors near housing complexes reduces pol-lution levels as residents do not need to use cars or two-wheelers to buy their daily requirements.

There is no clear picture of the number of women vendors, except in Ahmedabad where around 40 per cent of the 80,000 street vendors are women. In other cities they are an invisible category. Male vendors are more visible as they sell a greater variety of goods—clothes, fruits, household items, etc. Most food vendors are men. The level of unionisation is higher among them and they are thus able to protect themselves better than the women vendors. There is, therefore, a need to make a proper assessment of women vendors. At a rough guess, they should constitute 30 per cent of the total population of vendors. They are mainly small vendors and they are hardly unionised (except in Ahmedabad). These factors add to their invisibility.

The NASVI study found that the incomes of women vendors are lower than the men's because of two main reasons. Most of the women belonged to families that were poorer than those of male street vendors. They had less capital to invest in their business. Second, they could not spend as much time on their work as the men because they had to take care of the home as well. Moreover, in cities like Kolkata and Patna, women vendors were harassed by the male vendors and were not allowed to sit on the pavements. In Patna, the women prefer to carry their wares in baskets on their heads and move from house to house. In cities where they are unionised, as in Ahmedabad, their problems were not as acute.

In Mumbai, studies indicate that most of the women street vendors belong to families in which the male members were employed in better paid, secure jobs in the formal sector. They were unemployed when their enterprises closed. Their wives took to street vending to make ends meet. In contrast to these petty hawkers, the flower sellers at Siddhivinayak temple at Prabhadevi, also in central Mumbai, represent a higher income group. This temple attracts a large number of devotees on all days; more so on Tuesdays. The flower sellers around the temple are exclusively women. These women too are wives of textile workers who are now unemployed. They faced a lot of harassment by the police and municipal authorities while plying their trade. They then got together to form an informal association through which they tried to get legitimacy for their work. The municipal authorities finally agreed to allot them space on the pavement where they could construct kiosks. They are now among the better-off sections of street vendors. This is unfortunately the only success story in this city, which has a quarter of a million street vendors.

## Food Vendors

Studies on food vendors have been conducted by the Food and Agriculture Organisation (FAO) in some of the cities. These included Pune, Hyderabad, Mumbai, Bangalore, and Kolkata. The Kolkata study was the most important one conducted to date. The Pune study looked into varieties of food available, socio-economic status of vendors and con-sumers. The Mumbai study included types of food sold, timings and en-vironmental conditions prevailing and types of consumers. The Hyderabad study looked into types of vending, food sold and unpermitted adulterants present. The Bangalore study covered hygiene and sanitation conditions in small hotels and way-side restaurants. The Kolkata study looked into all aspects of the street food vending situation of the city, including type of vendors and consumers, timings of operation, costs and profits, nutritive value, physical, chemical and detailed microbiological analysis of all varieties of foods and water.[1]

There are a few other studies that deal with important aspects of street food vending. Mini Bhattacharya's (1997) doctoral dissertation on street food vendors in Guwahati in north-east India highlights their role in providing cheap food to the people and their employment potential. She notes that the food vendors face the problem of capital. They depend mainly on loans to run their business. They rarely approach banks because of the huge paper work involved in getting loans.

In most of the cities the street vendors have their trade unions. This is one of the means for survival for them. The NASVI study, in fact, collected most of its data with the help of local trade unions. Many of these trade unions are independent, local unions that operate in certain areas only. The national trade union federations too have their unions for street vendors. This would appear as a promising sign for the informal sector.

The national federations have their membership mainly in the formal sector, hence, their diversifying to the informal sector would imply that they are trying to bring about a link between the workers of the two sectors. This is not necessarily correct. In most cases street vendors' unions who were affiliated to the national or other federations were in fact operating as local unions. The federation concerned seemed to accept the union merely for increasing its total membership. Most leaders of the federations are invariably leaders of unions in the formal sector. They rarely addressed meetings of the street vendors or took up their issues at the higher levels of the federation. The main reason for the unions of street vendors to affiliate with national federations was to gain some credibility while negotiating with the municipal authorities.

The Self Employed Women's Association has played an important role in unionising women vendors in Ahmedabad that has helped them gain visibility. In 1998, it also initiated the formation of the National Alliance of Street Vendors of India, which is an all-India-level coalition of trade unions and voluntary organisations working for street vendors. Now based in Patna, NASVI started off as a networking organisation of street vendors. It advocates for the basic rights of street vendors. It creates awareness about the usefulness of vendors and hawkers, brings to light their plight, so that the urban planners and authorities can no longer ignore them, and publishes a quarterly newsletter in Hindi and English called *Footpath ki Awaz* (Voice from the Pavement/Sidewalk). The National Alliance of Street Vendors of India gives vendors a forum to raise their voice for just demands and rights. Today, more than 350 street vendor organisations from 22 states of the country are part of NASVI.

The Ministry of Urban Development and Poverty Alleviation had set up a National Task Force on Street Vendors in 2002 mainly as a result of the initiatives of SEWA and NASVI. The task force was entrusted with the task of formulating the national policy.

This policy mainly aims at legalising street vending and has several positive features. It recommends that the licensing system be replaced by provision of identity cards to street vendors. Decisions regarding street vending will be made by Ward Committees (for each municipal ward) which will have street vendors as representatives along with others. The policy also makes provisions for social security, insurance and pension for street vendors. On 20 January 2004, the cabinet formally accepted this policy. The implementation of this policy will depend largely on the attitudes of the state governments. Therefore, the next task of the unions of street vendors should be that of trying to convince the state governments to accept this policy.

## Sri Lanka

Street vendors in Sri Lanka appear to be in a slightly better position than their counterparts in Bangladesh and India. In most urban areas street vending is not totally illegal and vendors can ply their trade on the pavements by paying a daily tax to the municipal council. However, on a closer look, we find that their fate is no different from street vendors in other countries. Despite gaining some legal recognition, vendors are evicted if the municipal council feels that they cause problems to the general public. In most cases evicted vendors are not provided alternative sites. Sri Lankan delegates who participated in the Asian Regional Workshop of StreetNet reported that not only did the street vendors face evictions, the municipal authorities burnt their stalls during these drives.

In its report (23 July 2002), Sevanatha, an NGO working for the empowerment of street vendors in Colombo, notes that 'the street hawkers of Colombo have had their livelihoods threatened by the Colombo City planners' attempts to cleanse the city streets of the informal sector'. These planners 'keep to the outdated western concept that pavements are to be clear and clean for pedestrians whereas in the West and many Asian cities planners have realised the benefits of providing space for pavement sellers and maintaining a lively inner city culture'. Hence, though street vendors are somewhat recognised by the municipality as they pay taxes, it does not necessarily provide security to them. In most cases, provision of alternative space depends largely on how strongly their union can press for this demand. According to Sevanatha, there are 8,000 to 10,000 street vendors in Colombo, mostly in the formal city centres. They are from urban poor settlements and street vending is the only source of employment for these families. Women and children play active roles in this occupation. Their main problem is the lack of security of livelihood and the lack of access to credit.

Delegates who participated in the workshop said that it was possible to influence government policy through trade unions of street vendors. It was through their pressure that the government agreed to accommodate street vendors in the World Market Day and Night Bazaar. The goods sold by street vendors were cheaper than those offered by the big stores.

## Food Vendors

The figures of street vendors mentioned earlier do not include street food vendors, who form a large and significant part of the urban population. The project on food vendors conducted by the Intermediate Technology Development Group (see Tedd et al. 1999) notes that the number of food vendors in Colombo is fairly large and is increasing because of the needs of the customers. 'The food is relatively cheap and readily available. It is sometimes brought to the doorstep of the customers and sold on credit as done by the vendors operating at Manning Market in Colombo' (Tedd et al. 2002: 10).

The income of food vendors is higher than that of other vendors. According to a report, 'The average daily income of a street food vendor is around Rs. 1,250 while the average daily profit generated . . . is approximately Rs. 575. Most street food vendors operate for an average of 25 days a month. This means that they are able to generate a monthly average income of Rs. 31,250 and an average profit of Rs. 14,375. In comparison, the monthly income in urban Sri Lanka is Rs. 23,436 and the national monthly household income is Rs. 13,036 (Govt. of Sri Lanka 2002, quoted in Tedd et al. 2002: 11). This indicates that the contribution of street food vendors to the country's economy is significant, though they face similar problems as other street vendors, namely, lack of security and lack of institutional facilities.

The Colombo Municipality has tried to set up a model for street food vendors. According to Keerthi Mafasinghe, a food inspector in the Colombo Municipal Council, the municipality has organised a group of 35 food vendors called the *Galle Face Green Food Vendors*.[2] Carts are provided by the municipality and they maintain high standards of hygiene. The activities of this group are highlighted by the Public Health Department as an ideal project.

## Nepal

Nepal is perhaps the poorest country in South Asia. Industries in Nepal are found mainly in the plains bordering India and they offer little employment to the local population. In the larger towns such as Kathmandu, the main source of income of the urban poor is the informal sector. The tourist trade in these areas provides some support to activities in the informal sector, which includes street vending. The urban poor depend on street vendors for cheap goods.

Unfortunately, not much is known about these street vendors. Neither are there any studies on them nor do the government/municipal authorities provide any statistics. They are, for all practical purposes, an invisible group. Though not too invisible, because we do get information about their evictions by the police. Unionisation is almost non-existent and they are unable to articulate their interests. The delegate from Nepal who participated in the Asian Regional Street Vendors' Workshop noted that there were 30,000 to 40,000 street vendors in Nepal. They were largely unorganised because they were not aware of their rights.

The only union of street vendors—initiated by General Federation of Nepalese Trade Unions (GFONT), the largest federation in the country—was started barely three months prior to the StreetNet workshop. Even before unions had started, GFONT had taken up the case for street vendors. On the eve of the South Asian Association for Regional Co-operation (SAARC) meeting in Kathmandu, the government had ordered that the streets be cleared of hawkers. Tension mounted in the city as this move would jeopardise the interests of the street vendors and also cause inconvenience to the poor. Finally, at the intervention of GFONT, the government was forced to reconsider its decision.

## Bangkok (Thailand)

The most observable fact about Bangkok is its street vendors. Almost every street in this city has street vendors selling an array of items—clothes, curios, electronic items, and a wide variety of cooked and raw food. In fact, the food vendors of Bangkok are known for their cheap but nutritious fare. For the local population, the food stalls are an integral part of life in Bangkok, particularly the makeshift restaurants. Hundreds of people rely on them for a good meal at a low price.

The municipal authorities in Bangkok have demarcated sites where street vendors can operate. There are 287 such sites in the city. There are also 14 sites on private land. The sites officially allotted for street vending are not sufficient for accommodating all street vendors. Moreover, these areas do not cover all sections of the city and hence the customers are not catered to. This has led to street vendors operating in unauthorised areas. There are 407 sites where vendors conduct their business but these are unofficial areas. This means that the majority of street vendors in the city operate on sites that are unauthorised.

Street vending is an important source of income for the urban poor. I visited some slums in Bangkok in May 2003 and found that most of the slum dwellers were engaged in street food hawking. The number of street vendors in the city increased rapidly after the monetary crisis of 1998 which affected the group of countries known as the 'Asian Tigers'. Many of the workers who lost their jobs as a result of the crisis and others who could not find jobs, took to street vending as a source of livelihood.

An FAO study on street food vendors in South East Asia notes that in 1993 there were 6,040 street hawkers operating in the city selling raw food stuff (vegetables, fruits, meat, and sea food) (Pizzali 2001). This represented around 30 per cent of the total street hawkers at that time. In other words, the total number of street vendors was around 19,000–20,000. When the FAO study was conducted in 2001, it found that there were 26,000 food hawkers operating in authorised areas. This means that the number of food vendors in the authorised areas was higher than the total number of street vendors in 1993. If we take into account the unauthorised areas—which are much larger than the authorised areas—and the private sites, the number of street vendors in the city should be over 100,000.

## Food Vendors

The proliferation of food vendors in Bangkok is due to a number of reasons. First, there is a tradition of eating out among the population. Hence, food vendors form a part of the cultural tradition of the urban population. Second, rapid urbanisation as a result of migration from rural areas and the long hours of work for the low-paid workers in the informal sector often leave the urban poor with little time to cook proper meals. They thus depend on street food vendors to provide them with cheap but nutritious meals. Third, food vendors attract tourists who are on the look out for local foods. Fourth, according to the FAO study, 'low-income families purchase their food (including fish) on a daily basis, since they don't have enough money to purchase large amounts of food'. People buy fish by the small dish in street markets. Sale of fish by the small dish is a traditional service offered only by street food hawkers and the poor benefit from this.

Despite the service provided by street vendors to the general public, their contributions are not viewed in the same light by the authorities. Street vendors, especially those in unauthorised areas, are subject to frequent raids and evictions. In fact, at one time the government was thinking of passing a law banning street vendors in Bangkok as they caused clogging of the pavements and the streets. The famous traffic snarls of Bangkok are attributed to street vendors. There is no evidence that street vendors cause traffic problems; they operate from pavements and not on the roads. In reality, the road space is not sufficient to accommodate the growing number of private vehicles and that is what causes traffic problems. After the sky-rail was commissioned, the traffic problems, at least in areas where the rail operates, have lessened considerably as many car-owners now prefer to take the sky-rail to their work places.

Significantly, vendors in Bangkok are not unionised. This seems surprising given their large numbers and the problems that they face from the authorities. Perhaps unionisation could have been a means of getting protection to carry out their activities, recognition and possibly government support.

## Singapore

If we go by the reports of the Hawkers' Department of the Government of Singapore, this must be the only country in the world where all street vendors are licensed. It is the duty of the Hawkers' Department to check that there are no unlicensed hawkers and issue licenses to those wanting to hawk goods on the pavements. As in most South East Asian countries, in Singapore too food hawkers predominate. In 1971, a national programme aimed at building food centres and markets to resettle licensed street food hawkers was taken up. The programme provided basic stall facilities and services such as piped potable water, electricity and garbage collection and disposal. By 1996, all street hawkers had been completely resettled into food centres and markets (Pizzali 2001). In 1988, there were 23,331 hawkers operating in 184 centres; of these, 8,878 were engaged in selling cooked food. At present there are nearly 50,000 street vendors in this city-state.

The Hawkers' Department plays an active role in ensuring that the hawkers keep their environment clean and do not pose constraints on pedestrians. Its officials inspect all stalls and see that they abide by the Environmental Public Health Act of 1968. It also organises regular training courses on food hygiene, personal hygiene and nutrition. Between 1990 and 1996 the department had trained more than 10,000 hawkers.

The composition of the city's street vending population is changing. There is an emergence of younger, better-educated street vendors (*Star Malaysia* 2003). This change is attributed to the rising unemployment that has put 13,000 graduates out of jobs. Many of these have taken to street vending. The change is more noticeable in food hawking. The variety of food offered is wider than the earlier traditional fare. The younger, educated food vendors are willing to experiment with new international dishes and this has increased their popularity. The government decided to upgrade the food stalls in the densely populated residential areas. By 2003, 45 such centres were upgraded. Though the rents increased, the street vendors still got a lot of clientele because the items they sold were still cheaper than the shops.

A significant fact about street vendors in Singapore is that over the past 30 years they have helped to keep down the costs of living; workers, students and the poorer sections depend on them for their daily necessities, including their meals. This is true of other places as well, but unfortunately the planners rarely consider their contributions to the local economy.

## Kuala Lumpur (Malaysia)

Malaysia is one of the few countries in Asia that has given some form of recognition to street vendors.[3] In 1990, Malaysia initiated the National Policy on Hawkers. It is a comprehensive plan to tackle the social and economic problems associated with street vending. Its implementation includes the provision of funds to support credit schemes and training programmes for street vendors to improve their facilities. The regulation and control of street vendors is under the Department of Hawkers and Petty Traders (DHPT) established in 1986. The objectives of the department include the development, modernisation and management of the street vendors, in line with the objective of making Kuala Lumpur a clean, healthy and beautiful city for the local people and tourists.

As in the case of the other South East Asian countries, the number of street vendors in Kuala Lumpur has risen sharply since the Asian financial crisis. According to DHPT the number of licensed street vendors rose by 30 per cent between 1999 and 2000. The total number of licensed street vendors in 2000 was nearly 35,000. In addition, it was believed that there were more than 12,000 unlicensed street vendors operating. This figure could be an underestimation as there is no proper survey on the actual number of street vendors in the city. The increase of unlicensed street vendors is mainly because the DHPT has stopped issuing licenses after 1996. The financial crisis took place three years later and most people who lost their jobs at the time took to street vending.

The objective of the DHPT is to relocate street vendors; in the case of food hawkers, to food centres in buildings or to central sites. It also helps in designing vans for mobile hawking. Around 35 per cent of the total number of street vendors are food hawkers. However, there are other sites where street vendors can carry out their business. These are the densely populated residential areas and the industrial estates. There are hardly any hawking sites in these areas. More licenses could be granted for these areas. Licensed street vendors have access to institutional credit as the government has provided funds for this. Training programmes are organised regularly for these vendors in which they are taught about health and hygiene, business skills and accounts. The DHPT organises some of these programmes and seeks the cooperation of NGOs too. There are 60 NGOs engaged in this activity. The unlicensed street vendors do not get any of these benefits.

In 1970 only 4.4 per cent of Malays were engaged in street vending. However, in 2000 there were 11,170 (31 per cent) Malays, 20,812 (59.3 per cent) Chinese and 3,138 (9.0 per cent) Indians licensed as street vendors. It is believed that this change is due to the licenses issued by the DHPT which preferred to grant more licenses to the indigenous Malay population.

## Manila (Philippines)

Like Kuala Lumpur, the city of Manila (comprising seven municipalities) has devised some plans for street vendors. The Business Promotion and Development Office of the metropolis has a division known as the Hawkers Permit Services. This division was created by City Ordinance No. 79–2 to receive, process, review, and analyse applications for street vending. It has inspectors who are expected to regulate street trade and collect daily fees from regular (licensed) and other street vendors.[4] The objective, it appears, is to increase the revenue of the municipalities.

In 2001 the Philippines government decided to legalise street vending by issuing street hawkers identity cards, thus allowing them to ply their trade in certain areas (Vanzi 2001). This decision was taken to protect and uphold the rights of the informal sector. A memorandum of understanding (MoU) was signed by the Department of Interior and Local Government, Department of Labour, Department of Trade and Industry and League of Provinces.

According to the MoU, city and municipal governments should designate markets, vacant areas near markets, public parks and side streets as certified places for hawking. A head count of street vendors would be made to register them as informal workers. The MoU also mentions that the vendors' associations would be encouraged to take on the responsibility of regulating street vendors by ensuring cleanliness on the streets and proper hygiene for food vendors.

Despite these promises, the actual fate of street vendors in the Philippines, especially in Metro Manila where a third of the country's vendors operate, is no better than in most of the other countries mentioned earlier. Though the promised head count never took place, it is estimated that there are around 50,000 street vendors in Metro Manila, most of whom are unregistered and hence illegal. The paper presented by Celerina F. Sangil, a recreation and welfare service officer with the Department of Social Welfare, mentions that according to the Hawkers Permit Services, there are about 15,000 street vendors in Metro Manila and only 5,000 of them are legal. Other reports show that these figures are grossly underestimated.[5]

The main problem faced by the street vendors is that there are no demarcated areas for them to operate. Street food vendors do not have access to piped water and they are hence rendered illegal on health grounds. Street vendors are also blamed for the filth on the pavements and for causing traffic problems. The attitude of the government towards them can be gauged from a report, quoted here, on the latest moves to get them off the streets.

> Officials in the Philippines are planning to clear illegal street sellers off pavements by spraying their goods with kerosene. Manila Development Authority chairman Bayani Fernando says the move will make the goods unsellable (sic) and soon make street vending unprofitable. He has lost patience after the failure of other moves to combat illegal sellers. He plans teams of officials armed with plastic spray bottles filled with kerosene to hit vendors' stalls without warning.
>
> Human rights groups are criticising the measure, but Mr. Fernando seems unconcerned about the fire safety aspect of dousing materials in flammable liquid. He is unhappy about the litter left behind by street sellers and occasional traffic jams they cause by blocking streets, reports the Straits Times, quoting the Manila Standard newspaper.
>
> Mr. Fernando said: 'They can run, but they can no longer sell their goods once we have sprayed these with gas. Eventually, they will lose capital and stop illegal vending. People will no longer buy items that smell of, or are soaked in gasoline, particularly edible goods' (Ananova 2002).

Incidentally, Fernando was planning to contest for the post of vice-president in the next elections. Another important parliamentarian who supports Fernando's moves to keep the city streets clean is Ramon

Magsaysay, Jr., the son of the late president after whom the Magsaysay award is named. Hence, it is clear that though governments pretend to show sympathy to informal sector workers, they hardly ever translate their laws into practice.

This view was reiterated by the two trade union leaders who participated in the StreetNet regional conference. Maria Mercedes I Nicholas (of Katinig, a federation of workers in the informal sector) and Maria R. Buanghug (of Cebu City United Vendors' Organisation, an affiliate of Katinig), spoke of how, despite laws, street vendors are victimised. Though there are laws for legalising street vending, as discussed earlier, these are never implemented properly. Most vendors are not given licenses. It was through Katinig's efforts that the government signed the MoU. However, since most of the street vendors were not regularised by law, they are victims of police harassment and evictions. Besides fighting for the rights of street vendors, the two unions have also initiated cooperatives among them. The Kamansi cooperative was initiated by the union at Cebu City. It provides loans for hospitalisation and death assistance. In 2001, the assistance released was Pesos 8.3 million.

In general, in Philippines, women vendors are more easily unionised than the males.

## Hanoi (Vietnam)

Street vendors play an important role in urban Vietnam's commerce. They provide a variety of low-priced goods and generate employment for a large number of people, especially women. In the case of food vendors, around 30 per cent are women.[6] In 1989 the Vietnamese government adopted a law on protection of people's health. A survey of food samples in Hanoi showed that 47 per cent were microbiologically unsafe. Within a few years the scene transformed and 23.4 per cent of the food vendors had changed their unhygienic practices. This was achieved by regular surveillance of food vendors and by training them in hygienic practices. The government has adopted two practices for ensuring safer street food, namely, monitoring street food vendors through a licensing system and educating and training them on hygiene.

A study by Darunee Tantiwiramanond (undated) notes that women are at the forefront of Vietnam's economy. To overcome high unemployment, the government is focusing on promotion of the formal sector. The progress is, however, not in keeping with the rising poverty. This seems to be the age-old fallacy of most governments in developing countries. They seem to think that the only way to overcome the unfavourable situation of the informal sector is by trying to expand the formal sector, instead of trying to introduce reforms in the informal sector. The informal sector creates employment, fights poverty and subsidises urban living. Street vendors, especially in Hanoi, are an important component of this sector.

Tantiwiramanond's study finds half the women vendors are young, below 29 years of age, and a quarter of them are single. Most of them come from large poor families with at least five siblings. Though a majority of them have some education (up to 12 years) it is not sufficient for getting them secure employment. Street vending is the major means of their survival. Most of the female vendors move from door to door carrying their wares in two baskets slung on two ends of a pole that is carried on the shoulder. Most of them sell single items, that is, either food (vegetable, eggs and processed foods) or household items. A small proportion sell a combination of food and household items. The male vendors on the other hand are engaged in motor cycle repairs or sale of higher priced goods such as personal products, souvenirs, etc., and their earnings are higher.

Tantiwiramanond's study notes that the sexual divide is very prevalent in Vietnamese society. There is a sexual division of labour through which certain types of work are designated to women and others to men. For example, he finds that even women vendors feel sorry for male vendors who are into door to door vending by carrying two baskets strung on a pole as they feel that this is not a man's job. It is rather surprising to find such division of labour existing in a society that has, in the past, shown remarkable resistance to the super powers.

Women vendors face problems on the street, most of which are gender-related. Tantiwiramanond notes that customers often tease, disrespect or sometimes violate the human dignity of women vendors. There is also a social bias that women cannot perform certain activities such as motor cycle repair, polish shoes or work as taxi drivers at night. Moreover, women are expected to look after the home which reduces the time they spend on vending and adds a strain to their activities.

Tantiwiramanond finds that Vietnam is a good case study to understand the determination of people to struggle against all odds not only for self-rule but also for building a different society. Unfortunately, the current policy neglects the needs of micro-traders, especially women, in the informal sector. The street vendors are not unionised, nor are there any NGOs working for their empowerment. He warns that such policies of neglect may turn the creative urges of the poor to deviant behaviour. This is of course not the problem only of Vietnam but of most developing countries that are intolerant to street vendors.

## Cambodia

The Kingdom of Cambodia, like its neighbour Vietnam, has seen a lot of political upheavals in the recent past. Though there has been peace since 1997, Cambodia's economy has been shattered and the government is almost bankrupt. Regular jobs, provided by the government, are few and not well-paid. According to the Urban Sector Group (USG), an NGO working among slum dwellers and workers in the informal sector, 95 per cent of all employment is in the informal sector and 80 per cent of the GDP is from this sector (Agnello and Moller 2003).

Street vending is an important source of employment for the urban poor in Cambodia, especially women. There is no estimate of the actual number of street vendors in Phnom Penh, the capital, or in the other towns. The data in this section is based on two studies conducted on women vendors (Agnello and Moller 2003; and Kusakabe 2003). According to the USG study a majority of the street vendors in Phnom Penh (60 per cent) are in the age group 30 to 60 years and most of them (97 per cent) are women. These women represent the poor and they come from large families having two to four income earners. Cambodia has two poverty lines—the food poverty line and the general poverty line. The food poverty line represents the bare minimum required for basic food and nothing else. Those who come under this line are the poorest. The poverty line represents those earning barely enough to meet the needs of food, clothing and shelter. Street vendors fall below the poverty line but above the food poverty line.

According to the USG study, women have to put in hard work and have to spend around 12 to 13 hours a day at their work. However, they feel that street vending gives them self-respect as they do not have to depend on others (male members of their family) for their sustenance. According to the study by Kusakabe (2003) women vendors in Phnom Penh are from poor backgrounds and have low levels of education. Street vending is the only way they can earn a living with dignity. She finds that these women are less dependent on their husbands as they are the main bread winners in the family. In most cases the husbands do not have regular jobs and because of 'male superiority' they do not do housework, including taking care of the children's education. Kusakabe finds that street vendors who are widowed or divorced are not interested in finding husbands because they feel that they are independent and do not need the support of males.

The USG study finds that one of the objectives of women vendors to earn more is to educate their children. However, long hours of work outside of their homes leaves them little time to look into their children's studies. Most of the vendors said that though they could send their children to school they could not supervise their studies or their homework as they were busy with their work.

The main problem faced by street vendors is that the government does not recognise the existence of the informal sector. The street vendors do not have any permanent places to sell their goods. They thus cannot retain regular customers. They are frequently harassed by the police and the market security officials. The USG study notes that rent-seeking is high and the only way the women can stay on the streets is by paying bribes to these officials. If they don't pay, their goods are confiscated or even destroyed. The study also found that some of the women vendors could sell more goods if they had more space. But, this would mean more bribes which they could not afford to pay.

Access to credit is also a major problem for the women. They either use their own savings to run their business or they borrow from money lenders at high rates of interest. In fact, Kusakabe notes that some of the street vendors she interviewed told her that they worked for three reasons—to eat, to educate their children and to repay their debts.

## Seoul (South Korea)

The economic crisis in South Korea in 1998 resulted in massive restructuring.[7] As a result, several workers in the formal sector lost their jobs and had to move to the informal sector. After the Asian financial crises the number of street vendors increased even more and at present Seoul has around 800,000 street vendors.

The government, like most other governments in Asia, is insensitive to the problems of the urban poor. Street vendors and slum dwellers are under constant attack by the government. However, a peculiar feature of South Korea is that the government hires gangsters to evict street vendors and slum dwellers. The delegates at the first conference of StreetNet International held at Seoul (16–19 March 2004) mentioned that despite changes in governments, the plight of street vendors remained unchanged. According to the representative of the Korean Congress of Trade Unions (KCTU), the main federation of trade unions, 57 per cent of the workers are in the informal sector at present. This sector accounts for the earnings of 70 per cent of the women workers and 60 per cent of the male workers in the country. Yet this sector is not recognised by the government.

Faced by constant harassment, the street vendors of South Korea have formed a national alliance known as the National Federation of Korean Street Vendors (NFKSV). This federation estimates that the total number of street vendors could number around 1 million, which seems an inflated figure. However, the fact remains that street vendors form an important component of South Korea's workforce and their problems should not be ignored by the government.

Street vendors face problems especially during international events taking place at Seoul. These are the times when the street vendors are forcibly evicted by the authorities, aided by gangsters. In 1986, the first crackdown took place as the Asian Games were hosted in Seoul. This was followed by crackdowns in 1988 for the Olympics and then in 2002 for the FIFA World Cup (football) tournament. Street vendors' organisations have reacted strongly to such evictions. The clashes between them and the authorities have been violent. The street vendors appear to be more militant than their counterparts in other Asian countries. This mainly comes as a reaction to the extremely harsh attitude of the government towards them.

The street vendors have, on occasion, managed to negotiate with the government on specific problems. For example, after the eviction drive for the Olympics, the street vendors' union negotiated with the local government for alternative space. They were given a space in a street close to the Olympic stadium. Today this area has become an important centre for hawkers' trade and has become an attraction for tourists. Similarly, StreetNet and NFKSV were able to avert some of the major eviction drives that were to take place before the FIFA World Cup football tournament. The Bodh Gaya regional conference of StreetNet passed a resolution urging the South Korean government to take into account the problems of street vendors. Later, representatives of StreetNet and NFKSV met the government representatives and convinced them that eviction of street vendors was not a solution.

If the government continues to ignore the existence of the growing numbers of street vendors, the crisis is bound to worsen. It is therefore necessary to convince the government to take a positive view on street vendors and legalise their trade. This can be done through negotiations, but prior to that it will be necessary to assess the actual number of people engaged in this trade. The South Korean representatives at the StreetNet International conference laid greater stress on this aspect.

## Summary and Conclusions

We have been able to collect information on street vendors for most of the countries in South and South East Asia. The information presented is in no way comprehensive, covering all aspects of street vending. Unfortunately, there are not many studies on the socio-economic conditions of street vendors in Asia and this is one of the main handicaps of the present study. Moreover, there is little knowledge of the actual number of street vendors in the various Asian countries. We shall try to summarise the main findings of this chapter in the next few paragraphs and raise the important common issues.

A noticeable feature of the cities in Asia is the growing number of street vendors. The growth is mainly related to the changes in the economy of these countries. Street vending increases with the shrinking of jobs in the formal sector and with lack of gainful employment in rural areas. The rural unemployed tend to move to the cities in search of employment. They usually possess low skills and have low levels of education. Both factors make it almost impossible for them to find regular jobs in the formal sector. Street vending is one of the few options they have for earning a living. Entry into this trade is easier because it does not require high skills and the capital involved is low. This is seen in the case of Bangladesh, Nepal, Vietnam, and Cambodia.

In the other countries, especially the 'Asian tigers'—Thailand, Singapore, Malaysia, Philippines, and South Korea—there was a rapid increase in the number of street vendors after the monetary crisis of 1998. In India, the number of street vendors increased after the economic liberalisation policy was initiated in 1991. The traditional industrial cities, such as Mumbai, Ahmedabad and Kolkata saw a decline in the formal sector as large factories closed down and started outsourcing to the small-scale industries. A section of the workers in the formal sector, or their wives, took to street vending after they lost their jobs.

Unfortunately, the governments in these countries have more or less refused to recognise street vending as a legal activity and they, in fact, view these vendors as irritants to the city's development. Even in countries like Vietnam and Cambodia, which did not have a large formal sector, the governments do not give legal recognition to street vending. This is disappointing as the governments of both these countries are ideologically committed to the interests of the working class. However, in both countries street vendors are harassed. As a result, street vendors in most Asian countries live a precarious existence as they face the constant threat of eviction and destruction of their property.

Malaysia, Philippines and India have policies for regulating and protecting street vendors. Of the three, only Malaysia seems to be sincere in implementing the policy. It has been the only country where licensed street vendors (most of them are licensed) are provided facilities for conducting their trade and the government also provides for credit facilities for them. In Singapore too, the condition of street vendors is somewhat better; although there is no policy for street vendors, the state has tried to regularise all street vendors by providing licenses. This enables them to have proper stalls and maintain proper hygiene. Though Philippines has a national policy, the government refuses to recognise most of the street vendors and it takes harsh measures to clear them off the pavements. India too, has recently framed a national policy for street vendors which, if implemented, will provide security to them. At present, the street vendors face constant harassment from the authorities and rent-seeking is very high.

Most of the street vendors in Asia are not unionised. The reports of the regional conference of StreetNet International show that trade unions of street vendors are few. In most cases, with the possible exception of Nepal, the larger unions are not interested in drawing street vendors into their fold. In Nepal, GFONT has taken the initiative of unionising street vendors. In fact, most problems of the street vendors are related to their lack of unionisation. The delegates from Asian countries participating in the StreetNet conference all spoke of lack of awareness of rights among the street vendors. Unionisation would provide them with a common platform to press for their rights and protect them. In this way they could intervene in policy matters relating to their right to carry out their activities. In general, street vendors are not represented in local bodies. The Self Employed Women's Association as a union is an exception as it has been able to intervene in the policies of the municipal corporation in the Indian city of Ahmedabad. It provides an example of how unionisation could benefit street vendors.

Only two countries in Asia have federations or alliances of street vendors: South Korea and India. The two are a contrast where the intervention of policies is concerned. In South Korea the federation (NFKSV) was formed mainly to resist the oppression of the state. The battle lines between the two are clearly drawn and both are hostile to each other. The government appears unduly harsh on street vendors as it has spared no means to evict them. It must be the only country where the government hires gangsters to evict street vendors. This makes it almost impossible for the federation to enter into a policy dialogue with the administration. In India, the NASVI has been more successful. It has been able to intervene at the national level, and at local levels in some cases, to initiate policy dialogues with the concerned authorities. Its greatest success has been the initiation of the national policy, which was done along with SEWA.

Finally, it is necessary to summarise the condition of women street vendors in these countries. Women vendors form the lowest rung among street vendors. In most cases they take to this trade because of poverty and because the male members in the family do not have jobs. They are found in greater numbers in Vietnam and Cambodia where they form the majority. In other countries they form a lesser, but nonetheless significant component. Unionisation among them is low and their incomes are also lower than those of male vendors. In India most trade unions of street vendors, with the exception of SEWA, tend to ignore them. There are a few instances of trade unions having a women's wing, as in Bangladesh and

India, but these do not play a significant role in influencing the policies of that trade union. Their low income, double burden of having to work on the streets and look after the home and low level of unionisation make them the invisible section of street vendors.

Street vendors are an important part of the informal sector not only because of their numbers but because of the crucial roles they play in preserving this sector. The goods sold by street vendors are usually consumed by those in the informal sector, as they are cheap. Moreover, a significant amount of goods produced by small industrial units in the informal sector are marketed through them. In fact, we have a situation where a section of the urban poor (street vendors) help the other sections of the urban poor by providing them low-priced goods and by marketing their products. Unfortunately, instead of recognising their contributions to the economy, governments view street vendors as encroachers or criminals.

In conclusion, Asian countries have witnessed a sharp rise in the numbers of street vendors and they constitute the mainstay of the economy. Street vendors perform an important role in providing services to the urban population, especially the poor. But the governments are by and large indifferent to the specific needs of this sector. It is time that these governments acknowledge the contributions of this sector and afford them security and sustainability.

## Notes

1. Regional Seminar on Street Food Development, Bangkok, Thailand, 29 September–1 October 1999, FAO, Rome, 1999.
2. Paper presented at the Regional Seminar on Street Food Development, Bangkok mentioned in note 8.
3. The data presented in this section is collected from Pizzali (2001); Regional Seminar on Street Food Development, Bangkok mentioned in note 8; and Hassan (2003).
4. See http://www.cityofmanila.com.ph/hawkers.htm.
5. The extract is from the Regional Seminar on Street Food Development, Bangkok mentioned in note 8.
6. Regional Seminar on Street Food Development, Bangkok mentioned in note 8.
7. The section on South Korea is based on the author's visit to Seoul for the StreetNet International conference. He interviewed a large number of street vendors and functionaries of the unions then.

## References

Agnello, Francesca and Joanne Moller. 2003. Cambodia: Women Micro Entrepreneurs and Their Business Needs, Urban Sector Group, November.

Ahmed, Qazi Saif Uddin. 2000. 'Role of Dhaka City Corporation in Urban Food Security'. Paper presented at The Regional Seminar on Feeding Asian Cities, 27–30 November 2000, Bangkok, Thailand.

*Ananova*. 2002. 11 August.

Bhattacharya, Mini. 1997. 'Street Food Vending in Urban Guwahati: An Anthropological Appraisal', unpublished Ph.D. thesis, Guwahati University.

Bhowmik, Sharit K. 2000. 'Hawkers in the Urban Informal Sector: A Study of Street Vending in Seven Cities of India'. National Alliance of Street Vendors of India, available at www.nasvi.org, www.streetnet.org.

Hassan, Norhaslina. 2003. 'Accommodating the Street Hawkers into Modern Urban Management in Kuala Lumpur'. Paper submitted to the 39th IsoCaRP Congress.

Kusakabe, Kyoko. 2003. 'Market Class and Gender Relations: A Case of Women Retail Traders in Phnom Penh', *International Feminist Journal of Politics*, 5(1).

National Alliance of Street Vendors of India (NASVI). *Report of the Asian Regional Workshop on Street Vendors* (held in Bodh Gaya, India, 10–12 February 2002), available at www.nasvinet.org.

*New Age Metro*. 2003. 17 August, available at www.newagebd.com

Pizzali, A. F. Medina. 2001. 'Low Cost Fish Retailing Equipment and Facilities in Large Urban Areas of South East Asia'. FAO Fisheries Technical Paper No. 405, FAO, Rome 2001, available at http://www.fao.org/DOCREP/005/y2258E.htm.

Sharma, R. N. 1998. Census of Hawkers on BMC Lands, Mumbai: Tata Institute of Social Sciences.

SNDT Women's University and ILO. 1999. 'Study of Street Vendors in Mumbai' (mimeo).

*Star Malaysia*. 2003. 18 May, available at www.singaporewindow.org/sw03/030518ss.htm

Tantiwiramanond, Darun. not dated. 'Changing Gender Relations and Women in Micro Enterprises: The Street Vendors of Hanoi', available at http://www.2.century.edu/vietnam/lairson/Hanstrevend.htm.

Tedd, Leonard, Susul Liyanarachchi and Ranjan Saha. 2002. Energy and Street Food. Project conducted by Intermediate Technology Development Group and funded by DFID, available at http://www.itdg.org/docs/energy/energy_and_street_foods_final_report_r7663.pdf.

*The Bangladesh Observer*. 2003. 9 September, available at www.bangladesh observeronline.com

*The Hindu*. 2001. 26 June.

Tiwari, Geetam and Dinesh Mohan. 2000. 'Street Vendors', *Seminar* 491, July, available at www.seminarindia.org

Vanzi, Sol Jose. 2001. 'Metro Manila Street Vendors to be Legalised', Philippines Headline News Online, 28 June 2001, available at http://www.seasite.niu.edu/vanzi

# 3

# Street Vending in Delhi

Sanjay Kumar and Sharit K. Bhowmik

The state of Delhi was formed in 1992. The urban areas of Delhi, comprising Delhi and New Delhi, account for the overwhelming majority of the population of the state. The total population of the state, in 2001, was 13.85 million of which only 944,727 lived in rural areas (Government of Delhi 2001). Hence, the total urban population was 12.91 million (ibid.) making it the largest urban centre in the country. This is certainly a unique distinction for Delhi. Till the Census of 1981, Kolkata (then Calcutta) was the largest city followed by Mumbai (then Bombay) and Delhi was a poor third. At that time Delhi was regarded primarily as a bureaucratic city that lacked the working-class culture of Mumbai or Kolkata.

## Changing Population Composition

Over the recent decades, Delhi's character has changed. Although, being the political capital of India, it is still a city of bureaucrats, its manufacturing and trading base has expanded considerably. Two basic features have emerged in the city's demographic make-up. First, Delhi is now attracting the largest number of migrants. The city's net migration during 1991–2001 has surpassed all other cities in the country. Second, it is the fastest growing city in the country.

Between 1991 and 2001, Delhi's population increased by 47.02 per cent (Government of Delhi 2001). In comparison, the second largest city, Mumbai, had a growth of 20.03 per cent during the same period.[1] In absolute terms, Delhi's population increased by 4.43 million between 1991 and 2001; the population of Mumbai, on the other hand, went up by only 1.9 million.

The rapid growth of Delhi's population is certainly not due to expansion of the government sector. In fact, after 1991, when the policy of liberalisation was introduced, the government sector has not expanded. Delhi is rapidly shedding its character as a city of bureaucrats and petty government personnel and is emerging as a leading city for trade and manufacture. Writing in *The Hindu*, Rao (2005) notes that the composition of employment is no different than that of Mumbai. The break-up of the main heads of employment is: 23 per cent manufacturing, 29 per cent trade, 27 per cent public administration, health and education. The figures for manufacture and trade are the same as in Mumbai (see Table 3.1).

**Table 3.1**
**Delhi: Composition of Employment, 2001 (Per Cent to Total)**

| | |
|---|---|
| Manufacturing | 23 |
| Trade, hotels | 29 |
| Public administration, education, health | 27 |
| Transport, communications, finance | 13 |
| Construction | 16 |
| Agriculture, mines | 02 |

*Source*: Bhanoji Rao, 2005, 'India Beyond Delhi and Mumbai', *The Hindu*, 1 February.

An overwhelming majority of the manufacturing units are in the small-scale sector or in home-based industry and as such the workers in these units are in the informal sector. Similarly, an overwhelming majority of those engaged in trade are street vendors or petty shop owners. They are self-employed and form the majority of the informal sector workers.

## The Informal Sector in Delhi's Workforce

Delhi's total workforce was 4.55 million, or 32.82 per cent of the population in 2001 indicating that the dependent population is high. Of the total workforce, only 585,133 were women, constituting 9.37 per cent of the female population. There were around 4 million male workers. That is, 52 per cent of those eligible were in the workforce.

The important sections of the workforce for our study are those in household industries. The definition of household industries, according to Delhi's Master Plan (DMP 1998), is those industries that employ up to five workers and do not consume more than 5 KW of electricity or, a unit employing up to nine workers and not drawing any power. Though it is very difficult to gauge the actual number of units in household industries as the majority are not licensed, it is possible to get the number of workers engaged in this sector through census data. The census shows that the total number of workers is 140,032 of whom 112,522 are males and 27,510 are females. Street vendors form another major section of the informal sector. In fact, the number of street vendors in Delhi is much more than workers in household industries. According to one study (Manushi Trust 2001), street vendors in Delhi number 500,000.

According to the 55th Round of the National Sample Survey (NSS) data (Government of India 2004a), the total employment in the urban informal sector in Delhi was 1.7 million persons. The establishments they were engaged in were: manufacturing, construction, trade, hotel and restaurants, transport, storage, and other services. Trade offers the maximum employment where 850,000 people work. This is followed by manufacturing which provides employment to 412,000 people. The third largest is the category named 'other services' where the total employment is around 256,000. Distribution of employment among the different activities shows that 48.72 per cent of the employment is provided by the trading sector. The manufacturing group accounts for 23.60 per cent and 'other services' contribute 14.88 per cent.

Just as Delhi's workforce is predominantly male, the break-up of employment in the informal sector is also similar: 93.62 per cent of the total employed in this sector are males and only 3.38 per cent females. The NSS report also notes that hired employment accounted for 42.14 per cent and other employment for 57.86 per cent. This perhaps shows that this sector has good potential for employment.

Another important indicator is the average employment per enterprise. The employment in household enterprises is 1.2 persons and that of establishments is 3.7 persons. Establishments obviously have greater potential of providing employment. If we look at the activities separately the differences in the potential for employment are clear. In manufacturing, employment in household industries was 1.5 persons whereas in establishments it was 4.8. For trade, the figures are 1.2 and 3.1 respectively and in hotels and restaurants they are 1.2 and 4.0. There are a greater number of household industries than establishments. The total number of enterprises was 838,427 of which 549,346 were household industries and 289,081 were enterprises.

## Street Vendors

Street vendors form a major part of the urban informal sector in Delhi. According to some estimates mentioned earlier, the total number of street vendors number around 500,000. This seems to be an exaggerated figure as no survey or census has been conducted on this section of the working population. The National Policy for Urban Street Vendors (Government of India 2003: 1) mentions that approximately 2 per cent of the urban population is engaged in street vending. By this estimate the number of street vendors in Delhi should be around 260,000, considering Delhi's urban population is 12.9 million. This seems a more realistic figure as it is unlikely that 500,000 street vendors could sustain themselves in the city as there would be too many hawkers for the existing population.

In this chapter we will briefly discuss the legal status of hawkers in Delhi and then deal with the type of hawkers that exist in the city. After this we will discuss the case studies.

## Legal Status

Street vending in Delhi is regulated by the municipal laws. We must add here that the municipal laws relating to the poorer sections, namely, hawkers, slums, home-based producers, etc., are based on nineteenth-century British practice and 'are outdated and detrimental to the peaceful conduct of business by vendors' (Shah and Mandava 2005: 89). Most of the laws were based on Britain's experience in dealing with the urban poor and migrants in the eighteenth century. They were also designed to facilitate control over the Indians by the colonial rulers and regulate the economy to suit their administrative capabilities and to enhance their sense of security. In fact, most laws pertaining to street vendors, slum dwellers and unskilled migrants of the Bombay Municipal Corporation Act of 1882 were identical to the laws passed in England (ibid.). This Act was a model for other municipal corporations in the country and their laws too were framed accordingly. These laws persisted even after India attained independence from colonial rule. The municipal and police acts were changed but the sections that affected the urban poor remained unchanged.

The Municipal Corporation of Delhi (MCD) has certain rules that regulate street vending. These are found in Section 420 of the Delhi Municipal Corporation (as it was earlier known) Act of 1957. These rules are based on the Bombay Provincial Municipal Corporation Act of 1949.[2] The sections relating to hawking state that hawking could be done only after the municipal commissioner grants licenses for this purpose. Moreover, the vendors cannot put up a stall or even a cover to protect themselves and their goods from the elements of nature. The commissioner can dismantle or destroy these structures without notice. Hence, we can see that as far as vending is concerned only the municipal commissioner has the discretion to regulate it. The municipal bodies are expected to be run by elected representatives known as municipal councillors. In any democracy, the elected representatives have greater authority to make and enforce laws. However, in the case of municipalities, despite a Constitutional Amendment (74th) that decentralises power to the urban local bodies (ULBs) the officials still enjoy significant decision-making powers.

The municipal laws dealing with street vendors have all sorts of restrictions making the pursuit of vending on the streets extremely difficult, if not impossible. For example, hawkers must sell their wares at least 100 m away from educational institutions, hospitals, temples or religious places. They must be at least 150 m away from municipal markets. Ice cream sellers cannot raise their voices to attract customers and they cannot sit on their trolleys. The surfeit of rules and regulations only help to increase rent collection (bribes) by the municipal authorities. According to the Manushi Trust (2001), the municipal staff and police collect around Rs 500 million in rent every month. The Central Vigilance Commission too has supported this view.

The MCD also grants licenses of different kinds for street vendors known as *tehbazari*. These were laid down by the Supreme Court of India. According to the guidelines, there are basically four categories of tehbazaris. First, the regular tehbazari, that gives the hawker the right to squat at a particular spot on a more or less permanent basis. These could be fixed by MCD on an yearly basis. These vendors had to prove that they had occupied the spot in a survey conducted in 1982. This survey accepted those hawkers who were operating since 1979. The hawkers had to prove their existence at the place that they were occupying when the survey was done. Ironically, one of the proofs they could furnish was the receipts they had of evictions done by the municipal authorities.

The second category is the casual tehbazari. This was meant for licensing vendors who sell their goods in weekly markets. We shall look into the problems of this section of hawkers in our case studies. The third category is the open tehbazari meant for those who have started hawking after 1982. These hawkers cannot set up permanent covering and they must prove that they have been continuously engaged in the trade and they must have proof of residence and nationality. The fourth category is mobile hawking. This category does not come under tehbazari which deals mainly with hawkers who squat at their places of work. Under Section 420 of the DMC Act of 1957, the corporation can grant licenses to those who move in specified areas with their goods on their heads or on bicycles, trolleys or push carts. These four categories more or less cover all types of hawkers in the city.

The main drawback of this system is that it covers only a fraction of the total number of hawkers in the city. As in the case of most bureaucratic procedures, the system of tehbazari, especially the temporary categories, is fairly elaborate and at times too complicated for the neo-literate hawker to comprehend. Moreover, there are no provisions for the new entrants. The last entrants are those who entered the profession after 1982. There is continuous entry into the categories of street vending. These newcomers are denied licenses and are forced to operate without licenses. The MCD loses a lot of its income as taxes because of this (though its officials can collect bribes and increase their personal income!).

In sum, the existing rules relating to street vending are not very conducive to the trade. Worse, there is another Act that can overrule the rights of street vendors—the Police Act of 1951. Section 34 of this Act reads:

No person shall cause obstruction in any street or public place by:

- Allowing animals or vehicles.
- Leaving any vehicle.
- Using any part of a street or public place as a halting place for vehicles or cattle.
- Leaving any box, bale package or other things whatsoever upon a street for an unreasonable length of time or contrary to any regulation.
- *By exposing anything for sale or setting out anything for sale in or upon any stall, booth, board, cask, and basket or in any other way whatsoever* (emphasis added).

According to the last clause, the police have the right to remove any form of trade on the streets even if it has been permitted by the municipality. This obviously creates a contradiction. In fact, this is the main reason why the income of the police through bribes is more than that of municipal staff. Since the police has the right to evict even a licensed vendor, it can extract substantial bribes from the vendors.

## Case Studies on Street Vending

In this section we shall deal with case studies relating to street vending. We start with a look at the weekly markets in the city and the vendors that participate in them. After this we will look at the old Red Fort Sunday Market, and the trials and tribulations of its vendors in making a relocation plan successful. Another landmark of Delhi is the Sunday Book Bazaar in Daryaganj. However, there are threats to its existence. We will look at how these book vendors have managed to stay on the streets and serve the needs of the readers. Finally, we shall look at the making of a women's market in the heart of Delhi.

## Weekly Markets

Almost every locality in Delhi, except for the restricted areas where VIPs reside, has markets that operate on one day of the week. These markets are like fairs. A large number of street vendors assemble, usually in the late afternoons, to sell their wares. They occupy a particular area that is usually common land which could be a broad road and pavements or a vacant piece of land. For that half day, the traffic is diverted. The people residing in the locality usually get used to the idea of having a part of their road closed for traffic. Most do not complain because they can buy what they need from these markets.

Over the years these markets have increased in number mainly because of the support they get from the local people, especially the poor. The vendors that participate in these markets sell a wide variety of goods ranging from clothes, bed sheets, kitchen ware, furniture, and other goods for the household. These goods are cheap, much cheaper than those in large shops. It is not just the poor that benefit from these markets but the better-off sections too buy from these markets because of the competitive prices. In 1992, when the Supreme Court gave its guidelines on tehbazari, there were 67 weekly markets operating in the city. This number has grown several times since then. We conducted a study of some of the markets and spoke to some vendors. Though there were few women vendors, we spoke to them to understand their special problems.

### Adarsh Nagar

Adarsh Nagar in north Delhi has a weekly market on Saturdays. The older vendors told us that the market had been around for 40 years. The police confirmed this too. Pradeep Kumar Khanna, an elderly vendor who has been operating in this market for long, and is regarded as the leader of the market, says the market has 372 vendors. He sells readymade garments in his stall. As he is a senior and respected vendor, the others view him as their spokesperson. He also negotiates with the police when things go wrong and, at other times, he tries to solve issues regarding space.

The vendors pay Rs 5 to MCD as tehbazari. This is official as they are given receipts by the men engaged by MCD for collecting the tax. Besides this, vendors pay to the police to ensure that there is no eviction drive. They also pay some money to a local residents' association so that they do not complain to the police about encroachment on public space by the hawkers. However, despite these contributions, the vendors face harassment by the police mainly because of the connivance of the residents' association.

Adarsh Nagar was not an upmarket residential area. Its residents were mostly the lower middle class and the poor. However, during the past few years, new buildings have been raised that are more expensive than those in existence. Parts of this area have become a residential centre of the better-off classes. The residents in these housing societies have started raising their concerns against the market. They have complained to the police and MCD saying that they face a lot of problems while returning from work in their cars as the roads are blocked by hawkers. The vendors were afraid that the market would be closed at this rate. The market leader and some others have jointly approached the office bearers of the residents' associations to try and make them understand the financial problems of street vendors and the effect this market has on the poorer sections in the vicinity. They are hopeful of a solution in the future but till then they trade with a high degree of fear.

## Dhaka Village

Dhaka village, situated near Mukherji Nagar in north Delhi, has a weekly market that operates on Thursdays. This market has been held regularly since the past 35 years. It is larger than the Adarsh Nagar market and has around 500 vendors. They pay Rs 5 as tehbazari to MCD. They pay Rs 10 to the police as bribe in order to sit at their places. Anyone not paying the bribe is forcibly evicted by the beat constable. The president of the vendors is the same person who is president of the Adarsh Nagar market. The vendors sell a wide array of goods such as household and kitchen appliances, woollen goods (they start selling these goods after October, when the winter season is imminent), readymade garments, artificial jewellery, etc.

The vendors told us that they bought their goods from various wholesale markets specialising in those goods. These goods are made by home-based workers in different parts of the capital or in other towns. Thus, the vendors selling garments get their supplies from Gandhi Nagar Market and Shahadra Bazaar in east Delhi, which are the larger markets for readymade clothes. The woollens are bought from markets in Panipat in the state of Haryana, which is close to Delhi.

The hawkers usually cannot afford to employ extra hands to take care of their stalls. Instead, family members help in the work. These vendors sell in two markets every week. The rest of the time is spent in buying items from different markets. Their profits vary, depending on the investment they can afford for buying goods and the amount they sell. On an average, a street vendor makes a profit of Rs 500 in each market.

We noticed a virtual absence of women vendors in both these markets. In fact, as we have stated earlier, the participation of women in the informal sector in Delhi is low. However, we thought that we should track down some of the women in the weekly markets and speak to them about their work. We spotted nine women vendors in Sant Nagar market. The vendors display their wares on wooden platforms measuring 6' by 3', called benches, hired out by people who own them. We found that in Sant Nagar the charges range from Rs 7 to 14 for the evening.

Sunita Devi sells utensils of cast iron made by her husband at Sant Nagar and another market every week. Her profit is about Rs 300 per market, or Rs 600 per week. She paid the bench owner Rs 10 and had to pay tehbazari of Rs 5 with a bribe of Rs 10 to the police. Another vendor, Kamala, and her daughter sell clothes every week. They pay Rs 5 to MCD and Rs 10–20 to the police. They earn around Rs 50 at each market. Their appearance showed that they were very poor. Their clothes were in tatters. Initially they were afraid to speak to us but after a while, they started to open up. They face a lot of harassment from the police. In fact, they got emotional and started to weep while telling us their problems. A few weeks before when they did not have enough money to pay the police, two constables came to threaten them; they pleaded that they had no money and that they should be spared that week, but the policemen abused them, slapped the daughter and scattered their goods on the pavement. Some of the goods were spoilt because of this.

There were nine women vendors in that market. Their appearance suggested that they were all poor. They sold woollens, iron products (for the kitchen) and spices. They all spoke of similar ill-treatment by the police. They said that single women faced greater harassment because they were viewed as being more vulnerable. If their husbands came along the police harassed them less. They told us that the other vendors do not help them out. They have an association but the women are not members. The association mainly helps its male members and the leader is also indifferent to the problems faced by the women.

## Malkagunj

Malkagunj, near the University of Delhi campus, has a weekly market on Fridays. This market has been functioning for the past 30 years. There are about 300 hawkers participating in the market. They display their wares on benches that belong to one person. He charges them Rs 7 per bench. They pay Rs 5 as tehbazari to MCD. There are six women vendors who, like the ones in other markets, are very poor. They sold woollen garments bought from Gandhi Nagar market, artificial ornaments bought from Sadar Bazaar and bed sheets and pillow cases from Chandni Chowk market. Their profit margins are low, hence they earn around Rs 70 from the market. The men earn much more than women as their volume of sales is higher.

## Subhadra Colony

The weekly market held on Tuesdays at Subhadra Colony, Sarai Rohilla is fairly large. According to the *pradhan* (market leader), it has 580 vendors, 60 of whom are women. Besides paying the mandatory Rs 5 as tehbazari, the vendors pay between Rs 7 and 15 for the benches. These are owned by a former vendor. They also pay Rs 5 to the pradhan who ensures that there is no harassment by the police.

Bhagwan Devi has been setting up her shop in this market for the past 30 years. She sells cast iron kitchen implements. She makes them herself on other days of the week. She lives alone as her children have separated from her after they married. She is independent and does not expect friends and relatives to help her. She is very poor and earns Rs 70 from the market. Surprisingly, the police do not charge her anything, not even a small amount. Bhagwan Devi told us that they knew she earned very little. The three weekly markets fetch an income of Rs 1,000 a month, well below the poverty line. However, though Bhagwan Devi is poor she lives her life with dignity. Street vending has given her that opportunity.

Kavita sells low-cost footwear (slippers, sandals made of rubber or plastic). She gets her products from the small, household industries in Mongolpuri. She pays Rs 14 for the bench that she occupies in Subhadra Colony market. This is more than what others pay, but she is a new entrant and she has to pay more. Kavita has been in the market for the past four years. She took to street vending because of problems at home. Her husband lost his job in a factory due to ill health. The only option to support the family was street vending. Her husband had tried his hand at vending but he was unsuccessful because he was ill most of the time. Kavita finally decided to take over. She started visiting weekly markets to find space for selling her goods. Her husband sold footwear so she took up the same goods as well. She could get the contacts of manufacturers from her husband. Kavita sells her wares in four markets every week. She procures the goods and sells them all by herself. Her husband is not capable of helping her. She did not tell us how much she earned but she insisted that it was a hand-to-mouth existence.

Sangita Devi is a *mehndi* artist, which means that she makes spiral designs with henna (a herbal dye) on the palms of women. Although this is an art, Sangita Devi gets a pittance for her artistic skills. She does this in different weekly markets as she needs to work in order to maintain her family. Her husband is incapable of doing any type of hard work. He stays at home while Sangita Devi goes from market to market trying to eke out an income out of her mehndi art.

After studying the different weekly markets we found that they were stable places for street vendors because most of these markets have been in existence for several decades. This gives them some stability. Moreover, they operate once a week and not on all days. This reduces the obstructions, if any, caused by the markets. There may have been opposition from the public if they had been operating daily.

We also find that women are few in number in these markets. The few that are there form the poorest section of street vendors. In fact, we find that street vending in Delhi is largely a male-dominated profession. The few women who venture into this profession do so out of dire necessity. There are no earning members in the family and the women do not possess skills that would allow them to take up any other profession. The incomes of the women are much lower than that of men. This is because they belong to the poorer sections and do not have enough capital to invest in order to increase profits. Moreover, in a male-dominated patriarchal society, women are expected to do the housework like cooking, cleaning, washing clothes, etc., in addition to their work as vendors. This reduces the time they spend in selling their wares.

There is of course some opposition, as we have seen in the case of Adarsh Nagar market. The residents are complaining about this market and the problems of free flow of traffic because of the market. Such objections come from the wealthier sections of society. There are no complaints from the majority community comprising the lower middle class and the poor. Yet the complaints from those who comprise an elite, microscopic minority are taken seriously by the authorities. The action taken destroys the livelihoods of the vendors and also causes a lot of inconvenience to the poorer sections who are deprived of cheap goods.

After looking at weekly markets in general, let us look at a particular weekly market that has been in existence for centuries. We will also see that women vendors have played a role in bringing the problems of this market to the fore and seeking solutions.

## The Trials and Tribulations of Red Fort Market

The Sunday market at the historic Red Fort has been in existence for several centuries. It began initially as a Friday market only for women, during the Mughal rule in India. Friday is the weekly holiday for Muslims, hence this market used to be held every Friday. During the British rule (over 200 years ago) the market changed its character. It was no longer a market exclusively for women. It was turned into a market for selling used goods (*kabadi bazaar*, in local parlance). The fact is that despite its chequered history, this bazaar was always functioning in some form or the other. Even at the time that the Emergency was clamped by the then prime minister, Indira Gandhi (1975–77) and all political institutions were suspended, the market continued to exist, though not at the same place. It was removed to another location near Red Fort.

Unfortunately, in early October 2001, the market was closed by the Union Government, through an order of the minister of tourism, Dr Jagmohan. The vendors were forcibly evicted and their goods were confiscated. It was explained at the time that the market was a threat to the historical monument as the vendors and the multitude of shoppers were degrading the historical monuments, namely, Red Fort and Jama Masjid. Ironically, the same person, Dr Jagmohan, who closed the market was, during the Emergency, responsible for moving the market to Ring Road. He was then a bureaucrat and deputy chairperson of Delhi Development Authority (DDA).

The July–August 2001 removal of the market was different from other times when the market was shifted to other places. This was the first time that the market was actually stopped with no alternative arrangements. By 5 August 2001, 10 days before Independence Day, all street vendors from the vicinity of Red Fort were removed. The situation is best narrated by Kuldeep Nayyar, a veteran journalist from Delhi in the national daily, *The Hindu*.

> Behind the historical Red Fort, a weekly bazaar had come up from the days of Bahadur Shah Zafar, the last Mughal ruler, more than 150 years ago. It died early this month, without any tears or protest. Policemen came one day and forcibly removed around 2,000 hawkers, who used to peddle everything from a needle to a second-hand computer. The bazaar was a veritable treasure-trove where people would often chance on things they desperately wanted. It was a poor man's market, but now it is a stone wall. Some hawkers are still sitting cross-legged nearby, wondering where to go . . . (Nayyar 2001)

The government announced that the area would be landscaped and developed as a park. The street vendors were viewed as a security threat to the fort and being unaesthetic. The heritage and environment protection organisation, INTACH, conducted a survey of the area. It found that there were a little over 4,000 street vendors in the area and all were paying tehbazari, though a little more than 1,000 were licensed.

After a series of negotiations, the government decided to look for alternative sites. There are several trade unions of the street vendors. Three of them are the most prominent and they are the main actors of what followed. One of the unions is affiliated to the Congress Party and has the largest membership. The second union comprises older street vendors. These vendors reside in the areas near Red Fort and Jama Masjid and are mainly Muslims. The leader of this group, Jamil, is a senior vendor who has knowledge about the history of the market.

The third group is the Self Employed Women's Association (SEWA). Its entry into Delhi is fairly recent. It has been organising home-based workers and street vendors in the Jahangirpuri area. Some of these women sold used clothes in the Red Fort market and they had lost their livelihood. The Self Employed Women's Association thus got involved in the Red Fort vendors' case.

The government first suggested that the market be shifted to a village on the outskirts of the city. This was an isolated area with poor transport facilities. The lack of proper transport would make it difficult for vendors and customers to reach the place. The vendors hence refused to go there. This led to a deadlock in the negotiations for the next few months. In the meantime, vendors continued to sit in various places near Red Fort. They were chased out by the municipal authorities and the police frequently. They also paid large sums as rents to prevent harassment from these officials. For most of the vendors, especially the women, street vending is their only means of eking out an existence and they had no choice but to face all odds to carry out their work.

The next site suggested was at Mata Sundari Road in New Delhi. This place would be ideal as it was approachable. The market took place on one Sunday but there were protests from the Gurudwara (place of worship of the Sikhs) committee. The members said that worshippers were inconvenienced by the market. Since this was a religious issue, the government had to withdraw permission for holding the market. The vendors were back to where they were earlier.

The unions were trying to help but they showed no unity. The hawkers faced similar problems and if they united and articulated their demands as a collective, the solution could be arrived at earlier. Even though all the unions wanted the same thing, namely, proper rehabilitation of their members, unfortunately, each had plans that differed from the other. The largest union, the one owing affiliation to the Congress, would try to use its political clout to corner the benefits. The other unions too would try to get the best deal for their members. This led to division among the ranks of the street vendors. It led to suspicion, as members of each union were suspicious about the motives of the others. This actually slowed down the process of negotiations.

After the failure to set up a market at Mata Sundari Road, the unions and the authorities started looking for an alternative site. A possible venue was Gastion Bastion Road (G.B. Road). It was deserted on Sundays and the market could easily be held there. However, G.B. Road is the red-light area of Delhi. The Self Employed Women's Association protested strongly at this plan, as its members, solely women, would find it difficult to operate from a red-light area. Another site suggested was the lane behind the police head quarters close to Indra Prastha Estate. This lane connects Indra Prastha Estate to Bahadur Shah Zafar Road. It is not far from the original Red Fort market; hence the customers too would not be inconvenienced.

The plans were almost finalised and the market was to be set up on a Sunday when there arose objections from the offices nearby. They complained that by blocking the lane the market would prevent people from having easy access to the two areas although offices on both sides of the lane, namely Bahadurshah Zafar Road and Indra Prastha Estate, are closed on Sundays. Surprisingly, the government accepted these protests and decided not to allow the market there. A significant point is that the entrance to the head quarters of Delhi Police is on this lane, yet they did not object.

Once again the vendors were left in the lurch. They had to continue their make-shift arrangements near Red Fort and carry on their cat-and-mouse game with the authorities. Negotiations continued for the next few weeks. In January 2003, the government decided on another site in east Delhi, across the river Jamuna (trans-Jamuna in local parlance). This area was Jamuna Pushta, a lower-middle-class area. This too was a good site as there would be a lot of customers there. The street vendors were happy that they would finally get a good place to trade. The volunteers from the unions went to the area on the previous Saturday with municipal officials and marked the areas where street vendors could squat. There was a general feeling of jubilation among the vendors. Finally, after two-and-a-half years, they could trade at a place where they would not be under constant fear of eviction.

That next day, Sunday, the vendors and the union leaders, in a mood of jubilation, went to the new area. They were confronted with a scene they could not imagine. The area they had cordoned off for their market was filled with workers of the Delhi Development Authority to prevent the market from being held. The DDA claimed that it owned the land and no other authority could usurp it for any purpose. The vendors were baffled. Once again they had hit a wall. They had to return without selling any of their wares.

Though the vendors were frustrated they did not lose hope. The unions tried meeting all sections of the government. Office bearers of SEWA met the lieutenant governor of Delhi, the leader of the Congress union talked to the concerned minister, and Jamil kept meeting several municipal officers hoping to find a solution.

After several rounds of negotiations a new site was suggested. This was Valedrome Road off Ring Road, near Raj Ghat. This area is fairly deserted, and has few pedestrians. The road was one of the entrances to the Indira Gandhi Indoor Stadium. The vendors were not too happy with this site, but had no choice but to accept the offer. Permission for starting the market was sought from the DDA, Public Works Department, Traffic Department, Delhi Police, and the New Delhi Municipal Committee (NDMC). The Traffic Department cautioned the street vendors not to squat within 200 m of the main road (Ring Road), a precautionary measure so that vendors would not clog the road and later spill over to Ring Road.

The only way this new market could be successful was if the market at Red Fort, functioning illegally, was shut down. Regular customers would then come to this market. The police had given an assurance that the market at Red Fort would not function. The new market was to start in early May 2005, which was three years after their removal from Red Fort.

The new market came as a hope to many. They could now hawk in peace. The municipal commissioner and other officials visited the market on the first day in May 2005. At the launch the market was a success. The Red Fort market had ceased to function. The vendors could occupy space on the broad pavements. The police had cordoned off the front part of the road (200 m from the main road) with the other part kept free for traffic flow. The police barricade was the dividing line on the first day.

The market had provision for a little over 1,000 vendors and the women vendors belonging to SEWA managed to get space on the pavements.

The Self Employed Women's Association had played a significant role in securing the place. The municipal authorities were well-disposed towards the union and they came in full force on the first day. The municipal commissioner, the deputy commissioners, senior officials of the police, and a myriad assortment of government officials of various levels were present and gave the vendors some confidence in the market's continuance. Though provisions were made for around 1,200 pitches, more than 2,000 vendors turned up. They had to form two rows on the pavements. The market thus started successfully. Customers thronged the market and there were brisk sales.

This euphoria lasted for only a few weeks. By June 2005, the crowds started thinning. One did not have to inquire deeply to know why. Some of the vendors continued to sell their wares from the Red Fort market with the tacit, but illegal, support of the authorities. These vendors paid high rents for conducting their activities. The buyers who had come to Valedrome Road found it more convenient to go to Red Fort for their shopping.

By the end of June the buyers at Valedrome Road had reduced to a trickle and there seemed to be more vendors than buyers. The Red Fort market, on the other hand, seemed to flourish. There were larger crowds there and the number of sellers had increased tremendously. Besides the pavements and the road, street vendors had occupied even the traffic islands and road dividers. There was traffic congestion and the public walks were congested. The vendors said that they were secure because the authorities (police and municipality) had assured them that they would not intervene to block their business, as vendors had doubled the rents they used to pay to these local authorities. It was money-making time for all—at the expense of the registered vendors at Valedrome Road.

Typically, the vendors at Valedrome Road would start packing up around noon, mostly moving to the Red Fort area. These people, wise enough to have anticipated trouble, had kept their pitches at Red Fort occupied nominally. The worst sufferers were the women vendors as they had given up their pitches at Red Fort. Their incomes had dropped drastically.

The vendors at Valedrome Road tried their best to rectify the situation. Their unions negotiated with the authorities but to no avail. All they got were empty promises. The authorities even said that if they tried to forcibly evict the vendors from Red Fort there would be a law and order problem, resulting in riots. The Congress union went to the High Court of Delhi for redressal. The Court had earlier directed MCD to remove all encroachments from the No-Hawking zones. Red Fort area had been declared a No-Hawking zone hence the hawkers from the Sunday market had to be removed. The union filed a contempt of court case against MCD and Delhi Police with the plea that since these two bodies had not evicted hawkers from Red Fort, they had violated the Court's orders. Given the work load of the courts, this case was to come up for hearing only in January 2006, with the likelihood of further postponement. The matter did not come up but the situation had changed soon after.

The other union, led by Jamil, suggested that the pitches should be numbered and then allotted to the registered vendors. If a vendor did not occupy his/her pitch for more than a specified number of weeks, the allotment would be cancelled. This, he felt was the only effective way of making the vendors come to their pitches. The thinning of buyers was because the number of vendors had decreased. If more vendors came there, there would be more buyers. His views made sense as this was a positive way of solving the problem. Unlike the other union, he was not asking for eviction of Red Fort vendors so that the buyers could then come to Valedrome Road. He was thinking of the new place with a variety of vendors as a counter magnet for attracting buyers. He also felt that this was one way of preventing the vendors of Valedrome Road from returning to Red Fort.

In August 2005 the Red Fort market was again cleaned up prior to Independence Day (15 August) for security reasons. This gave a boost to the Valedrome Road market again. It is functioning well, but new problems have arisen. Since the pitches have not been numbered by the authorities, there is intense competition among vendors to get the better ones (those closer to the entrance). The women again are the losers as the male vendors tend to usurp the better pitches. The Self Employed Women's Association is busy trying to sort out the problems and reach an amicable settlement.

There is another looming problem: the government had asked for clearances from MCD, DDA, NDMC, and other bodies before allotting the space to the vendors. None of these bodies had objected. However, the Sports Authority of India (SAI) has now claimed that the road and the pavements are under its jurisdiction and it has asked the government to clear the vendors from there. The objections do not seem to have much weight because the market, held on Sundays, does not block the entrance to the stadium. There are other entrances as well. But once again, the future of the new market hangs in the balance. It is almost certain that the vendors will not be allowed at the time of the Commonwealth Games in 2010. The question is whether they will be allowed to return after the games are over.

## Sunday Book Market

Daryaganj is a busy business centre in the heart of Delhi. It is situated in what is known as the 'walled city', commonly known as Old Delhi. The road is also one of the busiest in the city. On a working day the road is clogged with heavy traffic and noise. On Sundays, however, when the roads have little traffic and the shops and offices are closed, the streets come alive with book sellers who operate from the pavements. The place is crowded, not by cars and buses, but by book-loving pedestrians who traverse the pavements picking and choosing books offered by the street vendors.

This book bazaar has existed for 40 years in the same place and around 5,000 people visit it every year. There are around 200 book sellers occupying an approximately 1.5 km of land stretch. The books offered range from popular fiction to text books, and even specialised books on science, technology and social sciences. Rare and out-of-print books are frequently found there. The place has been described as a 'virtual feast' for book lovers. The vendors told us that not all books were old or second hand. Many are new but sold here at low prices. They claim that these books are not pirated. Often distributors auction unsold stocks and vendors pick up the lots at very low prices, selling them on the streets at marked down prices. One vendor had even ordered a container of new (but unsold) books from the U.S.

The vendors display their books directly on the pavement, laying them out on plastic sheets. Each vendor earns between Rs 1,000 and 1,500 a week through his sale. There are few women in this market—only five independent female book sellers, all of whom are SEWA members; other women assist their husbands. These vendors earn far more than most other street vendors. Their monthly income is more than Rs 8,000 whereas the hawkers in the weekly markets described earlier earn around half this amount.

The book bazaar attracts all types of buyers. There are students who look around for best sellers or cheaper text books. There are writers and poets, many of whom are well-known names in their field. There are lovers of old and rare books that are sure to find a treasure there. The book sellers scout for books the whole week and sell them at the market.

The book sellers did not have a union because, after seeing how unions operate in the informal sector, they decided not to form one or get affiliated to a union. Instead, they have formed a welfare association which in effect acts as a trade union. It negotiates with the police and municipal authorities about the terms which will allow them to function. The association has a president, general secretary, treasurer, and five members of the executive committee (they refer to themselves as 'cabinet members'!). Every vendor paid between Rs 50 and 100 to the municipal authorities and the police as bribe.

Though the market has existed for such a long time, it has still not acquired legal status. The authorities regard it as an encroachment. In the first week of June 2005, the government decided to remove the market on the basis of complaints from the residents of the area who had said that the market clogged their house approaches and the pavements and roads were blocked by book sellers. The police promptly acted on these complaints and a notice was served on the vendors asking them to desist from selling on Sundays. The street vendors were in a quandary. They did not know where to go.

The market remained closed on two consecutive Sundays. Their association pleaded with the authorities to allow them to function. Finally, they were told that they could move to Valedrome Road, the same place where the Red Fort vendors had been relocated. When they reached there on that Sunday, they found to their dismay that there were no places for them. The SEWA unionists spoke to them and tried to help them. Though SEWA is a union of only women workers, the volunteers decided to help out the vendors. Press conferences were organised in favour of the vendors and writers and artists who had been frequenting the Sunday Book Market for years were requested to take up their cause. Several important writers and politicians wrote to the chief minister.

These efforts bore fruit and soon after, on 26 June 2005, they were allowed to return to their street—three weeks since their ousting. The market seems stable, as neither the police nor the municipality are interested in removing them now. Their staying on will depend largely on the support they can muster from different sections of people.

The vendors realised that they need to press their case in an organised manner. For this, they needed broad-based support from all the vendors on the street. Soon after the market reopened there was bickering between the secretary and the president. They had formed two groups and each was engaged in denigrating the other. One accused the other of selling pirated books. The other retaliated by saying that his rival was arm-twisting other vendors to follow his leadership. There was bitterness between the two. Most of the committee members were disgusted with the state of affairs and decided to withdraw from the association's activities.

Once again SEWA came to the rescue. Both sides complained to the coordinator of SEWA.[3] Both proposed that the coordinator lead the association as all book sellers had faith in SEWA. The coordinator promptly refused and suggested that each committee member should come to the SEWA office on a weekday. The meeting, as expected, was fiery. However, since other committee members were present they intervened to broker peace. It was finally decided that regular elections would be held with secret ballot. The existing team had been nominated through consensus and not through elections where every member participated.

The elections were held on 4 December 2006, as scheduled. Though the former secretary had boycotted the elections, he found little support for him among the others. In fact, his son too voted. The voting figures showed that 198 of the 210 voters had cast their votes. The president had been re-elected but the other members were new. The democratic election indicates that the book sellers from now onwards would fight a united battle for retaining their weekly space.

## Proposed Women's Market

Women form a small part of the total number of street vendors in Delhi. The few women vendors that are found in the weekly markets are very poor and it is their poverty that drives them to vending. We could draw two inferences from this. Either women are not interested in taking to street vending or, they are kept out of the better and more lucrative types of vending by the men. The latter seems to be correct. Male dominance in this field dissuades women from taking to street vending. They are frequently harassed by men—more often than not, by the hawkers themselves.

The Self Employed Women's Association had been pondering over this issue ever since it started its work in Delhi around 2000. The experience here was different from that of Gujarat, where women actively participated in street vending and also in other activities in the informal sector. In all cases they worked alongside men.

In order to overcome this problem and also increase the visibility of women in the informal sector, SEWA conceptualised a market exclusively run by women. They would not then face harassment by male colleagues. The idea slowly grew and the members discussed the possibilities of starting such a market. Volunteers from SEWA scouted for a place and finally found one on Asaf Ali Road (this road runs perpendicular to Daryaganj). The offices of the MCD are located there. In fact, they found that the ideal place for the women's market would be the roof of the car park. Members of SEWA spoke to the municipal authorities and they finally agreed that such a market could function on the roof of the car park. This was a major victory for SEWA.

The next task before SEWA was of identifying members who would sell there. The women readily agreed and some decided to go to the place as soon as possible. The sites were then fixed. They approached Kapil Sibal, the member of parliament from the area for help, who readily agreed to fund this scheme from the funds that are allotted to the Parliament Quota.[4] Meanwhile, the young architects helping SEWA decided to design some of the stalls. This market appears to be different from other markets. It would be a boost for women vendors who have for long been on the receiving end in street trading. The establishment of this market may pave the way for more such women's markets in the capital.

The market did start functioning from October 2008. The Self Employed Women's Association had approached the municipal councillor of the area and sought her support. Initially, the councillor was helpful. In fact, when SEWA asked her if she would like to include her people she declined saying that SEWA was doing a good job and she did not have any preference to nominate vendors. All this happened before the state elections. She also said that she would ask the Residents' Welfare Associations (RWAs) of the area not to oppose the setting up of the market.

However, soon after the elections when her party returned to power in the state assembly she changed her tune. She stopped cooperating with SEWA and it so happened that the RWAs too started protesting to the Municipal Corporation that this market was causing inconvenience to them. Residents were unable to move freely because of the obstructions caused by the market. The Self Employed Women's Association has been trying to negotiate with all parties for running the market. Its main battle is in fighting opposition to the market.

## Conclusion

We have tried to show the problems faced by the street vendors in Delhi. The Municipal Corporation of Delhi is one of the first to accept the National Policy for Urban Street Vendors. However, it has done nothing else to implement the positive aspects of the policy. For example, it has not set up the vending committees at the ward level. The policy states that unions of street vendors should comprise between 25 to 40 per cent of the total membership. The policy has specifically stated that these committees should have stakeholders and RWAs and shop owners' associations are not stakeholders (NCEUS 2006). It states that the stakeholders are the police and traffic police, the Municipal Corporation, public owners of the property (in Delhi this would mean Delhi Development Authority), and street vendors. Yet, the officials keep quoting the objections of the RWAs in removing street vendors. The policy states that the municipality should consult the RWAs but the municipal officers make the support of RWAs mandatory. Hence, any complaint from an RWA against street vendors is taken up promptly by the municipal authority and the vendors are evicted. Organisations like SEWA are new in the field in Delhi but they have been able to make their presence felt among the policy makers. However, none of the ward committees have representatives from SEWA. It has been systematically excluded. Perhaps the rent-seeking authorities find SEWA a hurdle in their nefarious activities. The Delhi case shows that strong and honest unions are needed among street vendors as only then can they get their rights.

## Notes

1. The population data on Mumbai is taken from the website of Bombay First (www.bombayfirst.com). It is an analysis of different census data.
2. The Bombay province or state comprised the present states of Maharashtra, Gujarat and parts of Karnataka. The states were bifurcated in 1960. The Bombay Municipal Corporation Act, therefore, applies at present to municipal corporations in the two states of Gujarat and Karnataka. Other states too have adopted this act.
3. The president and the secretary approached the coordinator separately and asked him to intervene. They had faith in SEWA as it had earlier helped the book sellers regain the bazaar. The coordinator got both of them together to sort out their issues. This became impossible with just the three of them (the coordinator of SEWA and the two office bearers).
4. Each member of parliament is sanctioned Rs 10 million for development activities in the constituency. These are recommended by the MP but are executed by the concerned state agencies.

## References

Bhowmik, Sharit K. 2000. 'Hawkers in the Urban Informal Sector: A Study of Street Vending in Seven Cities' (mimeo), Patna: National Alliance of Street Vendors of India.

DMP (Delhi Master Plan). 1998. *What Will Delhi Be in 2001? Delhi Master Plan 1990*. Delhi: Akalank Publications.

Government of Delhi. 2001. *Census of India 2001*, available at www.delhigovt.nic.in/labour, accessed on 16 August 2005.

———. 2003. *Economic Survey 2002–2003*, Ministry of Finance, available at www.nic.in/finance.

Government of Delhi. 2004a. Ministry of Labour, available at www.labour.nic. in/ss/INFORMALSECTORININDIA, accessed on 14 August 2005.

———. 2004b. *National Policy for Urban Street Vendors*, National Commission on Enterprises in the Unorganised Sector, available at www.nceus.gov.in.

———. 2005. *Economic Survey 2004–2005*, Ministry of Finance, available at www. nic.in/finance.

Manushi Trust. 2001. 'Memorandum Submitted to the Lt. Governor on Behalf of Delhi's Street Vendors and Rickshaw Pullers & Owners', 2 October.

NCEUS. 2006. 'National Policy for Urban Street Vendors', Delhi: National Commission on Enterprises in the Unorganised Sector, available at www. nceus.gov.in.

NCTD (National Capital Territory of Delhi). 2004. *Industrial Profile of Delhi, 2004*, Office of the Commissioner of Industries, NCTD.

Nayyar, Kuldeep. 2001. 'Hounded and Harassed', *The Hindu*, 8 October, available at www.hindugrouponnet.com.

Rao, Bhanoji. 2005. 'India Beyond Delhi and Mumbai', *The Hindu*, 1 February.

Shah, Parth J. and Naveen Mandava (eds). 2005. *Law, Liberty and Livelihood: Making a Living on the Street*, New Delhi: Centre for Civil Society and Academic Foundation.

# 4

# The Politics of Illegality: Mumbai Hawkers, Public Space and the Everyday Life of the Law*

Jonathan Shapiro Anjaria

'They said they will make Shanghai, instead they made *kabristan* [cemetery],' says Syed, a clothes seller, as we stand on the side of the road, watching as a municipality truck looms down on its way to clear the area of hawkers. It is the third time the municipality has come for a demolition this week. The mere sight of the grey truck inching its way through the traffic fills him with apprehension. Frustrated by the interruption caused by the truck, he told me, 'The police blame us whenever something goes wrong. This city is full of criminals, but the government targets us. If there is an accident on the street in front of us, even though we are just sitting here, the police blame us. The state treats us as if we are the biggest criminals, even though we are businessmen too.' Fortunately, there is heavy traffic on this day, so the hawkers have ample time to pack up their goods. It takes 30 seconds to take down a display of sheets, towels and children's clothes. With the help of some people loitering around, the vendors' tables with all the goods on it are swiftly carried into a small lane located just off the main street. With their tables safely stashed inside, Syed and his friends stand and wait. 'The government's slogan was *garibi hatao* [get rid of poverty], but now it's become *garibon ko hatao* [get rid of the poor]!' Syed adds with wit, inverting the well-known 1970s-era slogan associated with Prime Minister Indira Gandhi. At this point, the municipality truck arrives at the spot in front of us, only to continue down the road without incident. Syed tells me that it is headed for a hawker

---

* Parts of this chapter were originally published in *Economic and Political Weekly*, 2006 (41[21]: 2140–146).

demolition raid in Saat Bungalow, a nearby neighbourhood. The hawkers bring their goods back onto the street and resume business. Says Syed, 'If not today, tomorrow. They will come back.'

In recent years, scholars have identified how disempowered, yet numerically vast, populations such as street vendors, slum residents and squatters have reconfigured the political landscape of cities in the Global South. Holston (1991), Bayat (2000) and Appadurai (2001), for instance, have documented the ability of such marginalised groups to claim resources and entitlements denied to them by the state. Taking this further, Mike Davis (2004), suggests that groups who make claims to space and livelihood outside of the formal structures of the law represent a vast, and as yet only partially explored, site of transformative politics. For Davis, despite their heterogeneous social make-up and alienation from 'the culture of collective labour or large-scale class struggle' (2004: 28) they may represent the future revolutionary subject which has the potential to be 'reincorporated in a global emancipatory project' (2004: 28). In light of these perspectives on urban informality, how should we understand Syed, quoted earlier? While he engages in daily struggles with the municipality and the police, he does not conform to the model of the radicalised, or subversive, urban subaltern; he does not urge an overturning of the discourses of urban development which render him a criminal, but instead insists, 'we are businessmen too'. Moreover, instead of critiquing the law, he critiques the state itself for not following the law, for pursuing hawkers rather than real criminals. This is an unlikely urban 'informal proletariat' (Davis 2004: 5) of a future emancipatory politics.

Syed's aspirations, like those of other hawkers, are humble, and relate more to the realities of everyday experience on the street than to a larger transformative political agenda. In interviews, informal conversations and public statements, hawkers often say they want licenses, hawking zones, a stable hawking policy and an end to corruption. These are claims that, from the perspective of a scholar expecting a politics that more directly addresses structural inequalities, might seem surprising. For instance, despite working illegally, and working under the daily threat of having his goods confiscated, Syed does not reject the state, but instead seeks greater enmeshment with it. Moreover, he responds to the discourses of an orderly, modern city which render his presence on the streets unacceptable not by rejecting them, but instead by asserting his own, alternative and inclusive sense of urban order and morality. In this way, defying expectations, Syed's 'politics', if they can be identified as such, are characterised more by legitimation than rebellion.

## Hawkers' Place in the City

Street vending has been a central component of Mumbai's urban landscape for at least the last two centuries.[1] Nineteenth-century diaries of daily life in the city discuss the 'diversity of cries from those who hawk about their goods and wares in streets and roadways' (Ali 1823: 11), while early twentieth-century observers note that the ethnically varied hawker population epitomised the city's cosmopolitanism (Edwardes 1912). Colonial-era photos of the 'native' parts of town document the presence of hawkers in street and sidewalk scenes containing people engaging in a variety of purposes *other* than walking (Dwivedi and Mehrotra 1995; Rohatgi et al. 1997). Moreover, pre-World War II Bombay Municipal Corporation reports of the general condition of the city mention streets lined with stationary (in a fixed location) hawkers (Monak 1935), while accounts of specific neighbourhoods, such as the red-light area, note that '[m]ale petty traders . . . had a noticeable physical presence on the principle streets' (Krishnen 1923, cited in Tambe 2006: 226). The centrality of hawkers in the city's landscape continues to the present day, in which food hawkers, as well as book, *paan* and clothes hawkers count among the city's primary landmarks.

However, despite hawkers' long historical presence, continued centrality to the city's retail structure, as well as the direct employment hawking provides to over 300,000 people, and the indirect employment it provides hundreds of thousands more (Bhowmik 2003), most street vending in Mumbai is officially illegal, and is seen as a detriment, rather than an asset, to the city. Since the late 1990s, for instance, middle-class non-governmental organizations (NGOs) and residents' groups have been actively promoting, with some success, the idea that hawkers are to be blamed for many of the city's problems. To them, hawkers are one of the city's primary nuisances because they inappropriately use streets and footpaths, block traffic, depress real estate values and are, more generally, eyesores that prevent Mumbai from being a livable city.

Arguments for the removal of hawkers are often based on their presumed outsider status which, it is believed, causes them to have little concern for the urban spaces upon which they earn their livelihood. Towards this end, hawkers are often portrayed to be ignorant of what is proper behaviour in cities due to their bucolic origins in the distant northern states of Uttar Pradesh (U.P.) and Bihar. Nevertheless, the way street markets function makes it extremely unlikely that the newly arrived migrant from a village would set up a stall selling vegetables in a wealthy, and hence relatively more lucrative, residential neighbourhood. Farooq, who hawks shirts in the north-western suburb where he grew up, explains: 'We are not new to this road. We have been [hawking] here for 15 years.' Pointing to another group of hawkers down the road, he continues, 'Those hawkers' father worked here 30 years ago; I was brought up here, raised here and now work here. That is how it is for most people. We have nowhere to go. We are not from England or Pakistan; we have rights here in Bombay.' By contrast, newly arrived migrants to the city are more likely to establish themselves in the lesser-serviced marginal areas of the city, such as around the edges of *jhopadpatties* (shanty towns) in the northern suburbs or around unauthorised settlements at legally liminal areas of the Mumbai metropolitan area, such as the western fringes of Sanjay Gandhi National Park. Thus, because hawkers at the city's edges are largely outside the radar of civic campaigners, ironically, it is hawkers with the longest claims to city space (located in the most high-profile parts of the city) that are most often the targets of anti-hawker efforts.[2]

Despite the appearance of many hawker-lined streets, which might give the impression of a certain chaos, there are, nevertheless, unofficial rules strictly guiding who can work in these spaces. Often, hawkers gain 'ownership' over a space by slowly normalising their presence on the street. In this way, rather than a collective act of seizure of urban land, hawkers' presence is more often a result of what Bayat calls a process of 'quiet encroachment' (2000: 545–49). This is often an individual process involving a lone hawker occupying a spot continuously (it is not uncommon, for instance, for a hawker to be physically present on the same space on the side of the road for over 12 hours a day, seven days a week) and slowly accruing unofficial ownership rights through the relationships he or she forms with people who live and work in the area. For instance, one sandwich hawker with whom I spoke with regularly succeeded in securing his claim to a relatively lucrative spot off a main road by slowly inserting himself into the lives of nearby residents. He helps residents with small chores and acts as an informal security guard for the adjacent house, whose owners in turn allow him to store his cooking equipment overnight in their compound. The children in the area take great delight from his presence, play at his stall, call him 'uncle', as they would other respected adults, and eagerly accept the small cucumber snacks he freely hands out.

Even for those hawkers with a more secure access to space on the side of the road, the occupation is difficult, with little pay, and physically demanding. Farhana, a young vegetable hawker and organiser of the women's wing of a major street vendor union, describes the daily routine of her mother, also a vegetable hawker. 'Each day she wakes up at 4 a.m., leaves the *room* [shanty] at 4:30 a.m. for Vashi market [the wholesale market outside the city], returns at 7 a.m. with the vegetables, washes, cleans, cuts and arranges them until 9 a.m., sells until 10 p.m., and then returns back home again.' There is little time for entertainment. Days off to care for sick children or to take trips to the village to attend family events cause significant financial difficulties.

Says a tomato vendor who is a member of Farhana's union, 'Our work is difficult and it is dirty. Look at this shirt, see all the dirt on it. This comes from lifting the crates, moving the tomatoes, washing them, sitting all day outside in the sunshine, sweating. It is dangerous work too. We sit next to this busy road. If a car goes out of control and swerves off the road, who does it hit? Us.' The hazards of this work also include the long-term effects of exposure to vehicle pollution for extended periods of time. Men such as Syed complained of chest ailments resulting from standing for over 10 hours a day, for more than a decade, only a few feet from a densely trafficked road.

In addition to these difficulties, women face additional troubles while working on the street, which include sexual harassment and the pressures of family responsibilities. Explains Farhana,

> A woman sits on the footpath only when all her other sources for jobs are cut off. It is painful to sit on the footpath but a poor person has no other option. A woman sitting on the footpath for the first time faces the greatest problems. Ill-behaved men harass them by making rude comments. But as she gets old and gains experience on the road, she understands how to tackle the situation.

In addition, the near complete absence of public toilets disproportionately affects the health of female street vendors, who cannot avail of public urination as men can. Female hawkers also face even greater difficulties than vendors of non-perishable goods. In the lonely hours before sunrise, they must either travel by train or ride in the uncomfortable muddy hulls of trucks to wholesale markets, or even take long-distance trips to farms far outside the city. Says Farhana:

> The women who have to buy vegetables from Vashi have to get up 4 a.m. everyday. In the morning, traveling is very painful. They have to leave their kids; no one is there to take care of them. They are on their own. After coming back they clean vegetables and sit at the stall. At 2 p.m. some go home and cook food and feed the children. Again come back to the stall till evening. Then go back home late night, cook food and go to sleep by 11 p.m.

## The Politics of Public Space

Hostility towards hawkers and others considered to be encroachers on public spaces is of course not unique to Mumbai. For instance, since the 1960s, scholars working in the United States have studied the effects of imposing a modernist ideal of public space on what are considered 'disorderly' urban environments. In her 1961 classic work, Jane Jacobs urges urban researchers and planners to understand streets and sidewalks for how they actually function rather than for their intended use. She argues that, contrary to dominant opinion, it is those streets with the greatest outward signs of chaos—for instance, with children playing, old people sitting on steps, and street vendors—that are the most vibrant, safest and livable urban spaces. She identifies particular individuals whose continuous, daily street presence makes the streets safe, arguing that such people act as the 'eyes on the street', who, due to their long, continuous presence on the streets, are able to quickly detect when something goes wrong and provide help. Other urban researchers such as Mitchell Duneier (1999) have specifically focused on the way street vendors in New York, although a public nuisance in the eyes of city authorities, play essential social roles in the neighbourhoods in which they work.

There is ample evidence too that hawkers' vigilance produces a healthy public space in Mumbai as well. In casual conversations with Mumbai residents, stories abound of street hawkers preventing violence and sexual harassment against women at night. This is supported by the research by the PUKAR Gender and Space group on the way women envision public space in Mumbai. The research team has found that women living in Mumbai feel safer on streets marked by the presence of hawkers. "'Our watchman changes more often than the *bhelpuriwalla* at the corner," said one woman at Pali Hill. A group of corporate women in Nariman Point agreed that the food stalls that dot the area add to the familiarity of the place making it less potentially threatening, especially after dark. Women living in Kalachowkie who use Cotton Green station felt less safe since the three food stalls on the platform shut down'. The researchers conclude, '[c]lean lines and people-less streets do not equal comfort or safety. In fact, contrary to commonsense notions of urban beautification, women often prefer a degree of chaos, ambiguity and multiplicity to univalent notions of cleanliness and order' (Khan et al. 2005).

Moreover, the security which hawkers help maintain further enables their own claims to the public space. For instance, it is common practice for jewelry store owners to encourage hawkers to work in front of their shops, and store owners are known to have long, close relationships with particular hawkers. As Syed explains:

'The shopkeepers get worried that if we move from the front of their shops, then who will stop the thieves? We are one kind of protection for them. If there is a robbery, we [the hawkers] will yell out, create a scene and catch the thief. But if we are not sitting in front then it will be easier for them to rob the store and run away.'

As a result of this arrangement, on a number of occasions the store owner had defended him and other nearby hawkers in confrontations with the Brihanmumbai Municipal Corporation (BMC) and the police, further reflecting how a politics of 'slow encroachment' (Bayat 2000) profoundly shapes the urban landscape.

## Hawkers and the Law

Both the colonial and post-colonial Indian government have viewed street vending primarily as a problem, resulting in hawkers' persistent condition of legal insecurity. Similar legal attitudes towards street vending can be found in other former British colonies in Asia and Africa. Like the post-colonial states that succeeded it, the British government understood hawking in its colonies as a 'nuisance' to be eliminated (McGee 1973; Robertson 1997; Vahed 1999). For instance, McGee describes how colonial laws pertaining to street vending in Hong Kong 'conceived of [hawkers] as a problem—obstructive, noisy, unhygienic individuals—[rather than] view them as a constructive element, contributing to the effective functioning of the city' (1973: 22).

For at least a century, the official approach of the state towards street vending has been to eradicate the practice.[3] While official policy is that, with a license, street vending may be permitted, the municipality has not issued a new license since 1978. This has resulted in the current situation in which nearly all of the 200,000–300,000 (Bhowmik 2000) hawkers in Mumbai are illegal.[4] However, the official illegality of unlicensed hawkers in Mumbai does not preclude other forms of recognition by the state (cf. Chatterjee 2004). Unlicensed hawkers, although officially outside the purview of the law, have frequent, if not daily, interactions with a wide range of representatives of the state, including police constables, BMC staff and traffic officers, which profoundly shape hawkers' everyday experiences. This produces a complex relationship between street vending, the law and how the law works in practice.

In 1998, the Citizens' Forum for the Protection of Public Spaces (CFPP, later to change its name to CitiSpace), filed a petition in the Bombay High Court. The CFPP, an umbrella organisation of wealthy South Mumbai residents' associations, complained that the BMC had failed to implement an earlier ruling of the Supreme Court to demarcate hawking and non-hawking zones in the city. The CFPP petition referred to the 1985 Supreme Court judgement on two cases concerning municipal actions against squatters (Bombay Hawkers' Union vs. BMC and Olga Tellis vs. BMC).[5] In the Bombay Hawkers' Union vs. the BMC case, the BMC defended their right to evict squatters by citing the 1888 BMC Act, which authorises the municipality to remove encroachments on streets and footpaths without prior warning.[6] In turn, the street vendors' union noted the inappropriateness of the BMC deriving its powers from a colonial-era law. In a rare instance of noting the colonial origins of Mumbai's municipal governance structure, the union argued that the 1888 BMC Act was passed 'in an era [when] the consciousness of the modern notion of a welfare state was not present to the mind of the colonial legislature' (BHU vs. BMC 1985). While the final court judgement recognised that the problem was more than simply a technical issue relating to urban governance and the rule of law, but one of 'setting the tone of values in a democratic society' (Olga Tellis vs. BMC 1985), the court, nevertheless, granted the BMC the right to continue carrying out evictions without warning, while ordering the municipality to establish a system for regulating street vending through a city-wide system of hawking and non-hawking zones. Moreover, in the final judgement, the court, in an oft-quoted passage, declared that the constitutional right to life (Article 19[g]) does not merely mean the right to survival, but a right to livelihood as well.[7]

However, there is not a simple one-to-one relationship between official government policy towards street vendors—as demonstrated in court documents, policies and the public statements of municipality and police officials—and the everyday encounters hawkers have with the state. For Mumbai hawkers, the bewildering complexity and length of litigation regarding street vending (now stretching eight years), the plethora of (often conflicting) interim orders, the large number of concerned parties (including, but not limited to, CitiSpace, residents' and business associations, the municipality, various hawkers' unions, the Road Transport Office, and the police) and, since 2004, the active involvement of the three, three-member committees surveying potential sites for hawking and non-hawking zones, produces, among other things, a bewilderingly complex relationship between the law as it is found in the courts and the law as it manifests on the streets.

The current regulations on street vending originate from the 1985 Bombay Hawkers' Union vs. Brihanmumbai Municipal Corporation Supreme

Court judgement. This judgement included a letter submitted in 1983 by the then BMC commissioner suggesting a list of regulations for street vending. Over time, this list of suggestions took on a life of its own, and has subsequently become the basis on which rules on hawking have been written. Most importantly, the 2003 Bombay High Court regulations on hawking were taken verbatim from the 1983 commissioner's letter. These restrictions include a ban on cooking food from an open flame; a ban on selling items from a table, stall or handcart; a ban on street vending within 150 m of train stations, municipal markets, colleges, schools, and hospitals, in residential areas, on roads less than 8 m, or on major thoroughfares. Moreover, street vendors must be licensed (only one is to be issued per family), work in hawking zones, and work no later than 10 p.m.

These restrictions are remarkable for their disconnect with the already existing hawking practices in Mumbai, as well as with the overall functioning of the city more generally. As a number of observers have noted, the regulations forbid street vending at precisely those places where vendors are needed the most: train stations, municipal markets, colleges, and religious institutions are where the vast majority of Mumbai residents purchase cooked and uncooked food, household items and other items of daily convenience.

Yet while these draconian laws should have had the effect of radically altering the landscape of Mumbai, in the years since the High Court ruling, hawker eradication efforts have been rendered inconsistent by, among other things, the ongoing battle among hawkers and representatives of the state. Instead of a systematic anti-hawker campaign, the authorities use the new regulations and ongoing court cases to justify subtle harassment, daily threats and periodic confiscation of goods. As a result, hawkers often understand their work in terms of the skirmishes that are fought throughout the city. As Farhana explained one afternoon, 'today there is a great amount of trouble going on.' She continued, '*sahib* [the union leader] is in Kandivali, [his son] is in Jogeshwari, other union*wale* are in Goregoan.' Each activist, she explains, is dealing with the aftermath of a BMC 'action' against hawkers in different parts of the city. She speaks as if there is a low-running war going on throughout the city in which the street vendors and the municipality are the principle combatants. For their part, the BMC describes the situation in similar war-like terms. Says V. N. Kalampatil, a deputy municipal commissioner, 'Earlier we used to swoop on them, but now we first mark off a huge area and surround it with our officers. So even if there is a tip off we are able to catch the fleeing hawkers' (*Midday*, 18 April 2005). Nevertheless, despite periodic media reports documenting the latest major municipality campaign against hawkers operating near train stations, selling food late at night, or on a road declared a 'non-hawking zone', much of the city's vast hawker population remains.

## Everyday Life of the Law

Near the spot where Syed works is a bustling, mixed commercial area with stores selling sweets, clothing and electronic goods, a 1940s-era 'Irani' cafe, a McDonalds, as well as a bus station, colleges, training institutes, a large mosque, and municipal offices. Hawkers line the lanes selling shoes, clothes, fruits, fruit juices, fried snacks, and VCDs. In recent years, hawkers' presence in this area has become increasingly contentious, as the municipality and police have been put under greater pressure to de-congest the area. After a plan to move the existing hawkers to a fixed location on a nearby street was blocked by the residents' associations, the state has resorted to periodic hawker demolitions to open the roads. Nevertheless, the demand from commuters and other people using the station area has ensured that hawkers remain, regardless of the various pressures against them.

Nearly every afternoon the BMC parks one of its grey trucks in front of the station. To the hawkers, the mere sight of the parked, hulking truck elicits fear, for it is well-known from previous hawker demolitions. Thus, the truck represents the threat of their goods being confiscated, and loss of a week's profit or more. On most days the hawkers are able to run away and hide their goods in nearby shops before the truck's arrival. After the truck is parked at its usual spot facing the station, the BMC workers go off to their usual restaurant for some tea; the actual presence of the state officials isn't necessary to assert power, so, as the hawkers say, they can make better use of their time chatting with their friends at a nearby restaurant than sitting in their truck. In the meantime, the hawkers stand on the side of the road, watching the empty truck, speculating about the BMC's latest moves. By 7 p.m. in the evening, the trucks roll away, and the hawkers return to work for the remainder of the night.

While the media and civic activists attribute the continued presence of hawkers to a lack of 'political will' on the part of the municipality and the police—therefore reducing the problem to one of implementation—this does not explain the complexity of the situation. Forgotten in much of the discussion about enforcing *particular* regulations—such as the ban on hawking near train stations—is the fact that nearly *all* street vendors are, technically, illegal anyway. This has created some unusual situations, such as public announcements of bans on activities that have already been declared illegal. For example, amid the fear of an epidemic following the 26 July 2005 floods, and at the recommendation of prominent doctors, the BMC commissioner declared a two-week ban on street food vending. Of course, as per the Bombay High Court judgement in 2003, cooking food on the street was already declared illegal and, regardless, most food vendors operate without licenses as well. Nevertheless, newspapers quoted BMC officials saying they had requested food vendors to close shop (*The Times of India*, 18 August 2005).

The announcement of a ban on illegal activities reveals much about the everyday experience of the law. Following the widely publicised two-week ban on food-vending, Raju, a sandwich vendor, received a visit from a BMC official, requesting him to close his shop for a few days. Raju does brisk business throughout the day, in large part because he is located in a residential area with few other food vendors and a hungry population of school children and college students. However, his high sales make him a bigger target for the police and BMC. On this occasion, Raju's business was deemed illegal on three accounts: he does not have a license, he cooks food and he continued to cook food during the post-flood ban.

For over eight years, Raju, along with his father, has been working at the same spot, selling vegetable sandwiches from a 1 sq m booth. As he explained to me, every two weeks an off-duty police constable or BMC worker comes by and collects money (Rs 1,200–1,600 at a time) for his superiors. The arrangement allows him to stay, but at the cost of over a third of his monthly income. Following the 2005 street food ban, he was instructed to close his stall for a few days. However, after paying the requisite *hafta* (informal payments to the authorities, often loosely translated as 'bribe'), Raju was allowed to re-open. (Indeed, despite the BMC's claims that vendors had been requested to shut down, there was little evident change; in the weeks of the epidemic scare, street food was as widely available as ever.) Raju explained the logic of the regulation matter-of-factly: 'Because of the floods, they asked for double hafta this month,' suggesting how lower-level municipal workers successfully use their superior's directives to their financial advantage.

The effects of laws regarding street vending often far exceed, and at times invert, their intent, which suggests the need to focus on the 'life' of laws, rather than on the question of whether or not they are successfully implemented. As we can see in the case of Raju, by banning cooking food for a finite period of time, the state legitimised the practice at other times. Ironically, it is this double illegality—the fact that they are un-licensed *and* momentarily subject to regulations—that contributes to hawkers' continued presence on the streets. In other words, the constant adjudication of groups of hawkers has the effect of legitimising others, as well as of legitimising those same vendors at a different time. In this way, the convoluted and often conflicting laws and regulations inconsistently result in hawker eradication.

The most important problem hawkers say that they experience is not lack of sales, access to credit, or even work conditions, but the constant fear of demolitions and daily harassment for bribes from the authorities. The demand for illicit payments by state authorities and the concomitant insecurity it brings is the single biggest source of worry for most hawkers with whom I conducted research. As hawkers often say in conversation, their desire is to simply 'work here in peace [free from state harassment]'. It has been estimated, for instance, that street vendors pay the equivalent of tens of millions of dollars in hafta each year. On average, each vendor pays Rs 1,200–1,400 a month, which is taken by officials in the form of unofficial fines. These payments are made to the police and the BMC (always collected through intermediaries at the lowest rung of the bure-aucracy) in the form of money, or in kind. For instance, vegetable vendors on a popular stretch of road declare that they are compelled to give the police 100 kg of vegetables free of charge every week.

With great frequency, laws and regulations created by officials in the higher rungs of the bureaucracy and in the courts are translated by lower officials to greater demands for illicit payments. In turn, threats of impending demolition or confiscation of goods, pressure from above, and 'complaints' made by NGOs and local residents are often cited as an excuse for higher payments. And, since 2003, the suggestion made by the High Court–appointed committee that an area should become a non-hawking zone has also been used as justification for greater hafta demands. In this way, in certain areas, the inclusion of streets on the non-hawking zone list by the committee, although not yet a law, has become law on the ground. In parts of Andheri and Kandivali, the BMC has started to install non-hawking zone signs (which read, in Devanagari script, '*Bina Pheriwala Kshetra*'), which has led to the confiscation of some hawkers' goods, but more often, to increased demands for money from hawkers in those areas. In one area, stories circulate about non-hawking signs that have come up following a 1.5 lakh bribe to the BMC by the local residents' association with the financial backing of a prominent hotel owner. In another area, a non-hawking zone sign was installed amidst 150 vegetable vendors.

This was particularly illogical, as these hawkers are the primary providers of vegetables for a large and densely populated (and under-serviced) part of the city. To one hawker, however, there was clear rationality behind the installation of this sign: 'Why would they put this sign halfway down the road, with hawkers located on both sides? Now they will come, point at the sign and say "non-hawking zone". And that way they will be able to collect more money.'

## The Politics of Illegality

When I first met Syed, I was struck by the unassuming nature of his political demands. As I sat next to his table, he turned away from the rush of pedestrians and potential customers and told me:

> We don't want to fight with anybody and cause a commotion. We want to earn our daily bread. We don't have anything against the BMC or the police. If they are not giving us any place then give us some other service job. They say that it is not good that educated people stand on the road and work. So give us work elsewhere. Give us a space and we will go there and work.

While on the one hand Syed's awareness of stereotypes of hawkers as troublemakers may have shaped his comment that he does not 'want to fight with anybody or cause a commotion', these words also reflect a sense of frustration with a government that, in failing to provide jobs to people with education, plays a significant role in producing these fights. The resignation in Syed's voice on that day was due not only to the daily harassment he experiences, but to the inversion of right and wrong his presence on the street represents; thus, his sense of the 'problem' of the situation was directed at the state's role in creating an immoral society, where even 'educated people stand on the road and work'.

While street vendors might appear to represent an unregulated, and therefore problematic, population, finding a long-lasting solution to the 'problem' of street vending is not desirable to many in the municipality. Ali, a *raddiwala* (recycled paper trader) explains: 'The BMC and the police wants to keep things on a boil.' He continues, 'They don't want a solution to the hawker issue. Because if there is an end to the issue, then they won't get their hafta.' In this context we can see how, as Begoña Aretxaga (2003: 402) writes, 'the power of the state is harnessed not so much from the rationality of ordering practices as from the passions of transgression, in which the line between the legal and illegal is constantly blurred'. Here, the local state's power over street vendors does not come from acts of legalising, but from keeping their legal status in a constant state of flux. Thus, the persistent insecurity of hawkers stems from threats of municipality- or police-imposed fines, bribe demands or the confiscation of their goods. And yet, hawkers such as Syed, quoted earlier, do not reject the state, but talk of the potential for state intervention on their behalf; their politics and collective aspirations do not index rebellion, or subversion, but desires for legitimation. Syed, like others, desires legitimacy and security, not anarchy.

Indeed, hawkers' collective aspirations are quite humble. They are often for hawking zones, licenses, local registration, *pautis* (official receipts for fines paid), regularised vending fees, and the end of corruption and other forms of harassment (cf. Bhowmik 2003). Put simply, they desire positive recognition by the state, which they claim would enable a long-lasting solution to the contentious issue of street vending. These claims do not represent the kind of subversive politics one might expect of a population whose livelihood is so tenuous. To return to the question with which I began this chapter, how are we to understand a desire for regulation and increased state intervention when, at the moment, the state is itself a primary source of the problem? Does this represent a certain naiveté, a capitulation to an elite discourse, a failure of the imagination or an 'ad hoc' politics, à la Davis (2004: 29), that lacks a coherent vision? This disjuncture between the politics scholars might assume this marginal population to have, and their actual collective aspirations raises some additional issues relating to the everyday working of power in Mumbai. For, this disjuncture is in part due to a priori assumptions of the way the state works.

From a Foucauldian analytic perspective, a desire for a formal hawker policy might seem paradoxical or misguided, as such things as licenses or registration would seem to heighten vendors' 'surveillability' (Rajagopal 2001: 104) and '[render] them subject to all manner of regulation' (ibid.: 109). Such a plan to bring street vendors in Mumbai within the legal fold, for instance, would be considered problematic because it would heighten their subjection to a state regime of surveillance and regulation. From this perspective, a project to legalise vendors would not represent a profound change, but rather a mere reorganisation of power.[8]

Here, as I hope to have shown, power works differently. In Mumbai, as Veena Das also observes in New Delhi, 'the forms of governmentality are themselves instituted through sporadic, intermittent contact rather than an effective panoptic system of surveillance' (Das 2007: 167). From this 'intermittent' state contact many Mumbai hawkers understand the problem to be not so much a *regulatory* state, but a particular kind of predatory state, a state that constantly demands bribes and threatens demolitions—against which formal recognition provides security. While on the level of discourse (as found in official pronouncements to the media, for instance), hawkers might be unacceptable within the modern, ordered city, at the level of everyday practices of the municipality, hawkers represent something different: not simply a problem, but also a *possibility*. Thus, the experience of Mumbai's hawkers is defined less by their transgressive symbolic presence on the street, than by their peculiar relationship with the state. As Ali, quoted earlier, explains, the municipality exerts power through a very deliberate process of keeping hawkers perpetually in an uncertain condition between legality and illegality, from which municipal workers are able to extract a rich bounty of gifts and money. In this context, the subversive act of the Mumbai hawker is, ironically, not to circumvent the law or the surveilling eye of the state, but to find a place within it.

## Notes

1. In this chapter I refer to the city as 'Mumbai', because it is the official name of the city. In everyday speech in English, however, the city is commonly referred to as 'Bombay'. Hindi speakers, such as those included in this study, call the city '*Bambai*'. Marathi and Gujarati speakers most often call the city '*Mumbai*' (see Patel 2003).

2. The politics of nativism aside, the significant demographic question for Mumbai is not where the migrants are coming *from*, but where the migrants are coming *to*. Recent census data indicates that the vast majority of migrants to the Mumbai region are not settling within the city proper, but in satellite townships such as Thane, Kalyan and Bhayander (Shekhar 2005). This problematises the assumption that an influx of immigrants from rural areas is causing problems of congestion, traffic and crowding in the centre of Mumbai.

3. As early as 1909, Bombay hawkers were 'engaged in a running battle with the police' (Kidambi 2007: 152).

4. In the absence of an up-to-date, comprehensive survey of hawkers in Mumbai, current estimates of the total hawker population range from 200,000 to well over 300,000.

5. The Olga Tellis vs. BMC case related to the rights of slum dwellers. Olga Tellis, a well-known Mumbai-based journalist, initiated this case in response to BMC demolitions of squatters and other slum dwellers living adjacent to the highway in Mahim, central Mumbai. The petitioners argued that the slum developed in the 1960s to house the labourers constructing the highway adjacent to which they were currently living. The BHU vs. BMC case was initiated by the hawkers union to stop demolitions of street vendors without prior warning. They argued that the colonial origins of the 1888

BMC Act, which grants the BMC the authority to demolish hawkers' stalls, contradicted India's constitutional guarantees to a right to livelihood and the right to engage in whatever occupation one may please (Article 19[g] of the Constitution).

6. Section 313 of the Bombay Municipal Corporation Act states, 'Except under and in conformity with the terms and provisions of a license granted by the Commissioner in this behalf, no person shall hawk or expose for sale in any public place or in any public street any article whatsoever whether it be for human consumption or not'. Section 314(b) states, 'The Commissioner may without notice, cause to be removed any article whatsoever hawked or exposed for sale in any public place or in any public street' (From *Legal Status of Hawkers in India*, quoted in *Seminar* 2000). It has also been noticed that the BMC laws were taken nearly word for word from English vagrancy laws (*Seminar* 2000).

7. This passage has subsequently been interpreted by hawkers' unions as a tacit endorsement by the court of the right of street vendors to work in public spaces. However, residents' associations, citizens' groups, the police, and BMC officials fiercely object to the interpretation of the court judgement to grant a constitutional right to hawkers to work wherever they please.

8. Having said this, such a theory of power may very well be useful for understanding street vending in certain contexts. For instance, the anthropologist Paul Stoller writes on the experiences of African immigrant street traders in New York, for whom a street vending license brings with it constant monitoring by state officials, who perpetually fine hawkers for even the most minor infractions concerning the use of public space (2002: 88–90). This, of course, profoundly affects the politics of New York street vendors, for whom it is financially and physically more viable to operate *without* a license.

## References

Ali, Meer Hassan. 2004 (1823). 'Observations on the Mussulmauns of India'. Electronic Document, available at http://www.gutenberg.org/catalog/world/readfile?fk_files=86447, accessed on 16 February 2007.

Appadurai, Arjun. 2001. 'Deep Democracy: Urban Governmentality and the Horizon of Politics', *Environment & Urbanization*, 13(2): 23–43.

Aretxaga, Begona. 2003. 'Maddening States', *Annual Review of Anthropology*, 32: 393–410.

Bayat, Asef. 2000. 'From "Dangerous Classes" to "Quiet Rebels": Politics of the Urban Subaltern in the Global South', *International Sociology*, 15(3): 533–57.

Bhowmik, Sharit K. 2000. 'A Raw Deal?' *Seminar*, 491, July.

———. 2003. 'National Policy for Street Vendors', *Economic and Political Weekly*, 38(16), 19 April: 1543–546.

Chatterjee, Partha. 2004. *The Politics of the Governed: Reflections on Popular Politics in Most of the World*, New Delhi: Permanent Black. 'City Steers Clear of Chaat', *The Times of India*, 18 August 2005.

Das, Veena. 2007. *Life and Words: Violence and the Descent into the Ordinary*, Berkeley: University of California Press.

Davis, Mike. 2004. 'Planet of Slums: Urban Involution and the Informal Proletariat', *New Left Review*, 26 (March/April): 5–34.

Duneier, Mitchell. 1999. *Sidewalk*, New York: Farrar, Straus and Giroux.

Dwivedi, Sharada and Rahul Mehrotra. 1995. *Bombay: The Cities Within*, Bombay: India Book House Pvt Ltd.

Edwardes, S. M. 1912. *By-Ways of Bombay*, Bombay: D. B. Taraporevala Sons & Co.

Holston, James. 1991. 'Autoconstruction in Working-class Brazil', *Cultural Anthropology*, 6(4): 447–65.

Jacobs, Jane. 1992 (1961). *The Death and Life of Great American Cities*, New York: Vintage Books.

Khan, Sameera, Shilpa Phadke and Shilpe Ranade. 2005. 'Women Want Bright Lights, Safe Parks & Female Cops', *The Times of India*, 30 January.

Kidambi, Prashant. 2007. *The Making of an Indian Metropolis: Colonial Governance and Public Culture in Bombay, 1890–1920*, Burlington, Vt.: Ashgate.

Mcgee, T. G. 1973. *Hawkers in Hong Kong: A Study of Planning and Policy in a Third World City*, Hong Kong: University of Hong Kong.

*Mid Day*. 2005. 'Bhaago, Bhaago, BMC is Coming!', 18 April.

Monak, N. V. 1935. 'The City's Public Works', In Clifford Manshardt (ed.), *The Bombay Municipality at Work*, pp. 55–70, Bombay: D. B. Taraporevala & Sons.

Muralidharan, Sukumar. 2000. 'The Legacy of the Emergency', *Frontline*, 17(14), 8–21 July. Electronic Document, available at http://www.hinduonnet.com/fline/fl1714/17140290.htm, accessed on 10 January 2007.

Patel, Sujata. 2003. 'Bombay and Mumbai: Identities, Politics, and Populism', in Sujata Patel and Jim Masselos (eds), *Bombay and Mumbai: The City in Transition*, New Delhi: Oxford University Press.

Rajagopal, Arvind. 2001. 'The Violence of Commodity Aesthetics: Hawkers, Demolition Raids, and a New Regime of Consumption', *Social Text*, 19(3): 91–113.

Robertson, Claire. 1997. *Trouble Showed the Way: Women, Men and Trade in the Nairobi Area, 1890–1990*, Bloomington, Ind.: Indiana University Press.

Rohatgi, Pauline, Pheroza Godrej and Rahul Mehrotra. 1997. *Bombay to Mumbai: Changing Perspectives*, Mumbai: Marg Publications.

*Seminar*. 2000. 'Legal Status of Hawkers in India' (Street Vendors: A Symposium on Reconciling People's Livelihood and Urban Governance), 491, July.

Shekhar, Vaishnavi. 2005. 'Share of Migrants in Mumbai Halves Over 100 Years', *The Times of India*, 29 September.

Stoller, Paul. 2002. *Money Has No Smell: The Africanization of New York City,* Chicago and London: University of Chicago Press.

Tambe, Ashwini. 2006. 'Brothels as Families: Reflections on the Histories of Bombay's Kothas', *International Feminist Journal of Politics,* 8(2): 219–42.

Vahed, Goolam. 1999. 'Control and Repression: The Plight of Indian Hawkers and Flower Sellers in Durban, 1910–1948', *The International Journal of African Historical Studies,* 32(1): 19–48.

# 5

# Integrating Street Vendors in City Planning: The Case of Vadodara

Shreya Dalwadi

Street vendors in India act as an efficient distribution network for articles of daily necessities. The fact that they account for a substantial population in Indian cities indicates that there is a demand for street vendors in these cities. In spite of this, today street vendors are regarded as 'illegal'. A ray of hope is the fact that the acceptance of street vendors is increasing worldwide with talks about their rights and security. In India, with the formulation of the National Policy on Street Vendors in 2004, the status of street vendors has been recognised. With the acceptance of the policy by states and subsequently by cities, a methodology of integrating street vendors in the city will be required.

Through the case of Vadodara (erstwhile Baroda) city, a comprehensive framework for the integration of street vendors in city planning, which can be replicated for other cities, has been attempted in the research reported in this chapter. Beginning with the need and ways to integrate street vendors, it touches upon the existing situation of street vendors in Vadodara and further elaborates on the urban planning measures, regulation and monitoring mechanism, and in the end, the legislative support for successful integration of street vendors in the city.

## Background

Before getting into the nitty-gritty of the magnitude of street vendors, their location, their characteristics, it is important to take an overview of the current scenario of vendors at the global scale. It is also important to look closely at some fundamental concepts of street vending and their relevance. The chapter begins with an orientation of the readers on the issue of street vending activity.

## What is a 'Street'?

The very word 'street', as its etymology suggests, denotes a delimited surface—part of an urban texture, characterised by an extended area lined with buildings on either side (Rykwert 1991). There are two social functions of streets: the instrumental function which enables movement of goods, people, etc., and the expressive function which includes their use for casual communication, recreation, conversation, entertainment, as a site for processions, ritual observances, etc. (ibid.). So, streets have many functions, of which, connectivity is one. Streets are institutions for sociability, sources of entertainment and also an extension of living spaces (Anderson 1991), which is all the more applicable to streets in Indian cities. Street vending should be looked upon as one of such functions of streets. Occurrence of street vending is not a recent concept in India. Open markets, street corner markets and weekly *haats* are a part of Indian tradition (Jhabvala 2000) and can be dated to generations back.

Street vendors tend to concentrate in areas of high residential density, high transportation transfer or near commercial centres where there is a flow of a large number of people per day.[1] Distribution of street vendors varies according to the city's layout. It also depends on the type of commodity sold and space availability in the city.

## Classification of Street Vendors

Vendors can be classified on the basis of the commodity sold into two main types:[2] food item vendors, that is, those selling processed and non-processed food, and non-food item vendors, that is, those selling household articles, clothes, flowers and services (Table 5.1).

## The Need to Organise Street Vendors

In the context of Indian streets, traffic is often characterised by a lack of effective channelisation and control of speeds (Tiwari 2000). There are other problems like haphazard vehicle parking on streets, unauthorised auto-rickshaw stands, cattle on streets, etc. Since street vendors do not have a legitimate place in cities, they get located haphazardly in public spaces among which streets are the most favourable. Street vendors add to the mentioned problems on the street and often act as hindrances to traffic flow. Hence, street vending can be looked upon as one of the issues of street management. Street vendors also disturb the appearance

**Table 5.1**
**Classification of Street Vendors**

| Commodity Sold | Type of Vending Activity | Items Sold by Vendors |
|---|---|---|
| Food items | Processed food | Lunch, dinner, *paratha-sabzi*, snacks (*bhajiya*, *dalwada*, *samosa*, sandwich), *puri-pakodi*, *pav-bhaji*, tea–coffee, *juices* |
| | Non-processed food | Fruits, vegetables, ice-creams, packed foods, cold-drinks, water, soda, *pan–bidi, sharbat* |
| Non-food items | Household articles | Utensils, women's jewellery, bathroom accessories (tiles, fixtures, etc.), electrical fixtures (plug, bulb, etc.), show items, paintings, sanitary cleaning material (phenyl, acid), decorative articles (chandelier, lamps), safety products (helmet) |
| | Clothes | Cloth-pieces, readymades |
| | Flowers | Artificial flowers, plants, fresh flowers |
| | Service providers | Barber, mechanic, painter, cobbler, potter, cycle repairer, electrical goods repairer, newspaper kiosk |

*Source*: Field study, 2004.

and hygiene of the place/streets where they are located because of lack of proper infrastructure facilities.

From another point of view, it is important to understand that street vendors cater to the daily needs of people of different income groups, of which the lower income group shows more dependency. In India the population of street vendors in urban areas is found to have increased by 1.75 per cent in the last decade (CSO 2000; Jhabvala 2000).[3] Bhowmik (2003) in his study on seven cities, has estimated that around 2.5 per cent of the urban population is engaged in street vending.[4] The study for Vadodara shows approximately 3.54 per cent of the population directly involved in vending and approximately 10 per cent of the total population (for details, refer to the sub-section titled 'Number of Vendors and Space Reservation' in this chapter) dependant on vending as an economic activity.[5] Because of the lack of legal status, street vendors use the resources of the city but do not contribute in financial terms. There is hence a need to integrate street vendors in the city physically and socially.

## Requirement of a Comprehensive Framework

The laws framed during British India (implemented in cities even today) restricted the use of streets to circulation only and so street vending began to be considered an 'illegal activity'.[6] But with the formulation of the

Draft National Policy, legal recognition is being given to street vendors.[7] The policy has recommended that the laws considering street vending as illegal should be modified with the rider rendering street vending as legitimate use of the street under regulated conditions. When the policy is finalised and adopted by the states, a comprehensive framework will be required to integrate vendors for translation of the policy into groundwork for cities.

## Attempts at Organising Street Vendors

The first attempt at preparing a legal document for street vendors was made in 1995 in the form of the 'Bellagio International Declaration'. The declaration urged the governments of all countries to modify laws in order to support street vending and give licenses and social security to vendors (Horn Pat, StreetNet International 2003). Though street vending has been legally recognised in India only recently, the phenomenon is common in many cities of Europe and other developed countries. The district-level policy for vendors in the city of Durban in South Africa details roles and duties of the governing body/ies in order to organise street vending (Moser 1984). In Peru, reorganisation of street vendors has been undertaken in the programme of revitalisation of public spaces (see www.unhabitat.org).[8]

In the regional context, similar attempts in the city of Ahmedabad (with characteristics and lifestyle similar to Vadodara) are worth reviewing. A study of the process of organising vendors at Mansi Apartment, Satellite and at Jivraj Park crossroads, Vejalpur (both locations in Ahmedabad), reveals that in order to allocate physical space to vendors, studying the typology of vending activity is very important.[9] Typology of vendors is city specific and influences the area requirement, timings and customer size for the vending activity.[10] There are other ancillary facilities like toilets for vendors, electricity, drinking water, and wash area that need to be provided along with physical space. Waste management is a very important component of street vending, inefficiency of which renders the activity to be a nuisance for the surrounding land uses. If space is allocated to vendors on the street side, it should be such that it does not hinder the important function of circulation on streets. It should not conflict with the usual or the actual uses of the space/street. If the space to vendors is allocated on a lease/quasi-legal basis, the accountability of users increases and there is ease in management of the space. Local non-governmental organisations (NGOs) are found to be an effective link between the governing bodies and the vendors/vendors' organisations.

## Context of Vending in Vadodara

The classification mentioned previously in this chapter had been adopted for the purpose of research by the author and will be referred to in this chapter from this point onwards. Before reviewing the scenario of vending in Vadodara, it is essential to overview the profile of Vadodara city and attempts at organising vendors made in the past.

Vadodara is one of the premier cities of the state of Gujarat. The major transportation spine, NH-8, provides north–south linkages, linking Gujarat with the rest of the country, and Vadodara is located approximately in the centre of this corridor. The city is spread over an area of 108.26 sq km (1 kilometer is equal to 0.6 miles) and is administratively divided into 10 wards (Desai 2003). In terms of population (2001), Vadodara ranks 18th in India and third in the state of Gujarat. During 1971–81, the population in the Vadodara Municipal Corporation area grew by 57.11 per cent, and by 40.42 per cent during 1981–91. In 1991–2001, the city registered a growth rate of 26.63 per cent, the lowest in the history of the Municipal Corporation (School of Planning 2002). The city has a high literacy rate—87.85 per cent in 2001—and the city's economy depends mainly on the tertiary sector (58.89 per cent in 1991) (ibid.).

## *Declaration of Hawking and Non-hawking Zone Scheme in Vadodara in 1987*

The intervention of the Municipal Corporation to organise street vendors began with the declaration of the Hawking and Non-hawking Zone Scheme in Vadodara in 1987 (Desai 1987). The Supreme Court of India passed an order dated 2 May 1986 in Writ Petition No. 657 of 1986 filed by the Hawkers' Association of Baroda and others against the Municipal Corporation of Baroda, directing the Municipal Corporation to formulate a scheme for 'Hawking and Non-hawking Zones' in each ward of the city of Baroda (ibid.). Under this scheme, 30 major roads of Vadodara were declared 'Non-hawking Zones'. The scheme was prepared on a participatory basis and conditions for allocation and use of spaces and those for granting of licenses had been given in the scheme. As per the scheme, vending was not allowed on and up to a distance of 25 m on both sides of the demarcated streets (ibid.).

An inventory of vendors on major roads (width >18 m) of Vadodara in 2004 shows that the major concentration of vendors is on the same roads demarcated as Non-hawking Zones by the scheme of 1987.[11] After about 17 years of the proposal of Non-hawking Zones if the same roads show maximum concentration of street vendors, it points towards an important fact that a flat policy of declaration of Non-hawking Zones would not be successful in Indian conditions. It is also noteworthy that vendors are highly concentrated on the Outer Ring Road in Vadodara and the national and state highways. The cluster size is found to be high on all major roads, and even higher in the walled city of Vadodara.

## Vending in Vadodara—Important Results

The aggregate study of vendors in Vadodara by the author looks at the number, typology, location, and distribution of street vending in Vadodara and their relations with density and road width.[12] There has been an attempt to judge the total number of vendors and to decipher the rotation of vendor typology during the day, the space requirements, the customer timings for vendors, etc., for the city of Vadodara after detailed study.

### Typology of Vendors in Vadodara

In Vadodara, the majority vendors are engaged in the business of selling non-processed food items—fruits, vegetables, *pan-bidi*, cold drinks, packed foods, ice-cream, items like *sharbat*, fruit salad, cold cocoa, etc. (Table 5.2).

**Table 5.2**
**Distribution of Vendors by Type of Vending Activity**

| Type of Vending Activity | % Distribution |
| --- | --- |
| Processed food | 26.80 |
| Non-processed food | **42.33** |
| Household articles | 9.65 |
| Clothes | 2.62 |
| Flowers | 3.82 |
| Services | 14.78 |
| Total | 100.00 |

*Source*: City-level primary survey, Vadodara Municipal Corporation (VMC), 2004.

In terms of mobility, there are two major types of vendors: stationary and mobile. Among the stationary vendors (which was the scope of action in the author's research), there are two further sub-types: static vendors—the vendor would continue his business at the given place for the whole day, that is, morning to evening; and semi-static vendors—the vendor would carry out his business for some portion of the day either morning or evening (maybe a few hours in the morning and a few in the evening).

**Table 5.3**
**Distribution of Vendors by Duration of Vending Activity**

| | Duration of Vending Activity | |
| --- | --- | --- |
| Type of Vending Activity | Static | Semi-static |
| Processed food | 11.08 | 15.73 |
| Non-processed food | 16.98 | 25.36 |
| Household articles | 2.35 | 7.30 |
| Clothes | 0.83 | 1.78 |
| Flowers | 0.97 | 2.85 |
| Services | 13.98 | 0.79 |
| Total | 46.19 | **53.81** |

Source: City-level primary survey, VMC, 2004.

It has been found that 53.81 per cent of vendors in Vadodara are semi-static. Since the majority of vendors are semi-static, irrespective of the type of activity, this gives an indication that the 'timing of operation of vendors' is an important consideration for space allocation. It also gives a clue that different activities can be permitted alternatively at the same place. Provision of services by vendors, which includes barbers, mechanics, painters, and cobblers, is the only activity that requires stationary place of business due to the natural characteristic of the activity, but since it is small in proportion, it can be controlled and allotted fixed destinations.

The location of vendors in Vadodara on road junctions is of serious concern. Of the total vendors of the city 40 per cent are at junctions which cover only 10 per cent of the total length of major roads. The reason is that more numbers of people pass through a junction at any given point of time resulting in high business potential. Due to high traffic count at junctions, the high concentration of vendors adds to the congestion and disturbs traffic flow. The design of junctions does not account for the presence of street vendors.

Some 54 per cent of total vendors on major roads are located on road stretches. Though the absolute number of street vendors at road stretches might be more, it is of less concern because the spread is almost even along the whole street, with little potential for clogging of traffic and pedestrian flows. At first thought, moving the vendors away from the junction seems to be an easy solution to solve the problem of congestion. This is an attitude adopted by administrative authorities. However, the most favourable place of business for vendors is at the junctions of roads. An attempt, therefore, could be made to make vendors a part of street design and/or junction design.

## *Relation between Gross Density, Income, Land Use, and Street Vendors*

Table 5.4 shows the relationship between gross density of a ward and number of vendors. From medium to high density residential areas, the number of vendors per unit length of road increases.

**Table 5.4**
**Relation between Gross Density and Unit Number of Vendors**

| Ward No. | Density (Persons/sq km) | Density Range | Vendors/10,000 Popn. | |
|---|---|---|---|---|
| 4 | 6,356 | Low | 87 | *Low Density Range (<10,000 persons/sq km)* |
| 3 | 14,889 | Medium | 57 | *Medium Density Range (10,000–25,000 persons/sq km)* |
| 5 | 18,051 | Medium | 56 | *High Density Range (>70,000 persons/sq km)* |
| 2 | 1,03,636 | High | 82 | |

*Source*: City-level primary survey, VMC, 2004.

In low-density residential areas, which are on the outskirts of the city and inhabited usually by the higher-income group (HIG) population, the number of vendors is more since the potential for business is more. This has been observed to be true for two reasons: one, peripheral areas are generally far from the old Central Business District (CBD) and therefore require a stronger distribution network for daily commodities, and two, the residents being HIG, the profit margin obtained by vendors is very high. It must be understood here that many externalities, other than density, can affect the number of vendors. More than half of the population in the lower-income group (LIG) depends entirely on vendors for daily needs (Jhabvala 2000). Therefore, the number of vendors is high in areas of LIG residences, which are characterised by high residential density (Table 5.5).

**Table 5.5**
**Relation between Income Groups and Unit Number of Vendors**

| Typology of Residential Area | Vendors/km Length of Road |
|---|---|
| LIG (lower income group) | 450 |
| MIG (middle income group) | 178 |
| HIG (higher income group) | 198 |

*Source*: Ward-level primary survey, 2004.

The comparative situation of vendors with respect to different land uses is shown in Table 5.6. The demand of vendors is more in commercial hubs and transport nodes where the circulation of people per day is more.

**Table 5.6**
**Variation of Vending Activity with Change in Land Use**

| Land Use Type | Vendors/km Length of Road |
|---|---|
| Transport node | **555** |
| LIG residential area | **450** |
| Commercial hub | **258** |
| Hospital | 250 |
| HIG residential area | 238 |
| MIG residential area | 178 |
| Recreation place | 178 |
| Industries | 160 |
| Institution | 136 |

*Source*: Area-level primary survey, 2004.

The figures derived for the number of vendors/km length can be used as a generic statement for making respective predictions and further provisions at town planning (TP) scheme levels. The TP scheme is the tool of area planning constituted through the Gujarat Town Planning and Urban Development Act (GTPUD Act) (Government of Gujarat 2000).

In the preparation of a TP scheme, a rough idea of the expected land use in the region for which the scheme is being prepared can act as the basis for predicting the number of vendors probable to come up in the future. Space provisions for vendors can accordingly be made in TP schemes.

## Relation between Street Width and Street Vendors

Regression analysis for vendors/km length of road and width of road shows a positive relation between the occurrences of the two. It has been observed through field study that in all density ranges the unit number of vendors increases with the increase in road width (Table 5.7).

**Table 5.7**
**Regression Analysis between Vendors/km Length**
**of Road (Nos) and Width of Road (m.)**

| Density of Residential Area | Regression Equation | Value of $R^2$ |
|---|---|---|
| Low gross density ward | $y = 0.59x - 1$ | 0.68 |
| Medium gross density ward | $y = 1.1734x - 7.7173$ | 0.7937 |
| High gross density ward | $y = 0.3379x + 4.6531$ | 0.2742* |

*Source*: Ward-level primary survey, 2004.

* In the region with high gross density, the value of regression co-efficient is low because the region is a part of the old city and major roads are 21 m or less in width. Therefore, distribution of vendors on these roads, though of lesser width, is very high.

This indicates that provision for vendors needs to be made on major roads (on and above 21 m width) due to two reasons: first, the density of vendors is high on major roads, and second, traffic load on these arterial or collector roads is high and therefore conflicts due to the haphazard presence of vendors are high. Table 5.7 also shows that there is a possibility of predicting the number of vendors on a particular road width if gross density is known.

## Number of Vendors and Space Reservation

For Vadodara city, the number of vendors on all roads has been surveyed in the three sample wards (each from different density range). In order to arrive at the total number of vendors for the city, the proportionate distribution of vendors for the sample wards has been applied to the whole city (Table 5.8).

**Table 5.8**
**Proportionate Distribution of Vendors on Major and Minor Roads of the City**

| Density Range | Proportion of Vendors (Major Road: Minor Road) |
|---|---|
| Low density range (<10,000 p/sq km) | 1 : 0.50 |
| Medium density range (10,000–25,000 p/sq km) | 1 : 0.78 |
| High density range (>70,000 p/sq km) | 1 : 0.61 |

*Source:* Ward-level primary survey, 2004.

In order to estimate the number of vendors in the city, the average proportion of vendors on major roads as to those on minor roads could be taken as 1:0.7 (from Table 5.8).

The total number of vendor enterprises on major roads of Vadodara city is 7,365, hence, their proportion on minor roads, taking the above proportion, could be about 5,744. Therefore, the total number for Vadodara city could be estimated approximately at 13,109 vendor enterprises. The number of people employed in a vending enterprise is found to be two to five per enterprise. Taking an average of 3.5 persons per enterprise, the total number of people in Vadodara employed as vendors could be approximately 46,000, which is 3.54 per cent of the city's population. The work participation rate in Vadodara is 30 per cent (Census Data 1991). Accounting this, it could be derived that approximately 1,53,300 persons are dependant on vending as an economic activity for survival, which is 10 per cent of the population of Vadodara city. This derivation stresses the need for incorporating street vendors as a part of city planning.

Considering a minimum space of 1 sq m per vendor enterprise, the total space required for vendors in the city as a thumb rule would be 0.1 sq km, which is only 0.01 per cent of the total land use area of Vadodara (VUDA 1993). Considering higher value, that is, 3.5 sq m per vendor enterprise, the total would be 0.04 per cent of the land use, which is also a very low proportion of the total land use area of the city (108 sq km). Hence it is recommended that space reservations for vendor markets, which are low in proportion as compared to the city's total landuse, should be made mandatory in the Development Plan. This type of space reservation could be compared with that for housing schemes for the economically weaker sections (EWS).

## Urban Planning Guidelines for Vendors

The typology of street vending as an economic activity is informal. Due to this, vendors prefer the place with high circulation of traffic and pedestrians for their business. So, streets have become the favourite place of business for vendors in the absence of any other space allocation. Evicting vendors from their original place and placing them somewhere else would dilute location-specific problems if any, but is risky in terms of absence of business potential at the new location (from the vendors' point of view). The space allocation for vendors should be in tune with the market forces for their sucessful acceptance. This chapter further discusses measures for physical space allocation/s to vendors.

### *Provisions for On-street and Off-street Vending*

Physical space provision can be given to vendors in two forms:

- On-street vending activity—vending incorporated as a part of street section.
- Off-street vending activity—vending incorporated in a plot/land just adjoining the major street.

Here, the street and its width is regarded as a base since it is an independent variable of physical planning and is planned as a part of the Town Planning Scheme or Development Plan. It is recommended that selected roads of width 24 m and above could be declared as 'Category SV' (Category Street Vending), that is, those roads adjoining whom street vending activity can be allowed either on-street or off-street. The following are the pre-conditions to be checked before declaration of any road as Category SV:

- The road should be of strategic importance, that is, major connecting road of the city.
- There should be at least two vendor concentrations of size 45–50 on the road.
- There should be evidence of disturbance in traffic flow due to vending acitivity.
- The road should be a 'Sub-Arterial road' or 'Collector Street'.

The 'On-Street Vending Provisions' for existing roads could be done by modification of street sections and could be applied for new roads to be planned as a part of the town-planning schemes as well as, if possible, for the already existing roads declared Category SV. The ideal street section given by the Indian Road Congress (IRC) could be modified to suit specific requirements.[13] Usually, space allocation for cycle tracks and pedestrians remains misused, abused or unused in present conditions. So it is suggested that the IRC road sections could be modified as shown in Table 5.9, keeping the building lines and carriageway as per IRC recommendations. It is essential to enable physical separation of vending spaces so that disturbance to traffic is avoided while designing the road section.

The newly designed street section could be similar to that shown in Figure 5.1.

For on-street vending, the space requirement in terms of length of road section could be determined in two ways:

(a) For already developed (existing) road sections: In order to house all the existing vendors for the respective road stretch, the total length could be decided based on their current area requirements.[14] In case of space constraints in already developed roads, the number of vendors to be permitted could be fixed before hand based on space availability, and prioritisation for vendors could be adopted.

(b) For newly developing roads: This situation would arise while preparing the TP Scheme. The number of vendors could be deduced from expected land use on or around the proposed roads in the TP Scheme (refer to Table 5.4). Considering average space requirements of each vendor typology (see Appendix 1), respective space provisions could be made for on-street vending.

For 'off-street vending activity' provisions, the major typology of vending activity on the road and influence zone of the activity should be considered. 'Local area level markets' could be provided considering the

**Table 5.9**
**Street Designs for Different Street-Widths to Incorporate On-Street Vending Activity**

| Road Width (in Metres) | Vending on Both/ Single Road Side | Vending Platform (Metres) | Vendor Extension* (Metres) | Pedestrian Path(Metres) | Street-side Parking (Metres) | Carriage Way (Metres) | Median(Metres) |
|---|---|---|---|---|---|---|---|
| 24 | Single | 3 | 3 | 3 | 2.5 | 3.5 (4) ** | 1.5 |
| 36 | Both | 3 (2)*** | 3 (2) | 2 (2) | 2.5 (2) | 3.5 (4) | 1.5 |
| 36 | Single | 3 | 3 | 3 | 2.5 | 3.5 (6) | 1.5 |
| 40 | Both | 3 (2) | 3 (2) | 1.5 (2) | 2.5 (2) | 3.5 (2) | 1.0 |
| | | | | | | 3.0 (4) | |
| 40 | Single | 3 | 3 | 3 | 2.5 (parking) | 3.5 (6) | 1.5 |
| | | | | | 0.5 (separator) | 1.0 (2) (for 2W) | |
| | | | | | 3.5 (service road) | | |

* This portion caters to circulation adjoining the vendor establishment. It has been separated so that it does not hinder the pedestrian movement of non-users of vending activity.

** 3.5 (4)–traffic lane of 3.5 m and four numbers of such lanes, two on each side of road.

*** 3 (2)–width of 3 m multiplied by 2, because it is on both sides of the road.

*Source:* Compiled by author.

**Figure 5.1**

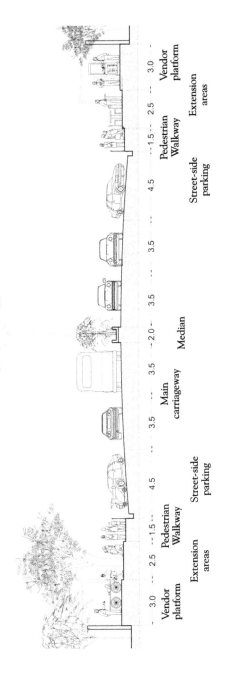

*Source:* Author.

radius of influence zone as shown in Table 5.10. Considering the zone of influence, the distribution of vending activity could be decided.

**Table 5.10**
**Influence Zone for Different Types of Vending Activities**

| Type of Vending Activity | Influence Zone of Respective Activity |
|---|---|
| Processed food | 0.5–2.5 km |
| Non-processed food | 1.0–1.5 km |
| Household articles | 1.5–2.0 km |
| Clothes | More than 2.5 km |
| Flowers | 1.0–1.5 km |
| Service providers | 0.5–2.5 km |

Source: Primary Survey, March 2004.

For off-street vending, cluster size could be determined in two ways:

(a) For already developed (existing) road sections: Wardwise zone of influence circles could be drawn from the nodal points for the respective vending activity which would already be existing. The total number of existing vendors multiplied by average space requirements would give the total area required for the 'local area level vendor market'. Respectively, the location of plots and their allocation could be decided.

(b) For newly developing roads: This situation would arise while preparing the TP Scheme. According to zone of influence, circles could be drawn for areas under the TP Scheme. Preferably, a centralised location could be alloted to the local area level vendor market which could house the total number of vendors (predicted as per earlier section titled 'Relation between Gross Density, Income, Land Use, and Street Vendors').

The recommended space provisions for off-street vending on eight roads under the SV Category in Vadodara city are as shown in Table 5.11.

While allocating plots for off-street vending or local level vendor markets, it would be essential to recognise the 'complimentarity' of vending typologies. The term complimentarity means that there is a certain interdependency within vending typologies and between other land uses and the vending typology. For example, usually, eateries' vendors agglomerate outside a public park or other public land use; vegetable markets are located near transport nodes; jewellery and fancy items are sold near

**Table 5.11**
**Space Provisions for Roads under Category SV (Street Vending)**

| Name of Road | Road Width (in m) | Provisions to be Made |
|---|---|---|
| Ring Road | 40 | 15 clusters each of size 65 at every 1.5 km of road length |
| Inner Ring Road | 36 | 4 clusters each of size 55 vendors at every 2.0 km of road length |
| State highway | 36 | 6 clusters each of size 100 vendors at every 1.5 km of road length |
| Old NH | 36 | 9 clusters each of size 50 vendors at every 2.0 km of road length |
| Ajwa Road to R C Dutt via Mandvi | 36, 21 | 8 clusters each of size 100 vendors at every 1.5 km of road length. |
| Genda Circle to Gorwa | 30 | 4 clusters each of size 100 vendors at every 1.0 km of road length |
| Bird Circle to Gotri | 24 | 5 clusters each of size 100 vendors at every 1.0 km of road length |
| Waghodia Road | 36 | 2 clusters each of size 100 vendors at every 1.0 km of road length |

*Source*: Compiled by author.

cloth wholesale markets; goods related to worship are sold near temples, etc. If the off-street or on-street vending provisions are made in tune with the complimentarity mentioned here, the probability of successful implementation of the same would increase.

Out of all types of street vending activities, eateries and sale of fruits and vegetables should not be allowed 'on-street' since the wet solid waste generated by these activities is high and the stay of customers for these varies from 30 minutes to 75 minutes. For such activities, local level vendor markets should be established as mentioned in 'off-street provisions'.

## Development of 'Urban Squares'

In the present conditions, there are no special regulations for buildings adjoining the junctions of roads. In order to allocate space for 'urban squares', the possible option could be to include the area of private property around a junction as a part of the junction design. This provision could be made at junctions of major road to major road only, and not all junctions of the city. Some space in these properties could be declared as reserved for vending, and the space lost by the boundary plots (and their owners) could be added to the allowed Floor Space Index (FSI) (in order to give incentive to the property owner). The reserved land could be officially sold to vendors for setting up stalls or could be given on rent. For commercial property on junctions, in both cases the income would be to the building/complex authorities. There could also be an option whereby the space could be transferred to the Municipal Corporation's authority. It is usual that commercial shops are on the ground floor of complexes and so, in order to avoid obstruction to the shops, the vendor stalls in these spaces could be limited to 5 feet in height from ground level. Options of this nature would result in a win-win situation for the vendors and property owners as well as users.

## *Vending as Part of Private Commercial Property*

Looking at a level smaller than city roads and junctions, provisions could be made at plot level through modification in the Development Control Regulations (DCRs).[15] This option would cater to plots for commercial uses (for each commercial building). Commercial complexes have space reservations for parking and so similar space reservation could be allocated for vendor stalls also. These stalls could be of the form between a *larri* or cabin and a formal shop. The ownership of the stalls could be with the Municipal Corporation. The other details for such stalls could be as follows:

- Restriction of height of 5 feet.
- Maximum area of stall 30 sq ft.
- Ownership options:
  - Stall could be sold through auction, or
  - Could be leased by the corporation, or
  - Cooperative society of complex could accept ownership of stall.
- Rules could be framed for running stalls.
- Special licenses could be obtained for ownership/operation in this kind of stalls.
- In case of manipulation, license of vendor could be confiscated.

Not applying the mentioned options to all commercial properties of the city, it could be made applicable to plots in the Central Business District or where on-street vending is not permissible. It would also be very beneficial in areas where land is of prime value and increase in road width might not be possible. For streets where flow of traffic would be so high that it would not be possible to allocate vending, this recommendation could be used. The authorities could auction such stalls or give them on lease on an yearly basis. The areas where this option/regulation needs to be followed could be specified in the DCRs. The areas/streets to be covered under this regulation could be decided after due consultation with builders and vendors.

## Process of Integrating Street Vending in Area Plans

The TP scheme is the tool of area planning constituted through the GTPUD Act (Government of Gujarat, 2000). In the preparation of a TP scheme, a rough idea of the expected land use in the region for which the scheme is being prepared can act as the basis for predictions of the number of vendors (as discussed in the sub-section titled 'Relation between Gross Density, Income, Land Use, and Street Vendors' in this chapter). The space provisions for vendors can be accordingly made in TP schemes.

The process consists of the steps mentioned in Table 5.12.

**Table 5.12**
**Process of Integrating Street Vending in Area Plans**

| | *Steps for Area Planning of Vending Activity* |
|---|---|
| Step I | Predict the land use most probable to come up in the respective area of TPS (T. P. Scheme). In case the TPS is to be prepared for an entirely undeveloped area, the trend of development in land use should be taken into account (predicted/ proposed land uses are mentioned in the Development Plan document of the city). |
| Step II | Identify the main street/s or area/s where vendor locations might arise. For this the 'influence zone' of vending activity should be considered (as described in the sub-section titled 'Provisions for On-street and Off-street Vending'). |
| Step III | The approximate number of vendors can be obtained by the no. of vendors/ km length of major roads (as described in the sub-section titled 'Relation between Gross Density, Income, Land Use, and Street Vendors'). |
| Step IV | Next is the judgement of typology of vending activity likely to come up. Though the most probable typology of vendors in the area could be obtained through field study, it is difficult to judge the mix of vending activity exactly. A rough idea could be obtained by viewing the comparison of typology of vending activity for each land use. It is advised that the prevalent vending trends in areas with similar characteristics be reviewed. |
| Step V | Each typology has specific space requirements (see Appendix Table 1). Therefore, the total land required for off-street local level vendor market or on-street vendor cluster could be obtained. |
| Step VI | Potential land abutting the major road where 'local vendor market' can be allotted should be located; it is essential that the plot is abutting the major road; otherwise it is not likely to work successfully as a vendor market. In any case the location should be decided in due consultation with vendors so that the business potential is not over-ruled. For on-street vending cluster design, street extension could be carried out through due consultation with vendor associations and urban planning authorities. |
| Step VII | Point should be made that the plot marked as 'local vendor market' should not be overridden by any other land use. |

*Source*: Compiled by author.

The change in vending activities follows a particular pattern. The characteristic feature of vending activities is that they are specific to timings of day, specific to festivals and specific to seasons. Illustrating the same, during the field study it was observed that in all residential areas, service providers work from 9 a.m. to 6 p.m. and vegetable vendors (non-processed food providers) work from 4 p.m. till 9 p.m. After 7 p.m., eateries (processed food providers) get good business till 11 p.m. This is an indication that all three types of vending activities could be allocated space to be operated in the same place/plot of land. The timings allotted to each activity could be: service providers—9 a.m. to 4 p.m.; non-processed food vendors (vegetable vendors)—4:30 p.m. to 7 p.m.; processed food vendors (mainly eateries)—7:30 p.m. to 11 p.m., all at one particular location only. This approach could minimise land requirements and still accommodate street vending.

## Regulation and Monitoring Mechanism for Vending Activity

Street vending, when formalised, would result in an increase in number and participation in the activity initially. When the transition period is over this phenomenon will cease. Management of the activity during this phase and in the long run is more important than the physical accommodation of the activity. A subtle control over the activity is also required from the administrators' point of view. Hence, a participatory approach involving all stakeholders could be adopted for management of street vending.

### *Stakeholders*

In the process of integrating street vendors the main stakeholders in the process of integrating vendors would be from three sectors—the public, private and social sector (Table 5.13).

In order to judge and formulate strategies, analysis ranking of influence, interest and capacity is done in order to conclude role players in the management process (Table 5.14). The conclusions of this analysis are:

1. Involvement of NGOs as an intermediary would be essential in the process.
2. Capacity-building process would be required for vendor association, which could be carried out by the NGO.
3. The municipal commissioner could be the final decision authority.
4. Interest and capacity of the NGO and the town-planning department will need to be high and would have to be subsequently tapped.

**Table 5.13**
**Stakeholders in the Process of Integrating Street Vending in City Planning**

| Sector | Description of Institution/Body | Officer/In-Charge of Institution/Body | Interest of Stakeholder |
|---|---|---|---|
| Public | Member of the urban governing body, in case of Vadodara, the VMC | Municipal commissioner | Integrating vendors in city planning being an issue of urban governance, the interest would be to organise the activity with relevant and successful administration strategies |
| | The traffic department | Traffic commissioner | The activity, if permitted at all, should not conflict with the basic function of streets—traffic circulation |
| | Planning authority of the city, VMC | Town planning officer | Maintenance and efficient use of land allotted; efficient system to monitor and regulate the activity |
| Private | Corporate sectors | ED, corporate body | To invest money for betterment as a part of social expenses, if possible with some kind of beneficial return |
| Social/Community | Eminent citizens | Individuals/ professionals | The chaos due to unregulated vending activity on streets could get solved |
| | Non-governmental organisation/s | Director, NGO | Fulfilment of objective of community organisation and achievement of a social cause |
| | Vendor association | President | Attainment of right to carry out business with security and without exploitation |

*Source*: UN Habitat; Information: Discussions with respective person/s.

**Table 5.14**
**Stakeholder Status**

| Stakeholder | Influence | Interest | Capacity |
|---|---|---|---|
| Municipal commissioner | 3 | 2 | 1 |
| Traffic commissioner | 2 | 1 | 1 |
| Town planning officer | 2 | 3 | 3 |
| Corporate body | 1 | 3 | 1 |
| Eminent citizens | 2 | 2 | 1 |
| NGO | 2 | 3 | 3 |
| Vendor association | 3 | 3 | 1 |

3 = High; 2 = Medium; 1 = Low
*Source*: UN Habitat; Information: Discussions with respective personnel.

Though the formal responsibility of integrating vendors lies with the Municipal Corporation (in the case of Vadodara, or the respective authority for other cities), it is observed that in the present context the Municipal Corporation lacks enough resources to plan and implement the process of integration of this activity. Hence, the intervention of NGOs as an intermediary between the governing authority and the grassroot stakeholders is recommended. The responsibility could be assigned to NGOs having experience of working for diverse issues in urban areas.

## Administrative Committees

In the present context, land management is the responsibility of the Municipal Corporation and street management is that of the traffic department. As a result it is found that vendors have to pay extortion charges to both authorities under different sections of law.[16] Hence, for the new framework the current administrative structure could be carried forward with some modifications. As an important modification, it is recommended that the role of the traffic department in regulation of street vending activity be deleted. The lowest level of administrative committee could be the vendors' cluster. Three per cent members of each cluster could be the cluster leaders. They could be directly answerable to the ward officer and sanitary inspector, which would be the lowest in the hierarchy of corporation staff. The ward officer could be responsible for the registration and licensing of vendors in consultation with NGOs and collection of charges from vendors. The sanitary inspector could be responsible for solid waste management in the street/market cluster of vendors. The NGOs could facilitate the process by monitoring the functioning of the ward officer, sanitary inspector and by resolving conflicts between vendors. It could also assist the commissioner in overall management of vendors in the city. The hierarchy suggested is shown in Table 5.15 and duties of the administrative committee are elaborated in Table 5.16.

**Table 5.15**
**Hierarchy of Suggested Administrative Committee**

| Name of Stakeholder | Description | Position in Hierarchy |
|---|---|---|
| Municipal commissioner | The administrative head of the Municipal Corporation | Level 5 |
| President, vendor association | To be elected by the association of vendors | Level 4 |
| Ward-wise NGO representatives (2 nos) | To be elected/appointed by the NGO in due consultation with the administrative authorities | Level 3 |
| Ward officer | Administrative officials from the existing Municipal Corporation structure | Level 2 |
| Ward sanitary inspector | | |
| Cluster leader/s | One leader for each cluster | Level 1 |
| Vendor cluster | Group of vendors | Grassroot level |

*Source:* Compiled by author.

## Execution Through Public–Private Participation

Lack of financial provisions for the execution of urban plans is the most common problem faced by the urban local bodies (ULBs). In such a scenario, private operators like corporate bodies can be invited for partnership in the detailing and execution of citywide 'local vendor markets'. The role of these private operators could be:

- To carry out financial analysis for execution and setting up of the infrastructure at vendor markets.
- To provide financial aid to the municipal corporation for the same.
- To execute construction of vendor markets as per details of street design.

They could receive return benefits in the form of:

- Advertisement rights at 'local vendor markets'.
- Collection of parking charges.
- A portion of the monthly amount paid by the vendors as rent for using the allotted locations.

**Table 5.16**
**Duties of Members of the Administrative Committee**

| *Candidate* | *Post* | *Duties* |
|---|---|---|
| Municipal commissioner | Committee head | Overall management and control of vending activity and supreme decision-making authority. |
| President, vendor association | Team leader | Negotiation between vendors and authorities;Regular consultation with NGOs;Aid in resolution of internal conflicts. |
| NGO representative | Associate leader | Negotiation between vendors and authorities;Aid in resolution of internal conflicts;Assistance in land allocation and locations of vendor markets. |
| Ward sanitary inspector | Head (SWM) | Responsibility of solid waste management (SWM) from allotted vendor location/s |
| Ward officer | Head (collection) | Collection of charges from vendors. Maintaining official records of registration and number of vendors; Granting of licenses to vendors. |
| Vendor cluster leaders (3–5 nos per ward, or 1 per cluster) | Representatives | Co-ordination among member vendors;Maintenance of law and order in 'local vendor market' or the allotted location;Aid in capacity building and training of vendors;Keep track-record for vendor members. |

*Source:* Compiled by author.

A formal Built Operate Transfer (BOT) project could be prepared for the process. The Terms of Reference (ToR) for both the parties could be written down. Recovery of charges/fees/rent on the part of private operators could be mentioned in the MoU. After the specified term, the operator could hand over the ownership again to the municipal corporation. The operator's contract could be renewed for the operation of asset. Such partnerships are found to be working very successfully in organising street vending at the Mansi complex, Ambavadi, Ahmedabad.[17]

## Collection of Charges

In the present context, the extortion amount paid by vendors on an average varies from Rs 25 to Rs 100 per day (for the city of Vadodara), depending upon the area of vending.[18] This amount is collected by the traffic police officials of the respective locations through a middleman, one of the vendors nominated by the group. It is suggested that the charge collection system be formalised in the same hierarchy. The cluster leaders could collect charges on behalf of the Municipal Corporation, which the authority could utilise for maintenance of the space/street provided. The vendors who already pay high extortion charges would not have any objections to paying them legally to the corporation in exchange for security of business.[19] The Corporation (or Private Sector) executing the construction of the local level vendor market/street could provide facilities like electricity, drinking water and toilets to the vendors, in return for the paid amount. The maintenance of the infrastructure could be the responsibility of the vendor group.

The advantage of the charge collection system would be that it would induce 'self-regulation'. Those who pay for their business would themselves not allow 'free-raiders' to be opportunists.[20] Hence, regulating the number of vendors will not depend only on the whims of the traffic police. However, in case of disputes/problems related to regulation, the administrative committee could be given power to take appropriate decisions.

### Legislation to Support Integration of Street Vendors

The Ministry of Urban Development and Poverty Alleviation formulated the 'Draft National Policy on Street Vendors' (DNP) in May 2002 (Ministry of Urban Development and Poverty Alleviation, 2002). Prior to the DNP, under the Bombay Provincial Municipal Corporation Act, 1882, 1949 (BPMC Act), the Bombay Police Act, 1951 and under the Indian Penal Code street vendors could be evicted on the pretext of creating disturbance or hindrance on streets. But the Supreme Court in the case of Sodhan Singh versus NDMC, 1989 gave a significant judgement that 'if properly regulated, street vending could not be denied on streets'. With this argument and on the basis of the Fundamental Rights given in the Constitution of India, there have been several movements in favour of street vendors which have led to the formation of policy at the national level.

The DNP regards street vendors as citizens with the right to an adequate means of livelihood, deserving a supportive environment for earning their livelihoods. The main objective of the policy is to 'provide and promote a supportive environment for earning livelihoods to the street vendors, as well as ensure absence of congestion and maintenance of hygiene in public spaces and streets'. Elements of the DNP are:

- Planning norms—spatial planning, natural markets, norms on the amount of space to be provided for vendors' markets in towns and cities and facilities which should be provided by civic authorities.

- Regulatory processes—involving registration of street vendors and 'non-discriminatory regulation of access to public spaces in accordance with planning standards', revenue and how it should be collected and establishment of democratically constituted committees for implementation of agreed regulatory measures.
- Monitoring mechanisms for street vending activity—to monitor and amend the activity through the ward committee, the city-level committee and state-level nodal officers.

## Summary

There is a strong association between streets and street vendors. Street vendors are a part and parcel of the Indian lifestyle. Street vending activity is a concern of street management and could be organised in the city through a specific methodology. From research, it is found that street vending has a direct relationship to the density of population, income level of surrounding population, surrounding land use, and street width. Hence, it would be possible to have an approximate idea of the number, typology and magnitude of vendors in the city (as done by the action research by the author in the city of Vadodara).

Based on these, two main options of incorporating vending activity in the city are recommended. First, 'on-street' vending in the form of an extension of the street section and second, 'off-street' vending on plot/s adjoining major streets of the city which could take the form of 'local level vendor markets'. Other options would be to develop 'urban squares' and to make vending a part of private commercial land uses. In either of the options, management of the activity after provision of physical space would become an important feature. Management would include formation of vendor groups for the respective market or cluster, allocation of space to vendors and resolution of internal conflicts.[21] Hence, there could be an intermediary agency (preferably an NGO) between the existing administrative structure and street vendors at the grassroot level. Maintenance of the market, collection of charges and decision power could rest with the governing body, whereas execution of market/cluster design could optionally be done through public-private participation. There is a Draft National Policy on Street Vendors formulated by the Government of India in 2002 to support the process legally. The process of integration of vendors may be summarised as shown in Table 5.17.

This chapter has attempted to depict the urban planning guidelines, the regulation mechanisms required and supporting legislative framework in order integrate street vending into city planning.

**Table 5.17**

**Process of Integration of Vendors**

| | |
|---|---|
| Step I | Allocation of 'local level vendor market' place by corporation |
| Step II | Consultation with vendors' association |
| Step III | Street design/plan for 'local level vendor market' |
| Step IV | Consultation with all stakeholders and surrounding residents |
| Step V | Implementation of plan by private sector/corporation |
| Step VI | Licenses to vendors by corporation against payment of charges(will induce competition among vendors and therefore self-regulation of the activity) |
| Step VII | Deletion of traffic department, municipal corporation responsible,and therefore,Organizing vendors would become transparent, fast and accountability of Ward Authority increases |
| Step VIII | Successful integration of street vending would become a continuous process |

*Source:* Compiled by author.

# Appendix 1

## Table A

**Space Requirements (in sq ft) of Different Types of Vending Activities for Different Land Uses on a Comparative Basis**

| | | Types of Land Use | | | | | | | | |
|---|---|---|---|---|---|---|---|---|---|---|
| | | Residential Areas | | | | | Institutional Areas | | | |
| Parameter | Type of Vending Activity | HIG | MIG | LIG | Commercial Centre | Transport Node | Educational Campus | Medical Campus (Hospital) | Recreational Area (Park) | Industrial Area |
| Average space requirements (in sq.ft.) | Processed food | 24–48 | 24 | 24 | 24–60 | 24–44 | 24–32 | 40–50 | 30–50 | 40–50 |
| | Non-processed food | 18–300 | 30–100 | 24 | 6–10 24 | 18–24.24 | 24 | 24 | 18–24 | 24 |
| | Clothes | 24 | 24 | 24 | 10–18 | 24–150 | 60–80 | – | 50–60 | – |
| | Household articles | 500 | 24 | 24–36 | 10–18 | 18–150 | 24 | 24 | 24 | – |
| | Flowers | 18–200 | 18 | 6–18 | 6–18 | 24 | 18 | 24 | – | 18 |
| | Service providers | 24–88 | 24 | 24 | 24 | 36 | 24 | 24–50 | – | 24-52 |
| Higher proportion of vending activity | Processed food | * | * | * | 24 | * | * | * | * | * |
| | Non-processed food | * | * | * | | * | * | * | * | * |
| | Clothes | | | | * | * | | | | |
| | Household articles | | | | * | | | | | |
| | Flowers | | | | | | | | | |
| | Service providers | * | * | * | * | * | * | | | * |
| No. of vendors/km length of major road abutting | | 238 | 178 | 450 | 258 | 555 | 136 | 150 | 178 | 160 |

* Indicates existence of the activity.

## Notes

1. Deduced from survey of street vendors at city level during dissertation study by the author.
2. Classification of vendors has been attempted in the past by Patil, De and Bhattacharya, McGee, the references of whom have been used and modified further by the author to suit the study area.

   Street vendors can be classified based on:

   (a) Commodity sold—as mentioned in the sub-section titled 'Classification of Street Vendors' in this chapter.
   (b) Business asset used—based on the type of business asset used the vendors are classified into five categories:
      - *Larri*—Structure of wood with four wheels attached to it for movement. It is popular among mobile vendors and vegetable selling vendors;
      - *Galla*—Box type structure, can house one/two persons along with articles of sale; also called cabin;
      - Box—It is a box of wood or aluminium which during business timings, acts as a place for sitting and at the end of the day all goods are packed into it;
      - *Pathari*—In this type of asset usually a cloth or jute bags are laid on the ground on which business activity is carried out. Sometimes a slightly raised platform made of bricks or a cot acts as *pathari*;
      - *Tokri*—Also called basket, this type of asset is essentially a basket of cane or iron which is rested on the ground during business hours; it is carried on the head by the vendor if the vendor is a moving vendor.

   The space requirement varies with the type of vending asset used. The space requirements for a mobile *larri* which is popular for multi-purpose use are: Length = 1.8 m, Width = 1.2 m, Height = 0.9 m and Area = 2.16 sq m.

   The area requirements for various assets of vending are as follows:

   | Type of vending asset used | Space required |
   | --- | --- |
   | *Larri* | 2.16 sq m (6' × 4' = 24 sq ft) |
   | *Galla* | 3.24 sq m (6' × 6' = 36 sq ft) |
   | Box | 0.54 sq m (3' × 2' = 6 sq ft) |
   | *Pathari* | 2.25 sq m (5' × 5' = 25 sq ft) |
   | *Tokri* | 0.36 sq m (2' × 2' = 4 sq ft) |

   *Source*: Field study, 2004.

   (c) Duration of vending—Based on duration, vendors are static or semi-static.

   Static vendors—the vendor would continue his business at the given place for the whole day, i.e., morning to evening. The business asset is not withdrawn from the spot of business at the end of business hours. The business asset used is either a *larri* (with stands and extensions), *galla*, box, etc.

Semi-static vendors—the vendor would carry his business for some portion of the day, either morning or evening (maybe a few hours in the morning and few in the evening). The business asset is withdrawn from the spot of business at the end of business hours. In this case the business asset used is usually *larri*, *tokri*, cycle, tempo, cycle-rickshaw, etc.

3. The preliminary results based on the data collected from July 1999 to December 1999 by the National Sample Survey Organisation (NSSO) indicated that the estimated number of workers in the informal sector enterprises in the country was 83.2 million and of those 41.3 million (approximately 41 per cent of the total population working in the informal sector) were in urban areas (CSO 2000). Considering the number as same in 2001, if not increased (due to non-availability of the data for 2001), it can be said that 41 per cent of the population of the country works in informal sectors in urban areas. According to studies by Jhabvala, estimates show that about 15 per cent of the urban informal sector workforce are street vendors (Jhabvala 2000). From the above two results, it can be estimated that approximately 6 per cent of the country's population would constitute street vendors in the year 2001. The NSSO gives the number of street vendors in the country in 1991 as 3.6 million (4.25 per cent of the total population in 1991). This leads to the fact that the number of street vendors in the country has increased by about 1.75 per cent in the last decade.

4. The study was conducted by Bhowmik on behalf of the National Alliance of Street Vendors in India (NASVI) in 2001 in seven cities—Mumbai, Kolkata, Ahmedabad, Patna, Bangalore, Bhubaneshwar, Imphal, and Indore.

5. Results obtained from the action research conducted by the author. Methodology for the action research was at three levels of study: first, city-level survey of street vendors on all roads of the city, second, ward-level survey of street vendors for three selected wards of the city (based on density distribution), and third, area-level studies for street vendors (based on land use characteristics). For more details refer to the sub-section titled 'Relation between Gross Density, Income, Land Use and Street Vendors' in this chapter.

6. The Bombay Police Act, 1951.

7. The Ministry of Urban Development and Poverty Alleviation formulated the 'Draft National Policy on Street Vendors' in May 2002. The main objective of the policy is to 'provide and promote a supportive environment for earning livelihoods to the street vendors, as well as ensure absence of congestion and maintenance of hygiene in public spaces and streets'. Elements of the policy are: planning norms, regulatory processes and monitoring mechanisms for street vending activity.

8. The case is the best practice documented by UN Habitat; see http://www.unchs.org/best practices briefs.

9. At Mansi Apartment, Satellite, Ahmedabad, 150 vegetable vendors have been given a built platform for carrying out their business activity by the Ahmedabad Urban Development Authority in return for collection of charges. At Jivraj

Park crossroads, Vejalpur, Ahmedabad, 400 vegetable vendors have been registered and allowed to carry out business on the street side in exchange for charge payment by the Vejalpur Nagarpalika. The condition placed is that vendors themselves manage segregation of waste and resolution of internal conflicts.

10. Learnings from the case study during the dissertation conducted by the author.

11. Results from action research conducted by the author; for detailed methodology see endnote 12.

12. As mentioned in note 5, this section contains results obtained from the action research conducted by the author during her dissertation. Methodology for the action research was at three levels of study: first, city level survey of street vendors on all roads of the city, second, ward level survey of street vendors for three selected wards of the city (based on density distribution), and third, area level studies for street vendors (based on land use characteristics). For city-level studies, a detailed inventory of vendors on all major roads of the city (greater than or equal to 21 m in width) has been conducted. From city-level studies, results related to distribution of vending activity, its duration and its locational aspects have been deduced. For ward-level studies, the 10 wards of Vadodara have been classified according to Gross Densities into:

- Low Density Ward (<10,000 p/sq km);
- Medium Density Ward (10,000–25,000 p/sq km);
- High Density Ward (>70,000 p/sq km).

One ward from each density range has been studied and the mentioned results are from the three wards of typical densities. From ward-level studies, relations between vending and gross density, income, land use, etc., have been deduced. For area-level studies, nine land uses have been selected and important streets have been studied in detail as representative samples. Results for prediction of scale of vending activity have been deduced from the same.

13. From road sections for urban roads by Indian Road Congress (IRC 1977).

14. See Appendix 1.

15. This sub-section has been written after a study of the existing General Development Control Regulations (GDCRs), published by VUDA (VUDA 2000).

16. The extortion charges are as high as Rs 80–100 per day, as found during action research in the study area.

17. Deduced from case studies at Mansi complex and Vejalpur, Ahmedabad, conducted by the author.

18. Also found as an inference from the action research conducted by the author.

19. As found by the author during action research for dissertation.

20. The case can be compared to principles of Natural Resource Management, where 'everyone's resource is no-man's resource'. As payment of charges is advocated in environmental economics to increase accountability towards management of resources, similarly, payment of rent is advocated by the author to increase accountability of vendors towards resources of the city.
21. Market in the case of off-street vending; cluster in the case of on-street vending.

## References

Anderson, Stanford. 1991. 'People in the Physical Environment: The Urban Ecology of Streets', in Stanford Anderson (ed.), *On Streets*, England: MIT Press.

Bhattacharya, K. P. and Dey Prashant. 1991. 'Problems of Hawkers in Metropolitan Cities: A Case Study of Calcutta'. Occasional Paper No. 20, Habitat Centre: Centre for Human Settlements, Calcutta.

Bhowmik, Sharit. 2001. 'Hawkers and the Urban Informal Sector: A Study of Street Vendors in Seven Cities', (on behalf of) NASVI (National Alliance of Street Vendors), available at streetnet.org.za and www.nasvi.org.

———. 2003. 'National Policy for Street Vendors', *Economic and Political Weekly*, 18(16).

Census of India. 1991. 'Census 1991, Series-7 Gujarat, District Census Handbook', Vadodara District, Ahmedabad: Central Government Publications.

CSO. 2000. 'Informal Sector Statistics: A Report of the Work of the Delhi Group', Ministry of Statistics and Programme Implementation, Committee on Statistics, Economy and Social Concerns for Asia and Pacific, Bangkok.

Desai, Mona. 2003. 'The VUDA Development Plan, A Critical Appraisal' (Unpublished Dissertation), Vidyanagar.

Desai, M. K. 1987. 'Report for Hawking and Non-Hawking Zones for the City of Baroda', Vadodara Municipal Corporation.

———. 2003. 'The VUDA Development Plan, A Critical Appraisal' (Unpublished Dissertation), Vidyanagar.

Ellis, William C. 1991. 'The Spatial Structure of Streets', in Stanford Anderson (ed.), *On Streets*, England: MIT Press.

Factfile. 2000. 'Factfile', *Seminar*, July, 491.

Gallion, Arthur B. and Eisner Simon. 1963. *Urban Pattern*, New York: Van Nostrand Reinhold.

Government of Gujarat. 2000. 'The GTP and UD Act, 1976', Gujarat State: Government Printing, Publications and Stationery.

Green Eminent Consultants. 1999. 'ABC . . . of Vadodara, Our City Guide', Vadodara: Jindal Hotels.

Gurumukhi K. T. n.d. 'Land Pooling Technique: A Tool for Plan Implementation— An Indian Experience', (Chief Planner) Town & Country Planning

Organisation, Government of India, New Delhi, available at www. gisdevelopment.net/application.

Gutman, Robert. 1991. 'The Street Generation', in Stanford Anderson (ed.), *On Streets*, England: MIT Press.

International Alliance of Street Vendors. 1996. 'What is Illegal about Vending in Cities?', Durban.

IRC. 1977. *Space Standards for Urban Roads, IRC:69-1977*, Indian Road Congress, New Delhi: Sagar Printers & Publishers.

Jacobs, Allan. 1995. *Great Streets*, USA: MIT Press.

Jhabvala, Renana. 1999. *Poor Women in Urban Areas*. Ahmedabad: SEWA.

———. 2009. 'Roles and Perceptions', *Seminar*, July, 491.

McGee, T. G. 1971. *The Urbanization Process in the Third World*, London: Bell and Sons.

McGee, T. G. et al. 1977. *Hawkers in South-East Asian Cities: Planning for the Bazaar Economy*, Qltawa: IDRC.

Ministry of Urban Development and Poverty Alleviation. 2002. *Draft National Policy on Street Vendors*, New Delhi: Government of India.

Moser, C. 1984. 'The Informal Sector Reworked: Viability and Vulnerability in Urban Development', *Regional Development Dialogue*, 5(2), Autumn.

NASVI (National Alliance of Street Vendors). 2002. 'Drafting Committee (Definition)', *Footpath ki Aawaz*, Patna: NASVI.

———. 2003. 'The Unorganised Sector Workers Bill 2003', *Footpath ki Aawaz*, Patna: NASVI.

Papola, T. S. 1980. 'Informal Sector: Concept and Policy', *Economic and Political Weekly*, 3 May, 15(18): 817–24.

Patil, Vishram. 1987. 'Hawkers in Ahmedabad: A Study of Spatial and Economic Aspects', unpublished dissertation, School of Planning, CEPT, Ahmedabad.

Proudlove, A. and A. Turner. 1990. 'Street Management', in H. Dimitriou and G. Banjo (eds), *Transport Planning for Third World Cities*, London: Routledge.

Rao, M. K. 1994. 'The Urban Informal Sector and Urban Development', in M. K. Rao (ed.), *Growth of Urban Informal Sector and Economic Development*, Delhi: Kanishka Publication.

Rykwert, Joseph. 1991. 'The Street: The Use of its History' in Stanford Anderson (ed.), *On Streets*, England: MIT Press.

School of Planning. 2002. *City Development Strategy, Vadodara*, Ahmedabad: CEPT, School of Planning.

SEWA. 2003. 'Guidelines for Street Vendors and Hawkers in Gujarat', Unpublished Compilation.

Sharma, R. N. 2000. 'The Poitics of Urban Space', *Seminar*, July, 491.

StreetNet International. 2003. 'StreetNet Influences Government Policies', *StreetNet News* (No. 2), October 2003.

Tiwari, Geetam. 2000. 'Encroachers of Service Providers?', *Seminar*, July, 491.

Tiwari, D. P. n.d. 'Challenges in Urban Planning for Local Bodies in India', available at www.gisdevelopment.net/application.

Vadodara Urban Development Authority. 1993. *Vadodara Urban Development Area-Draft Development Plan-Revised (1993–2011), Part A,* Vadodara: VUDA.

———. 2000. *Varied Revised General Development Control Regulations 2000,* Vadodara: VUDA.

Wang, Stephanie and SEWA. 2000. 'SEWA's Vendor Campaign and Legal Interventions', Ahmedabad, unpublished compilation, SEWA.

www.nasvi.org

www.streetnet.org.za

www.unhabitat.org

www.urbanindia.nic.in

# 6

# Street Vendors in Phnom Penh, Cambodia*

## Kyoko Kusakabe

In Cambodia, the informal sector constitutes 85 per cent of the workforce and accounted for 62 per cent of the GDP in 2003 (EIC 2006). According to the Asian Development Bank (ADB), 95 per cent of all employment is provided by the informal sector (Agnello and Moller 2004). Street vending is a significant component of the informal sector, and has been and still is an important means of livelihood for many of the poor in Phnom Penh, the capital of Cambodia.

Street vending was the main occupation of people coming back from the rural areas to the emptied Phnom Penh in 1979–80, immediately after the People's Republic of Kampuchea regime took over, and has remained as the major source of income for many households throughout the 1980s and 1990s. Street vending is considered to be an occupation that is an extension of women's role in the family and society. As Horn (1994) has said, street vendors 'cultivate customers' like they traditionally cultivated their backyard gardens to feed the family. Even when it is the main income earner, street vending is considered to be a 'light' job—justifying low returns. Because of this image of being 'kampik kampok' ('petty' in Khmer), and because of the cultural construction that retail trade is less prestigious than working in the government even though the income is much more, street vendors do not receive the recognition that they deserve (Huseby-Darvas 2001; Brenner 1998).

A distinctive feature of street vending as compared to other informal sector occupations is that it occupies public space, which is still defined

---

* An earlier version of this chapter has been published as 'On the Borders of Legality: A Review of Studies on Street Vending in Phnom Penh, Cambodia', *Informal Economy, Poverty and Employment*, Cambodia Series, Number 4, International Labour Office, Bangkok, 2006.

as men's space in Cambodia. Women's labour force participation is high in Cambodia, but decision making is dominated by men. Women street vendors occupy public places but their spaces are considered an extension of their household spaces. They bring their children to the market, serving to blur the demarcation between home and workplace. As Brenner (1998) described in the case of Indonesia, if women become too successful in vending, they are seen to be transgressing the place where women belong and are considered to be a sexual threat to men. In order to be accepted by the society, women vendors need to be confined to a space that can be considered an extension of the household—not claiming power and influence in society. Such confinement makes women micro-vendors the most visible in the city, but among the most invisible in policy and decision-making arenas.

This chapter describes the development of street vending in Phnom Penh, Cambodia. It will first review the economic changes in Phnom Penh since the end of the Democratic Kampuchea regime, then describe the operation of street vendors and the challenges that they face. Part of the problems that street vendors face can be attributed to how the state and society perceive women street vendors even though the Micro-Vendors Association has been trying to work with the state to claim their position in the market.

## Economic Changes and Street Vending

During the ultra-Maoist Democratic Kampuchea regime, from 1975 to 1979, the population was sent to the rural areas to be engaged in communal production. Phnom Penh was virtually empty in 1979, when the Democratic Kampuchea regime collapsed with the invasion from Vietnam. When people came back to the city, they survived by barter trade. This was the beginning of retail trade after 1979. Traders gradually started assembling at the place where markets used to be before the regime abolished them. The space was up for grabs, and women and men claimed the place on a first-come-first-serve basis. Since the market was still small, most of the vendors preferred to sell at the fringe of the market place rather than securing a proper place inside the market, and only those who had extra labour to secure a place inside the market could occupy a stall in the market place (Kusakabe 2003).

Retail trade provided a lucrative option for many business persons in Phnom Penh. In the 1980s, retail trade flourished with goods from black markets. Since the late 1980s, small-scale retail trade has become a popular business for wives of government officials, who were increasingly unable to make a living only on government salaries. In the 1980s, selling places were not very difficult to obtain. Up until 1985, people occupied whatever places they preferred. In 1985, the government reorganised the market place and reallocated stalls to people who were already there. At that time, there were still many vacant stalls in the major markets in Phnom Penh.

However, in the 1990s, when Cambodia opened its markets, and invited the United Nations Transitional Authority in Cambodia (UNTAC) to oversee its first general election in 1995, Cambodian economy went through a rapid change. It experienced a very high economic growth (17.8 per cent growth rate in GDP per capita in US dollars in 1995), and also a very high inflation rate (41.1 per cent in 1994). Phnom Penh markets became rapidly crowded. New migrants came to Phnom Penh, not only returning from the border refugee camps but also from impoverished rural areas where they were struck by a series of natural disasters. In 1993–94, only 0.9 per cent of migrants in urban areas were new migrants (having spent less than a year in Phnom Penh), while in 1998, the ratio was 12.6 per cent (NIS 2000). In 2004, 56.2 per cent of Phnom Penh's population were migrants, and for women, the ratio was higher at 58.2 per cent (NIS 2004).[1]

Kusakabe's (2001) study showed that current street vendors came to Phnom Penh much later than traders with shops and stalls. Street vendors came to the city mostly in 1990, while shops and stall owners came in 1980–82. Street vending was one of the first occupational options for migrants. There are several peaks in the years when street vendors started business; 1979 and 1980, immediately after the Khmer Rouge regime fell, was the first peak. Over 40 per cent of the street vendor respondents came to Phnom Penh during this period (Kusakabe et al. 2001). The second peak came in 1993, when UNTAC was deployed in Cambodia for the first general election. These two peaks were marked by high economic growth.

The third peak around 1998 was marked by economic recession, political crises and natural disasters. Cambodia's economy showed negative growth during this period due to the political crisis of 1997, the Asian Economic Crisis, droughts, and flood. This resulted in an influx of migrants into Phnom Penh, and consequently, an increase in the number of street vendors. Pou (2005) pointed out an increase in the number of street vendors in 2001–2. This was the period of economic recovery, and reflecting brisk sales, the number of street vendors increased. In Cambodia, where employment options are limited, street vending increases during both boom and bust periods.

By the early 1990s, markets were crowded and it became difficult to find places in them. Small vendors settled on the roads around the public market places, which led to conflicts between them and the market committee.

Table 6.1 shows the percentage of people working in wholesale and retail trade and repair services. Although there is a high possibility that many of the street vendors are excluded from these official statistics, the above figures show the importance of trade as an employment option for women in the urban areas. However, it is noted that the relative percentage of women working in trade is slightly decreasing. This reflects an increase in women's working options in the manufacturing sector. In 2001, there were only 4.1 per cent women working in manufacturing, while in 2004, this increased to 11.4 per cent (NIS 2001, 2004). In around 1999, for the first time the number of women working as employees out-numbered women as own account workers (mainly engaged in trade activities) in Phnom Penh.

**Table 6.1**
**Proportion Working in Wholesale and Retail Trade**
**in Urban Areas in Cambodia, 1993–2004***

(% of total employed population in Phnom Penh and other urban areas)

| Year | Women | Men |
|---|---|---|
| 1993/94 | 45.9 | 17.4 |
| 1996 | 39.1 | 15.5 |
| 1999 | 29.0 | 8.8 |
| 2001 | 37.0 | 16.6 |
| 2004 | 31.3 | 14.2 |

*Source:* National Institute of Statistics, 2000, *Cambodia: Statistical Yearbook 2000*, Ministry of Planning, Phnom Penh, Cambodia; National Institute of Statistics, 2001, *Labour Force Survey of Cambodia 2001*, available at http://www.nis.gov.kh/SURVEYS/ LFS2001/table_1.htm; National Institute of Statistics, 2004, *Cambodia Inter-censal Population Survey 2004*, NIS, Phnom Penh, Cambodia.
* This also includes those engaged in repair of motor vehicles, motorcycles, personal & household goods.

Even with the increase in women employed in manufacturing, the importance of the trade sector remains high among women migrants in urban areas; 32.7 per cent of economically active women migrants in urban areas were engaged in services and were shop and market sales workers in 2004 (Morris 2007: 81). However, the concentration of people working in the trade sector might have increased in some cities. For example, Analyzing Development Issues (ADI) (2008) reported that in Kampong Cham market, more than half of the vendors started the occupation after 2000 taking advantage of the economic boom. It is also noted that there are more women who are divorced among the tertiary sector employment compared to other sectors in 2004 (see Table 6.2), a fact which has not changed since 2001. This suggests that retail trade, which typically becomes street vending for poor women, still seems to be an important option for their survival.

**Table 6.2**
**Percentage Distribution of Employed Females**
**in Industries by Marital Status, 2004**

| Industry Category | Never Married | Married | Widowed | Divorced | Separated |
|---|---|---|---|---|---|
| Cambodia-total | 27.1 | 60.9 | 7.8 | 3.3 | 0.9 |
| Primary sector | 25.6 | 62.9 | 7.6 | 3.0 | 0.9 |
| Secondary sector | 47.4 | 44.0 | 4.9 | 3.1 | 0.6 |
| Tertiary sector | 25.6 | 59.1 | 9.6 | 4.5 | 1.1 |
| Wholesale and retail trade | 21.4 | 62.9 | 10.3 | 4.1 | 1.3 |
| Repair of motor vehicles, motorcycles and personal and household goods | | | | | |
| Health and social works | 9.9 | 76.6 | 6.6 | 5.9 | 0.9 |
| Other community, social and personal service activities | 40.7 | 43.6 | 9.9 | 4.8 | 1.1 |
| Private households with employed persons | 60.2 | 22.0 | 6.4 | 9.8 | 1.6 |

Source: National Institute of Statistics, 2004, *Cambodia Inter-censal Population Survey 2004*, NIS, Phnom Penh, Cambodia.
Note: For tertiary sector, only selected sub-sectors are presented.

## Profile of Street Vendors in Phnom Penh

There are currently 31 public markets in Phnom Penh. Banwell (2001) reported that there are around 300 poor women working as street vendors in one market. Pou (2005) estimated that the number of vendors is around 5,000. This includes only those who are vending in and around public markets, excluding itinerant sellers or vendors along the street outside market places. The number of street vendors appears to have increased rapidly in recent years. For example, Pou (2005) said that the number of vendors in Daum Kor Market increased by 50 per cent in four years since 2001.

Most street vendors sold items that required little initial capital such as vegetables. Banwell's study (2001) showed that 83.2 per cent of respondents sold vegetables or fruits. In the study by Agnello and Moller (2004), vegetable sellers comprised 43.9 per cent of their respondents, while 17 per cent sold prepared food. Vegetables are the most popular items for selling among poor street vendors, since they require the least capital.

Almost all the street vendors are women. Agnello and Moller (2004) reported that only 3 per cent of the vendors were men. Most of the street vendors were in the working age of 30–50 years (Banwell 2001; Kusakabe et al. 2001). The education level of street vendors is lower than the average for the city. According to the census of 1998, 50.7 per cent of all women in the city have completed primary education or higher. Banwell's (2001) study revealed that only 12.3 per cent of the street vendor respondents completed primary education or higher and 34.8 per cent did not have any schooling. Agnello and Moller (2004) said that 75 per cent of the street vendor respondents had been to school, but only 18 per cent completed primary school. Kusakabe et al. (2001) found that the average years of schooling were 3.34.

A high number of women-headed households are found among street vendors. In 1998, 13.5 per cent of the women in Phnom Penh were widowed/divorced/separated (NIS 1998), and in 2004, 12.9 per cent of the women in urban areas were recorded as having similar status (NIS 2004). Kusakabe's (2001) study showed that compared to vendors who have stalls and shops, street vendors are more likely to be widowed/divorced (17.5 per cent for the former, and 31.5 per cent among the latter). Other studies of street vendors in Phnom Penh found 30–40 per cent of their respondents to be widows/divorcees/separated (Banwell 2001; Agnello and Moller 2004; Kusakabe et al. 2001), and found that the average number of children is three to four.

Street vendors' contribution to their household income is very high, even for those who are living with their husbands. Nearly 90 per cent of the respondents contributed half or more of the household income (Banwell 2001), while 52 per cent of the respondents were the sole income earners in the household. Kusakabe et al. (2001) reported that 26.9 per cent of respondents were the sole income earners. Agnello and Moller (2004) reported that 60 per cent of respondents live with 5–10 family members and have two–four income earners. Kusakabe et al. (2001) reported that on average respondents lived with five people and 2.16 persons contributed to the household income. Although street vending contributes to a significant portion of the total household income, since their income is small, without being supplemented by other income sources, it is very difficult for them to survive. Banwell (2001) reported that 23.7 per cent of the widows and divorcees have other income earners in the household.

Despite making a significant contribution to the household income, how much influence they have over expenditure decisions depends on their age. Banwell (2001) reported that over 70 per cent of the vendors aged 40 and above said that they take decisions themselves, while only 58.5 per cent of those aged below 40 years said that they make the decisions.

Street vending is not a temporary occupation. Agnello and Moller (2004) reported that most respondents have been in this occupation for 7–10 years. They have long working hours, averaging 8–13 hours a day, seven days a week. The long hours of work for street vendors are reflected in the person that they speak with most. Kusakabe et al.'s (2001) research showed that street vendors had spoken with other vendors more than with family members in the last one week before the interviewing period.

The average net income of street vendors is around US$1.5 per day (6,000 Cambodian *riels*). The National Poverty Reduction Strategy of Cambodia, 2003–5 calculated the overall poverty line for Phnom Penh as 2,470 *riels* per day per person and the food poverty line as 1,737 *riels*. If the street vendor is the sole income earner supporting three people in the family, with an average of 6,000 *riels* per day, street vendors will fall below the poverty line (Agnello and Moller 2004). Banwell (2001) also indicated that street vendors live below one US dollar a day, and with most of the street vendors being the major earners in the family, street vendors and their families can be categorised as the poorest of the urban poor.

Most of the street vendors are not originally from Phnom Penh. Kusakabe et al. (2001) showed that only 18.7 per cent of the respondents were born in Phnom Penh. The highest number of respondents (26.9 per cent) were born in Kandal, 9.3 per cent in Takeo, 9.9 per cent in Svay Rieng, and 9.3 per cent in Prey Veng.

Kusakabe et al. (2001) showed that 55.5 per cent of the respondents currently lived near the market, while 4.9 per cent lived in the market, sleeping in market stalls. Around 60 per cent owned houses, while others rented houses. Even those who owned houses owned them in squatter areas, and their ownership is precarious. Banwell (2001) showed that street vendors averaged 23 minutes travel time from home to the market with a median of 15 minutes. Most stayed close to the workplace in order to economise on transportation costs.

Even though many street vendors have resided in Phnom Penh for a long time, most still maintain linkages with their native villages. Kusakabe et al. (2001) showed that only 8.2 per cent of the respondents do not have relatives in the provinces. Nearly 70 per cent of those who have relatives in the province visit them at least once a year, while nearly the same percentage have their relatives from provinces come and visit them in Phnom Penh at least once a year. However, among the 182 respondents, only 15 respondents remitted money regularly to their relatives in provinces. Some of them go back to their province for festivals and other occasions, collecting contributions from fellow vendors to contribute to ceremonies back home. The large sum of money that they could collect through contributions from fellow vendors gives them 'face', an importance, when they go back to their village. However, few street vendors said they want to go back to the provinces even if business collapses in the city. Their relatives in the provinces are not always considered a safety net that can be relied upon in difficult times.

Agnello and Moller (2004) reported that 41 per cent of the respondents chose the occupation because they did not have enough capital to start any other business, and 26 per cent said they did not have other choices. However, the level of confidence that can be seen among street vendors is impressive. The economic independence and the sense of being able to take care of family contribute to this positive feeling. As one street vendor said, 'It is dignified. I can earn money by myself. No one will look down upon you. It is independent. I am my own boss. If I want to stop [selling] I can. I have money to pay for my house rent. I have enough to spend for each day.'

Their ability to provide for their families leads to a high sense of satisfaction among street vendors. Kusakabe (2003) compared the perception of street vendors to other more established entrepreneurs, such as those who have stalls or shops or sell goods requiring higher capital.[2] In this study, 64.6 per cent of the street vendors were satisfied with their business, and 50 per cent considered themselves successful. The main reason for the positive assessment of their business was that they were able to support their family as well as sustain their business.[3] At the same time, for the women the sense of satisfaction and success is not as high as other better-off retail traders because their income is often too small to support the family on its own. They need the support of husbands to maintain the family. So, for the women, finding and retaining husbands is important, and weakens their bargaining power in the household.

## Operation of Street Vegetable Vending

Street vendors sell various kinds of goods, vegetables being the most common due to low initial capital requirement. A striking characteristic of the operation of street vendors in many of the major public markets in the city (such as Chbar Ampeau and Daum Kor Markets) is that most street vendors buy from other vendors in the same market (Banwell 2001). Banwell showed that 73 per cent of the street vendor respondents said that their suppliers were from the same or nearby markets. By buying in bulk or by buying at odd times of the day, they can purchase vegetables at a cheaper price.

The distinction between wholesalers and retailers is quite vague in the city's markets, and many vendors who sell to street vendors also continue retail sales in the same market. Sometimes, street vendors themselves sell wholesale to mobile vendors who hawk vegetables in nearby communities. Agnello and Moller (2004) showed that 95 per cent of their respondents sold only to individual customers, while 2 per cent sold to other street vendors.

Although the advantage of street vendors coming together and buying in bulk is quite obvious, there is very little attempt among them to do so. In Agnello and Moller's (2004) study, 5 per cent of the street vendor respondents (nine out of 196) bought goods in bulk by grouping with others to reduce the cost. Some vendors said that it is difficult to buy vegetables in bulk, since the quality of vegetables is not standard and there will always be quarrels over who got the better quality vegetables.

Figure 6.1 shows the market chain of vegetables. As seen from the figure, the commodity chain for vegetables in Phnom Penh markets is short. In the absence of proper storage facilities for vegetables, they have to be delivered from the farm to the market in a day or two. Agnello and Moller (2004) pointed out that 85 per cent of the respondents bought their goods from wholesalers and 10 per cent from farmers. Only a handful of street vendors grow their own vegetables. Most of the vegetables come from nearby provinces.[4]

Local collectors collect vegetables on-farm and/or buy them at Daum Kor Market, where trucks loaded with vegetables come from nearby provinces. Collectors often have contracts with farmers and farmers are obliged to sell vegetables to them. These local collectors sell the vegetables to wholesalers as well as larger retailers directly.[5] Most of the wholesalers operate in Chbar Ampeau and Daum Kor Markets, where retailers come to buy vegetables in the early hours of the morning. As one vendor puts it, 'This market never sleeps.' The largest retail market is Orrusey Market, while Thmei (Central) Market is the second largest.

Contrary to more established retail traders, street vendors are often unable to buy on credit, thereby limiting the quantity of goods they can trade.[6]

**Figure 6.1**
**Market Chain of Vegetables in Phnom Penh**

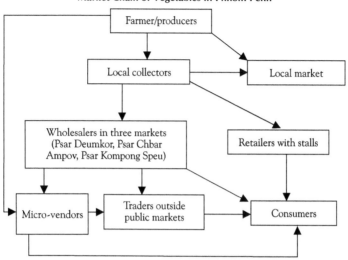

Source: Sovann Pou, 2005, *Fighting Poverty, Fighting the Market: Street Vendors in Cambodia*, unpublished report, Phnom Penh, p. 28.

Since they do not have a stall, there is nothing that they can put up as guarantee. Only those who have long-term relationships with wholesalers can buy on credit, and even then only for a day.[7] Agnello and Moller (2004) found that 26 per cent buy goods on credit, and almost 40 per cent of the street vendors interviewed buy goods partially on credit. That is, by paying half of the price immediately and the other half at the end of the day. Agnello and Moller (2004) said that if street vendors borrow money from money lenders, the interest rate is often 20 per cent per month. Information on credit sources is not easily shared among street vendors. Even though some NGOs provide micro-credit, it is not widely known among street vendors (Kusakabe et al. 2001).

All the studies showed the subsistence level of street vendors' business operations. Kusakabe et al.'s (2001) report noted that the average initial investment capital is 137,504 *riels* (around US$35), while the median is 20,000 *riels* (around US$5).[8] Among the respondents, 12.6 per cent did not have any start up capital. Working capital was on average 165,398 *riels* (around US$42), with a median of 50,000 *riels* (around US$12.8).[9]

Agnello and Moller (2004) noted the main costs incurred by street vendors. They include rent paid to the stall or house owner to sell in front of the building, market security fee and transportation costs. Securing and retaining a place to sell goods is identified as one of the most expensive and significant problems. Twelve per cent of their respondents reported negative profits. According to their survey data, the cost for rental (from umbrella to space) is on average 1,405 *riels* (US$0.35) per day. Some pay 7,000–8,000 *riels* (US$1.75–2) daily for the space, while the umbrella costs a few hundred *riels*. The average daily market fee was 1,133 *riels* (US$0.29), while the median was 1,200 *riels* (US$0.31) (Banwell 2001).[10] On an average, Agnello and Moller's (2004) data showed that street vendors earn 102,698 *riels* (US$25.7) per day, while their expenses stood at 96,773 *riels* (US$24.2), leaving 5,925 *riels* (US$1.48) as profit.

In this very limited business condition, with low capital and relatively high cost of operation, vendors rely on public relations tactics to keep up their sales. One of the strategies is to encourage customer loyalty. How long they are able to keep regular customers is seen as the most important skill for their work.[11] Street vendors also exercise trial and error to look for better business opportunities. Kusakabe et al. (2001) noted that 59.3 per cent of the respondents never changed the items they sold, while 22.3 per cent of them changed more than twice. Agnello and Moller (2004) pointed out that street vendors want to expand or diversify business by selling more or selling different types of goods, but few feel brave enough to do so. According to their study, 72 per cent of the respondents noted that the major obstacle to business expansion is lack of capital, while 21 per cent said that finding a reasonably priced selling place is the major obstacle.

Street vendors' willingness to improve their business can also be seen in their willingness to invest in training to improve their skills. Fifty-five per cent of respondents in Agnello and Moller's (2004) study showed their willingness to receive training and business advice, and among them, 75 per cent were willing to pay a minimal fee for training (2,000 *riels*). Of those who do not wish to be trained, 58 per cent replied that they do not have time to be trained as they are busy with their activity in the market; 11 per cent said that they are unable to attend training because they do not have relatives to replace them while they dedicate themselves to training.

According to Banwell (2001), problems that street vendors face are: bad smell (93.3 per cent), rats and mosquitoes (92 per cent), other pests, flooding (82 per cent), health and hygiene (78.4 per cent), air pollution/dust (76.4 per cent), access to credit (66.3 per cent), personal security (53.9 per cent), sanitation (46.4 per cent), food preservation (38.2 per cent), children and childcare (30.6 per cent), security of goods (25.8 per cent), and access to clean water (18.2 per cent). Agnello and Moller (2004) showed that harassment from market security and police is the most serious complaint made by 51 per cent of the respondents.

Banwell (2001) also noted that there is no water source available in and around the market, and the vendors need to buy water from pushcarts. Dangers of working in the market for an extended period of time also include security of their home. Many street vendors live in squatter areas and other low-income housing areas vulnerable to fire. Cases of kidnapping of children and thefts worry street vendors. Agnello and Moller (2004) noted that street vendors also fear for their personal safety when going to the wholesale markets early in the morning when it is still very dark. They are afraid that goods may be stolen by gangsters or glue sniffers or they would be mugged by motor taxi drivers.

Agnello and Moller (2004) showed that street vendors are also worried that their work might have a negative impact on their family, particularly on their children's health and schooling, as seen in some of their quotes: 'There is no time to take care of children and take care of the home'; 'If I cannot cook on time for my husband he will be angry with me'; 'I am always at the market, but I am always worrying about the security of my family at home. I am afraid of burglars, of people burning down my shelter, killing my husband, my children, and so forth.'

## Street Vendors in Policy Documents

Figure 6.2 shows the structure of a public market. Market committees work with the local district government (*Khan*), but are answerable to the municipal government and ultimately to the Ministry of Interior. Market committees set internal rules and regulations for the market. Rules governing daily taxes are drafted, approved and annually amended by the municipality. The market committee also supervises tax collectors in the market. Tax collection (*pasi*) has been auctioned off from 1998, and each contract lasts for five years.

Banwell (2001) reported that when the Ministry of Finance complained in 1997 that tax collectors in charge of Phnom Penh markets owed the Ministry of Finance more than 700 million *riels* (US$205,000), pressure on street vendors to pay more in daily taxes and fees increased. Because there are other bidders in the auction, the present tax collector tries to fulfil the payment in order to continue the contract. The tax contractor as of 2007 was Phan Y Mech Investment Company, whose five-year contract started from 1 January 2003. This tax is the only legal fee that business operators have to pay.

**Figure 6.2**
**Structure of Public Market in Phnom Penh**

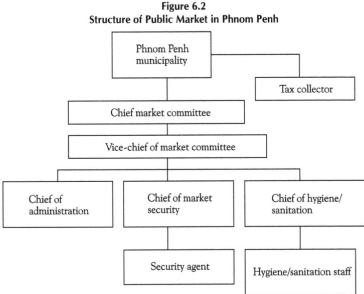

*Source:* Modified from Sovann Pou, 2005, *Fighting Poverty, Fighting the Market: Street Vendors in Cambodia,* unpublished report, Phnom Penh, p. 16.

Articles 8 and 11 of the business operation tax book describe the method and rate of tax collection. Article 14 specifies the punishment for collectors who demand more; first time violators will be fined 20 per cent of the total monthly tax collection, and second time violators will be fined 50 per cent. Article 15 states that vendors can complain to the Sub-district (*Sangkat*) or Tax Management Committee to take action if asked to pay a higher rate of tax. Tax collection itself is relatively transparent. After the formation of Micro Vendors' Associations, street vendors were informed of the tax rates. Tax collection is not a major problem since then, and only 4 per cent of the respondents complained of high taxes (Agnello and Moller 2004). Most vendors complained of 'other fees' collected as security and rentals, and harassment from security and police personnel.

Agnello and Moller (2004) noted that selling space is one of the most expensive and significant problems street vendors face. Included in the expenses are not only the fees for security guards but also the monthly rentals charged by market committees (80,000–90,000 *riels* per month). In the absence of any written regulation that elaborates on the process of deciding such rental rates, market regulation and fee policies are murky and unclear. Street vendors who sell in front of other people's houses pay rent to the house owners—around 2,000–4,000 *riels* per day.

Street vendors also face heavy fee collection by police. Khan police as well as Phnom Penh municipality police collect money from street vendors—around 1,000 *riels* per day, or between 10,000 to 30,000 *riels* per month (Pou 2005). There is no written regulation that allows police to collect fees nor is there a statement on the amount to be collected. The police and Sangkat/Khan chief explained that this is based on the Sub-Decree of Public Order Articles 12 and 13 (Pou 2005).

The Sub-Decree on Public Order signed by the first and second prime ministers on 10 August 1994, states that street vending is illegal. Article 12 states that selling goods and disturbing the public order are prohibited. In case of violation, the violators will be fined 10,000 *riels*. Article 13 states that selling goods by cart along the road is prohibited. In case of violation, the fine is 2,000 *riels*. Even though in the Sub-Decree street vending is defined as illegal, the business operation tax book includes in the types of taxes items such as 'rent one big umbrella', 'sell in one basket', 'mobile baggage cart', which are payments particularly related to street vending. This contradiction in law and regulation creates a space for fuzzy fee collections to occur. Hence, even though street vendors pay taxes and fees, they are still not entitled to their business and space.

Despite all these payments, street vendors' rights to space are not secured, and there is no guarantee that they will retain business places for the long term. This can be gathered from these quotes from Agnello and Moller's (2004) study:

> 'It is better to sell at the same place every day, because then we will have regular customers.'
> 'I paid security guards money [for the place] but when the fish seller comes, they let them sell there [in the place where I was selling].'
> 'Market security people always chase us. As a result, we have no selling space, and don't know where to sell.'

Control over the area around the markets is divided between the market committee and the local government. Street vendors are chased away or their goods confiscated by local authorities to maintain order in the area of their responsibility. When street vendors move to the other side of the road, they are chased away by the market committee responsible for the area around the market (Pou 2005).

The Urban Poverty Reduction Strategy recognised the importance of access to a secure business space. After extensive consultations with organised communities, NGOs and community-based organisations (CBOs), the Municipality of Phnom Penh and UN Habitat jointly developed the strategy in 1999. This strategy, based on lessons from earlier collaborations, aims at:

- Improving access to basic services for the urban poor—by securing affordable land and housing, enabling the delivery of physical infrastructure (water supply, drainage, roads, sanitation, electricity, transport, solid waste collection), social infrastructure (education, health care, family planning) and implementation of disaster management (against fire and floods).
- Enhancing local economic potential (especially for women)—by providing education, vocational and business skills, credit and savings, industrial employment, marketing information, and space for small businesses and marketing.
- Strengthening participatory urban governance mechanisms—by facilitating community organisation and leadership, setting community development management committees, creating land and housing policies for the urban poor, simplifying procedures for government services, eliminating corruption, and securing tenure.

Although the Urban Poverty Reduction Strategy recognised the importance of a secure space for street vendors, better skills, better living and working environment, it fell short of being translated into concrete policies and programmes. It also did not problematise the legal status of street vendors and the extra fees they pay to stay in operation. It did not define street vendors' access to space as their entitlement, and also did not challenge the contradictions in policies and regulations. As a result, there has been no change in the status of street vendors in the legal and developmental framework.

The Poverty Reduction Strategy Paper (PRSP) 2003–5, issued in 2002 by the Council for Social Development, three years after the Urban Poverty Reduction Strategy, reiterated the problems including the lack of attention to the situation of the urban poor. The paper pointed out that the urban poor, which include all the street vendors, are seen more as a hindrance to city development rather than a target for support:

> The urban poor, who are predominantly squatters, or even worse, street dwellers, have been seen as an obstacle to urban development because they often hinder the development of infrastructure by occupying state public land and because their rural appearance and habits are out of step with modern

city life. . . . The usual response from middle class people and from officials is that the urban poor should be sent back to the rural areas where they belong. (Council for Social Development 2002: 85–86)

The PRSP concludes that the urban poor are given much lower priority in assistance since they are considered to be 'responsible for their predicament' (ibid.: 86), whereas the rural poor are seen as a victim of underdevelopment. Recognising this lack of attention to the livelihood of the urban poor, the PRSP includes the following recommendations for adequate economic opportunities/income generation, particularly for women:

- Improve understanding of informal sector and apply measures to regularise it.
- Review policies and practices in city markets and city streets to ensure affordable space for poor vendors; make regulations and charges known to the poor and monitor implementation.

However, the operationalisation of these recommendations is a challenge, and so far no concrete policy and programme has come out of this recommendation. The PRSP again, does not challenge the legal status of street vendors or the contradictions in policies nor does it see street vendors' access to space as an entitlement. Six years after the Urban Poverty Reduction Strategy, there has been little change in the status of street vendors.

A more recent policy paper, the Cambodia rectangular strategy (2004–8) is a guiding principle for development issued by the prime minister. It has four strategic 'growth rectangles': agricultural productivity, diversification, and competitiveness; private sector growth and employment; rehabilitation and construction of physical infrastructure; and capacity building and human resource development. Each strategic 'growth rectangle' has four sides;

Growth rectangle 1: (i) improved productivity and diversification, (ii) land reform & mines clearance, (iii) fisheries reform, and (iv) forestry reform.
Growth rectangle 2: (i) strengthened private sector and investments, (ii) promotion of small- and medium-sized enterprises (SMEs), (iii) creation of jobs and improved working conditions and (iv) establishment of social safety nets for workers.
Growth rectangle 3: (i) transport infrastructure, (ii) water resources management and irrigation, (iii) energy and power grids, and (iv) information and communication technology.

Growth rectangle 4: (i) enhanced quality of education, (ii) improved health services, (iii) greater gender equity, and (iv) a rational population policy.

This policy puts emphasis on rural development as well as the formal sector and manufacturing sector. Although Growth Rectangle 2 includes some focus on employment creation and improved working conditions, the wording shows that the focus is more on the formal manufacturing sector employment.

In 2005, the Phnom Penh Municipality announced the Phnom Penh Development Master Plan. It is a grand urban infrastructure development plan with a US$59 million investment including road and canal development, and demolition, relocation, and land sharing plans for slum areas. It also includes improvement of Kandal, Chas (Old) and Thmei (Central) Markets. All decision-making in the process of improvement will be done by the market committee and the investment company. There is no notion of vendor-participation in this process. Under this plan, Daun Penh district is to be developed as a tourism zone. It should be noted that Daun Penh district has the second largest number of street vendors, second to Prampi Meakkara district (Pou 2005). Daun Penh district hosts Thmei (Central) Market, Chhas (Old) Market, as well as Victory Monument New Garden, which has a high concentration of street vendors. Again, street vendors' participation in the design and decision-making of the tourism zone development is absent.

In short, there is a strong rural bias in strategies for poverty alleviation and provisioning of social support in Cambodia. If any support is discussed for the urban poor or urban development, the focus is on housing. This focus on housing also leads to residential bias in terms of support to the urban population. Almost all support for the urban poor is provided at the place of residence rather than at the place of work. Thus, the PRSP as well as the Urban Poverty Reduction Strategy emphasise community development and not workplace organisation. It should be noted that street vendors spend most of their time in the market. The policy documents demarcate urban spaces into workplace and residence, and fuzzy in-between places that the street vendors occupy are not recognised. As a result, they are often excluded from information that is provided to the community.

Street vendors, along with other informal sector workers, are still seen as temporary workers in policy documents. As was evident in the Rectangular Strategy, the state is hoping that street vendors and other informal sector workers would be absorbed into 'formal' manufacturing sector employment with the expansion of private sector investment and growth in SMEs. Since the state considers it a temporary phenomenon, they continue to perceive street vending as illegal and just acknowledge the necessity of the occupation for the time being. Thus, no revision of law is made to strengthen the status of street vendors and no programme is introduced to support the business of street vendors except for initiatives by NGOs.

Pou's (2005) study showed that most government officials and police acknowledge that street vending is a necessary occupation. He interviewed urban planners, *Sangkat* chiefs, district and municipality police officers. They all agree that street vending is a necessary occupation especially for the poor, although according to the Sub-Decree, it is illegal. The police officers also admitted that street vendors provide them an opportunity to collect some fees to complement their low salaries. Middle-ranked officers of the government said that street vending provides convenience for consumers, because they can buy things without going to public markets far from their houses. They cited the Khmer saying, 'Even a millionaire has a muddy frying pan'. That is, everyone needs to do basic activities such as eating, and street vendors contribute by offering consumer-friendly services for these basic activities. Tax collectors were happy to see more vendors, since more vendors translated into higher incomes for them.

Although most policy makers acknowledge the necessity of street vending, they do not plan to actively support the activity. Thus, street vendors remain invisible in policy actions, although they are an integral part of any city market in Phnom Penh. As Bromley (1997: 134) noted in his study in Columbia, the main objective of those who administer law and order on the streets is 'usually "containment"—to hold down the numbers of people working in the streets'— and 'street occupations conflict strongly with the prevailing approaches to urban planning'. City planners are concerned with reserving the streets for motorised transport and short-distance pedestrian movement, and consider street occupations as 'an unfortunate embarrassment'.

## Micro-Vendors' Association—Social Capital of Street Vendors

In the face of a precarious status and lack of entitlements to their employment, street vendors' main source of security is their family. Building trust among street vendors is not easy. Because of physical proximity and the length of time that they spend in the market, they talk a lot to their fellow vendors. However, they do not trust other vendors as seen in

Kusakabe et al.'s (2001: 15) study: 'If I ask them to help me, they will tell me that I am lazy and look down on me. When I am suffering, if others look down on me, the suffering will be much harder. So, I normally tolerate and keep to myself.'

Kusakabe et al.'s (2001) study also showed that 62.1 per cent of the respondents said that they had no one to entrust their business to if they had to attend to something else for a week. Nearly 30 per cent of the respondents said that they had no one to entrust their children to, either. Some 47 per cent recorded that they had never discussed the problems they faced in their workplace or residence with others. This again shows that they do not trust others, and are afraid that others might use the information against them.

Having a precarious status in the public place and at the same time not being able to build up trusting relationships with other street vendors makes street vendors very vulnerable to shock, since they have few people to rely on. The Micro-Vendor's Association has been organised in some of the major public markets with the help of an NGO, the Urban Sector Group, since 1998.[12] The association provides micro-credit, some support for access to health services, childcare services, as well as legal and rights training. They also negotiate with market authorities collectively. It should be noted that significantly more vendors who are association members discuss their problems with others (61 per cent for members and 46.7 per cent for non-members) than others (Kusakabe et al. 2001). One association member remarked that 'Business is not only for selling. It is also for relating with each other (*roap ann kania*)' (ibid.: 23).

Forming an association improved some members' confidence and their sense of being recognised in society: 'We can talk with each other easier. When people are fighting, I stop them. If we talk correctly (*niyui trew*), they will listen. After I joined the association, people come to talk to me about their problems' (ibid.: 28).

There are significant differences in perception between association members and non-members concerning the following issues:

- People in the market look out mainly for the welfare of their own families and are not much concerned with the improvement of the market.
- If I do a good thing to my fellow vendors, they will also be nice to me.
- People are always interested only in their own welfare.
- I think my life will be better in the future.

- I will be able to improve my life in the future. (Kusakabe et al. 2001)

Association members displayed a higher sense of reciprocity, co-operation and mutual help and hope for the future. The same study noted that association members also showed higher trust in the possibility to make changes, look up to the state for law and order, and display a higher tendency to inform and demand from the state. Significantly more association members notify problems to the police, the court or other authorities (33.8 per cent for members, 3.8 per cent for non-members) when wares are confiscated or stolen from them or others. This reflects the association members' trust in the system and their engagement and confidence in improving theirs and fellow vendors' livelihoods.

The sense of being supported by fellow vendors and others leads to a positive perspective of the society. They believe that things can be made better, and trust other people in the market as well as in the neighbourhood. The study concludes that welfare support to street vendors has a long-lasting positive effect by creating a sense of trust in the system and society.

The same study also warns that creating an association and building up trust itself does not allow women to challenge existing gender ideologies that subordinate women. Even though gender ideologies contribute to women's concentration in this precarious occupation and their vulnerability to harassment, the study showed that association members actually had more 'traditional' gender views, conforming to the existing gendered expectation. It is important that the vendor's association become a place where women can discuss their problems in the family and workplace, and lead to higher realisation of their subordinated position in society.

## Concluding Discussion

Street vending is an important livelihood option for the urban poor, even when other employment options are increasing. Most street vendors are major breadwinners in poor households. Due to lack of facilities, vegetables have a very short commodity chain, and street vendors squeeze out a meagre profit from re-selling products in the same market.

The importance of street vending as an option for the poor is well-recognised among policy makers. However, it is still defined as illegal, and development policies/programmes have little focus on supporting street vendors. Their entitlement to their means of livelihoods, that is, their space to sell, is not guaranteed and left precarious, even when they are contributing to the state coffers through legal taxes. This ambivalent status makes street vendors vulnerable to all sorts of extortions. As discussed in the beginning of this chapter, women street vendors are one of the most invisible in policies and planning, and among the physically visible informal workers in Phnom Penh. This is because their workplace is not considered a workplace from a policy perspective. They are not supposed to be occupying the space that they are occupying, but it has been so far tolerated because it is seen as an extension of women's household activities—to feed and maintain the children and family. The difference in geographical scale that they occupy makes them invisible in policy and city planning discussions.

As Gough et al. (2006: 29) noted, poverty policy is about managing the relations within 'poor areas' and between these and the 'prosperous areas'. Policies on poverty are not contained within a particular scale, but they 'typically relate and contrast the different scales'. It is the case, as Bromley (1997) says, that urban planners' obsession in reserving the streets for transportation purposes causes much difficulty for micro-vendors; street vending policies are not merely about allowing the poor to sell in a small corner of the market. They should also examine how these spaces are integrated in relation to other urban spaces, and how space management is strategically positioned within urban development policies.

To rephrase it, the whole framework needs to be inclusive towards the urban poor and marginalised women and men in cities, and city beautification should not be prioritised at their expense. Perera (1994) demonstrated how accommodating the informal sector both in physical and economic terms contributes to sustainable urban development. Most approaches see urban space as a mono-function unit. It is interesting that Perera included sidewalks and street corners, which street vendors normally occupy, in his definition of urban voids. He included them because 'the same spaces have been identified as having potential to accommodate a secondary function without disrupting the primary function' (Perera 1994: 56). Such a multi-layered concept about the use of space is crucial to accommodate street vendors in urban spaces.

The Micro-vendors' Association is attempting to claim the space that the micro-vendors deserve, but it has also uplifted the confidence and dignity of street vendors. The challenge for the association now is how much they are able to exert their influence in decision-making regarding city planning and the use of space in the city. A multi-layered concept of use of city space can make the micro-vendors visible in city planning by giving them a legitimate claim on the place that they occupy.

# Notes

1. Based on previous residence.
2. Kusakabe (2001, 2003) classified street vendors, hawkers and traders in squatter areas as well as market traders without stalls as one group.
3. Those who felt the most satisfied (91.7 per cent) were shopowner-traders, luxury item traders in market stalls and non-perishable item traders in market stalls who have husbands working in the government. The main objective of this group of women retail traders is to support the meagre salary of their husbands and enable them to maintain the government position. In Cambodia, government officers have higher social status than business operators, thus for them, it was important that their husbands remained government officers. Those who considered themselves the most successful (90.3 per cent) were perishable item (e.g., vegetable, fruits, fish, meat) traders in market stalls. This group of traders are professional traders who take total control of their business as well as take pride in the product that they are selling. In this group of retail traders, nearly half were widows and they had a great sense of independence.
4. According to Pou (2005), provinces supplying vegetables to Phnom Penh markets are: Kandal, Kompong Speu, Takeo, Kampong Cham provinces as well as suburbs of Phnom Penh itself. Some vegetables come from Vietnam (Lam Dong province), and are normally off-loaded at Chbar Ampeau Market.
5. Collectors pay business operation tax to the wholesale market (200–500 *riels* per day).
6. According to Kusakabe (2001), over 90 per cent of perishable goods (fish, meat, vegetable, and fruits) sellers with stalls buy goods on credit, and 88 per cent of non-perishable goods (grocery, stationeries, etc.), sellers with stalls buy goods on credit, while only 67 per cent of the traders without stalls buy on credit. Sellers with stalls said that no capital is needed to start a business. Once one has a stall, middle merchants will fill the space with goods at no cost. Such benefits are not available to street vendors.
7. Retail traders with stalls can buy on credit for longer periods. Luxury item (watch, gold, etc.), traders or non-perishable item (stationery, grocery, etc.), traders with stalls can extend the repayment up to two weeks, and many said they can repay anytime. If they have a stall, perishable item (fish, meat, vegetable, fruit) traders can also buy on credit for an equally long time, even though 17 per cent of the traders need to repay within a day (Kusakabe 2001).
8. This is almost the same as in the provinces. Analyzing Development Issues (2008) noted that in Kampong Cham market, the initial capital of their respondents was around US$38.
9. A few of the street vendors operated with large capital, thus the average has increased. One used clothes seller had a working capital of US$1,500.

10. This includes taxes, fees for security, use of latrines, and other fees/ services.
11. This echoes the 'clientelization' of Geertz (1978).
12. Aside from the Micro-Vendors' Association mentioned here, Goods Transportation and Labour Protected Association in Cambodia (GTL-PAC) also organises workers in the informal economy including street vendors. They support their members in collective actions. For example, they assisted their street vendor members to seek compensation from a market security guard who hit a street vendor (EIC 2006: 44).

# References

Agnello, Francesca and Joanne Moller. 2004. *Vendors Purses: Women Micro Entrepreneurs and Their Business Needs, Phnom Penh, Cambodia*, Phnom Penh: Urban Sector Group, March.

Analyzing Development Issues (ADI) Trainees (Round 18) and Team. 2008. *Market Vendors in the Informal Economy of Kampong Cham Town*, Phnom Penh: Cooperation Committee for Cambodia.

Banwell, Suzanna Stout. 2001. *Vendors' Voices: The Story of Women Micro-vendors in Phnom Penh Markets and an Innovative Program Designed to Enhance Their Lives and Livelihoods*, Phnom Penh: The Asia Foundation, February.

Brenner, Suzanne April. 1998. *The Domestication of Desire: Women, Wealth, and Modernity in Java*, Princeton: Princeton University Press.

Bromley, Ray. 1997. 'Working in the Streets of Cali, Colombia: Survival Strategy, Necessity, or Unavoidable Evil?' in Josef Gugler (ed.), *Cities in the Developing World: Issues, Theory, and Policy*, pp. 124–38, New York: Oxford University Press.

Council for Social Development, Kingdom of Cambodia. 2002. *National Poverty Reduction Strategy 2003–2005*.

Economic Institute of Cambodia (EIC). 2006. *Decent Work in the Informal Economy in Cambodia: A Literature Review*, Informal Economy, Poverty and Employment, Cambodia Series, Number 2, International Labour Office, Bangkok.

Geertz, Clifford. 1978. 'The Bazaar Economy: Information and Search in Peasant Marketing', *American Economic Review*, 68(2): 8–32.

Gough, Jamie, Aram Eisenschitz and Andrew McCulloch. 2006. *Spaces of Social Exclusion*, London: Routledge.

Horn, Nancy. 1994. *Cultivating Customers: Market Women in Harare, Zimbabwe*, London: Lynne Rienner Publishers.

Huseby-Darvas, Eva. 2001. 'Hungarian Village Women in the Marketplace during the Late Socialist Period', in Linda J. Seligmann (ed.), *Women Traders in Cross-cultural Perspective: Mediating Identities, Marketing Wares*, Stanford: Stanford University Press.

Kusakabe, Kyoko. 2001. *Women's Participation in the Market: Women Retail Traders in Phnom Penh, Cambodia*. Gender Studies Monograph 9, Gender and

Development Studies, School of Environment Resources and Development, Asian Institute of Technology, Thailand.

Kusakabe, Kyoko. 2003. 'Market, Class and Gender Relations: A Case of Women Retail Traders in Phnom Penh', *International Feminist Journal of Politics*, 5(1): 28–46.

Kusakabe, Kyoko, Chan Monnyrath, Chea Sopheap, Theng Chan Chham. 2001. *Social Capital of Women Micro-vendors in Phnom Penh (Cambodia) Markets: A Study of Vendors' Association*. UMP-Asia Occasional Paper No. 53, United Nations Urban Management Programme, Thailand.

Morris, Elizabeth. 2007. *Promoting Employment in Cambodia: Analysis and Options*, Bangkok: International Labour Organization, ILO Subregional Office for East Asia.

National Institute of Statistics (NIS). 1998. *Population Census of Cambodia 1998*, available at http://www.nis.gov.kh/CENSUSES/Census1998/educat.htm.

―――. 2000. *Cambodia: Statistical Yearbook 2000*, Phnom Penh: Ministry of Planning.

―――. 2001. *Labour Force Survey of Cambodia 2001*, available at http://www.nis. gov.kh/SURVEYS/LFS2001/table_1.htm.

―――. 2004. *Cambodia Inter-censal Population Survey 2004*, Phnom Penh, Cambodia.

Perera, L. A. S. Ranjith. 1994. 'Urban Void as a Spatial Planning Tool for Accommodating Informal Sector Enterprises in the Urban Built Environment: An Exploratory Study in Colombo, Sri Lanka', Ph.D. Dissertation, Asian Institute of Technology, Bangkok.

Pou, Sovann. 2005. 'Fighting Poverty, Fighting the Market: Street Vendors in Cambodia', Phnom Penh, Unpublished Report.

# 7

# Street Food Vending in Bangkok*

Narumol Nirathron

> The household with the least flexibility, as total income goes down, is the
> household most dependent on wage income, since the ability to obtain
> wage income (or a certain level of wage income) is a function of the offer by
> someone outside the household of that wage employment. A household can
> most readily affect its total income by investing its labour power *in activities it
> can autonomously launch.*
>
> —Smith and Wallerstein 1992: 15

Street food vending is a type of self-employment activity that normally
uses a small space, such as a pavement or alley as a trading area. This
study examines the many aspects of street food vending activities in
Bangkok, particularly their role in poverty alleviation and entrepreneurial
development; in other words, de-marginalisation of the marginals.
Following from a brief interdisciplinary perspective on street food
vending in Bangkok the chapter presents survey findings and qualitative
information followed by policy recommendations.

## Background

In the early period (1782–1851), street food vending in Bangkok took
place both in the canal and on land. Vending on the street became more
popular after the construction of roads starting from the reign of King
Rama IV (1851–68).

---

* This article is excerpted from the International Labour Organisation 2006
publication *Fighting Poverty from the Street: A Survey of Street Food Vendors in
Bangkok* (Bangkok). The publication is also available at http://www.ilo.org/
asia/whatwedo/publications/lang—en/docName—WCMS_BK_PB_128_EN/
index.htm.

The author wishes to thank the International Labour Organisation for granting
the permission to reproduce an excerpted text of the publication.

Chinese vendors dominated street vending in Bangkok. The majority of the Chinese vendors were men while Thai vendors were predominantly women. Thai women were keen to be street vendors because of the *Sakdina* system (Kiat et al. 1982: 8).[1] Thai women had to take care of the family as the husbands had to leave for their duty. Additionally, due to the expansion of rice exports and the high prices of rice in the world market, farmers earned higher incomes than those in other occupations in the city (Porphant 1996: 140). Thai men also preferred to serve in the court as there were higher opportunities for social mobility (Kanchanakhaphan 2002: 13). Statistics from 1952 highlight the significant numbers of Chinese vendors in Bangkok.

**Table 7.1**
**Street Vendors in Bangkok in 1952**

| | Male | | Female | | Total | |
|---|---|---|---|---|---|---|
| *Occupations* | *Thai* | *Chinese* | *Thai* | *Chinese* | *Thai* | *Chinese* |
| Market vendors | 290 | 4,390 | 450 | 400 | 740 | 4,790 |
| Street vendors | 120 | 1,880 | 230 | 170 | 350 | 2,050 |

*Source:* G. William Skinner, 1957, *Chinese Society in Thailand: An Analytical History*, Cornell University Press, New York, pp. 301–2.

Three factors that resulted in swelling the ranks of Thai vendors in Bangkok were:

- Economic mobility of Chinese vendors which was partly the result of their eagerness to upgrade their economic and social status (Skinner 1957: 91–92).
- Thai government's encouragement to Thai people to engage in trade and industry (ibid.: 262).
- Difficulties of Thai farmers due to the depression after World War I. Farmers in suburban areas such as Sukhumvit, Klongtoey and the central plains gave up their lands and migrated to Bangkok for wage work as many factories were built in Klongtoey and Bangsue (Nalinee et al. 1999: 291). Between the years 1947 and 1954, there were approximately 37,800 rural migrants that entered Bangkok annually (Skinner 1957: 305). The total population of Bangkok increased from 750,000 in 1950 to 1.2 million in 1954.

Street vending for the Chinese offered upward mobility and turned them into entrepreneurs. Wage workers engaged in street food vending were able to accumulate capital and expand into a business of larger scale. Some owners of large Thai conglomerations also started out as vendors.

The development strategy of the country induced mass rural–urban migration even before the inception of the First National Economic Plan in 1961 (Ammar and Suthad 1989). This was partly facilitated by the construction of the road that connected the north-eastern provinces and Bangkok. The emergence of many slums in Bangkok, including Klongtoey, was the testimony of such developments (Nalinee et al. 1999; Sompong 1984: 1). Research by Prachum et al. (1980) found that half of the street vendors in Bangkok were rural migrants. Subsequent research by Kusuma (1983) showed that street food vending was one of the most popular occupational choices among women migrants.

Most of the succeeding research on street vending tended to regard it as a 'survival strategy' rather than an activity that can be 'expanded' (Chomlada 1991; Napas 1994; Narumol 1996; Vichanya 1998; Ajchariya 2001). Prachum et al.'s (1980) work confirmed that street food vending offers cheap goods to the workers, enabling them to subsist in low wage conditions. However, some studies argue that consumption of street food was not limited to people in the low-income households (Van Esterik 1992; Vichanya 1998).

Trade liberalisation and globalisation since the 1980s created fluctuation in employment as a result of high competition at the global level. Self-employment became a viable option for income generation (Redclift and Mingione 1985: 1–11). The economic crisis which started in Thailand in 1997 resulted in mass lay-offs. Many laid-off workers took up street vending (Homenet 2002: 38). Statistics in 2000 indicated that there were 380,000 street vendors in 2000 as compared to 250,000 in 1997 (National Statistical Office, various years).

The demographic characteristics of street vendors in 1980 were as follows: (1) the proportion of Bangkok vendors and migrant vendors was close; (2) the percentage of women vendors was much higher than their male counterparts; (3) most vendors did not have higher than primary education or had no education at all; (4) most vendors were 16–40 years of age; and (5) most vendors were married. Subsequent research on street vendors revealed similar demographic and social characteristics and thus confirmed the marginality of street vendors.

Cultural dimensions play a crucial role in the persistence of street food vending in Bangkok. Food culture particularly explains both the demand for and supply of street foods in Bangkok. In the early period in Bangkok, foods sold by vendors were mostly fresh foods and semi-processed foods which needed to be cooked as eating out or buying cooked foods was not popular. The buying of cooked foods was limited to vendors who had to leave home early to catch the sale in the floating market (Sombat 2001: 59). Cooking was transformed from a household activity into an activity under division of labour, and a market-oriented activity as the country entered the capitalistic economy (Pawewan 1993: 6). The persistence of street foods in Asia is the result of urbanisation in Asian countries (McGee and Yeung 1977; Drakakis-Smith 1990).

Changes in food strategies of the people of Bangkok created what Yasmeen (1996) called 'public eating'. Yasmeen traced 'public eating' back to the time when cooked foods were catered for Chinese migrants in the early period. In modern Thailand factors such as migration from rural areas to Bangkok, the small places of residence, the skills, time and other resources needed for the preparation of foods, and the changing role of women, contribute to the culture of 'public eating' in Bangkok. In modern times, many different varieties of foods are sold on the streets.

The varieties of foods reflect earning opportunities. Foods which have been around for a hundred years such as noodles, pork rind, dumpling, deep-fried dough stick are still available, whereas some have disappeared and new ones such as 'Siriwat sandwich' have come onto the scene. In a guide to street foods in some areas in Bangkok including Klongtoey, the authors recommended 113 kinds of foods (Yee and Gordon 1993: 12–28). Besides the diversity in types of food, different cooking methods can also provide variations. For instance, two vendors selling grilled pork spareribs, of which one vendor uses soy sauce to marinate spareribs and the other vendor uses garlic and chilli, were found in Tha Prachan area (Pawewan 1993: 74). Three vendors selling the Chinese flour snack in Nang Lerng market offer the same kind of snack but the tastes are different and the consumers can choose to buy either (Nalinee et al. 1999: 22–23).

Consumption of street foods in Bangkok is almost a culture in itself. This is not only manifested in 'public eating', but also in the variety of foods that can be consumed during the day and in the rituals and religious activities that call for a diversity of foods. The abundance of raw materials encourages creativity in food production (Suthon in *Post Today* 2003).

## Legal and Policy Dimensions

The attempt of the Thai government to monitor street food vending in Bangkok took shape in 1941 when the then Bangkok Municipality enacted separate regulations monitoring fixed vending and mobile vending. After the establishment of Bangkok Metropolis in 1972, it enacted a new law to monitor street food vending in Bangkok. The attempt to clear the vendors from pavements began in 1973. But it was marred by the oil crisis. The Bangkok Metropolitan Administration eventually supported the 'return' of street foods on the pavements (Bangkok Metropolitan Administration 1995). In fact, the task of the restoration of street vending has always been on the Bangkok governor's priority list (ibid.: 55).

Policy at national and local levels reflected the 'dualism' of attitudes towards street vendors. In the Fourth Bangkok Metropolitan Development Plan (1987–91) and the Fifth Bangkok Metropolitan Development Plan (1992–96) street vending was depicted as a 'threat' to Bangkok's orderliness, as a city must be systemic, orderly and liveable (Bangkok Metropolitan Administration 1991: 47). Street vending also represented 'underdevelopment'. The Plans, therefore, set the goal of reducing the number of street vendors in all districts of Bangkok, limiting the increase of street vendors and prohibiting the preparation of foods on the streets. On the contrary, the Plans stated that petty trade was a means to reduce poverty. Nevertheless, during the years of both Plans, the National Statistical Office indicated that the number of street vendors in Bangkok increased.

Despite the direction set out in the Plans, measures with regard to street vending in Bangkok depended on the individual governor (Siripunya 1995). As of 2003, legal measures concerning street food vending were found in a number of Acts and Regulations. The Regulation of Bangkok Metropolis on Hawkers B.E. 2519 (1976) provides definitions for 'fixed vending' and 'mobile vendor'. The Act on Maintaining Public Cleanliness and Public Order B.E. 2535 (1992) authorises the Bangkok Metropolitan Administration with the approval of the Traffic Police Bureau to designate areas for street vending. The Act on Maintaining Public Cleanliness and Public Order B.E. 2535 (1992) authorises the Bangkok Metropolitan Administration to designate areas prohibited from vending. The Regulation of Bangkok Metropolis on Selling in Public Spaces B.E. 2545 (2002) stipulates that vendors must have an authorisation to sell, and also stipulates guidelines for food sellers such as dress code, personal hygiene and care for cooking utensils. While the regulations for mobile and fixed vendors are slightly different, the law has not been strictly enforced. The former Bangkok governor who took office in 2004 ordered that vendors could not sell on Mondays.

At the national level, the government's attempt to encourage self-employment was first outlined in the Sixth National Economic and Social Development Plan (1987–91). Measures such as provision of skills training, social protection schemes and capital money were introduced.

However, research reported that the initiatives were inaccessible to many people (Office of Urban Community Development 1993; Napas 1994; Narumol 1996; Pawadee 1996; and Vichitr, Vilaiwaj and Pradit 2003). The government's attempts to use petty enterprise to respond to the economic downturn were apparent in 1997. Free seed money of 4,000 baht was offered to the less-privileged people. In addition, funds were earmarked from the World Bank and Miyazawa loans in the name of the Social Investment Fund to support petty enterprise through occupational groups and savings groups in the community.

The significant step with regard to the support of petty enterprise was the establishment of the Bank of People's Project which is under the supervision of the Government Savings Bank. The Project, which offers a monthly interest rate of 1 per cent for an initial loan of 15,000 baht, was put into effect on 25 June 2001.

## Food Vendors in Klongtoey and Dindaeng Districts

Klongtoey and Dindaeng in Bangkok both 'started out' as low-income areas. Klongtoey district is near the port and is the site of the largest squatter slum in Bangkok. Dindaeng, previously a garbage dumpsite, is a sweatshop district where thousands of subcontractors in the garment industry work. It also has government offices, schools and universities. Dindaeng is also known for its network of little alleys and lanes which enable mobile food vendors to move easily through the area. These provide ideal sites for 'home delivery' eateries.

## Profiles of Vendors

This section presents findings on two types of vendors—mobile and fixed.

### *Mobile Vendors*

The socio-economic profile of vendors is as follows:

- The majority (88 per cent) came from provinces outside Greater Bangkok.
- The highest percentage of vendors came from the north-east, the region of lowest per capita income in Thailand.
- A high proportion (35 per cent) of vendors came to Bangkok only after the 1997 economic crisis.
- Seventy per cent of vendors were from the agricultural sector.
- The percentage of male and female vendors is close, indicating that women no longer dominate in selling food on the streets of Bangkok.

- The youngest vendor was 20 years of age and the oldest was 78, whereas more than half of the vendors sampled were between 30 and 50 years of age.
- The majority (80 per cent) had received less than six years of formal education.

Only 3.4 per cent of those sampled identified themselves as ethnic Chinese (see Table 7.2).

The length of time engaged in vending was:

- A significant proportion (53 per cent) were in business less than five years; 27 per cent were in business from five to less than 10 years.
- Fourteen per cent had spent more than 20 years in the vending activity (see Table 7.3).
- The duration in the vending business ranges from less than five years to more than 21 years.

More than 90 per cent of mobile vendors were in the 'true self-employment' category whereas around 3–6 per cent were in the 'disguised wage-work' and 'dependent work' categories respectively (see Table 7.4). More than half of them were individual operators (see Table 7.5).

The highest percentage (65 per cent) sold foods that can be consumed on the street reflecting the culture of 'public eating'. Only 16 per cent traded in uncooked and other non-ready-to-eat types of food (see Table 7.6). About a third or 30 per cent said they worked not more than 0.6 m walking distance from their place of residence.

A vendor may sell more than one type of food. The decision on the type of food sold is based on which type of food earned highest income. Papaya salad is categorised as 'food prepared on the street'. The different types of food sold by a papaya salad vendor in Dindaeng district (July 2003) are given in Table 7.7.

The variety of food that a vendor sells demonstrates the following:

- The vendor has knowledge of foods that enables him/her to fix more than one dish. S/he also has sufficient knowledge in cost accounting, enabling him/her to calculate the balance between various kinds of foods s/he sells.
- The types of foods sold indicated high stock value. The stock value for one day was 700–800 baht.[2]

**Table 7.2**
**Socio-economic Features of Food Vendors**

| Features | Mobile (n = 236) | Fixed (n = 505) |
|---|---|---|
| *Domicile* | | |
| Greater Bangkok | 11.9 | 33.3 |
| Other provinces | 88.1 | 66.7 |
| Central region | 17.3 | 38.6 |
| Northern region | 9.1 | 10.7 |
| North-eastern region | 70.2 | 38.3 |
| Eastern region | 2.4 | 4.5 |
| Western region | 1.0 | 7.9 |
| *Reasons for coming to Bangkok* | (n = 203) | (n = 303) |
| Seeking jobs | 92.2 | 83.2 |
| Accompany family members | 7.8 | 16.8 |
| *Duration of stay in Bangkok* | | |
| 1997–2003 (less than 7 years) | 34.5 | 11.8 |
| 1992–1996 (8–12 years) | 23.5 | 25.9 |
| 1987–1991 (13–17 years) | 18.5 | 17.6 |
| 1982–1986 (18–22 years) | 11.8 | 18.4 |
| Before 1982 (23 years up) | 11.7 | 26.3 |
| *Ethnicity* | (n = 117) | (n = 499) |
| Thai | 96.6 | 89.6 |
| Ethnic Chinese | 3.4 | 10.4 |
| *Age* | (n = 121) | (n = 499) |
| Less than 25 years | 3.3 | 6.8 |
| 25–less than 30 years | 10.7 | 9.2 |
| 30–less than 40 years | 42.1 | 27.2 |
| 40–less than 50 years | 26.5 | 31.7 |
| 50–less than 60 years | 12.3 | 18.4 |
| 60 years up | 5.1 | 6.7 |
| *Sex* | (n = 121) | (n = 503) |
| Female | 50.4 | 45.1 |
| Male | 49.6 | 54.9 |
| *Education* | (n = 101) | (n = 485) |
| None | 16.5 | 4.7 |
| Primary education | 68.6 | 73.6 |
| Secondary education | 9.9 | 9.6 |
| High school | 5.0 | 12.1 |

*Source*: Compiled by author.

- The vendor spends considerable time preparing the food s/he sells. Usually, s/he leaves his/her place before 1 a.m. to purchase materials at a market, where s/he spends two hours shopping. Food preparation begins shortly after s/he returns from the market, lasting for about

**Table 7.3**
**Length of Time in Vending Activity**

| Length of Time in Vending | Mobile Vendors | Fixed Vendors |
|---|---|---|
| Less than 5 years | 52.9 | 41.5 |
| 5–less than 6 years | 11.1 | 5.6 |
| 7–less than 10 years | 15.3 | 25.1 |
| 10–less than 15 years | – | 9.9 |
| 16–less than 20 years | 6.7 | 10.9 |
| 21 years up | 14.0 | 7.0 |

*Source*: Compiled by author.

**Table 7.4**
**Percentage of Vendors by Different Types of Self-employment**

| | Mobile Vendors | Fixed Vendors |
|---|---|---|
| True self-employment | 91.1 | 95.8 |
| Disguised wage work | 3.4 | 1.0 |
| Dependent work | 5.5 | 3.2 |

*Source*: Compiled by author.

**Table 7.5**
**Types of Operation**

| Type of Operation | Mobile | Fixed |
|---|---|---|
| Individual business | (n=236) | (n = 404) |
| | 56.4 | 37.1 |
| Family business | (n=103) | (n = 255) |
| –spouse and children | 99.0 | 86.2 |
| –other family members | | |
| Employees/family members | 1.0 | 13.8 |
| –employees | 1.0 | 9.3 |

*Source*: Compiled by author.

**Table 7.6**
**Percentage of Vendors Selling Each Type of Food**

| Types of Food | Mobile Vendors | Fixed Vendors |
|---|---|---|
| Fresh food | 8.1 | 19.6 |
| Prepared food | 30.8 | 36.1 |
| Food prepared on the street | 15.1 | 15.6 |
| Readymade food | 19.1 | 12.4 |
| Fruits | 18.9 | 8.5 |
| Others | 8.0 | 7.8 |

*Source*: Compiled by author.

**Table 7.7**
**Types of Food Sold**

| Types of Foods | Foods |
|---|---|
| Cooked foods/Foods prepared on the street | Fresh green papaya, mangoes which can be sold as fruit or prepared on the street as salad. |
| Packaged food/Cooked foods | Thai noodles with fish curry sauce—without coconut milk (The noodles are packaged food, the curry is home-cooked) |
| Cooked food | Boiled snails, fried noodles, boiled quail eggs |
| Packaged food | Boiled peanuts and corn, assorted Thai desserts such as layered cake, egg cakes, sugar-coated fried banana, etc.(purchased from Mahanak market) |
| Fruits | Fresh fruits in season |

*Source*: Compiled by author.

two hours. Afterwards, the vendor rests and gets up at around 8 a.m. to arrange his/her basket for the day's sale. Selling starts at around 10 a.m.

- The vendor buys food from small shops in the public market that are open around the clock, catering to buyers' taste and culture.
- The decision on what products to offer for the day requires some sort of 'consumer research'.
- With the variety of food that the vendor sells, his/her small eatery functions as a 'one-stop shop' that offers a complete meal consisting of several dishes and desserts.
- Mobile street food vendors provide 'home delivery service', which responds to the needs of sweatshop workers in Dindaeng districts who do not have time to eat out.

Unlike previous research (Kusuma 1983; Renu 1991; Chomlada 1991; Vichanya 1998; Ajchariya 2001), the vendors cited quick cash turnover as the main reason for food vending. The types of foods sold were determined by the amount of capital investment, knowledge about food, the number of sellers selling similar types of food and the complexity of the preparation. Many sellers didn't limit themselves to selling only specific types of food as 23 per cent of vendors reported to have changed the types of food sold. The reasons for changing types of food sold are mainly related to marketing. Under brisk competition, knowledge about food and savings is therefore very important.

In general, the majority of mobile vendors had stock worth 201 to 500 baht and 701 to 1,000 baht, respectively. The vendors in this study may be classified into three groups:

- Those with less than 500 baht value of stock (41.5 per cent).
- Those with value of stock between 501 and 1,000 baht (39.7 per cent).
- Those whose value of stock was 1,001 baht and up (18.8 per cent) (see Table 7.8).

Some of the vendors who had low value of stock worked as commission sellers or disguised wage-workers. A large proportion of vendors (84 per cent) said that earnings were adequate, confirming that street food vending was a means of livelihood among the less-privileged people of Bangkok (see Table 7.9). For most vendors, food vending was not their first occupation. This confirmed many previous research findings that self-employment required prerequisites such as capital, social network and experience about foods and market demand.

The most important reason for opting for vending was economic as 47.6 per cent indicated that they needed more income. Almost 22 per cent cited autonomy, 17 per cent said their previous company had closed down, 9.7 per cent referred to unproductive farming and 3.7 per cent had inherited the business from their parents. The most cited reason for selling foods was that food was easy to sell and promised quick cash compared to other commodities. This not only confirmed the notion of 'public eating' but was also linked to the quick cash inflow which guaranteed capital for investment for the following day. The most cited second reason was that the vendors knew about foods and the third one was low investment. Another reason also cited was that the food could also be consumed in the family. Low investment was cited as the reason for the selection of the types of food to be sold.

The majority (86 per cent) of vendors said they were satisfied with their occupation (Table 7.10); the reasons for which were both economic and social, as earning opportunity and autonomy were most often cited (see Table 7.11). Vendors who reported low satisfaction cited low earnings and homesickness as reasons. However, compared to the basic minimum wage of 169 baht in 2004, earnings from street food vending were relatively higher. If the earnings were adequate, it is interesting to inquire further if the vendors wanted to be in the occupation all their lives and if they wanted their children to follow suit. Data revealed that more than half the

**Table 7.8**
**Daily Value of Stock, Earnings and Net Profits**

| Amount | Mobile Vendors | | | Fixed Vendors | | |
|---|---|---|---|---|---|---|
| | Value of Stock | Earnings | Profit | Value of Stock | Earnings | Profit |
| Less than 200 baht | 9.9 ⎫ 41.5 | 5.1 ⎫ 29.4 | 21.4 ⎫ 83.0 | 4.9 ⎫ 21.2 | – ⎫ 21.0 | – |
| 201–500 baht | 31.6 ⎭ | 24.3 ⎭ | 61.6 ⎭ | 16.3 ⎭ | 21.0 ⎭ | 65.0 |
| 501–700 baht | 17.5 ⎫ 9.7 | 15.5 ⎫ 43.2 | 6.9 ⎫ 15.0 | 8.7 ⎫ 33.3 | 14.0 ⎫ 31.5 | 24.7 |
| 701–1,000 baht | 22.2 ⎭ | 27.7 ⎭ | 8.1 ⎭ | 24.6 ⎭ | 17.5 ⎭ | |
| 1,001–1,500 baht | 7.5 | 18.0 | | 9.5 | 18.4 | |
| 1,501–2,000 baht | 3.6 ⎫ 18.8 | 5.6 ⎫ 27.4 | 2.0 ⎱ | 12.4 ⎫ 45.5 | 11.9 ⎫ 47.5 | 10.3 |
| 2,001 baht up | 7.7 ⎭ | 3.8 ⎭ | | 23.6 ⎭ | 17.2 ⎭ | |

*Source*: Compiled by author.

**Table 7.9**
**Percentage of Vendors by Adequacy of Earnings**

| Adequacy of Earnings | Mobile Vendors | Fixed Vendors |
|---|---|---|
| Adequate | 83.9 | 81.2 |
| Inadequate | 16.1 | 18.8 |

Source: Compiled by author.

**Table 7.10**
**Satisfaction with Occupation**

| Satisfaction with Occupation | Mobile Vendors | Fixed Vendors |
|---|---|---|
| Yes | 86.0 | 87.8 |
| No | 14.0 | 12.2 |

Source: Compiled by author.

**Table 7.11**
**Would You Like to be a Street Food Vendor All Your Life?**

| | Mobile Vendors (n = 234) | Fixed Vendors (n = 505) |
|---|---|---|
| Yes | 47.0 | 62.0 |
| No | 53.0 | 38.0 |

| Reasons for 'Yes' | | | |
|---|---|---|---|
| Mobile Vendors ( n = 110) | | Fixed Vendors (n =225) | |
| Want to save money | 58.0 | Want to save money | 65.3 |
| Autonomy | 16.9 | Autonomy | 23.5 |
| Too old, have no other choices | 10.7 | Too old, have no other choices | 11.2 |
| Off-season occupation | 9.8 | | |
| Waiting for children to finish school | 3.4 | | |
| Until I get rich | 1.2 | | |

| Reasons for 'No' | | | |
|---|---|---|---|
| Mobile Vendors (n = 124) | | Fixed Vendors (n =150) | |
| Going home | 29.4 | Want to open store | 70.5 |
| Too old, want to rest | 21.0 | Going home | 15.0 |
| Tired | 8.4 | Want to do something else/change commodity | 10.5 |
| Want to do something else/change commodity | 23.5 | Too old, want to rest | 4.0 |
| Want to open store have fixed selling location | 17.7 | | |

Source: Compiled by author.

vendors (53 per cent) would not want to be in the vending business their entire lives citing different reasons as the work being too tiring, wanting to go home and opening shops, etc. Those who did want to continue cited reasons such as high earning opportunity and autonomy (see Table 7.11). Around 97 per cent said that the earning opportunity was high and that around 83 per cent would encourage friends to enter the business (see Table 7.12) but not their own children (see Table 7.13). It is therefore likely that after being able to accumulate savings, vendors changed their occupation.

**Table 7.12**
**Opportunity for Food Vending in Bangkok**

| *Attitudes towards Earning Opportunity* | *Mobile Vendors* (n = 234) | *Fixed Vendors* (n = 505) |
|---|---|---|
| Opportunity for food vending in Bangkok | | |
| Yes | 97.4 | 94.7 |
| No | 2.6 | 5.3 |
| Would you encourage friends into food vending? | (n = 233) | (n = 462) |
| Yes | 82.8 | 76.8 |
| No | 17.2 | 23.2 |

*Source*: Compiled by author.

**Table 7.13**
**Do You Want Your Children to be Street Food Vendors?**

| *Do You Want Your Children to be Mobile Street Food Vendors?* | *Mobile Vendors* (n = 234) | *Fixed Vendors* (n = 505) |
|---|---|---|
| Yes | 20.2 | 29.0 |
| No | 79.8 | 71.0 |

*Source*: Compiled by author.

This information has policy implications:

1. It confirms that street vending creates opportunity to fight poverty. It assures the livelihood of the new generation of less-privileged people.
2. Street food vending is a means for capital accumulation. This is remarkable considering the fact that these people were impoverished farmers looking for better livelihoods. They had limited education and skills and therefore limited employment opportunity. Street food vending de-marginalises the marginals.

3. Street food vending creates earnings and entrepreneurial skills. Many vendors (as seen in many case studies) have used their entrepreneurial skills to advantage. Many of them had more than a decade of experience. They are not newcomers looking for 'low interest loans'. Rather, they are waiting for the opportunity to expand their ventures.

4. Bangkok streets can also be regarded as 'spheres for entrepreneurial training' as they are arenas filled with brisk competition. Vendors must be well-equipped with numerous skills to survive. Vendors who were able to accumulate capital were those who were able to 'pass' the test of the entrepreneurial training ground.

5. The percentage of vendors who wanted to continue this occupation for life and those who wanted their children to follow suit reflected the significance of street food vending as a means for upward mobility. Agencies concerned should, therefore, instead of limiting their activities, provide opportunities both in terms of space and the information needed such as food hygiene and knowledge about food. Such positive policy would provide support for those who have potential to upgrade into larger business ventures. Food vendors have varying definitions of success:

- Around 12 per cent said they would feel successful if they earned enough simply to survive for another day.
- Most (63 per cent) define success as being able to accumulate savings.
- A quarter (24 per cent) felt successful when their trade expanded.

The vendors evaluated themselves as follows (see Table 7.14):

**Table 7.14**
**Percentage of Vendors at Different Levels of Success**

| Levels of Success | Mobile Vendors | Fixed Vendors |
| --- | --- | --- |
| Subsistence level | 56.0 | 53.9 |
| Have savings but not considering to expand | 38.0 | 31.4 |
| Have savings and considering to expand | 6.0 | 11.7 |

Source: Compiled by author.

- More than half (56 per cent) saw themselves at the subsistence level.
- Around a third (38 per cent) said they had savings.

- Only a small number, or 6 per cent, said they were considering expanding their venture.

## Fixed Vendors

The socio-economic characteristics of fixed vendors are as follows:

- They are more likely to be from Bangkok and the central region.
- Around 33 per cent of vendors were born in Bangkok.
- Almost an equal percentage was from the central and north-eastern regions.
- More than 80 per cent of migrants cited economic reasons for coming to Bangkok.
- The length of time of stay in Bangkok is much longer for these vendors compared to mobile vendors as around a quarter of fixed vendors came to Bangkok before 1982.[3]
- More than 60 per cent of vendors were between 30 and 50 years of age and 7 per cent were more than 60 years of age.
- The youngest vendor was 15 years of age and the oldest, 78 years old.
- More than 70 per cent of vendors were married. Spouses of more than half the total vendors helped in food selling, implying that fixed vending is a family enterprise.
- The percentage of male vendors was slightly higher than that of the female vendors probably because the wives preferred that their husbands respond to the interviewers' inquiries.
- More than 80 per cent of vendors had studied only up to the primary level of education.
- Ninety per cent of vendors identified themselves as ethnic Chinese (Table 7.2).

As for the vending experiences:

- Seventy-three per cent of vendors had less than 10 years of experience in the vending business.
- Around 21 per cent were in the business less than 20 years.
- Only 7 per cent reported to be in the business more than 21 years (see Table 7.3).
- More than 95 per cent of fixed vendors engaged in 'true self-employment' (see Table 7.4). Around one-third or 37 per cent

were individual operators. Only 1 per cent reported employing wage labourers (see Table 7.5).

- Only 30 per cent of vendors sold in the legally designated areas. The remaining 70 per cent sold in the non-designated areas which included public space in the community. The percentage of vendors selling in the community was 46 per cent.
- As high as 70 per cent of fixed vendors reported that they had worked as mobile vendors before.

When asked why they became food vendors, most cited the reason as autonomy, and the reason for selling food was mostly quick cash turnover. As for the types of foods sold by vendors, a high percentage (65 per cent) of vendors sold ready-to-eat foods. Nevertheless, the percentage of vendors selling fresh foods was much higher. The fixed vendors have more space for displaying fresh foods (see Table 7.6).

Fixed vendors sold a smaller selection of foods. The selection of food depends on not only knowledge of food and the capital needed, but also on the availability of foods in the area. More than half of the vendors acquired their materials from public markets. More than half of the vendors said they worked not more than 1.2 miles from their place of residence.

In general, the fixed vendors have a higher daily value of stock (see Table 7.8).

- Around a quarter had daily value of stock of less than 500 baht.
- Around one-third (33.3 per cent) had value of stock between 501 and 1,000 baht.
- Almost half (45.5 per cent) had stock of above 1,001 baht.

Daily value of stock varies by types of foods sold which is similar to the case of mobile vendors. Fresh food and fruit sellers had the highest daily value of stock. More than 80 per cent of vendors said their earnings were adequate (Table 7.9). Almost 90 per cent of vendors reported that they were satisfied with their occupation (Table 7.10). The most cited reasons were earnings and autonomy. Sixty-two per cent said vending would be their life-time occupation (see Table 7.11). Eighty per cent said they would persuade their friends to get into this occupation (see Table 7.12), but not their children (Table 7.13).

Asked if they wanted any support from the government, 42 per cent said they did not. Those who wanted government intervention said that the provision of selling space was the most important area for government action.

How do the vendors see their own performance as vendors?

- Around half (54 per cent) saw themselves as being at subsistence level.
- Around one-third (31 per cent) said they had savings.
- Around 12 per cent said they were considering expanding their ventures (Table 7.14).

Vendors were asked to indicate the level of importance of factors that contributed to their present level of success on a 3-point Likert scale with the categories 'very important', 'important', and 'not so important'. Findings on indicators of success led to the following conclusions:

1. There were indicators of success which were important to vendors at all levels of success: self-confidence, knowledge about cheap sources of materials, selling location and place of residence, appearance of vendors which comprised attire and good rapport, and the foods sold by vendors which comprised taste, food handling and prices.
2. There were indicators that vendors at different levels of success regarded the following differently: knowledge, family, capital, and social network.
3. Vendors whose success put them beyond the subsistence level tended to have a high regard for business and financial knowledge whereas vendors at subsistence level relied more on knowledge pertaining to cheap sources of materials. Vendors at a higher level of success also benefited from family support, social networks and low-interest loans.
4. Factors that contributed to unsuccessful ventures were lack of self-confidence and lack of knowledge and working capital and the addiction of vendors to gambling and over-spending.

## Case Studies

We present five case studies of vendors to complement data from the field survey.

## 1. Vendor who Earns Subsistence Income

### Mobile Vendor: Chilli Paste Seller

Auntie Ging, 56, is a native of Nakorn Ratchasima. Her husband who works as a taxi-driver is 70 years old. Ging has three grown-up children, two of whom are married and live in other provinces. The youngest daughter stays with her. She is 24 years old, married with three children. The daughter works as a mobile vendor selling desserts and her husband is unemployed. Ging has been living in the community for 18 years.

Ging came to Bangkok in 1985 when she was 38. She stayed with her aunt near St. Louis Hospital. It was from her aunt that she learned how to mix many kinds of foods such as papaya salad, chilli paste and assorted dishes. She started selling cooked food in Klongtoey after she got married.

The business was not very good and in 1991 she decided to change to manual labour in Klongton after six years of food vending. The earnings were inadequate and inconsistent. But above all she didn't like the work. She decided to change back to food vending. Ging said she liked selling food as she enjoyed cooking and she already had many regular customers. Since 2001, Ging has been selling assorted cooked foods as she can mix many kinds of foods. She manages to earn 700–800 baht daily and the profit is around 200–300 baht. The hours of selling are from 2 p.m. to 6 p.m.

Ging is a member of a savings group. She manages to save 100 baht monthly. The savings are for her granddaughter's education. Ging was the one responsible for the household expenses as her husband refused to chip in. The husband's earnings were spent on gambling and alcoholic drinks. Ging borrowed money from an informal creditor as the earnings from selling food were not adequate. She had to earmark 100 baht daily for her creditor. Ging attributed her success to perseverance and hard work. As for food selling, Ging said that she took care of her regular customers by selling clean food and listening to their requests. She also attributed her good sales to a good rapport with customers and her clean appearance.

## 2. Vendor who has Savings but Does Not Consider Expanding Trade

### Fixed Vendor: Grilled Chicken Seller

Prasert is a 27-year-old vendor selling fried chicken in Tesco Lotus Superstore. He is married with one son. His family stays in the Surin province. Before 1995, Prasert was working as a farmer on his own land which he inherited from his parents.

Income from rice farming was not sufficient for a family of three. Prasert decided to come to Bangkok to find work and for further education at an open university in 1995. During the first two years at the university he was able to juggle studies and work. After that, he decided to quit studying. Prasert opened a fixed stall selling grilled chicken in Klongtoey. The idea of selling chicken came from his uncle who also sold fried chicken in another community. The uncle, from whom Prasert learned to cook chicken, also lent him seed money to open the chicken stall.

The business did very well; after he quit studying he had more time to concentrate on work. His customers were from the nearby government agencies such as Klongtoey port and the Customs Department. According to Prasert, he earned around 1,000 baht daily making a profit of 300–400 baht. The value of stock was around 700–800 baht daily. Earnings doubled during the weekends. After six years of hard work, Prasert managed to save money for further investment.

In 2001, a friend persuaded him to apply for a selling location in Tesco Lotus Superstore's new branch in Klongtoey. He was selected to sell in the store due to his experience and the taste of his foods. Prasert had been selling in the store for two years at the time of the interview. The gross earnings were around 55,000 baht per month. He was able to make a monthly profit of 18,000 baht. The earnings were consistent as there is only one fried chicken vendor in the store. Prasert said he had no regular customer. After eight years of hard work, he was able to establish himself.

Prasert attributed his success to many factors. First, he had social capital: the uncle provided social and economic support. He added that the food had to be tasty and there shouldn't be too many sellers for the same products in the same area. Even though he had to borrow money from his uncle when he started his business he was able to pay it back. His savings enabled him to expand his trade. Prasert said his stay in Bangkok will be short term as he did not plan to settle down in the big city. He is satisfied with his present work as the sales were good and he had a secured selling location.

## 3. Vendor who Considers Expanding Trade
### Mobile Vendor: Papaya Salad Seller

Mali, 45 is a native of Roi-et, a north-eastern province. Her decision to take up activities other than farming came when the earnings from rice farming proved to be insufficient. Being the eldest child, Mali had to take care of the family. After working a few years as manual labourer, Mali was able to save some money. She invested the money in four pigs which she raised and later sold for a buffalo. After a year she sold the buffalo as well. Then, she invested the money in a small grocery store and a refrigerator. The business went well at the beginning only to collapse later, as she had many debtors who bought grocery on credit. She was then married and had a daughter. In 1980, seeing no future in her home town, Mali, then 19, and her husband decided to leave for Bangkok along with her younger sister and brother-in-law, leaving her daughter with her mother.

Mali took up her first job in Bangkok as a commission-seller of icecreams, about which she said 'it wasn't worth the effort, but I had no other choice'. Her husband worked as a 'tuk-tuk' driver. The 4,000 baht earnings in the first month, though not much, were far better than earnings from farming. After a year-and-a-half, Mali decided to be on her own by selling grilled eggs which required low investment. In less than one year she changed to grilled chicken and pork as both earned higher profits. Around the same time her sister who resided in Dindaeng persuaded her to move there. Seeing that Dindaeng district was at the centre of the city and there were many small factories in the area, Mali moved there in 1987.

After selling grilled pork and chicken in Dindaeng for six months, Mali saw the opportunity for a new venture. She persuaded a friend in the village to invest in a coconut pudding venture. Both Mali and her friend chipped in 5,000 baht, the largest investment she had ever made. She also persuaded five women in the village to work as commissioned sellers. Mali worked as a producer and seller. The business was good at the beginning but sales declined after two years. The saleswomen had to walk much longer distances and the pudding couldn't be kept long due to the heat.

In 1990, Mali gave up the business and turned into a curry vendor. The idea of selling curry came from one of her old customers. The business went quite well. From selling only curry, Mali gradually added products to her pole baskets to serve her customers' demand. At the time of the interview in 2003, Mali sold papaya salad, mango salad and assorted types of foods. Curry was no longer her top product. Mali also had boiled snails, boiled quail eggs and other kinds of foods and desserts which she purchased from the market. All the coconut pudding sellers turned into individual vendors selling similar foods.

Mali had a location near the University of Thai Chamber of Commerce where she would stop every day from 11 a.m. to 2 p.m. before moving to another location. Before acquiring the space, Mali had been selling in the area for a few years. Though the area already had two papaya salad vendors, being a big community with a university, dormitory, rented houses, and also the connected small alleys which linked to two major roads, the area is an ideal place for food vending. Mali did not have a good relationship with the city police as she refused to give them 'payment'.

For Mali, the decision to come to Bangkok originated from the debt that she had with the Bank of Agriculture and Cooperatives. But she admitted that even without the debt, she would have come to Bangkok as, according to her, 'We need to have more, for instance, television, microwave.' She added that some women in the village wouldn't come to be vendors in Bangkok because they were embarrassed at being one. She said, 'I would be more embarrassed to be poor.'

Mali no longer farmed her land as she had leased it out. She went back to her hometown twice annually during the Songkran festival in April and Bun Bang Fai in May. She said that she had to go back because of peer pressure and she would stay at home only for a brief period as she had regular customers waiting for her in the city. According to Mali, Bangkok 'would never run out of money'. She didn't want to open a shop as she said the rent was too high. But she was considering investing in other ventures after her daughter graduated from the university, of whose success, Mali was very proud. Her earnings from the more than two decades of hard work were spent on building a nice house in Roi-et.

## 4. Vendor who Plans to Expand Trade

### Mobile Vendor: Soft-Drinks Seller

Amnaj is 50 years old and his wife 46. Both have had four years of education. Amnaj has a daughter who is studying marketing at Rajabhat University. He is a native of Roi-et. Before coming to Bangkok in 1986, Amnaj worked on his rice farm but the earnings were not good. He and his wife decided to move to Bangkok and stayed with his sister who had moved there earlier.

Upon coming to Bangkok, his sister suggested that he work as a commission-seller for a friend who had opened a dessert shop in the market. Amnaj decided to take the job as it required no investment. He was able to make 20 baht profit on the first day. The profit increased gradually but was not sufficient for the family of three. After working as a commission-seller for a month, Amnaj decided to produce the dessert himself. He borrowed 200 baht from his sister to buy the materials. He was able to make a 300–400 baht profit. The earnings jumped from 3,000 baht to 9,000–10,000 baht monthly.

In 1990 Amnaj formed a group of drink sellers with relatives from his home province. He worked as a group leader and was able to form a six-member group. The group expanded into 15 members. In 1995, he began to expand his venture by adding assorted drinks. He started with the trial and error method, experimenting with various kinds of drinks until he knew which types sold well. In 1999, he received grants from the Social Investment Funds and Miyazawa Project. The money was used to buy pushcarts. He was also selected to join a field trip in Lopburi, where he learned some occupational skills that he later applied to his work.

In 2000, Amnaj and his group formed an occupational savings group. The savings accumulated to 40,000 baht in 2003. His savings group works well with the community's savings group. In 2003, Amnaj started selling 'pearl tea', a drink which originated in Korea. He got the idea from his supplier. The sales were good in the first few months but began to fall afterwards, as there were other vendors selling the same product. He was thinking of selling roselle drink as his brother owned a roselle farm in the province.

Amnaj believes that a mobile vendor has an advantage over the fixed vendor as the mobile vendor was able to get to the customer and conduct a 'consumer research'. He also said that for a beginner, having a place of residence close to the selling area was necessary but for those whose sale was already stable, other factors were more important. He suggested that vendors could sell many types of foods in Bangkok. But one must be careful that the initial investment was not high. The vendors must also have some savings for 'trial and error' of new products. He also warned against gambling, saying that many vendors who wanted to earn 'quick money' gambled and ended up being in debt.

Amnaj planned to set up a community enterprise. He believed that if the people in the community cooperate to form such an enterprise, it would help generate income and security for all, and the community would be strengthened. The most important thing was economic self-reliance. He would not encourage community enterprise from debt creation. He believes in the King's sufficiency economy philosophy.

## 5. Unsuccessful Vendor

### Fixed Vendor: Noodle Seller

Somsak, 45, came to Bangkok in 1983 and settled in Klongtoey. He had neither friends nor relatives in Bangkok. He got a job at the port. His wife, Suvaporn, worked in a nearby construction site. Both worked until they managed to have savings. Now they both work as manual labourers. He had six years of education. Their only son is 15 years old. The boy finished secondary education and gave up his studies.

When the son was born in 1989, Somsak decided to change his occupation. He bought a house in the community at 4,000 baht. The house was in a good location on a thoroughfare. Somsak decided to set up a noodles stall as he used to cook noodles for his family back in the province. Selling noodles didn't need much preparation. The investment was not high and there were no noodle-vendors in the area. His wife could also help out at the stall.

After two weeks of practice, Somsak set up a stall in front of his house. At first the earnings were not consistent as the stall was new to the customers. After two to three months sales began to pick up. The earnings were consistent and he had a number of customers from within the community. In 1998, the sales began to go down and the production costs increased. Earlier, he would buy materials every two days, but after the economic crisis, he had to buy materials every day. Besides, there were more food shops in the community as people began to engage in self-employment. The earnings fell sharply. In the meantime, Somsak got addicted to gambling and drinking. His sales became uncertain as he lost money gambling. Somsak decided to borrow money from a loan shark. He had an interest rate of 20 per cent per month. He also borrowed money from a friend. He had to pay back debt every day. Somsak had to close the stall as his bad reputation affected sales.

When the Bank of People's project came into operation, Somsak applied for a loan and was granted 15,000 baht. He was not able to meet the payment schedule and he knew that he would not be eligible for the next loan. In 2003 Somsak and Suvaporn set out to engage in manual work. Their son had to quit school.

## Study of Consumers

A survey of 385 buyers in Klongtoey and Dindaeng districts found that more than half of the consumers (57 per cent) were female. Almost 50 per cent of the buyers were under 30 years of age. Around 25 per cent were between 31 and 40 years of age. Almost half the respondents had undergraduate degrees. Data indicated that a high percentage of buyers were monthly wage workers, civil servants and public enterprise workers. Some 60 per cent of buyers earned less than 10,000 baht per month though up to 36 per cent earned more than 10,000 baht. Half of the buyers lived in their own house (see Table 7.15). Data on the educational level and income of buyers confirmed that consumption of street food was not limited to people of humble background.

**Table 7.15**
**Socio-economic Characteristics of Street Food Buyers**

| Socio-economic Characteristics | % |
| --- | --- |
| **Sex** | (n=385) |
| Female | 57.4 |
| Male | 42.6 |
| *Age* | (n=382) |
| Less than 30 years | 47.4 |
| 31–40 years | 25.4 |
| 41–50 years | 15.4 |
| 51 years up | 11.8 |
| *Levels of education* | (n=380) |
| Primary education or less | 14.7 |
| Secondary education | 11.1 |
| Higher secondary education | 27.6 |
| Bachelor's degree | 42.9 |
| Higher than bachelor's level | 3.7 |
| *Occupation* | (n=385) |
| Government/Public enterprise | 22.1 |
| Monthly employee | 29.9 |
| Self-employed | 9.6 |
| Daily wage worker | 5.7 |
| Housewife | 4.2 |
| Students | 19.7 |
| Others | 8.8 |
| *Average monthly income* | (n=368) |
| Less than 5,000 baht | 21.2 |
| 5,001–10,000 baht | 42.7 |
| 10,001–15,000 baht | 14.4 |
| 15,001–20,000 baht | 11.4 |
| 20,001 baht up | 10.3 |
| *Types of residential unit* | (n=383) |
| Rented house/room | 38.9 |
| Own house | 50.1 |
| Others | 11.0 |

*Source:* Compiled by author.

More than 70 per cent of the foods bought were foods which could be consumed at the point of purchase. Meals most frequently purchased were dinner. More than half the buyers bought street foods at least once daily. Around 75 per cent of buyers spent no more than 60 baht per purchase.

Around 50 per cent spent no more than 60 baht daily and 45 per cent spent 80 to more than 100 baht daily on street food (Table 7.16).

**Table 7.16**
**Purchasing Behaviour**

| Purchasing Behaviour | % |
| --- | --- |
| Frequency | (n=385) |
| More than once per day | 33.2 |
| Once per day | 21.3 |
| More than once per week | 29.4 |
| Once per week | 10.6 |
| Others | 5.5 |
| Foods most frequently purchase | (n=384) |
| Fresh food | 17.7 |
| Food cooked on the street | 8.9 |
| Cooked food | 43.5 |
| Readymade food | 20.6 |
| Fruits | 8.6 |
| Meals most frequently purchased | (n=384) |
| Breakfast | 19.3 |
| Lunch | 28.4 |
| Supper | 47.9 |
| Late supper | 4.4 |
| Purchasing behaviour | % |
| Expense per one purchase | (n=370) |
| Less than 20 baht | 27.0 |
| 21–40 baht | 27.6 |
| 41–60 baht | 25.1 |
| 61–80 baht | 3.0 |
| 81–100 baht | 10.5 |
| 101 baht up | 6.8 |
| Daily expenses on street foods | (n=327) |
| Less than 20 baht | 11.9 |
| 21–40 baht | 14.7 |
| 41–60 baht | 24.8 |
| 61–80 baht | 6.1 |
| 81–100 baht up | 26.6 |
| 101 baht up | 15.9 |

*Source*: Compiled by author.

This data has many implications. First, it confirms the importance of ready-to-eat foods. Second, the considerably high percentage of buyers who bought street food more than once a day implies that the purchase occurred at different times of the day which included the main meal and snacks. This confirms the earning opportunity of street food vending. Third, the value of purchase links to the economic value that street food contributes to the country's economy. Buyers cited many reasons for buying street foods such as 'close to home', 'close to office' 'time saving','variety of foods', and 'being a regular customer' (see Table 7.17). All of these confirmed previous studies on the consumption of street foods. Around 6 per cent cited compassionate purchase saying that they just wanted to 'help' the vendors.

**Table 7.17**
**Reasons for Purchasing Street Foods**

| Reasons | %* |
| --- | --- |
| 1. Proximity to home | 44.7 |
| 2. Cheap | 39.2 |
| 3. Time-saving | 34.0 |
| 4. Varieties | 33.0 |
| 5. On the way | 28.6 |
| 6. Proximity to workplace | 20.3 |
| 7. Regular customer | 15.3 |
| 8. Bargainable | 7.5 |
| 9. Compassion purchase | 6.0 |

*Source*: Compiled by author.
* More than one answer.

When asked to indicate the advantages and disadvantages of street food vending, a high percentage (70 per cent) cited convenience, employment opportunity and cheap foods. As for the disadvantages, buyers cited obstruction to traffic, lack of orderliness and unhygienic foods sold on the streets (Table 7.18).

Almost all (96 per cent) of the consumers said that street food vending was necessary for Bangkok's citizens.[4] Interestingly, this included manual labourers, students and respondents who hold more than bachelor's degrees (see Table 7.19).

When asked how they would like to see Bangkok street food vending, buyers' responses reflected their concerns about food hygiene and orderliness and selling areas. They were also concerned about the use of chemical substances in food. Low prices were the main attraction of street foods. As for orderliness, buyers suggested that vendors should not obstruct thoroughfares. This is in line with the suggestions that zoning by types of food should be applied, parking space should be provided and vendors

Table 7.18
Strengths and Weaknesses of Food Vending Activities

| Strengths | Per Cent |
|---|---|
| 1. Convenience/time-saving | 70.1 |
| 2. Employment and income generation | 68.8 |
| 3. Cheap food—good taste | 40.5 |
| 4. Traditional | 17.7 |

| Weaknesses | Per Cent |
|---|---|
| 1. Obstruction to pedestrians | 53.5 |
| 2. Inorderliness | 47.0 |
| 3. Unhygienic foods | 44.9 |
| 4. Unhygienic environment | 26.2 |
| 5. Cause traffic problems | 11.4 |
| 6. Noisy | 5.2 |

*Source*: Compiled by author.

Table 7.19
Are Street Food Vendors Necessary for Bangkok People?

| Response n = 385 | % | Daily Wage Worker n = 22 | Students n = 78 | Government/ State Enterprise Officers n = 85 | Higher than Bachelor's Degree n = 14 | Bachelor's Degree n = 163 | Own House n = 192 |
|---|---|---|---|---|---|---|---|
| Yes | 96.1 | 100.0 | 100.0 | 90.5 | 100.0 | 97.5 | 97.9 |

*Source*: Compiled by author.

should not be overcrowded in some areas. With regard to vendors, the suggestions were in line with the buyers' concern regarding food hygiene as buyers recommended that vendors wear clean attire and head cover (see Table 7.20).

## Policy Recommendations

'. . . nothing more unequal than the equal treatments of the unequal.'
—Harvey 2003: 40

Survey findings confirm that policy implications on street food vending should take into consideration the structural context and individual context, diversity of food vendors ranging from types of vending unit, economic performance, types of food sold, food hygiene and more importantly, the role of street food vending in the strengthening of grassroot economic reliance. Some policy recommendations regarding street vending in Bangkok are as follows.

## Table 7.20
## How Would You Like to See Bangkok Street Food Vending?

| Suggestions | % |
| --- | --- |
| 1. Orderliness (n=246) | |
|   – Not obstruct thoroughfare | 52.8 |
|   – Zoning by types of foods and parking provided | 44.8 |
|   – Cart should not be left on public space | 2.0 |
|   – Vending should be strictly prohibited in certain areas | 0.4 |
| 2. Accommodating buyers (n=90) | |
|   – Shouldn't be overcrowded | 61.1 |
|   – Zoning by types of food | 22.2 |
|   – Vending should be close to areas where people gather | 16.7 |
| 3. Foods (n=339) | |
|   – Clean in production | 32.5 |
|   – Free from chemical substances such as borax, saccharin and other dangerous substances | 25.4 |
|   – Clean selling area | 12.7 |
|   – Cheap | 29.4 |
| 4. Vendors (n=125) | |
|   – Clean attire with apron and head cover | 56.0 |
|   – Loyal, not selling substandard food | 24.0 |
|   – Good rapport | 20.0 |

*Source:* Compiled by author.

The goal of the government should be to help people to be self-reliant. The government should realign its attitudes towards street food vending and in the meantime understand the diversity among food vendors. Such understanding should reflect in policies that are realistic. It is not useful to implement a single policy for the diverse groups of vendors.

Besides being regarded as a survival strategy for the less-privileged people, street food vending should be regarded as expandable which implies vendors being supported as having potential for expansion, and not as the impoverished. They should be on par with small- and medium-enterprise owners.

To support these people as entrepreneurs would mean more than providing capital or funding for the venture. The policy must incorporate integrated measures considering the factors that contribute to the economic performance of the vendors, namely housing, sources of materials, selling location, etc. Findings based on tracing the backward linkages between street vendors and micro-enterprise and small business in many public markets indicate that street food vending can impact small business. These small businesses constitute a vital grass roots economy. Street food vending helps to support many small businesses, which are important in the globalising economy. The support of small business implies the rethinking of development strategies which favour large capitalistic establishments.

## Employment Generation, Poverty Alleviation and Economic Mobility

Data on indicators of success confirms that vendors who earned a subsistence level of earnings or below were likely to be elderly women who had to look after their children who, in fact, should already be independent. This causes the insufficiency of earnings and shortage of capital among the older vendors. In this aspect the real problems of the vendors were indeed not the shortage of funds, rather the economic burden caused by the dependents. It is likely that the situation will 'reproduce' another batch of a younger or new generation of low-income earning food vendors.

Factors that keep vendors at subsistence level were economic along with social factors. In this case, the measures which support the vendors in economic aspects such as accessibility to cheap credit, and opportunity for the activities were deemed insufficient as these deal only with the capital 'inflow'. Instead, measures should work on the cash 'outflow' side, particularly the measures to strengthen the community and family which helps generate a network of knowledge. Taken up through joint consultation, such policies would eventually lead to providing a 'cushion' for the younger generation and help support income-generating activities.

Measures to enhance employment opportunities should be holistic taking many enabling factors into consideration such as the proximity of residence to the source of materials and selling space, the provision of space for vending activities, the increase in family stability and the nurturing of thrift consciousness. It goes without saying that the government has been very selective in terms of measures to enhance the earning opportunity of the vendor. For instance, the low-interest loan has always been the flagship of the policy. But simultaneously the government does not think twice about relocating slums to another less developed area as the land they occupy currently becomes earmarked for projects that guarantee higher economic returns.

Information and knowledge is another important factor. This study confirms that knowledge is a prerequisite for successful ventures either at the very beginning or at the capital accumulation stages. Knowledge services of different relevance are therefore important. For instance, business planning is important for the beginning of the venture but for those who have already accumulated capital, other types of knowledge may be more important. Financial planning, cost-profit calculations are important for all groups of vendors. The dissemination of information and relevant skill building should be through social networks and not through formal institutions. The strengthening of social networks and community networks is therefore vital, both in terms of knowledge dissemination and for the organisation.

The fact that indicators of success are different for different levels of success confirms the diversity in measures. Vendors who are relatively better off need different kinds of support. More importantly, for these vendors, money or loans are no longer their priority. Rather, they need other types of support to sustain their level of success such as selling space and the strengthening of vendors in order to be able to cope with brisk competition from the newcomers. Selling space is more important to fixed vendors than to mobile vendors. However, though the study found that securing selling space is one of the indicators of success, lack of space was not mentioned as the cause of unsuccessful ventures. This implies that for the vendors, the problem of space is manageable. This is contrary to past researches on vending that stressed on the importance of secure selling spaces. This study points to the need to open spaces for the vendors in light of the understanding of public space as a production space.

## Food Vendors and Hygiene

Hygiene has been the weak point of street foods. Data on buyers confirms that they have high concerns for food hygiene and the vendors must adjust themselves to higher standards of food hygiene. Besides monitoring on the part of vendors, food buyers should be informed of food hygiene standards in order to have a role in the monitoring and be selective in buying foods from vendors who live up to the standard.

Despite the law concerning food hygiene, there is lack of practice on the part of vendors and monitoring on part of the officers. Food hygiene is an important matter both for the survival of street food vending and the buyers themselves. The authorities should focus more on the monitoring of food hygiene rather than pushing the food vendors out of the streets.

## Orderliness and Pedestrian Safety

Food vending has been regarded as the major cause of lack of orderliness and of making thoroughfares unsafe. Street vending has been regarded as a representation of outdated and underdeveloped trade. However, two former governors of Bangkok shared a similar opinion of street trade, that rather than being a representation of underdevelopment, street food vending portrayed the life of Bangkok's people. It is the city's cultural capital. To reduce the problems of inorderliness, the officials have to resort to monitoring and control. Vendors should also have a role in this monitoring effort. This is evident in the case of Soi Prachasongkroh in Dindaeng, where the vendors have a part in assuring the orderliness of the soi (street).

## Food Culture

Street food vending forms part of the cultural facet of Bangkok. Street foods in Bangkok are well-known for their ubiquity and taste. The Bangkok Metropolitan Administration itself uses this cultural capital in the publicity of Bangkok in a book *Bangkok Bangkok*, in which street food is portrayed as one of Bangkok's many tourist attractions.

The reputation of street foods is partly attributed to the popularity of Thai foods such as Tom Yum Koong, a well-known 'health food'. The policy on street food vending should take into consideration the popularity of Thai food and Thai identity. Vendors should have knowledge about Thai food and be creative in coming up with new dishes. Such knowledge will not only further popularise Thai food but also increase earning opportunities.

## Notes

1. The *Sakdina* system granted land ownership to the princes, noblemen and soldiers. Male adults had to spend six to eight months per year working or fighting in battles under the command of noblemen or soldiers, who were granted ownership of the land.
2. 1 baht is equivalent to US$0.285.
3. This may link to the migration of people from the central and north-eastern provinces during the time of the construction of the harbour in Klongtoey and the time when Dindaeng was still a dumpsite.
4. In response to one of the questions, 'Is street food vending necessary for Bangkok?'

## References

Ajchariya Charncherngrob. 2001. 'Naew tang karn Pitaksitiprayote Toneng Kong Puka Haabre Pangloy' (Guideline for Advocacy for Street Vendors in Bangkok), Master of Social Work Thesis, Thammasat University.

Ammar Siamwalla and Suthad Setboonsarng. 1989. *Trade, Exchange Rate and Agricultural Pricing Policies in Thailand: The Political Economy of Agricultural Pricing Policy*, Washington, D.C., World Bank.

Armstrong, Warwick and T. G. McGee. 1985. *Theatres of Accumulation: Studies in Asian and Latin American Urbanization*, London: Methuen.

Askew, Marc. 2002. *Bangkok: Place, Practice and Representation*, New York: Routledge.

Atthakor, Ploenpote. 2002. 'Devious Loan Scam Blasted by Senator', *Bangkok Post*, 24 March: 1.

Babb, Florence E. 1989. *Between Field and Cooking Pot: The Political Economy of Market Women in Peru*, revised edition, Texas: University of Texas Press.

Bangkok Metropolitan Administration. 1991. *Pan Pattana Krungthep Mahanakom Chabab Ti Si* (The Fourth Greater Bangkok Plan), Bangkok: Thammasat University Press.

———. 1995. *Yee Sib Song Pee Krungthep Mahanakom* (Twenty-Two Years of Bangkok Metropolitan Administration), Bangkok: D.L.S.

———. 1996. *Pan Pattana Krungthep Mahanakom Chabab Ti Ha* (The Fifth Greater Bangkok Plan), Bangkok: Thammasat University Press.

———. 1999. *Jak Tessaban su Krungthep Mahanakom* (From Municipality to Bangkok Metropolis), Bangkok: Chuan Pim Press.

———. 2001. *Pan Pattana Krungthep Mahanakom Chabab Ti Hog* (The Sixth Greater Bangkok Plan), Bangkok: Thammasat University Press.

Bangkok Municipality. 1941. *Pramuan Tessabanyat hang Tessaban Nakom Krungthep* (Bangkok Municipal Codes), Bangkok: Bangkok Municipality Printing House.

Bromley, Ray and Chris Gerry. 1979. 'Who are the Casual Poor?' in Ray Bromley and Chris Gerry (eds), *Casual Work and Poverty in Third World Cities*, pp. 3–26, New York: John Wiley and Sons.

Cartwright, Androw. 2003. 'Take Some Pride in Real Thailand', *Bangkok Post*, 20 October.

Charmes, Jacques. 2000. 'Informal Sector, Poverty and Gender: A Review of Empirical Evidence', Background paper for the World Development Report, 2001.

Chamaiporn Rungroekrit. 2001. 'Improving the Situations of the Urban Street Food Vendors in Thailand', Master's Thesis, Institute of Social Studies, The Hague.

Chomlada Loprayoon. 1991. 'Vending Activity in Bangkok', Master's thesis, Faculty of Economics, Thammasat University.

Core Planning and Development. 2000. 'Raingan Chababsomboon Karn Chadtum Panpung Pattanakhet' ( A Final Report on District Development), Bangkok.

*Daily News*. 1995. 8 February: 7.

*Daily News*. 1995. 9 March: 8.

Dararat Kaewsalapsi. 1999. 'Pajjai ti Mee Pon tor Karn Nam nayobai Pai Patibat : Suksa Chapoh Koranee Karn Ruam Klum Acheep Klongkarn Thai Chuay Thai

Krom Pracha Songkroh' (Factors Affecting Policy Implementation: A Case Study of Occupational Group under the Thai Help Thai Project Department of Public Welfare), Master of Social Work Thesis, Thammasat University.

Department of Regional and Urban Planning. 2000. 'Raingan Chababsomboon Karn Suksa Pua Chadtum Pan lae Pung Pattanakhet' (A Final Report on District Development), Bangkok: Chulalongkorn University.

Department of Labor, Ministry of Interior. 1992. 'Report on Workshop on the Role of Informal Activity on the Growth of Economy and Employment Creation in Thailand'. 23–24 January

Deosthgli, Ashkay. 2003. 'Street Vendors Pay Heavy Price', *Bangkok Post*, 28 October.

de Geus, Arie. 1997. 'The Living Company', *Harvard Business Review*, 77(2) (March–April): 51–59.

Drakakis-Smith, David. 1990. 'Food for Thought or Thought about Food: Urban Food Distribution Systems in The Third World', in Robert B. Porter and Ademloa T. Salau (eds), *Cities and Development in the Third World*, pp. 100–120, London: Mansell.

Faculty of Social Administratiion, Thammasat University. 1971. *Karn Samruaj Vijai Tang sangkom Songkroah Boriven Lang Suemsom Tha Rua Klongtoey Changwat Pranakorn* (A Social Work Research Survey on Klongtoey Slum Commnunity, Bangkok), Bangkok: Faculty of Social Work, Thammasat University.

Farbman, Michael. 1981. *The PISCES Studies: Assisting the Smallest Economics Activities of the Urban Poor*. Washington, D.C.: USAID.

Fujimaki, Motoki. 1995. *Informal Economic Activity: General Thinking and Case Study in Bangkok*. Bangkok: CUSRI.

Gaber, John. 1994. 'Manhattan's 14th Street Vendors Market: Informal Street Peddlers Complementary Relationship with New York City's Economy', *Urban Anthropology*, 23(4): 373–408.

Geertz, Cliftord. 1963. *Peddlers and Princes: Social Change and Economic Modernization in Two Indonesian Towns*, Chicago: University of Chicago Press.

Girod, Roger. 1986. 'Intra-and Intergenerational Income Mobility: A Geneva Survey, 1950–1980', in Robert V. Robinson (ed.), *Research in Social Stratification and Mobility*, pp. 261–79, Greenwich, Connecticut: JAI Press,.

Harvey, David. 2003. 'The Right to the City', *International Journal of Urban and Regional Research*, 27(4): 939–41.

Homenet Thailand. 2002. *Impact of the Economic Crisis on Homeworkers in Thailand*, Bangkok: HomeNet Thailand.

Hungry in Bangkok. '. . . And Let Visitors Enjoy Street Foods', *Bangkok Post*, 20 October.

International Labour Organisation. 1991. *The Dilemma of the Informal Sector*, Geneva: International Labour Office.

International Labour Organisation. 1996. *Entrepreneurship Development for Women: A Manual for Trainers*, New Delhi: ILO/South Asia Multidisciplinary Advisory Team.

———. 1996. *Know About Business: Entrepreneurship Education in Vocatonal and Technical Training*, Turin: International Training Centre of the ILO.

———. 2000. *Decent Work For All: Targeting Full Employment in Thailand*, Bangkok: International Labour Organization.

Kanchanakhaphan. 2002. *Krungthep Mua Wanni* (Yesterday Bangkok), Fourth Edition, Bangkok: Sarakadee.

Kiat Chivakul et al. 1982. *Talad Nai Krungthep: Kankhayai lae Pattanakarn* (Markets in Bangkok: Growth and Development), Bangkok: Chilalongkorn University.

*Kom Chat Luk.* 2002. 30 April: 4.

*Kom Chat Luk.* 2003. 29 July: 1.

*Kom Chat Luk.* 2003. 16 October: 4.

*Krungthep Turakij.* 2002. 25 July: 12–14.

*Krungthep Turakij.* 2003. 14 February: 11.

Kusuma Kosayayotin. 1983. 'Bab paen karn kao Su Acheep lae Kwam Pung Po Chai nai Acheep kong Satree ti Yai Tin Kaoma Tamngan nai Krungthep Mahanakorn' (Entry Pattern and Satisfaction in Occupation of Women Migrants in Bangkok), Master of Sociology and Anthropology Thesis, Thammasat University.

Lessinger, Johanna. 2001. 'Inside, Outside, and Selling on the Road: Women's Market Trading in South India', in Linda J. Seligmann (ed.), *Women Traders in Cross Cultural Perspective*, pp. 73–102, California: Stanford University Press.

Leiser, Roland. 2003. 'Thai Food in Strange New Incarnation', *Bangkok Post*, 2 March: Outlook: 1.

Lund, Frances and Smita Srinivas. 2001. *Learning from Experience: A Gendered Approach to Social Protection for Workers in the Informal Economy*. Turin: International Labour Office.

Lund, F. J. 1998. *Women Street Traders in Urban South Africa: A Synthesis of Selected Research Findings*, Durban: School of Development Studies, University of Natal.

*Manager Daily.* 1995. 12 July: 11.

MacEwen Scott, Alison. 1995. 'Informal Sector or Female Sector? Gender Bias in Urban Labour Market Models', in Diane Elson (ed.), *Male Bias in Development Process*, New York: Marchester University Press.

Meagher, Kate and Mohammed-Bello Yunusa. 1996. *Passing the Buck: Structural Adjustment and the Nigerian Urban Informal Sector*, Geneva: United Nations Research Institute for Social Development.

McGee, T. G. 1973 *Hawkers in Hong Kong: A Study of Planning and Policy in a Third World City*, Hong Kong: Centre of Asian Studies.

McGee, T. G. 1977. 'The Persistence of the Proto-Proletariat: Occupational Structures and Planning of the Future of Third World Cities', in Janet Abu-Lughod and Richard Hay, Jr. (eds), *Third World Urbanization*, pp. 257–70, Chicago: Maaroufa Press.

———. 1979. 'The Poverty Syndrome: Making Out in the Southeast Asian City', in Ray Bromley and Chris Gerry (eds), *Casual Work and Poverty in Third World Cities*, pp. 45–68, New York: John Wiley and Sons.

———. 1996. 'On the Utility of Dualism: The Informal Sector and Mega-Urbanization in Developing Countries', *Regional Development Dialogue*, 17(1): 1–15.

McGee, T. G. and Y. M. Yeung. 1977. *Hawkers in Southeast Asian Cities: Planning for the Bazaar Economy*, Ottawa: International Development Research Center.

Mishra, Ramesh. 1999. *Globalization and the Welfare State*, Cheltenham: Edward Elgar.

Moser, Caroline O.N. 1978. 'Informal Sector or Petty Commodity Production: Dualism or Dependence in Urban Development?' *World Development*, 6(9–10): 1041–64.

———. 1980. 'Why the Poor Remain Poor: The Experience of Bogota Market Traders in the 1970s', *Journal of Interamerican Studies and World Affairs*, 22(3) (August): 365–87.

Murray, Alison J. 1992. *No Money. No Honey: A Study of Street Traders and Prostitutes in Jakarta*, Singapore: Oxford University Press.

Narumol Nirathron. 1993. 'Karn Chad Sawaddikarn Sangkom Samrab Purabnganpaitumtiban' (Social Protection Scheme for Homeworkers).

Navarat Nophirun. 1997. 'Chewit Maeka' (Life of Market Traders: Botbat tang Sethakij lae Krobkrua nai Boribot Karn Ka', Master of Sociology and Anthropology Thesis, Thammasat University.

NESDB. 1981. *The Fifth Economic and Social Development Plan (1982–1986)*, Bangkok: National Economic and Social Development Board, Office of the Prime Minister. United Production.

———. 1986. *The Sixth Economic and Social Development Plan (1987–1991)*, Bangkok: National Economic and Social Development Board, Office of the Prime Minister. United Production.

———. 1991. *The Seventh Economic and Social Development Plan (1992–1996)*, Bangkok: National Economic and Social Development Board, Office of the Prime Minister.

———. 1981, 1996. *The Eighth Economic and Social Development Plan (1997–2001)*, Bangkok: National Economic and Social Development Board, Office of the Prime Minister.

———. 2001. *The Ninth Economic and Social Development Plan (2002–2006)*, Bangkok: National Economic and Social Development Board, Office of the Prime Minister.

Nalinee Tantuvanit et al. 1999. 'Wiwatthanakan Chum Chon Ae-at lae Ongkon Chumchom Ae-at nai Muang. Koranisuksa Krungthep Mahanakorn'

(The Development of Crowd Communities and Communities Organizations in the City: A Case Study of Bangkok), in Akin Rabibhadana (ed.), *Chumchon Ae-at Ong Kwam Ru kap Kwam Pen Jing* (Crowded Community: Body of Knowledge and Reality), Bangkok: Thailand Research Fund.

Nalinee Tantuvanit et al. 2000. *Klongkarn Vijai lae Patibatkarn Ruang Pattana Chumchon Ae Aut lae Ongkorn Chumchon nai Muang: Koranee Suksa Chum Chon Nang Lerng* (Urban Slum Community Development and Slum Organizations: An Action Research Project), Bangkok: Urban Community Development Foundation, Crown Property Bureau.

Napas Sirisamphand. 1994. *Raeng Ngan ti Took Bod Bang: Pu Ying nau Pak Sethakij Nok Rabob* (Hidden Labour: Women in the Informal Sector), Bangkok: Edison Press Products.

———. 1997. *Sawasdikarn Sangkhom pua Satree nai Pak Sethakij Nok Rabob nai Prathes Thai* (Social Welfare for Women in the Informal Economy), Bangkok: Edison Press Products.

Napas Sirsamphand and Christina Szanton. 1986. *Thailand's Street Food Vending: The Sellers and Consumers of 'Traditional Fast Foods'*, Bangkok: Social Research Institute, Chulalongkorn University.

Narong Petchprasert (ed.). 1998. *Khon Jon Thai nai Pava Vikrit*, Bangkok: Political Economy Center, Chulalongkorn University.

Narumol Nirathron. 1996. 'Homeworkers in Two Urban Poor Communities of Thailand', in Narumol Nirathron (ed.), *Practical Actions for the Social Protection of Homeworkers in Thailand*, pp. 94–110, Bangkok: International Lobour Office.

———. 1997. 'Plight of Women Homeworkers', in Virada Somswadi and Sally Theobald (eds), *Women, Gender Relations and Development in Thai Society*, pp. 163–86, Chiangmai: Ming Muang Navarat.

Nathanon Thavisin. 2001. *Bangkok Bangkok*, Bangkok: Conform.

National Statistical Office. Various years. *Labour Force Survey*, Bangkok: United Production.

Neufeldt, Aldred and Alison Albright. 1998. *Disability and Self-directed Employment Business Development Models*, Ottawa: Captus Press.

Nithi Aeuosrivongse. 2000. 'Kuen Thanon kae Kon Dern Tao' (Return the Streets to the Pedestrians), in Nithi Aeuosrivongse (ed.), *Song Na Sang khom Thai* (Two Faces of Thai Society), Bangkok: Amarin Printing and Publishing.

———. 2000. 'Satarana Sombat lae Subpayakorn', in Nithi Aeuosrivongse (ed.), *Kon Jon kab Nayobai Tam Hai Jon Khong Rath* (The Poor and the Poverty-Induced Policy) Bangkok: Amarin Printing and Publishing.

———. 2001. 'O Cha Kafae' (Delicious Coffee), in Nithi Aeuosrivongse (ed.), *Wattanatham Kwam Jon* (Culture of Poverty), Bangkok: Amarin Printing and Publishing.

Niti Kasikosol. 2000–2001. 'Haab Re Pang Loi: Tha Pra Chan' (Street Vending: Tha Prachan), Julasarn Thai Khadi Suksa (Thai Khadi Monograph), 2 (November–January).

Office of Urban Community Development. 1993. 'Karn Tidtam lae Pramernpon Karn Cahisinchua pur Pattana Archip' (The Follow-Up and Evaluation of Occupational Development Loans), National Housing Authority.

Panithee Suksomboon. 2002. 'Krueakai tang Sangkom lae Karn Sawaengha tang Luek kong Maeka' (Social Network and the Searching for Alternatives of Street Vendors), Master of Sociology and Anthropology Thesis, Thammasat University.

Pasuk Phongpaichit and Pradit Charsombat. 1988. *Urban Self-Employment in Thailand: A Study of Two Districts in Bangkok Metropolitan*, New Delhi: ILO.

Pasuk Pongpaichit and C. Baker. 1996. *Sethakij Kammuang Thai Samai Krungthep* (Political Economy of Bangkok Era), Bangkok: O.S. Printing House.

Pawewan Norapallop. 1993. 'Wattanatham Aharn Kong Konthai: Suksa Chapoh Koranee rabob Aharn kong Chumchon Tha Prachan' (Food Culture of the Thai: A Case Study of Food System in Tha Prachan), Master of Sociology and Anthropology Thesis, Thammasat University.

Pawadee Thonguthai. 1996. 'Role of the Informal Service Sector in Urban Poverty Alleviation in Thailand' in Pawadee Thonguthai (ed.), *Role of the Informal Service Sector in Urban Poverty Alleviation*, N.Y.: United Nations.

Pichet Saipun. 1998. '*Chewit Muang: Loakatat ti Prae Plian jak karn Kayai Muang kong Krungthep Mahanakorn*', Julasarn Thai Khadi Suksa (Thai Khadi Monograph), 2 (November–January).

Porphant Ouyyanond. 1996. *Rai Ngan Karnvijai Ruang Parvatsart Sethakij Krungthep* (Research Report on Economic History of Bangkok), Bangkok: National Research Council.

Portes, Alejandro and John Walton. 1981. *Labor, Class and the International System*, New York: Academic Press.

Prachum Suvatti et al. 1980. *Haab Re nai Krungthep Mahanakorn* (Mobile Vendor in Bangkok), Bangkok: Faculty of Applied Statistics, National Institute of Development Administration.

Redclift, Nanneke and Enzo Mingione. 1985. 'Economic Restructuring and Family Practices', in Nanneke Redclift and Enzo Mingione (eds), *Beyond Employment: Household, Gender and Subsistence*, pp. 1–12, New York: Basil Blackwell.

Renu Sungthongjeen. 1991. 'Karn Prakob Acheep kong Raengngan Ying nai Krungthep Mahanakorn' (The Work of Women Workers in Bangkok), Master of Social Work Thesis, Thammasat University.

Ross, David. 2003. 'Clear the Vendors Near World Trade', *Bangkok Post*, 1 August.

Rungsan Thanapornpun. 1986. *Patakata 'Tun Wattanatham'* (Cultural Capital), Bangkok: Sukhum and Son.

Safa, Helen I. 1995. 'Urbanization, the Informal Economy and State Policy in Latin America', in Michale Peter Smith and Joe R. Feagin (eds), *The Capitalist City*, pp. 252–72, Oxford: Basil Blackwell.

Samak Suntaravej. 2003. *Chim Pai Bon Pai* (Taste and Comments), sixth edition, Bangkok: Amarin Printing and Publishing Company.

Scott, MacEwen Alison. 1979. 'Who are the Self-employed?' in Ray Bromley and Chris Gerry (eds), *Casual Work and Poverty in Third World Cities*, pp. 105–32, New York: John Wiley and Sons.

Siripunya Tungkasamit. 1995. 'Karn Chadkarn dan Karn Jad Rabieb Haabre Paeng Loy kong Krungthep Mahanakorn : Punha lae Naewtang Kaekai' (The Organization of Bangkok Street Vendors: Problems and Solutions), Master Thesis, Krirk University.

Skinner, G. William. 1957. *Chinese Society in Thailand: An Analytical History*, New York: Cornell University Press.

Smart, Josephine. 1989. *The Political Economy of Street Hawkers in Hong Kong*, Hong Kong: Centre of Asian Studies.

Smith, Joan and E. Wallerstein. 1992. *Creating and Transforming Households*, Cambridge: Cambridge University Press.

Sombat Plainoi. 2001. *Chewit Tam Klong* (Life Along the Canal), fourth edition, Bangkok: Saitarn Printing.

Sompong Patpui. 1984. *Sapap Sithi Kong Slum: Mong Jak Ngae Sethakij, Sangkhom lae Karn Pattana* (Rights Situation of Slum: Economics, Social and Development Perspectives). Bangkok: Thai Khadi Institute and The Foundation and The Foundation for the Promotion of Social Sciences and Humanities Textbooks Project.

Suntaree Komin. 1995. 'Changes in Social Values in the Thai Society and Economy: A Post-Industrialization Scenario', in Medhi Krongkaew (ed.), *Thailand's Industrialization and Its Consequences*, pp. 251–66, London: St. Martin's Press.

Suthon Sukpisit. 2003. 'Alanka Aharn Thai' (The Magnificent Thai Food), *Post Today*, 13 February: C2.

———. 2003. 'Franchise, Traditional Style', *Bangkok Post*, 20 July: 5.

Tinker, Irene. 1997. *Street Foods*, New York: Oxford.

Titinop Komolnimi and Chatree Leesiriwit. 2003. 'Mong Puying kab Aharn Pan Mummong Satree Niyom' (Women and Food: A View from Feminism), Bangkok: Independent Women Studies Group, Thammasat University.

Teilhet-Waldorf, Saral. 1978. 'Self-employed in a Bangkok Neighborhood: An Anthropolical Study of an Informal Sector', Ph.D. Dissertation, University of New York.

'Vendors Moved Out of the Extortion Claim', *Bangkok Post*, 24 July: 2.

Vichanya Bamroongchon. 1998. 'Karn Mee Suan Chuay Sanubsanun Chumchon Muang Kong Kijjakam Tang Sethakij Nokrabob nai Ket Krungthep Channai kong Krungthep mahanakorn: Koranee Suksa Haabre Pangloy nai Khet Pathumwan, Bangrak, Rajthewee and Phyatai' (The Role of Informal Economy Activities in the Support of Urban Community in Inner Bangkok: A Case Study of Street Vendors in Pathumwan, Bangrak, Rajthewee and Phyatai Districts), Master of Regional and Urban Planning Thesis, King Mongkut Institute of Technology.

Vichitr Rawiwongse, Vilaiwaj Krisanaputi and Pradit Silabutr. 2003. *Satanakam Kon Jon lae Karn Kaekai Punha Kon Jon nai Pava Viklit* (Situation of the Poor and the Solving of the Problems of the Poor in the Time of Economic Crisis), Bangkok: Thailand Research Fund.

Van Esterik, Penny. 1992. 'From Marco Polo to Mc Donald's: Thai Cuisine in Transition', *Food and Foodways*, 5(2): 177–93.

Voravit Charoenloet. 1994. 'Utsahakam karn Palit Sua Pa Samret Roop Hong Thaew : Koraness Suksa ruang Raeng Ngan Nok Rabob nai Krung Thap' (Ready-To-Wear Manufacturing Shophouse: A Case Study of Labor in the Informal Sector in Bangkok), *Pu tai* Special Edition (November).

Wancharoen, Supoj. 2003. '70 Food Stalls Forced to Move as City Spruces Up for Apec Forum', *Bangkok Post*, 29 July: 2.

Winarno, F. G., and A. Allain. 1998. 'Street Foods in Developing Countries: Lessons from Asia', Available at http://www.fao.org/decrep/U3550t/u3550t08.htm.

Yasmeen, Gisele. 1996. 'Bangkok's Foodscape: Public Eating, Gender Relations and Urban Change', Doctoral thesis, the Faculty of Graduate Studies, The University of British Columbia.

Yasmeen, Gisele. 2000. 'Not "From Scratch" Thai Food Systems and "Public Eating"' *Journal of Intercultural Studies*, 21(3): 341–52.

———. 2001. 'Stockbrokers Turned Sandwich Vendors: The Economic Crisis and Small-Scale Food Retailing in Southeast Asia', *Geoforum* 32(1): 91–102.

Yee, Kenny and Catherine Gordon. 1993. *Thai Hawker Food*. Bangkok: Cliver Wing.

Yunus, Muhammad. 1998. 'Poverty Alleviation: Is Economics Any Help? Lessons From the Grameen Bank Experience', *Journal of International Affairs*, 52(2): 47–65.

# 8

## Street Trading Trends in Africa: A Critical Review*

Caroline Skinner

Despite the advances in modern retailing, millions of people throughout Africa still make their living partly or wholly through selling goods on the streets. A vibrant array of traders selling everything from fruit and vegetables, to clothes, to traditional medicine and even furniture is what characterises African cities. This chapter outlines broad trends about these activities on the continent. It critically analyses what is known about this phenomenon with a view to help frame future research.

The chapter first reviews urbanisation, migration and economic development trends. The little data about street traders that is available is reflected. The evidence suggests that there has been a surge in numbers of street traders, partly caused by economic restructuring processes, and that this is likely to continue. Trends in policy, planning and governance are then critically analysed. Research on the issue suggests that state responses to street trading form a continuum from violent sustained evictions to an inclusive approach, but that an inclusive approach is rare. What is clear from this is that the processes of incorporation or exclusion of street traders are part of everyday political struggle. The ways in which street traders are organised, articulate their concerns and wield power, are therefore critical. The next section thus focuses on trends in street traders' organisations. Although there are promising examples of street traders' organisations, existing

* This chapter is a summary version of a longer paper commissioned by the research and advocacy network Women in Informal Employment: Globalising and Organising (WIEGO). The paper can be downloaded from www.wiego.org. I would like to thank them for their support and Judith Shier for her assistance in finding literature.

evidence suggests that many traders are not part of such organisations. The conclusion makes the case for including street traders into urban planning and then identifies priority policy and advocacy research gaps.

This chapter draws on a substantial review of the literature. As will be detailed later, there have been studies on street trading in West Africa (Senegal, Guinea-Bissau, Ivory Coast, and Ghana); Central Africa (the Democratic Republic of Congo); Sub-Saharan Africa (Zambia, Zimbabwe, South Africa, Lesotho) and East Africa (Tanzania, Kenya). This leaves substantial regions in the continent un- and under-explored. The most striking gap is the absence of research on North Africa. Also, no research was found on street trading in Africa's biggest economy, Nigeria. The literature search was confined to research written in English and there is thus a bias towards Anglophone experiences. The broad trends identified need to be qualified by these biases.

## Street Trader Trends over Time

In Africa the informal sector as a whole is estimated to account for 60 per cent of all urban jobs and over 90 per cent of all new urban jobs. After home-working, street trading is estimated to account for the largest share of these jobs (Charmes 2000). Trends in street trading over time are integrally linked to urbanisation, migration and economic development processes. Therefore, before reflecting on what data there is, each of these will be considered in turn.

As Mitullah (1991: 16) notes, urbanisation in African countries is a relatively recent phenomenon except for West Africa and some coastal East African towns. Table 8.1 presents urbanisation figures in 1995 and 2007 as well as projected urban growth rates for 2005–10.

Despite the fact that, for the first time in history, in 2008 one in every two people lived in urban areas, overall urbanisation in Africa is lower than in Asia and in Latin America and the Caribbean. What, however, is clear from the table is that there are significant regional differences within Africa. North and Southern Africa are highly urbanised in contrast to, for example, East Africa. Further, there are increases over time. In the space of 12 years—a relatively short period in demographic time—the percentage of the total population that is urban has increased by 5 per cent. Again there are regional differences with increases in urbanisation figures being particularly pronounced in Middle, East and West Africa. The final column of the table uses current figures to project the urban growth rate. These predictions suggest that urbanisation processes in Africa will proceed faster than on other continents. Due to low barriers to entry,

**Table 8.1**
**Percentage of Total Urban Population**

|  | 1995 | 2007 | Urban Growth Rate 2005–10 |
|---|---|---|---|
| Latin America and the Caribbean | 74 | 78 | 1.7 |
| Asia | 35 | 41 | 2.4 |
| Africa | 34 | 39 | 3.2 |
| Eastern Africa | 22 | 23 | 3.7 |
| Middle Africa | 33 | 41 | 4.1 |
| Northern Africa | 46 | 52 | 2.6 |
| Southern Africa | 48 | 57 | 1.0 |
| Western Africa | 37 | 44 | 3.7 |

*Source:* United Nations, 1997, 'State of the World Population 1997, Reproductive Rights and Reproductive Health', available at www.unfpa.org/swp/1997/swpmain.htm; United Nations, 2007, 'State of the World Population 2007, Unleashing the Potential of Urban Growth', available at www.unfpa.org/swp/2007/presskit/pdf/sowp2007_eng.pdf.

newcomers to the city often opt for street trading as a way of surviving. These figures seem to suggest that the current congestion on the streets is likely to intensify.

A further dimension of urbanisation processes that swells the number of street traders is international migration. As Landau (2007: 61) points out, 'international migration is an inexorable response to regional economic inequalities'. Not only are there significant inequalities between African countries, but Africa has long been the site of a number of political crises and civil wars. Somalia, Liberia, Sierra Leone, the Democratic Republic of Congo, Rwanda, Burundi, Ethiopia, and Eritrea have generated high levels of forced migration. More recently, issues in the Darfur region as well as Zimbabwe are generating flows of migration both within Africa and elsewhere. In a continent where there is large-scale unemployment and under-employment, the trend is for migration legislation to be designed to protect locals from competition for jobs. Foreign migrants, like their rural counterparts, often have no choice but to work in segments of the economy where barriers to entry and set-up costs are low. Street trading is thus what many foreign migrants opt to do. Another group of foreigners involved in street trading are cross-border traders. Again this is an activity that has been going on for some time. Lonrenco-Lindell (2004: 87) points out that Dyulas—West African cross-border traders—have been active for centuries and that for many villages they are the primary source of supplies. Cross-border traders either supply domestic street traders or sell their goods directly to consumers (see Peberdy [2000] for one of the few surveys of this group). Given that foreign migrants are seldom in the recipient coun-tries with appropriate documentation, they are an extremely difficult group to gather statistics on.

A critical factor in increasing the numbers of street traders in Africa was the Structural Adjustment Programmes (SAPs) of the 1980s and 1990s. As has been discussed in detail elsewhere (see, among others, Iyenda 2001; Freund 2007; Lonrenco-Lindell 2004; Tsitsi and Agatha 2000), the cocktail of privatisation, restructuring of the public sector and the opening up of African economies to foreign goods, led to a dramatic shrinking of the formal economy in Africa. This resulted in a substantial increase in the numbers of those informally employed. Structural Adjustment Programmes, however, often encouraged a more tolerant attitude to the informal economy, particularly, for example, in the former socialist states. Lonrenco-Lindell (2004) details this for Guinea-Bissau and Nnkya (2006) for Tanzania.

Ongoing privatisation and liberalisation efforts on the continent continue to impact on the size, nature and dynamics within the informal economy, in general, and street trading in particular. Consider, for example, the implications on gender dynamics of the increase in numbers of those working informally. Although often more dominant in terms of numbers, in many countries, women tend to predominate in areas of trade which are less lucrative. With greater competition, there is evidence that either women get displaced or forced into even more marginal areas of trade (see, for example, Tranberg Hansen [2004: 72] on street traders in Zambia). The combination of greater competition among informal traders and a shrinking demand for goods due to shrinking economies, has led to individual incomes decreasing.

The implications of trade liberalisation for informal traders are also complex. Liberalisation of African economies has led to an increase of imports with the final point of sale for many of these goods being informal traders. This has become particularly pronounced with the dramatic increase in imports from China to Africa over the last 10 years.[1] The greater availability of a diverse range of goods can be positive for informal traders. But trade liberalisation has often had devastating impacts on local industry. Baden and Barber (2005), for example, reflect on the impact of the second-hand clothes trade on local clothing manufacturing in West Africa. This has not only led to job losses, especially for women, but also a shrinking customer base for informal trade. The overall welfare implications of recent economic policies for this segment of the informal economy require further interrogation.

The combination of urbanisation, migration and economic development trends suggests that there has been a rapid increase in the numbers of street traders operating on the streets of African cities.

As the International Labour Organisation's (ILO) (2002: 51) compilation of informal economy statistics outlines, despite the numbers and visibility of street traders, there are few good estimates of the number of traders. Many population censuses and labour force surveys do not contain a question on 'place of work' with relevant alternative responses. Over and above this, however, street trade is inherently difficult to measure. As the report notes, there is a great variance in the number of street vendors counted depending on the time of day, day of the week, time of month or the season of the year. It is noted (2002: 51) that

> The number of vendors can fluctuate from one season to the next, one day to the next, and even during a single day. This is because some vendors only sell in the morning, afternoon or evening; and others sell only during certain seasons. Some may move from one location to another during the day, appearing to settle at each; while others may change what they sell from one season, month or day to another.

A further complicating factor is that the same vendor family or unit may have several different stalls at the same market or in different markets.

Despite these problems the ILO managed to pull together estimates for selected countries. Using this data Table 8.2 represents street vendors in the African countries for which data was available and Table 8.3, the size and contribution of informal trade and women traders in informal trade. Unfortunately, there is no time series data.

**Table 8.2**
**Street Vendors in Selected African Countries**

|  | Number of Street Vendors | Percentage of the Non-Agricultural Labour Force | Percentage of Women |
|---|---|---|---|
| Tunisia (1997) | 125619 | 6 | 2 |
| Benin (1992) | 45591 | 5 | 81 |
| Kenya (1999) | 416294 | 8 | 33 |

Source: ILO, 2002, *Women and Men in the Informal Economy: A Statistical Picture*, International Labour Office, Geneva, p. 52.

As is clear from Table 8.3, informal traders in the African countries for which data is available contribute between 85 and 99 per cent of total employment in trade and between 46 and 70 per cent of total value added

Table 8.3
Size and Contribution of Informal Sector in Trade and Women
Traders in Informal Trade

| | Informal Sector as a Share of | | Female Informal Traders as a Share of | |
|---|---|---|---|---|
| | Total Trade Employment | Total Trade Value Added | Total Informal Trade Employment | Total Informal Trade Value Added |
| Benin | 99 | 70 | 92 | 64 |
| Burkina Faso | 95 | 46 | 66 | 30 |
| Chad | 99 | 67 | 62 | 41 |
| Kenya | 85 | 62 | 50 | 27 |
| Mali | 98 | 57 | 81 | 46 |
| Tunisia | 88 | 56 | 8 | 4 |

Source: ILO, 2002, *Women and Men in the Informal Economy: A Statistical Picture*, International Labour Office, Geneva, p. 53.

in trade. In most African countries, other than North African Muslim countries, women represent at least 50 per cent, if not more, of the total number of traders. In the matrilineal societies of West Africa there is a long-standing tradition of informal markets largely controlled by women (see Charmes 2000; Lyons and Snoxell 2005a: 1308; Mitullah 1991: 14, among others). Adiko and Anoh Kouassi (2003), in their survey of over 1,700 market and street vendors in Ivory Coast, for example, found that over 70 per cent of traders were women. Although there are regional differences, there appears to be a trend of women selling food products and men selling non-food products, which are often more lucrative.

While national data on street vending is scarce, city-level statistics are even rarer. The sample sizes of national data like labour force surveys in resource-constrained African countries are not, in most cases, large enough to be disaggregated to city level with any level of accuracy. Given the trend of increasing decentralisation of tasks to a local level, it is increasingly important for planning purposes for local authorities to be aware not only of the number of street traders but also their demographics and contribution to local economies. Some cities, however, have commissioned street trading censuses. For example, in 1997 the Durban City Council commissioned a survey and census of street trading in the metropolitan area (Lund 1998). There is an interesting initiative in Nairobi where a trader organisation, with the help of local academics and support agencies, has conducted its own census of numbers of street traders (Kamunyori 2007: 51). There are likely to be lessons to be learned from such initiatives.

The evidence suggests that street trading employs large numbers of people and, in many contexts, a disproportionate number of women.

Although there is no time series data, urbanisation and economic development trends suggest that their numbers have increased over time. With the global financial crisis this is likely to continue.

## Policy, Planning and Governance Trends

The coordinator of the international alliance of street vending organisations, who has substantial direct experience of city policies and street trading across Africa warns:

> There are no policy best practises with street trading. Where there have been windows where better practises emerge, there tends to be a continuity problem. There is a change in the bureaucracy, a big event or an election, and the approach changes. . . . With street vending things are particularly fluid. (Interview, 16 April 2007)

Mindful of the dynamism of state responses to street trading, this section reviews policy planning and governance trends.

There is substantial evidence of large-scale sustained evictions of street traders. Possibly the largest and most violent eviction of street traders in the continent in the last decade was in Zimbabwe in May 2005—Operation Murambatsvina.[2] Street traders and those living in informal housing were targeted. The UN Habitat mission to Zimbabwe estimated that some 700,000 people in cities across the country lost either their homes, their source of livelihood or both (Tibaijuka 2005: 7). Sites where informal sector workers gathered to market their wares, as well as formal markets, some of which had been in operation for decades, were targeted. Potts (2007: 265) estimates that in Harare alone 75,000 vendors were unable to work from late May 2005. A local civil society support group described the impact of Operation Murambatsvina on street traders as follows:

> The Government, under the auspices of the Ministry of Small and Medium Enterprises Development, began by arresting 20,000 vendors countrywide, destroying their vending sites, and confiscating their wares. Thousands more escaped arrest, but have lost their livelihoods. This process took one week in the first instance. Harare was among the worst affected cities: police action was brutal and unannounced. . . . Vendors, who have been operating in the same places without complaint or interference for their entire working lives, were confronted with riot squads without any warning, were rounded up, arrested, and watched helplessly while their source of livelihood was destroyed. Within days, bulldozers have moved in to take away remains.[3]

In explaining these events many analysts have pointed to the fact that since 2000 the urban electorate had voted overwhelmingly for the opposition—the Movement for Democratic Change (MDC). Since Tibaijuka (2005) estimates that one in every five Zimbabweans were affected by Operation Marumbatsvina and thus not only MDC supports were affected, political affiliations, although critical, are only one part of the rationale behind these actions.

Although not on the scale of Zimbabwe there are other cases of widespread evictions. Tranberg Hansen (2004: 66–67), in her study of street traders in Zambia, notes how in April 1999

> council workers, police and paramilitary in riot gear razed the temporary market structures of Lusaka's city centre, extending the demolition the following night and weeks all across the city, into townships and residential areas. . . . In June, similar operations took place on the Copperbelt and in the towns along the line-of-rail.

Tranberg Hansen identifies a leadership change in the local authority as a key reason for the evictions. She notes (2004: 68) that a new mayor and council members had come to office in Lusaka and they were 'bent on cleaning up the capital'. In a Ghanaian context, King (2006) reflects a similar finding. She argues that the new system of decentralisation where there are more frequent changes in local authorities leads to evictions of street traders which is seen as 'a common way to impress the public' (2006: 117).

There are a number of historical cases where national governments have established systems of trader repression. In South Africa the apartheid state's complex web of national and local laws effectively banned street trading. Rogerson and Hart (1989: 32) argued that South African urban authorities 'fashioned and refined some of the most sophisticated sets of anti street trader measures anywhere in the developing world'. This, however, was in a context of high levels of unemployment and poverty so traders continued to attempt to operate. They were consistently harassed and periodically violently removed. Rogerson and Hart (1989: 32) point out that until the early 1980s hawkers in South Africa were subject to 'a well-entrenched tradition of repression, persecution and prosecution'. Treatment in socialist states was equally harsh. In Tanzania, Nnkya (2006) relays how in the mid-1970s the Tanzanian government rounded up street traders operating in Dar es Salaam and forcibly removed them to villages on the coast. In 1983 a penal code was enacted that branded all self-employed people as 'unproductive, idle and disorderly' (Nnkya 2006: 82). These actions were justified on the basis that street trading was a subversive activity that challenged socialist principles. Lonrenco-Lindell (2004) describes a similar situation in newly independent Guinea-Bissau.

Sporadic evictions of street traders often precede major public events. In Maseru, Lesotho Setsabi (2006) lists the many times street traders were removed—in 1988 when Pope John Paul II visited the city, in 1991 when President Nujoma from Nambia came on a state visit, and street traders were also threatened with eviction when President Mandela came in 1995. In this last case the street traders diverted the action by agreeing to clean the streets. In Zimbabwe, Potts (2007: 270) notes that street traders were removed just before Harare hosted the Non-Aligned Movement in 1984. There are already cases of street traders being removed in South Africa ahead of the 2010 Soccer World Cup (www.streetnet. org). Bromley (2000), drawing on over two-and-a-half decades of related research and international policy in his review of street trading, confirms this as an international trend. He (2000: 12) notes, 'Aggressive policing (of street traders) is particularly notable just before major public and tourist events, on the assumption that orderly streets improve the image of the city to visitors'.

Ongoing and low-level harassment of informal traders is pervasive across African cities. Lonrenco-Lindell (2004) outlines that in Bissau, although a more permissive approach has been adopted since the SAP of 1986, municipal agents have essentially remained hostile to them. In surveys street traders cite that they are frequently forced to pay bribes, complaining of the 'oppressiveness and arbitrariness of public agents' (2004: 94–95). Of the 355 street traders interviewed in Abidjan in Adiko and Anoh Kouassi's study, 69 per cent feared being chased off their current site (2003: 55). A group that is particularly vulnerable to this are foreign street traders. Hunter and Skinner's (2003) survey of foreign street traders operating in Durban, South Africa, for example, found that they frequently reported that the police elicited bribes. Few of these foreigners have proper documentation, nor do they have access to bank accounts, and are thus easy targets. Kamunyori (2007: 33) reports that in Nairobi the council inspectors make several times their monthly salaries on bribing street traders. She records the monthly salary of these so-called 'askaris' as approximately US$50. This points to a more systemic problem; until local officials in African cities are better paid this kind of corruption will be difficult to root out.

There are, however, a few examples where street traders have been accommodated. In Dar es Salaam, Tanzania, by the early 1990s street traders had been issued licenses and were allowed to operate. Nnkya (2006: 88) states that 'street trading in the central business district (CBD) is well managed and trader associations have good relations with the city authorities'. Nnkya (2006) identifies the 1992 Sustainable Dar es Salaam Project (SDP) as a turning point from the state's previous approach of trader repression. This project, a collaboration between United Nations agencies and the state, identified petty trading as a key issue. By the mid-1990s, as a direct consequence of the SDP, a Working Group on Managing Informal Micro-Trade was established. This group identified constraints street traders faced and made numerous recommendations. A consequence of the SDP was the Guidelines for Petty Trade adopted by the City Commission in 1997 which set out the framework for managing street trade. Nnkya does, however, point out that there are implementation inconsistencies—with management being haphazard in parts—and that while some are included, others (most notably women traders) are not, particularly in the more lucrative trading sites in the CBD. In comparison to many other cities in Africa overall, he argues, Dar es Salaam has created an enabling environment for street traders.

The other case that has been cited as a better practice in the management of street trading is Durban, South Africa. In the last years of apartheid the South African government adopted a more tolerant approach to the informal economy. During the transition to democracy the 1991 Business Act was promulgated. This legislation disallowed local authorities from restricting street trading. This led to a dramatic increase in these activities in all South African cities and towns. Although during the 1990s a range of legislative measures were introduced that allowed regulation, local authorities were forced to grapple with the new reality of street traders.

Although there has been recent harassment of traders in Durban, there was a period when Durban's approach was identified as particularly progressive. A particularly innovative approach has been adopted in the inner-city district that contains the main transport node—the Warwick Junction. On an average day the area is estimated to accommodate 460,000 commuters, and at least 5,000 street traders. In 1996 the city council launched an area-based urban renewal initiative. In careful consultation with traders, trader infrastructure was established. For example, nearly 1,000 traditional medicine traders were accommodated in a new market and corn-on-the-cob sellers and those cooking and selling the Zulu delicacy, bovine heads, were provided tailor-made facilities. Through this, the project piloted an economically informed, sector by sector approach to supporting street traders. In parallel with infrastructure development there was a focus on improving management of the area. The area-based team established a number of operations teams to deal with issues as diverse as curbside cleaning, ablution facilities, childcare facilities and pavement sleeping. In 2001 the local authority in the city—the eThekwini Municipality—adopted an Informal Economy Policy. This policy acknowledges the informal economy as an important component of the city's economy and, drawing on some of the lessons learned from the Warwick Junction Project, suggests a number of management and support interventions. This was an attempt to standardise a progressive approach across the city. Like Dar es Salaam, the approach developed suggests that inclusive approaches to design, planning and management of public space for street traders are possible.

With respect to local-level planning, facilities, licences and user fees are particularly important to traders. Facilities created for street traders indicate the extent to which they are incorporated into urban plans. Street traders need shelter from the elements, places to store their goods and ablution facilities. In many of the countries for which there is information there seems to be an approach of building markets in which to house traders. Although street traders are often desperate for facilities, local authorities, in locating these markets, pay scant attention to the importance of foot traffic. Tranberg Hansen outlines how the local authority in Lusaka built a city market which opened in 1997 and, for this reason, many years later remains empty. There is much more of a tradition of markets in West Africa. Lyons and Snoxell (2005a) in their study of markets in Dakar, Senegal and Accra, Ghana point to more successful municipal efforts to provide and manage market space.

Case study evidence seems to suggest that licences can be used either as an inclusionary or exclusionary tool. Licensing street trading gives them the right to operate. If traders are to have a securer livelihood and invest both in their economic activities and their trading areas, security of tenure is critical. Licensing and site allocation are key components in better management of public spaces. The critical issue, however, is how many licences as a proportion of the total number of traders are issued. Lyons and Snoxell (2005b: 1078) suggest that in Nairobi, Kenya there were 7,000 licences and formal sites even though it was estimated that there were 500,000 street traders operating in the city. Given that in many African countries demand is constrained, there is a direct trade off between the numbers of licenses and sites allocated and individual earnings of traders. There are very few examples of cities making careful calculations of the carrying capacity of streets.

A related issue is how much traders pay for access to public space. In many contexts, particularly in West African countries, fees charged to street and market traders are a key revenue stream for the state. Adiko and Anoh Kouassi's (2003: 58) survey in the Ivory Coast outlines the numerous taxes and fees traders are subject to. In Ghana, King (2006: 117) finds that a significant proportion of total metropolitan revenue in Kumasi comes from trader fees. In East Africa while traders are being accused of being tax evaders in Tanzania (Nnkya 2006: 89), traders in Nairobi have used tax as a bargaining tool. The Nairobi Informal Sector Consultative Forum (Kamunyori 2007: 17) has argued that street vendors would be willing to pay taxes in return for guaranteed services (or at least the right to demand them). This has been key to establishing more cooperative relations between traders, formal business and municipal authorities in this city.

## Understanding Processes of Exclusion and Inclusion of Street Traders

In making sense of the trends identified earlier, city development and urban planning paradigms are critical. Each of these is considered in turn.

Kamunyori (2007: 11) points out that there is a tension between modernisation of African cites and what are often perceived as 'non-modern' activities like street trading. This issue of how street traders are perceived reoccurs. In the case of violent removal of street traders in Zambia, Tranberg Hansen (2004: 70) points out that these actions were condoned by the national government who argued that the presence of street traders was discouraging international investors. Further, as previously noted, street traders are often removed prior to international events as part of city 'beautification' processes. As Bromley (2000: 12) argues, there is a widely held view that street trading is 'a manifestation of both poverty and under-development', thus 'its disappearance is viewed as progress'.

This is connected to the focus in urban studies, policy and practise on 'world class' cities. Beaverstock, Taylor and Smith's work (2002) is a classic text in this literature. They establish a roster of world cities. In their analysis mention is made of only one African city—Johannesburg. As Robinson (2002: 563) outlines, the notion of 'world' or 'global' cities has the effect of 'dropping most cities in the world from vision'. The position and functioning of cities in the world economy thus becomes the dominant factor in urban economic development planning. The implicit economic development policy prescriptions are that international investment should be pursued above all else. Informal activities, like street vending, in this paradigm, are seen as undesirable and their contribution to local economies is not recognised. Robinson (2002: 531) argues that the notion of world class cities imposes 'substantial limitations on imagining or planning the futures of cities'. This is particularly the case in the developing world.

Urban planning traditions play an important role in shaping local authority responses to these issues. Freund (2007: 156), in his reflections on post-colonial African cities, argues that planning ordinances and decrees often show little real variation from colonial patterns. This lies at the heart of more nuanced analyses of the rationale behind Operation Murambatsvina. Potts (2007) details how colonial approaches extended on into the post-colonial period. She demonstrates that there was a long history of anti-informality sentiments in both national and local governments. She (2007: 267–68) notes that although street traders were present, they were 'very contained and on a minor scale *in comparison with* the bustle and competitive selling of goods and services so typical of cities from Luanda to Kinshasa to Lagos to Dakar'. She argues (2007: 283) that the 'adherence to the ideology of planned and orderly cities remained a core belief for many'. This combined with anger against the urban electorate was a fertile field for those who always desired urban 'order' to gain ground. In many other countries colonial laws remain in place. Tranberg Hansen (2004: 63) in the case of Zambia, for example, states that 'post colonial regulations on markets, trading licensing, town and country planning and public health restricted trading . . . to established markets'. Kamunyori (2007: 10) points out that in Nairobi, although street trading is legal according to the city by-laws, the colonial era General Nuisance by-law is used to supersede this provision. The General Nuisance by-law allows city officials to arrest any individual that they deem to be 'creating a "general nuisance" in public spaces'.

Adopting new approaches to urban planning is common to the more inclusionary practices cited here. In Tanzania the 1992 Sustainable Dar es Salaam project stemmed from an invitation by the state to the United Nations Development Programme to review the Dar es Salaam Master Plan. As Nnkya (2006: 83) notes, instead, the UN staff persuaded the city council to pursue a new approach to planning, based on participatory or collaborative principles.

The results from a project documenting the lessons learned from Warwick Junction suggest that participation was central to the project's success (Dobson and Skinner forthcoming). A street trader leader described the council's staff approach as affording 'informal traders the opportunity to participate on a sustained and continuous basis in negotiations about their needs and priorities . . . in a low-key way, often on an issue-by-issue basis' (Horn 2004: 211). Skinner and Dobson (2007) argue that consultation dissipated conflict, facilitated interventions genuinely informed by user needs and led to users having a sense of ownership of the area. This, in turn, led to high levels of volunteerism that resolved a number of urban management issues like crime and cleaning. These are good examples of what Healey (1998) would describe as planning by multi-stakeholder collaboration and planning by negotiation and contract. The dynamism of street vending lends itself to this style of management. Sandercock's (1998: 30) arguments, although reflecting largely on contexts in the north, are applicable to the challenges of planning in developing country contexts. She argues for the need to develop a new kind of multicultural literacy which she explains as follows:

> An essential part of that literacy is familiarity with the multiple histories of urban communities, especially as those histories intersect with struggles over space and place claiming, with planning policies and resistances to them, with traditions of indigenous planning and with questions of belonging and identity and acceptance of difference.

## Trends in Organising among Street Traders

Where traders have been incorporated into urban plans, traders tend to be well-organised. Nnkya (2006) identifies this as a factor in Dar es Salaam. He (2006: 84) points out that by 1997, about 240 self-help groups representing 16,000 members had been formed, 'enabling traders collectively to address problems and access services'. There is an umbrella organisation—the Association of Small Scale Businesses—which 'acts as a lobbyist and pressure group and is involved in the selection of public space for business activities'.[4] In Durban, street traders were well-organised during the redevelopment of the Warwick Junction area. Traders were organised into product groups and block committees (Dobson and Skinner forthcoming). The Self Employed Women's Union (a sister to the much larger Self Employed Women's Association in India), was also very active in the area (Devenish and Skinner 2006). In both cases this meant that there were negotiating partners for local authorities.

Unfortunately, existing information on street trader organisation is patchy. The research that is available suggests that many traders are not affiliated to any organisation at all. Where trader organisations do exist, they focus on one or more of three concerns—financial services, lobbying and advocacy, particularly at a local level and on product-specific issues. The role of trade unions appears to be increasingly important. Concerns about the internal organisational dynamics have also been raised. Each of these issues is considered in turn with a focus where possible on regional trends.

There is some evidence that organisation densities among street traders are low. Lund's (1998: 33–34) re-analysis of data in South Africa, for example, found that in the two large surveys of street traders that had been conducted, in Johannesburg 15 per cent of traders reported belonging to an association, while in Durban 12 per cent of the men and 16 per cent of the women traders were members of associations. Alilo and Mitullah's (2000) interviews with over 300 street traders operating in four different Kenyan cities found that 67 per cent had no knowledge of associations that addressed street vending issues (2000: 18). More recently, in Nairobi there has been the formation of the Nairobi Informal Sector Confederation (NISCOF). According to Kamunyori (2007: 14–15) NISCOF was re-gistered in 2005 and as of 2007 had 23 member associations representing approximately 15,000 individual traders. Although this is a positive develop-ment, Lyons and Snoxell (2005b: 1078) suggest there may be as many as 500,000 street traders operating in the city. The Nairobi Informal Sector Confederation thus represents 3 per cent of the total number of traders.

There is evidence of a high prevalence of rotating savings and credit associations (ROSCAs). As is the case in other parts of the world, through these, members deposit a mutually agreed sum with the group at regular intervals. Each member has a turn to receive the total money collected. Some ROSCAs also provide loans to their members. As Lyon and Snoxell (2005a: 1089) note, this guarantees the periodic availability of a capital sum through peer pressure to save. Of the 124 traders interviewed in Nairobi in Lyon and Snoxell's (2005b: 1089) study, 58 per cent were part of a ROSCA. They conducted a similar study in two markets in Ghana and found that 49 per cent of 144 traders interviewed were members of a savings group (2005a: 1312).[5] Although not quoting exact figures, Alila and Mitullah (2000: 11) and Tsitsi and Agatha (2000: 10) find a similar situation in Kenya and Zimbabwe respectively. All of these studies note that there is particularly high prevalence of membership of savings groups among women. In the face of poor access to banking services these systems of financial services and support play an important role.

In 2005, War on Want (2006), in collaboration with the Workers Education Association of Zambia conducted research explicitly focused on the organising and advocacy strategies of informal economy associations in Ghana, Malawi, Mozambique, and Zambia. Interviews were conducted with 62 organisations, the majority of which were street or market trader organisations. This research concluded that the majority of organisations were established in specific markets or trading areas and have been dealing with urgent issues arising in these locations, such as harassment from the police and solving disputes and conflicts among vendors. The relationship between organisations and the state was examined and the researchers concluded that street trader organisations largely had confrontational relations with local government (WoW 2006: 31–32). Lund and Skinner's (1999) study of 22 organisations of street traders in five cities in South Africa found that many of them focused on negotiating with local authorities. They were, however, not formally structured and tended to be vocal when issues arose but often difficult to find in-between. These trends were confirmed in more recent studies (Thulare 2004; Motala 2002).

There is evidence to suggest that traders are comparatively well-organised in West Africa. King (2006), for example, reflecting on the situation in Kumasi Ghana, found that trader organisations were well-established and widely respected. She notes that the Market Traders Association—an umbrella group of various product associations—has a representative on the Kumasi Municipal Authority's General Assembly. This association launched a successful challenge in court when the local authority threatened to increase market fees by 300 per cent (King 2006: 108–9). The Ghana Trade Union Congress (GTUC) has had an informal sector desk for many years. In February 2003 the GTUC initiated a national alliance of market and street traders—the StreetNet Ghana Alliance. As of 2006 they had 19 trader associations with a total of 5,810 individuals (War on Want 2006: 36). Adiko and Anoh Kouassi's (2003) study in the Ivory Coast found that organisational membership was high among traders—varying between 36 per cent and 42 per cent of interviewees depending on their location.[6] Traders were members of a range of organisations including unions, cooperatives and ROSCAs.

The research pays less attention to collective action that directly supports the business of trading. In Lund and Skinner's (1999) study they find that a number of street trader organisations in South Africa focus primarily on bulk purchase of goods. War on Want found a number of product-specific trader organisations in Ghana, Malawi and Zambia. They give the example of an organisation of wholesalers that supplies street traders—the banana sellers association. Their primary aim is to ensure regular and adequate supply of the product and to negotiate the terms of trade with the primary suppliers. Although this is not explored in any detail, Adiko and Anoh Kouassi's (2003) study in the Ivory Coast suggests cooperatives have been formed among traders.

Given the decreasing numbers of those formally employed in Africa, there is evidence of trade unions, particularly the national federations, paying increasing attention to organising among the informally employed. These initiatives either entail direct organising efforts, encouraging appropriate affiliates to organise or supporting or expanding on existing organising efforts. In May 2002 the Zimbabwean Congress of Trade Unions (ZCTU) launched an informal sector desk which is tasked with directly organising, among other groups, street traders (Tsitsi and Agatha 2000: 12).[7] The Malawi Congress of Trade Unions assisted in the formation of the Malawi Union for the Informal Sector. This Union has street traders among its members. As previously noted, the Ghana Trade Union Congress has been very actively involved in encouraging its affiliates to organise in the informal economy. The Mozambique trade union federation (OTM) played an important role in forming the Association of Informal Sector Operators and Workers (ASSOTSI). The ASSOTSI has 26 branch committees within 59 markets in Maputo and in 2005 claimed membership of over 40,000 (War on Want 2006: 43). The War on Want research does, however, find that there are often tensions between the national federations and informal worker organisations.

Concerns are raised in this literature about two aspects of internal organisational dynamics—how organisations are constituted and women's roles. War on Want (2006: 30) found that trader associations 'often show low level of participation and leadership accountability'. For example, of the 20 trader organisations interviewed in the Ghana study, nine reported that their method of choosing leadership was by appointment rather than elections (War on Want 2006: 95–96). Lund and Skinner's study (1999) raised a concern about organisations not being formally constituted. At the time of their study there was only one organisation—the Self Employed Women's Union—that had functioning democratic structures and regular elections.[8]

Although members are often predominantly women, the leaders of street trader organisations are often men. This was found in studies of street trader organisations in Malawi, Zambia and Mozambique (War on Want 2006) and in South Africa (Lund and Skinner 1999). For example, in Malawi, of the 16 organisations interviewed, only one had a majority of women in leadership positions (War on Want 2006: 97–98). Lyons and Snoxell's (2005b: 1082) study of markets in Nairobi found that both market committees were comprised entirely of men and that no woman had ever been an official. The opposite, however, held true in Ghana where, of the 33 organisations interviewed, 22 had women in leadership positions. Women seem to play a much more dominant role in leadership positions in markets in the matrilineal societies of West Africa. However, again there are exceptions, particularly in predominantly Muslim states. In Senegal, the Mouride Brotherhood largely controls trading activities and is very politically powerful.

Since its launch in 2002, StreetNet International, an alliance of street trader organisations, is an increasingly important player in street trader organising on the continent. Membership-based organisations directly organising street and market traders are entitled to affiliate to StreetNet. They currently have members not only in Africa but also in Latin America and Asia. One of StreetNet's primary foci is to build the capacity of street trader organisations so as to strengthen their organising and advocacy efforts. This is done through providing direct leadership training, exchange visits which allow sharing of experiences among traders and documenting and disseminating better practices. Another area of activity is assisting with the expansion of organising efforts to the national level. StreetNet was instrumental in the establishment of both the Alliance for Zambia Informal Economy Associations and the formation of the national alliance of trader organisations in Ghana. These kinds of formations will help traders to play a more influential role in policy, particularly at the national level. At an international level, StreetNet advocates for the rights of street traders within international bodies like the International Labour Organisation but also the international trade union federations. Their primary campaign at the moment is the World Class Cities Campaign. This aims to challenge the notion of 'world class' cities and the trend to remove traders when cities host international events. The campaign has started in South Africa in response to the upcoming 2010 Soccer World Cup (www.streetnet.org.za).

The research on street trader organisations thus suggests that many traders are not members of organisations. Given the importance of collective action to inclusive planning, this constitutes a challenge both to existing organisations and trade unions but also to local authorities. Concerns have been raised about the internal dynamics within organisations and who is represented in organisations. Bromley (2000: 14) claims street trader associations 'typically represent older, established and licensed traders'.

## Conclusion and Priorities for Further Research

There are a number of reasons why an inclusive approach to street trading is desirable. Pragmatically, demographic and economic trends indicate that these activities are on the increase, thus street trading is a reality that is unlikely to go away. From a developmental perspective street traders are often responsible for large numbers of dependents. There are also a disproportionate number of women working as street traders. Research demonstrates that women are more likely than men to spend their income on household needs (Levin et al. 1999 demonstrate this for vendors particularly). From a planning perspective, street traders provide urban residents and particularly the urban poor, with goods and services in appropriate quantities and forms, and at times of day and in parts of the city that contribute to the functioning of cities. Economically, although the individual incomes are often low, cumulatively these activities contribute to local economies and to local revenue collection. Inclusive planning, however, does not imply unbridled street trading. Local authorities need to balance the interests of many different stakeholders using public space. Traders themselves report not wanting to work in badly managed environments. Further, as previously noted, given limited consumer demand there is a direct trade off between the number of traders and individual incomes earned. Inclusive policy, planning, urban design and management holds the possibility of not only benefitting traders but enhancing the cityscape.

Informed by this and the review of evidence, a number of priority policy and advocacy research gaps are identified.

It is clear from the section titled 'Street Trader Trends Over Time' in this chapter that very few countries gather statistics on this segment of the labour market and those that do, seldom do so at a city level. For appropriate planning for this group, but also to address negative perceptions about street traders, reliable and regularly updated statistics on the numbers of street traders and their contribution to the economy at a national and local level are critical. In cases where a more developmental approach has been adopted, statistics have often played an important role (see Kamunyori 2007). Given how dynamic this group is, securing accurate estimates will require methodological innovations.

Not only is information needed on the contribution of street traders to local economies but about the economic dynamics of specific segments of the street trading economy. It has been argued elsewhere that given the heterogeneity of the informal economy, policy analysis and documentation should be sectoral (Chen et al. 2002). The same argument holds true for street traders. Although there are problems like harassment by the city officials that all traders face, there also product/trade-specific issues that warrant attention. Traditional medicine traders, for example, face dwindling supplies due to indigenous forests being over-exploited, while supply of second hand clothes is dependent on national tariff regimes. Understanding where different groups of traders fit into broader value chains would identify sector-specific constraints and allow for targeted national and local government policy responses.

The implications of the increased penetration of formal retail for informal livelihoods need to be explored. No studies were found on the impact of formal shopping centre developments on informal retail in the surrounding areas. Greater understanding of the overall welfare implications of these on low-income consumers is critical. Where there are cases where informal traders have been incorporated into these developments, these need to be documented. A dimension of this is that South African and foreign retailers are increasingly establishing themselves throughout Africa. Again little is known about what this means for informal traders.

In response to planning trends, documentation of those cases where cities have included street traders into urban plans, creatively resolved conflicts between different users of public space and developed approaches that have resulted in improved street trader management may help to introduce new possibilities in the minds particularly of spatial planners and urban managers. This would go some way to addressing Robinson's concern about current limits on the city imaginary. Both research, but also literature and art that celebrate the diversity and vibrant dynamic that street traders introduce into cities would go some way in changing perceptions among the general public. This is part of the contribution that Simone (Simone 2004; Simone and Abouhani 2005) and other urban scholars who draw on post-modernism are currently making.

The issue of legal reform has been neglected. Policy often suggests support interventions like microfinance and training. However, if traders do not have security of tenure these interventions can be irrelevant or even destructive. Legal reform and litigation strategies on how best to secure the right to operate and improve working conditions need to be further explored.

Finally, analysis about different organisational forms in response to different contexts may go some way in supporting existing organisations' efforts at collective action. This would be complimented with research on how the state can create an environment conducive to the development of organisations and more constructive street trader–government relations.[9]

Bromley (2000: 22), however, reminds us:

> Pressures on the authorities come from numerous different vendor groups, from a wide range of special interests, and from all sides of the political spectrum. Official responses are diverse, spasmodic, and often contradictory, and their effectiveness is severely constrained by the highly-visible and constantly fluctuating nature of the population involved, and by the operational limitations of a street-level bureaucracy. Policy interventions often have unforeseen consequences, and are rarely implemented consistently. Grand visions and linear causal models are inappropriate, and instead our understanding is likely to be enriched through consideration of interconnections, conflicts, complexity theory and system effects.

## Notes

1. During 1991–2000 China–Africa trade grew more than 700 per cent, albeit starting from a low base. Following the first China–Africa forum in 2000, bilateral trade grew to more than $20 billion over the four years to the end of 2004 (Brown and Lyons, forthcoming). This is estimated to increase to over US$100 billion by 2020 (*Mail and Guardian*, Online 15 June 2007).
2. While government translated this to mean 'Operation Clean-up', the more literal Shona translation of 'murambatsvina' is 'getting rid of the filth' (Potts 2007).
3. http://sokwanele.com/articles/sokwanele/opmuramb_overview_18june2005.html.
4. Unfortunately, he does not detail how the organisation is constituted nor how representative these organisations are, particularly of poorer and women traders.
5. Lyons and Snoxell (2005a) also surveyed a similar number of traders in two markets in Senegal and found only 17 per cent were members of a savings group. The majority of these traders were men. This reinforces again the importance of avoiding any blanket generalisations.
6. It should be noted that a number of traders were reluctant to report their organisational membership.
7. The ZCTU is aligned to the opposition in Zimbabwe. Given the current repression of the opposition it is difficult to get any recent information about, for example, how many informal worker members the ZCTU has organised.
8. This organisation has since closed.
9. StreetNet has started this process. In March 2007 they hosted a meeting in Senegal on collective bargaining and laws and litigation strategies. This meeting was attended by organisations from 14 countries and documented a range of strategies that informal economy organisations can employ to assist their members.

# References

Adiko, A. and P. Anoh Kouassi. 2003. 'Activities and Organisations of Traders on the Markets and Streets of Ivory Coast: A Case Study of Cocody, Treichville, Yopougon Communities and Some Streets in Abidjan'. Abidjan, University of Cocody, Paper Commissioned by Women in Informal Employment: Globalising and Organising.

Alilo, P. and W. Mitullah. 2000. 'Women Street Vendors in Kenya: Policies, Regulations and Organisational Capacities'. Nairobi, Institute for Development Studies, University of Nairobi, Paper Commissioned by Women in Informal Employment: Globalising and Organising.

Baden, S. and C. Barber. 2005. 'The Impact of Second-Hand Clothing Trade on Developing Countries Oxfam International', available at www.maketradefair.com/en/assets/english/shc_0905.pdf.

Beverstock, J., P. Taylor and R. Smith. 2002. 'A Roster of World Cities', *Cities*, 16(6): 445–58.

Bromley, R. 2000. 'Street Vending and Public Policy: A Global Review', *International Journal of Sociology and Social Policy*, 20(1–2): 1–27.

Brown, A. and M. Lyons. forthcoming. 'Has Mercantilism Reduced Urban Poverty in Sub-Saharan Africa? Boom, Bust and the China-Africa trade in Lomé and Bamako', *World Development*.

Charmes, J. 2000. 'Informal Sector, Poverty and Gender: A Review of Empirical Evidence'. Paper Commissioned for *World Development Report 2000/1*. Washington D.C., World Bank.

Chen, M., R. Jhabvala and F. Lund. 2002. 'Supporting Workers in the Informal Economy: A Policy Framework'. Paper Prepared for the ILO Task Force on the Informal Economy, available at www.wiego.org.

Devenish, A. and C. Skinner. 2006. 'Collective Action for those in the Informal Economy: The Case of the Self Employed Women's Union', in R. Ballard, A. Habib and I. Valodia (eds), *Voices of Protest: Social Movements in Post-Aparthied South Africa*, Durban: University of KwaZulu-Natal Press.

Dobson, R. and C. Skinner. Forthcoming. 'Working in Warwick: Integrating Street Traders into Urban Plans', Durban: School of Development Studies, University of KwaZulu-Natal.

Freund, B. 2007. *The African City, A History*, Cambridge: Cambridge University Press.

Healey, P. 1998. 'Collaborative Planning in a Stakeholder Society', *Town Planning Review*, 69(1): 1–21.

Horn, P. 2004. 'Durban's Warwick Junction: A Response', *Development Update*, 5(1): 209–14.

Hunter, N. and C. Skinner. 2003. 'Foreigners Working on the Streets of Durban: Local Government Policy Challenges', *Urban Forum*, 14(4): 301–19.

International Labour Organisation. 2002. *Women and Men in the Informal Economy: A Statistical Picture*, Geneva: International Labour Office.

Iyenda, G. 2001. 'Street Food and Income Generation for Poor Households in Kinshasa', *Environment and Urbanisation*, 13(2): 233–41.

Kamunyori, W. 2007. *A Growing Space for Dialogue: The Case of Street Vending in Nairobi's Central Business District*, Boston: Department of Urban Studies and Planning, Massachusetts Institute of Technology.

King, R. 2006. 'Fulcrum of the Urban Economy: Governance and Street Livelihoods in Kumasi, Ghana', in A. Brown (ed.), *Contested Space: Street Trading, Public Space, and Livelihoods in Developing Cities*, Warwickshire: Intermediate Technology Publications.

Landau, L. 2007. 'Discrimination and Development? Immigration, Urbanisation and Sustainable Livelihoods in Johannesburg', *Development Southern Africa*, 24(1): 67–76.

Levin, C., M. Ruel, S. Morris, D. Maxwell, M. Armar-Klemesu and C. Ahiadeka. 'Working Women in an Urban Setting: Traders, Vendors and Food Security in Accra', *World Development*, 27(11): 1977–91.

Lonrenco-Lindell, I. 2004. 'Trade and the Politics of Informalisation in Bissau, Guinea-Bissau', in Tranberg Hansen, K. and M. Vaa (eds), *Reconsidering Informality, Perspectives from Urban Africa*, Uppsala: Nordic Africa Institute.

Lund, F. 1998. 'Women Street Traders in Urban South Africa: A Synthesis of Selected Research Findings'. *CSDS Research Report No. 15*. Durban: University of Natal, available at www.sds.ukzn.ac.za.

Lund, F. and C. Skinner. 1999. 'Promoting the Interests of Women Street Traders: An Analysis of Organisations in South Africa', *CSDS Research Report No 19*. Durban: University of Natal. 50 pages.

Lyons, M. and S. Snoxell. 2005a. 'Sustainable Urban Livelihoods and Marketplace Social Capital: Crisis and Strategy in Petty Trade', *Urban Studies*, 42(8): 1301–20.

———. 2005b. 'Creating Urban Social Capital: Some Evidence from Informal Traders in Nairobi', *Urban Studies*, 42(7): 1077–97.

Mitullah, W. 1991. 'Hawking as a Survival Strategy for the Urban Poor in Nairobi: The Case of Women', *Environment and Urbanization*, 3(2): 13–22.

Motala, S. 2002. 'Organising in the Informal Economy: A Case Study of Street Trading in South Africa'. Seed Working Paper No. 36. Geneva: International Labour Organisation.

Nnkya, T. 2006. 'An Enabling Framework? Governance and Street Trading in Dar es Salaam, Tanzania', in A. Brown (ed.), *Contested Space: Street Trading, Public Space and Livelihoods in Developing Cities*, Warwickshire: Intermediate Technology Publications.

Peberdy, S. 2000. 'Mobile Entrepreneurship: Informal Sector Cross-border Trade and Street Trade in South Africa', *Development Southern Africa*, 17(2): 201–19.

Potts, D. 2007. 'City Life in Zimbabwe at a Time of Fear and Loathing: Urban Planning, Urban Poverty and Operation Murambatsvina', in G. Myers and M. Murray (eds), *Cities in Contemporary Africa*, New York: Palgrave Macmillan.

Robinson, J. 2002. 'Global and World Cities: A View from off the Map', *International Journal of Urban and Regional Research*, 26(3): 531–54.

Rogerson, C. and D. Hart. 1989. 'The Struggle for the Streets: Deregulation and Hawking in South Africa's Major Urban Areas', *Social Dynamics*, 15(1): 29–45.

Sandercock, L. 1998. *Making the Invisible Visible: A Multicultural Planning History*, Los Angeles: University of California Press.

Setsabi, S. 2006. 'Contest and Conflict: Governance and Street Livelihoods in Maseru, Lesotho', in A. Brown (ed.), *Contested Space: Street Trading, Public Space, and Livelihoods in Developing Cities*, Warwickshire: Intermediate Technology Publications.

Simone, A. 2004. *For the City Yet to Come: Changing African Life in Four Cities*, Durham: Duke University Press.

Simone, A. and A. Abouhani. (eds). 2005. *Urban Africa: Changing Contours of Survival in the City*, London: Zed Books.

Skinner, C. and R. Dobson. 2007. 'Bringing the Informal Economy into Urban Plans: A Look at Warwick Junction, South Africa', *Habitat Debate*, 13(2): 11.

Thulare, P. 2004. 'Trading Democracy? Johannesburg Informal Traders and Citizenship', *Centre for Policy Studies, Policy: Issues and Actors*, 17(1): 1–15.

Tibaijuka, A. 2005. Report of the Fact-finding Mission to Zimbabwe to Assess the Scope and Impact of Operation Murambatsvina by the UN Special Envoy on Human Settlements Issues in Zimbabwe, available at www.un.org/News/dh/infocus/zimbabwe/zimbabwe_rpt.pdf.

Tranberg Hansen, K. 2004. 'Who Rules the Streets? The Politics of Vending Space in Lusaka', in K. Tranberg Hansen and M. Vaa (eds), *Reconsidering Informality, Perspectives from Urban Africa*, Uppsala: Nordic Africa Institute.

Tranberg Hansen, K. and M. Vaa. 2004. *Reconsidering Informality, Perspectives from Urban Africa*, Uppsala: Nordic Africa Institute.

Tsitsi, N. and T. Agatha. 2000. 'Women Street Vendors in Zimbabwe. Women and Law in Southern Africa Research and Education Trust'. Paper commissioned by Women in Informal Employment: Globalising and Organising.

United Nations. 1997. 'State of the World Population 1997 Reproductive Rights and Reproductive Health', available at www.unfpa.org/swp/1997/swpmain.htm.

———. 2007. 'State of the World Population 2007 Unleashing the Potential of Urban Growth', available at www.unfpa.org/swp/2007/presskit/pdf/sowp2007_eng.pdf.

War on Want. 2006. 'Forces for Change: Informal Economy Organisations in Africa', London, available at www.waronwant.org.

# 9

# Street Trade in Latin America: Demographic Trends, Legal Issues and Vending Organisations in Six Cities

Sally Roever

Street commerce represents one of the most visible and dynamic segments of the informal economy in Latin America. Rapid rural-to-urban migration from the 1940s to the 1970s, economic crisis in the 1980s, and neoliberal reform in the 1990s combined to create a surplus of unemployed workers in the region's cities, so that by 2006 the region faced a formal employment deficit of 126 million jobs.[1] In the absence of formal wage employment, many workers have turned to the informal sector as a way to generate income. According to Tokman (2001: 20), six of every 10 new jobs generated since 1990 in Latin America have been in the informal sector, and nearly 50 per cent of workers in the region's cities engage in informal economic activity. Many of these workers, seeking an occupation with low barriers to entry, have taken to the streets to hawk merchandise for profit.

Street vendors' occupation of public space in crowded commercial areas has attracted the attention of local government authorities charged with maintaining order throughout the region. While vendors cite the constitutional right to work to justify their occupation of streets and sidewalks, city officials are faced with a choice between tolerating street trade, attempting to regulate it, or trying to eliminate it through the use of force. The resulting interplay between vendors and governments has made street trade a major issue in Latin American urban governance.

This chapter offers a review of street vending issues in six major Latin American cities: Bogota, Colombia; Caracas, Venezuela; Lima, Peru; Mexico City, Mexico; Santiago, Chile; and Sao Paulo, Brazil. The chapter examines three broad themes in each city. First, it explores demographic trends and working conditions among street traders, compiling available information on the size of the street vending population, its growth over time, gender and age breakdowns, and working conditions such as income stability and employment security. Second, it examines legal issues related to the governance of street trade in each city, including an analysis of laws, regulations and ordinances at the national, regional and local levels. Where information is available, it adds an assessment of the effectiveness of those laws, the legal status of vendors, and the broader attitudes of the authorities towards street traders. Third, the chapter compiles information on the extent of organisation among street traders, with a focus on unions and other types of associations, and their strategies and effectiveness. The chapter concludes by offering an outline of best practices emerging from the region. The analysis is based on data from national and international statistical agencies and secondary sources gathered through contacts with researchers in the region.[2]

## Overview of Regional Trends

The country studies reveal several interesting trends at the regional level. First, in terms of demographics and working conditions, available data indicates that the size of Latin America's street vending population has grown substantially over the past two decades, particularly in large urban centres where rural migrants have family members who can facilitate their entry into the sector. Contributors to this growth most likely include the regional economic crisis of the 1980s, neoliberal reforms in the 1990s that downsized or eliminated state-owned enterprises and increased employers' flexibility with regard to hiring and firing workers, and sluggish economic growth that has failed to generate sufficient demand for low-skilled workers.

While this trend is more or less universal in the region, working conditions among street traders vary substantially, both within countries and across them. Within countries, some street traders, particularly those who have occupied the same space over a long period of time, and who have thus established a regular clientele and informal 'rights' to their workspace, have established lucrative enterprises that generate a reasonably stable income and provide decent working conditions. Others remain on the margins of sustainability; this is especially the case with ambulatory vendors who have few entrepreneurial skills, who sell low-end merchandise such as candy and small trinkets, and who have been unable to establish a fixed, secure location from which to vend. Across countries, vendors who are subject to a clearer and more stable legal framework, as in Chile and

Colombia, tend to have better working conditions than those in countries where their legal standing is muddled by conflicting policies, such as in Peru and Venezuela.

With regard to legal issues, two trends are notable. First, existing research suggests the presence of a continuum along which Latin American cases might be arrayed in terms of the extent to which written legislation and actual practice coincide. At one end, countries such as Chile and Colombia have relatively clear legal frameworks and jurisdictional mandates that facilitate the enforcement of and compliance with written law. At the other end, countries like Peru and Venezuela have legal frameworks that do not easily and clearly accommodate street traders, as well as overlapping jurisdictional mandates that produce confusion and conflict between vendors and governments, resulting in a lack of adequate enforcement and low levels of compliance with written law. As noted earlier, the clarity of the legal framework seems to have an important effect on working conditions, particularly security of workspace for the street vendors.

A second notable trend in the Latin American region is the diffusion of models for cleaning up the historic centres of capital cities. Historic centres established during the Spanish colonial period attract hordes of street traders because of their centralised location and their high levels of tourist traffic. In several cases (most notably, Lima, Mexico City, Caracas, and Bogota), the proliferation of street vending posts in historic areas created intolerable conditions of pedestrian and vehicular congestion, trash accumulation, noise, and other problems in the mid-1990s. In response, metropolitan or capital district governments engaged in large-scale campaigns to expel vendors from these areas and relocate them to off-street commercial centres, sometimes resorting to the use of force in order to clear the streets. The positive effects of these projects, most importantly the restoration of order and cleanliness to historic areas, created a model that other local governments followed. However, their negative effects—particularly the displacement of low-income vendors who could not afford to participate in relocation projects—have also been replicated, to the detriment of some of the most vulnerable workers in the region.

Finally, in terms of the extent of organisation, street traders have formed thousands of associations in the region to facilitate their work and defend their interests in the political arena. This proliferation of associations indicates low barriers to collective action at the grassroots level, and at the same time a high potential for establishing a political voice. Typical functions of these associations include resolving conflicts among members (typically over the allocation of space in the streets), coordinating with other groups of vendors, and serving as interlocutors with local government officials. However, these organisations tend to remain very small and relatively weak politically, so that the interests of street vendors rarely get channeled into national political agendas. When vendors have achieved some political clout, they have been aided by broader political circumstances, including transitions to democratic elections at the local level and the availability of political parties to serve as allies for vending organisations.

The case studies in the following section of the chapter suggest that the best practices emerge when two conditions are met. First, a clear legal and regulatory framework for street trade facilitates stability in the sector and encourages both vendors and governments to invest in long-term strategies for sustainable solutions to traditional problems related to street commerce. Second, sustainable solutions are more likely when street vending organisations are incorporated into the decision-making process, particularly when they involve relocation projects. These conditions appear to be associated with the successful governance of street commerce in countries with diverse economic, political and social conditions (see Table 9.1).

## Case Studies

### Bogota, Colombia

In the context of regional trends, Bogota is an atypical case in several senses. First, armed conflict in the Colombian countryside in recent decades has been more severe and sustained over a longer period of time than in other countries, so that Bogota has become the refuge for a large population of internally displaced people (IDPs). Second, the economic recession that affected many Latin American countries in the second half of the 1990s hit Bogota particularly hard, so that socio-economic gains of the late 1970s–mid-1990s were reversed (World Bank 2001: 14). These two conditions have most likely contributed to a sudden and relatively rapid growth trend in the informal economy in the past decade or so. On the other hand, Bogota is also exceptional in the sense that its urban governance structure has relatively clear rules with regard to informal workers, in contrast with other cities in the region.

### Demographics and Working Conditions

According to Colombia's National Administrative Department for Statistics (Departamento Administrativo Nacional de Estadística, DANE), approximately 52.9 per cent (1,659,237) of Bogota's 3,136,000 workers

**Table 9.1**
**Economic and Social Indicators by Country, 2004**

| *Brazil* | | *Chile* | *Colombia* | *Mexico* | *Peru* | *Venezuela* |
|---|---|---|---|---|---|---|
| GDP (current US$, millions) | 603.9 | 94.1 | 97.7 | 676.5 | 68.6 | 110.1 |
| Annual GDP growth | 5% | 6% | 4% | 4% | 5% | 18%* |
| GNI per capita | 3,000 | 5,220 | 2,020 | 6,790 | 2,360 | 4,030 |
| Industry, value added (% of GDP) | 40% | 45% | 31% | 26% | 30% | ** |
| Life expectancy | 71 | 78 | 73 | 75 | 70 | 74 |
| Literacy rate | 89% | 96% | 93% | 91% | 88% | 93% |
| Population (millions) | 183.9 | 16.1 | 44.9 | 103.8 | 27.6 | 26.1 |

*Source:* World Bank, 2006, *World Development Indicators.* Available at http://web.worldbank.org/WBSITE/EXTERNAL/DATASTATISTICS/0,,content MDK:20899413~pagePK:64133150~piPK:64133175~theSitePK:239419,00.html (accessed 21 May 2006).
* This anomalous rate of growth follows 2 years of negative growth (–9% in 2002 & –8% in 2003).
** Missing data.

are informal.[3] This figure is slightly higher than the country-wide figure, which was just under 47 per cent in 1998 (ILO 2002) (see Table 9.2). Both estimates suggest that Bogota ranks among the Latin American countries with larger informal sectors, partly a result of armed violence in the countryside in the 1980s and the economic crisis of the late 1990s.

Street traders appear to form a large component of Bogota's informal sector. Data from DANE shows that in 1996, the total number of street traders in Bogota was 220,344 (Donovan 2002: 89, fn. 221). This figure represented 19.8 per cent of Bogota's informal labour force in that year. A 2003 DANE estimate suggests that the street vending population increased dramatically after 1996, as the total number of people working in the streets or in stands or kiosks by 2003 was 521,606. That number continued to increase through 2005, when it totaled 557,934.

In terms of gender breakdown, men and women form almost identical segments of the informal economy, as 49.7 per cent of Bogota's informal workers are women, while 50.3 per cent are men. However, the balance among street traders is much more lopsided. While the number of women working in kiosks or stands overtook the number of men in that category in 2004 (20,882 vs. 14,681), men represented 75 per cent of those working in the streets by 2005 (see Table 9.3). However, the rate of increase among women in street trade outpaced that of men between 2003 and 2005.

Street vendors in Bogota show significant variation in terms of working conditions (FVP 2001a: 3). Those who permanently occupy stands,

### Table 9.2
### Informal Sector as a Percentage of Employment, Latin America

| Country | % of Employment | Year of Estimate |
|---|---|---|
| Argentina | 47.7 | 1998 |
| Bolivia | 52.6 | 1997 |
| Brazil | 37.2 | 1998 |
| Chile | 32.4 | 1998 |
| Colombia | 46.9 | 1998 |
| Ecuador | 52.5 | 1998 |
| Mexico | 44.8 | 1998 |
| Paraguay | 57.9 | 1996 |
| Peru | 48.2 | 1998 |
| Uruguay | 33.7 | 1998 |
| Venezuela | 38.3 | 1998 |

*Source:* ILO, 2002, STAT Working Paper No. 1-2002: ILO Compendium of Official Statistics on Employment in the Informal Sector. Available at http://www.ilo. org/public/english/bureau/stat/papers/comp.htm, pp. 237–41.

*Note:* For each country (where possible), the series produced by the ILO regional office is presented for the year 1998. The table thus presents the most standardised data possible across countries.

### Table 9.3
### Colombia: Informal Workforce by Place of Work and Sex, 2003–5

| Place of Work | 2003 | | 2004 | | 2005 | |
|---|---|---|---|---|---|---|
| | Men | Women | Men | Women | Men | Women |
| At home | 282591 | 731183 | 238858 | 109113 | 256847 | 731174 |
| In another's home | 310233 | 464689 | 269798 | 445309 | 323225 | 494350 |
| In a vehicle | 448827 | 18554 | 452036 | 26833 | 501597 | 20417 |
| From door-to-door | 332065 | 202725 | 289404 | 181293 | 347238 | 191917 |
| In a kiosk or stand | 17535 | 13423 | 14681 | 20882 | 20272 | 23190 |
| On the street | 378478 | 112170 | 362243 | 121122 | 385941 | 128531 |
| In a fixed establishment | 2315334 | 1964959 | 2438378 | 2097822 | 2459766 | 2149658 |
| In the countryside | 66400 | 7921 | 75735 | 13884 | 81734 | 13779 |

*Source:* Departamento Administrativo Nacional de Estadística, www.dane.gov.co. Figures accessed in the year 2005.

posts and kiosks tend to have relatively stable incomes, the capacity for specialisation in the goods and services they offer, and some ability to generate savings. Some who lack permanent spaces, for example, many clothing and food vendors, still exhibit some degree of business savvy; though they may lack stable incomes and savings, these vendors are capable of adjusting their commercial strategies to capture clients in multiple strategic locations. An intermediate category, the vast majority of Bogota's vendors, has fluctuating incomes, unstable working conditions, and lack permanent stands from which to vend.[4] Ambulatory vendors—those whose sales are dependent on the flow of pedestrian traffic—are the most vulnerable, as they sell low-cost goods (candy, fruit, juice, and newspapers, for example) and lack any capacity for savings.

In terms of income and education, a 2001 survey of 6,382 ambulatory and stationary vendors in Bogota showed that 24 per cent earned a monthly income between US$80 and $200, and another 13 per cent earned between $200 and $285 (FVP 2001a: 6). Thus, although the majority generated incomes lower than $80 a month, there is still a substantial proportion who have made street vending into a reasonably lucrative activity. In addition, 50.7 per cent of vendors surveyed had basic education, and 41.8 per cent had mid-level education. The survey also showed that 35 per cent had been vending for less than five years.

Available evidence suggests that average incomes among street traders may have declined during the 1990s. For example, a 1995 DANE study showed that informal traders earned an average income of US$223, while a 1999 survey measured an average net income of US$197 (Donovan 2002: 89). Although the two studies used different methodologies and therefore are not directly comparable, negative economic conditions (economic crisis in 1998–99, high unemployment, devaluation, and reverse GDP growth) and political conditions (terrorism, internal migration) are likely to have driven an increasing number of people into the informal sector, which in turn may have reduced incomes in the sector.

## Legal Issues

In contrast to cities such as Lima and Caracas, Colombian law designates a single agency, the Fondo de Ventas Populares (FVP), as the entity responsible for governing street commerce in the capital. Created in 1972, the FVP is part of Bogota's mayor's office, and its board of directors consists of public officials appointed by the mayor (Donovan 2002: 9). The FVP is responsible for generating alternatives for the organisation, training, formalisation, and/or relocation of ambulatory and stationary vendors (FVP 2001b: 8). An FVP report (2001a) states that its relocation projects from 1998 to 2000 assisted more than 3,200 vendors. According to Donovan (2002: 8), the FVP invested a total of US$16.5 million in relocation projects during the 1998–2000 period.

Colombia is also unusual in that its Constitution (1991, Article 82) elevates the protection of public space to a constitutionally guaranteed right enforced by mayors (Donovan 2002: 10).[5] Although the Constitution, like others in Latin America, also protects the individual right to work, it explicitly privileges collective rights over individual rights, and in doing so privileges the preservation of public space over the individual's right to work (FVP 2001b: 4). In addition, the country's Constitutional Court has issued a series of rulings clarifying the implications of those provisions for the governance of street commerce. In particular, those rulings state that streets, sidewalks and other areas designated for vehicular or pedestrian transit may not be obstructed by vending stands; that when local authorities initiate projects to recuperate public space occupied by licensed or authorised vendors, they should design and execute adequate and reasonable relocation plans for the affected street vendors; and that such relocation projects should provide space in which vendors can work permanently, without fear of expulsion, with minimum guarantees of hygiene and security (FVP 2001b: 5–6).

The relative clarity of Colombian law with regard to street commerce has given vendors there a measure of security, which does not exist in other countries where vending rights are less explicit. One example of a Constitutional Court ruling that explicitly recognises the needs of street traders subject to relocation illustrates this point. It reads: 'Although the general interest in preserving public space outweighs the particular interest of stationary and ambulatory vendors, it is necessary, according to jurisprudence, to reconcile appropriately and harmoniously the rights and responsibilities in conflict' (Sentencia T-396 de 1997, M. P. Antonio Barrera Carbonell, cited in FVP 2001b: 7).

Expulsions from public space are constitutionally permitted only when there exists a judicial process that authorises it, in compliance with the rules established prior to the expulsion, and when policies that guarantee that the occupants will not be neglected are enacted. The ruling also states that measures such as training for vendors and improved access to credit are permissible alternatives to relocation.

## Experiences with Licensing

Licensing was the primary mechanism for governing street commerce in the pre-1988 era in Bogota. Street vendors who held licenses to vend in public space during this time were more likely to obtain credit and less likely to face police harassment than unlicensed vendors. However, according to Donovan (2002: 29), the process by which licenses were obtained was less than transparent; vendors needed intermediaries with influence or political connections in order to obtain them, and many found such intermediaries in street vendors' unions. Thus, clientelistic behaviour underpinned street governance; vending unions facilitated the distribution of licenses to their members, and in exchange provided political backing for local politicians, primarily city council representatives. Commercial wholesalers also performed the role of intermediary on behalf of client vendors who sold their products. After democratic elections were introduced in the Bogota mayor's office in 1988, the licensing process was decentralised, which in turn undermined the patron–client relations that predominated during the pre-1988 period.

## Experiences with Relocations

According to Donovan (2002), relocation projects headed by the FVP before 1988 tended to be unsuccessful, for two reasons: first, the Bogota mayor's office lacked the financial resources for conducting them successfully; and second, the public did not hold presidentially appointed mayors accountable for protecting public space, so the political incentives for long-term solutions to public space problems were insufficient. Reforms during the 1988–91 period, including political and fiscal decentralisation, the democratisation of the mayor's office, and the elevation of public space as a guaranteed collective right in the new 1991 Constitution, provided the groundwork for more successful relocation projects in subsequent years. These reforms made three specific contributions to the legal framework that facilitated the governance of public space in the Colombian capital: (1) they enabled the mayor's office to make binding decisions regarding the protection of public space; (2) they legally institutionalised agencies that were explicitly responsible for recovering and protecting public space (such as the Defensoria del Espacio Publico), and (3) they granted the mayor's office expenditure and revenue-raising powers to undertake public space recovery projects (Donovan 2002: 49).[6]

In terms of the working conditions of relocated vendors, Donovan's research shows that relocated vendors experienced 'significant gains in the quality of the environmental conditions in their work place' (Donovan 2002: 96–97). These environmental conditions included the quality of air, cleanliness, dust, garbage removal, light, noise, odour, space, temperature, and water. The greatest benefits of moving to off-street locations were in the areas of cleanliness, garbage removal and noise levels. Relocated vendors also reported safer conditions in official markets than on the streets, and reported a drastic reduction in police harassment. On the other hand, half of the relocated vendors surveyed for the study reported that they were earning lower incomes in off-street markets than they had on the streets. Another study found that 93 per cent of relocated vendors surveyed had lower incomes in markets than on the streets (Olea Suarez and Huertas Laverde 1996, cited in Donovan 2002: 100).

Higher administrative costs, including rent, utility payments and fees, most likely account for the reduced incomes. However, vendors relocated to markets that specialise in a single product, such as books or flowers, reported wider clienteles and increased incomes in the off-street markets (Donovan 2002: 103).

## Organisation

A 1995 ILO-commissioned study found that in 1995 the rate of unionisation among informal workers was below 1 per cent. Within the informal workforce, street vendors appear to have a higher rate of unionisation than other types of informal workers. For example, a survey conducted by Donovan (2002: 72) showed that among vendors occupying eight principal thoroughfares in the city, 22.4 per cent belonged to unions, associations or cooperatives.

According to Donovan, street vending unions in Bogota were relatively powerful in the pre-1988 era, when licensing was the primary mechanism for governing street commerce and vending unions acted as intermediaries between individual street traders and city councilors. At that time, mayors were appointed by the president rather than elected, and so mayors' failures to keep public space in order were viewed as a failure of the central government. Because mayors were not held accountable by the voters, local officials saw little reason to antagonise vending unions. In addition, the overall number of vending unions during this period was relatively low because of stringent labour laws that allowed the central government to easily deny legal status to unions. With few legal vending unions in existence, those that did gain legal status had large membership numbers and held considerable sway in the political arena.

These conditions were reversed during the reform period of 1988–91. The new public space laws made newly elected mayors responsible for protecting public space, which in turn created a powerful constituency for mayoral candidates: residents and formal business owners who wished to control the proliferation of vendors. The decentralisation of licensing programmes and the new emphasis on relocations removed the vote-buying mechanism on which city councilors previously relied, which in turn hindered unions' ability to recruit members on the basis of their ability to provide aid in obtaining licenses. Additionally, a 1990 Labour Law Reform reduced the barriers to entry for unions, and as a result the number of street vending unions proliferated. At the same time, their political power waned, as many of the new unions consisted only of a dozen or so vendors and few maintained formal relations with national political parties or labour federations. As is the case in Peru and Venezuela, many Colombian vending associations now encompass vendors only on a certain city block, or only vendors who sell a certain product in a certain part of the city. Associations of relocated vendors who have received support from the mayor's office to become 'formalised' have also broken alliances with associations of vendors remaining on the streets. This sort of atomisation among vending associations has reduced the political leverage of the sector.

## Caracas, Venezuela

Caracas is the chaotic capital of one of the region's most politically polarised countries. After almost 30 years of relatively stable democratic governance, a popular revolt among the country's marginalised poor in 1989 undermined the power of the two dominant political parties, Accion Democratica (AD) and the Social Christian Party (COPEI), and led to the election of Lieutenant Colonel Hugo Chavez in 1998. Chavez and his supporters wrote and passed a new Constitution in 1999 that dismantled the country's long-standing representative democracy and envisioned instead a more direct democracy with power centralised in Caracas (Ellner and Myers 2002: 96). Though Chavez has remained popular among the urban poor, his extremism has alienated the moderate middle class and his anti-capitalist rhetoric has destabilised the financial sector and increased the risk for foreign investors.

The consequences of political and economic upheaval are evident in the unruly capital; 'Caracas as a whole,' as one journalist put it, 'seems to be falling apart.'[7] The uncontrolled proliferation of street vending is a central part of the chaos that reigns in the city's public spaces. As Kaste reports, 'the subway is arguably the most pleasant public space left', as *buhoneros*, or street traders, are prohibited from vending on platforms so that passengers can make their way unimpeded (see Chapter 10 in this book on Venezuela).

### Demographics and Working Conditions

According to 2004 data from the National Statistical Institute (INE), 53 per cent of the Venezuelan workforce is informal, equaling 5.25 million workers. While Venezuela is atypical of the region in that a relatively stable democracy and vibrant economy based on the petroleum sector helped provide formal jobs and keep unemployment low in the 1970s and early 1980s, both the country's oil income and its democratic political consensus began to collapse in the late 1980s, and continued instability since then has fostered a rise in informality. According to Zanoni Lopez (2005: 27), economic recession, inflation and the absence of a legal framework to protect property rights effectively have reduced private sector investment, eroded household purchasing power and increased unemployment. Moreover, a large and inefficient bureaucracy constructed around the petroleum sector in previous decades has created similar legal and administrative obstacles to operating small businesses as those that de Soto (1989) encountered in Peru. Finally, Venezuela labour legislation makes the country's workers among the most expensive in the region, which in turn provides incentives for employers to hire informally (Zanoni Lopez 2005: 30).

In the Metropolitan District of Caracas, consisting of five municipalities, over 48,000 people work as street vendors (Garcia Rincon 2006a: 1). When those who work in markets (8,156) or in kiosks (4,603) are included as well as those who vend in the streets (48,675), the total documented street vending population in Metropolitan Caracas forms about 5.3 per cent of the city's economically active population, or over 61,000 people (ibid.: 1). According to Zanoni Lopez (2005: 42), the Capital District houses a total of about 18,000 vending posts.

As in many other countries, there are no reliable estimates of the growth of the street vending population over time. However, newspaper accounts and academic studies suggest that street commerce in Caracas is a relatively recent phenomenon in comparison to other Latin American capitals, such as Santiago and Lima. Street vendors did not appear in large numbers in Caracas until the 1970s, and it was not until the 1980s that street commerce became problematic for city officials (Garcia Rincon 2006a: 4). Thus, the first ordinance to govern street commerce in Caracas was issued in 1985, whereas similar ordinances date back several centuries in Lima and Sao Paulo and almost a century in Santiago.

Table 9.4 presents estimates of the size of the street vending population in Caracas from different sources gathered by Garcia Rincon (2006a). The data indicates an upward trend in the number of street vendors that began gradually in the late 1980s and early 1990s and then increased rapidly after 2000. However, in each case estimates were derived from different methods, so that the over-time estimates are not methodologically comparable.

Recent data from a municipal census indicates substantial heterogeneity within the street vending sector with regard to products sold. As Table 9.5 shows the largest group of vendors in Caracas sells clothing, followed by pirated electronic goods and other assorted products. According to

**Table 9.4**
**Estimates of Street Vending Population, Caracas, 1988–2002**

| Year | Estimated Number of Street Vendors |
|------|-----------------------------------|
| 1988 | 12,000 |
| 1996 | 28,950 |
| 2000 | 20,000 |
| 2001 | 48,000 |
| 2002 | 74,000 |

Source: Maria Fernanda Garcia Rincon, 2006, 'A Short Assessment of the Situation of Street Vendors in Caracas, Venezuela'. Unpublished manuscript, University of Cambridge (UK), p. 4.

**Table 9.5**
**Street Vendors by Product Sold, Caracas, 2002/2003\***

| Product | % of Street Vendors |
|---------|---------------------|
| Clothing | 26 |
| CDs, DVDs, music, software | 17 |
| Various products | 10 |
| Jewelry, accessories, sunglasses | 9 |
| Food, fruits, vegetables | 6 |
| Shoes, sandals | 6 |
| Books | 6 |
| Other | 6 |
| Mobile phones, accessories | 4 |
| Arts and crafts | 4 |
| Purses, belts, leather products | 3 |
| Religious articles | 3 |

Source: Municipal census, 2002 and 2003.
    \* Average November/December 2002 and February/March 2003.

data from CEDICE, women in the street vending population outnumber men (58 per cent to 42 per cent, respectively). Roughly a third of street vendors are between 30 and 39 years of age; another third are between 15 and 29 years of age, and the remainder are 40 and above (Garcia Rincon 2006a: 5).

## Legal Issues

Two national-level laws, the Ley Organica de Ordenacion Urbanistica (Art. 10) and the Ley Organica del Regimen Municipal (Art. 36), assign municipalities the responsibility for governing public space (Zanoni Lopez 2005: 64). The legal instrument with which municipalities are to do so is the Municipal Ordinance. In the case of Metropolitan

Caracas, however, the Special Law for the Caracas Metropolitan District states that the Metropolitan Mayor is responsible for urban planning within the metropolitan region, which encompasses five municipalities: Libertador, Baruta, Chacao, Hatillo, and Sucre. The national legislation also states that urban planning in the Caracas Metropolitan District is the responsibility of the Libertador mayor's office. This legal ambiguity creates a jurisdictional conflict between the metropolitan and municipal mayors' offices, as each can claim authority for managing issues relating to street vending and the use of public space.

The overlapping jurisdiction for urban planning can only be resolved through political negotiation between the two offices, and consensus has been difficult to reach in recent years. As Zanoni Lopez (2005: 43) puts it, the legal infrastructure that encompasses street vending in Venezuela is 'complex and unclear, to the point that it leaves many aspects open to interpretation, sometimes arbitrary for legislators or those who are expected to comply'.[8]

The jurisdictional conflict between metropolitan and municipal mayors' offices in the area of urban planning has constrained the ability of public officials and street vendors to establish a stable set of rules to effectively govern street markets. The case of Sabana Grande, one of Caracas's most important thoroughfares, is illustrative (see Chapter 10 in this book).

Persistent 'geopolitical feudalism' between levels of government adds to the ineffective governance of the sector.[9] For example, repeated efforts by the Caracas mayor, Antonio Ledezma, to establish order in the street vending sector after his election in 1995 resulted in some successful relocation projects in areas where markets had degenerated into crime-ridden areas. However, at the same time the Governor's Office of Caracas was issuing permits to vendors for the holiday season!

## Lima, Peru

Residents of Lima view their city as the 'capital of informality' in the Latin American region, in part because an enormous percentage of its land is occupied by squatter settlements formed in the middle of the twentieth century, and in part because a vast number of its workers engage in informal economic activity. Though publicly available official statistics do not provide estimates of the size of the informal sector in Lima, they do measure the size of the workforce engaged in small and micro-enterprises. According to the National Institute of Statistics and Informatics (INEI), Peru's national statistical agency, by June 2006, 74.7 per cent of Metropolitan Lima's economically active population worked in small and micro-enterprises, and 33 per cent worked independently, that is, as self-employed or own-account workers.[10] The ILO estimates from 1998 indicate that Peru has the fourth largest informal sector on the South American continent, behind Bolivia, Ecuador and Paraguay.

Like Bogota and Caracas, Lima experienced political and economic instability during the 1980s and 1990s, along with continued rural-to-urban migration. However, unlike those cities, Lima has had a large informal sector for many decades, as it never developed a robust industrial sector during the period of import substitution industrialisation (ISI) or a large petroleum sector to absorb the growing population of unemployed workers. Street vendors are likewise nothing new to the Peruvian capital, as Lima's Historic Center has featured informal traders since the sixteenth century.[11] Despite centuries of efforts to regulate street trade, the sector remains chaotic and unevenly governed, partly due to an unclear legal and institutional framework that to some extent resembles that of Caracas.

## Demographics and Working Conditions

Although street traders form an important part of the local economy in Lima, no government agencies or non-governmental institutions have attempted to measure the size of the street vending population over time. The Metropolitan Government of Lima (Municipalidad Metropolitana de Lima, MML) conducted the first census of street vendors in the modern period in 1976. This census produced an estimate of 58,284 vendors in 29 municipal districts within the metropolitan area, of which about 55 per cent were women. Nine years later, the Institute for Liberty and Democracy in Peru, headed by Hernando de Soto, carried out a second census in Metropolitan Lima. This effort focused on parts of the city that were home to known concentrations of vendors, and in these areas census takers counted 84,135 vendors. A survey of municipalities in 1994 that combined headcounts and estimates produced by local municipal authorities generated an estimate of 182,167 street vendors. As in other cities, therefore, the available estimates show an upward trend in the street vending population over the past few decades, although these estimates were all produced using different methodologies. Current estimates suggest that the number of street vendors at present may be as high as 360,000 (Roever 2005: 200).

In terms of gender and age breakdowns, two surveys conducted in the past five years suggest that women outnumber men both in the peripheral areas of the city near the squatter settlements where many vendors live, and in central-city commercial areas to which vendors commute in order to reach larger and more diverse customer bases. In Aliaga Linares's 2002 study of street traders in Independencia, in Lima's Northern Cone, 73 per cent of market vendors surveyed were women, while just 27 per cent were men. Among women included in the study, the majority (70 per cent) were married and, therefore, likely used street vending to supplement the head of household's income, but another 9 per cent were heads of household themselves, and thus dependent on the income generated through street sales to sustain their families (Aliaga Linares 2002: 41). Roever's 2005 study of street vendors in central-city areas suggests more gender balance, as 59 per cent of garment district vendors were women and 41 per cent were men, and 51 per cent of vendors in Caqueta were women versus 49 per cent men.[12] The two studies also found that the vending population is relatively young, as 60 per cent of vendors in Independencia were between ages 25 and 45 (Aliaga Linares 2002: 41, fn. 30), as were 53 per cent of the vendors in the central-city locations.

In terms of products sold, the two surveys showed substantial differences across the various research sites. In Independencia, the majority (77 per cent) of those surveyed sold food, most commonly fruits and vegetables, meat, dairy, and grocery items. Of the 33 per cent who sold non-perishables, most sold electronics, clothing and shoes (Aliaga Linares 2002: 46). In the garment district of Gamarra, not surprisingly, the largest group (52 per cent) sold textiles; yet vendors in that part of the city also hawk a variety of other goods, including footwear, fruits and vegetables, prepared food, and beverages. Vendors in Caqueta exhibited more diversity in terms of products sold, as an equal percentage offered produce and clothing (20 per cent each), and others hawked prepared food, footwear, household goods, and other items (see Table 9.6).

## Legal Issues

Peru is typical of many Latin American countries in that its national-level laws are designed to promote the small-enterprise sector and help micro-entrepreneurs grow their businesses, while local-level ordinances are designed to restrict the activities of street traders as petty entrepreneurs (UN HABITAT 2006). Comprehensive national laws from 1991, 2000 and 2003 aimed to promote the formalisation, growth, development, and job-creating capacity of small-scale enterprises through tax incentives, simplified registration procedures and state-sponsored programmes.[13] Street vendors operate small-scale enterprises and, therefore, in theory, are subject to these laws. At the same time, however, local ordinances tend to heavily regulate street vendors' activities, most commonly by designating

**Table 9.6**
**Street Vendors by Area and Product Sold, Central Lima, 2003**

| Product | % of Street Vendors in Gamarra | % of Street Vendors in Caqueta |
|---|---|---|
| Clothing | 52 | 20 |
| CDs, DVDs, music, software | 0 | 3 |
| Prepared food | 7 | 9 |
| Fruits and vegetables | 6 | 20 |
| Shoes, sandals | 5 | 4 |
| School supplies | 0 | 1 |
| Household goods | 2 | 4 |
| Arts and crafts | 3 | 2 |
| Beverages | 4 | 1 |
| Electronics | 1 | 1 |
| Other/Various | 26 | 41 |

Source: Sally Roever, 2003, '2003 Microbusiness Survey', May–June 2003. Totals are slightly higher than 100% because some vendors offered multiple responses.

certain areas as *zonas rígidas* (restricted zones where vending is prohibited) and requiring vendors to pay fees, purchase licenses, maintain their posts at a certain size, and comply with health and safety regulations. The vast majority of vendors are more directly affected by local ordinances that are enforced by local security services, whereas off-street vendors are more likely to enjoy the benefits of the national promotional measures.

Lima's Metropolitan Government enacted one of the most visible projects in the region to address problems associated with street vending in 1996. By that time, street vendors had overrun many of the city's downtown thoroughfares, causing hopeless traffic gridlock on the streets surrounding the main plazas in the Historic Center. Alberto Andrade, one of the candidates for mayor in the 1995 election, made the recuperation of the Historic Center an explicit part of his successful campaign. Shortly after taking office in January 1996, Andrade enacted the most sweeping relocation project in the city's history. Its aim was to completely 'eradicate' all but a handful of street vendors in the Historic Center proper, to relocate those with viable businesses to off-street commercial centres in other parts of the city, and to 'formalise' those who were relocated. In many respects, the project was a tremendous success, as the Historic Center became transitable once again and some relocated vendors saw their sales and job security increase. However, the diffusion of the Andrade model caused problems at the local level. Municipal mayors adopted his rhetoric of 'eradicating' the street vending problem, but lacked the resources to successfully relocate and formalise vendors who were removed from the streets.

Compounding the problems associated with efforts to replicate the Andrade model at the local level is the contradictory legal framework to govern street commerce in Metropolitan Lima. Lima is similar to Caracas (and unlike Bogota) in that its urban governance structure produces overlapping jurisdictions that have complicated the implementation of street vending regulations at the local level. At the national level, the Constitution grants all citizens the right to work, and the Law of Municipalities states that municipal districts are responsible for governing street commerce. At the metropolitan level, Metropolitan Ordinance 002 of 1985 establishes the regulatory framework for street commerce in the metropolitan region's 43 municipal districts. That measure calls on district governments to charge a daily tax, called the *sisa*, in exchange for the right to use public space for street vending, issue licenses to vendors, and establish a social fund and a consultative commission through which vendors could participate in policy design in each district municipality. In exchange, vendors are to comply with a series of regulations, including vending only in designated areas, wearing uniforms, maintaining their posts at a certain size, and complying with health and safety measures. In practice, however, no municipal district has effectively enforced the ordinance over time. Instead, district governments selectively implement the parts of the ordinance that serve their interests at any given time. Vendors, likewise, selectively comply with only certain parts of the ordinance, arguing that local governments are not holding up their end of the bargain (Roever 2006).

The legal status of vendors in Lima is ambiguous, particularly in comparison to their counterparts in Bogota. Without the weight of clear rulings issued by a high court, vendors and governments in Lima engage in endless disputes over vendors' occupation of public space, and most commonly, individual vendors or vending organisations negotiate their own agreements with the authorities, as in Caracas.[14]

Vendors in Lima also have a negative public image, for two reasons. First, the media often associates street vendors with urban problems such as crime, noise, congestion, and the accumulation of garbage. Second, street vending organisations were associated with the political left in the 1980s, whose radical elements brought the Shining Path terrorist movement to Lima late in that decade. Though vending organisations were not overt supporters of the guerrilla movement, their association with leftist parties left them politically isolated after 1990.

## Organisation

Street vendors in Lima have formed thousands of organisations since the 1960s. Organisation is most common among vendors with fixed posts, while mobile-post and ambulatory vendors are less likely to belong to organisations. Membership in organisations is common in central-city areas where dense commercial areas attract high numbers of vendors; for example, Roever's 2005 study found that 54.5 per cent of vendors in Gamarra and 73.5 per cent of those in Caqueta belonged to associations. At the same time, however, vending associations in Lima are weakly institutionalised. Formal rules established to govern the internal activities of organisations are rarely followed; many associations do not keep up-to-date paperwork on their membership or activities; and loyalty to these organisations among members tends to be fairly low, so that disagreements between leaders and members often lead to the organisation's dissolution. As in Bogota and Caracas, Lima's street vending organisations are mostly small, encompassing vendors on a block or a single street, and have just a few dozen members.

Nonetheless, organisations serve an important purpose for Lima's street traders. As Sulmont Haak (1999: 68) argues, base-level organisations, which operate at the level of blocks and half-blocks in Lima, perform the critical role of mediating disputes among members, primarily over the allocation of space on the streets and sidewalks. These base-level associations also promote cohesion among vendors, absorb pressure from formal merchants and neighbours, and negotiate with lower-level authorities. A higher level of organisation includes federations, 'fronts' and 'centrals', which mediate disputes among base associations and negotiate with higher-level authorities. Though leadership tends to be dominated by men and elections tend to be infrequent, these federations have made some important gains for the sector over the years. For example, Federacion Departamental de Vendedores Ambulantes de Lima (FEDEVAL), a Lima-wide federation, was relatively successful in the 1980s, when left-oriented parties offered a powerful political ally. However, that power waned in the late 1980s and early 1990s, and vending federations remain weak at present.

## Mexico City, Mexico

Mexico has the largest GDP and GNI per capita of any country included in this study, and in some senses it also has one of the most evolved political-legal infrastructures for street vending in the region. The Partido Revolucionario Institucional (PRI), Mexico's dominant political party for

70 years, incorporated street vendors into its organisational structure, and in doing so brought the governance of street commerce to the national policy table. Nonetheless, familiar patterns of patron–client relations and regulatory invasion persist in different local spaces within Mexico City. Despite major differences in political and economic structures, both Mexico City and Lima enacted Historic Center clean-up campaigns in the early- to mid-1990s designed to limit street commerce in downtown areas, with similar results.[15]

## Demographics and Working Conditions

According to the Population and Housing Census for Mexico City's Federal District, 73,154 street vendors worked in the Federal District in the year 2000.[16] Street selling in Mexico City employs more people than any single branch of industry (Williams 2006: 1). Moreover, street vendors represent one of the largest categories of workers in retail trade, along with food, drink and tobacco vendors in specialised retail shops, and workers in non-food specialised retail shops. Mexico City has more street sellers than workers in supermarkets, department stores, gas stations, and car sales (Williams 2006: 1).

Available statistics suggest that informal sector activities in Mexico, however defined, grew steadily between 1993 and 1998.[17] Growth in informal activities accompanied both negative growth in formal employment from 1993 to 1995 and positive growth in formal employment between 1995 and 1998, showing that informality is not only an outcome of poor economic conditions (Williams 2006: 5). In the Federal District, while the total number of sellers without an establishment fell between 1998 and 2000, the number of those selling house to house or in the streets (as ambulatory vendors) rose 12 per cent in that time period, and the number of those selling in street stalls or in market stalls also rose (1 per cent). The reason for the overall decline in vending without fixed establishments was a decrease in numbers of those vending from vehicles or from one's own home (Williams 2006: 8).

In terms of gender breakdown, the balance between men and women in trading (with or without an establishment) remained the same from 1998 to 2000, at about 60 per cent men and 40 per cent women. Though the total number of women traders without an establishment declined, the number of women selling from house to house or in the streets rose 5 per cent from 34,639 in 1998 to 36,299 in 2000. Meanwhile, the number of women selling from home and selling from street stalls or market stalls declined during that period. The increase in the number of women selling in the street paired with a decrease in the number of women selling from home is significant in that the most common strategy for providing child-care among women street vendors is to watch them personally at their place of work, and children are more exposed to health risks in the streets than at home (Hernandez et al. 1996). Meanwhile, the number of men in every category (with or without a fixed establishment) grew over the same time period (Williams 2006: 9). In terms of the age breakdown, 1990 data shows that more than 95 per cent of street vendors are in their prime productive years, between the ages of 15 and 60, and 50 per cent are between ages 21 and 35 (Cross 1998: 89–90).

In terms of products sold, the 1998 ENAMIN survey estimated that the most frequently traded goods among micro-enterprises without a fixed establishment are clothing and footwear (22 per cent), sweets, chocolates, soft drinks and ice cream (15 per cent), general foods (10 per cent), and fresh fruit and vegetables (10 per cent). However, these results are country-wide and do not include the Federal District, so they do not necessarily reflect categories of products sold in the streets of Mexico's capital.[18]

In terms of street vendors' working conditions in Mexico City's Federal District, data is available on two indicators: income and working hours. Income data suggests that incomes among street workers fell between 1990 and 2000 in comparison to the total occupied population, and the percentage of street workers earning no regular income (but rather commissions, tips, irregular payments, etc.), grew 100 per cent over that decade (Williams 2006: 15). Despite the 'earnings gap' between street vendors and the overall occupied population, the percentage of street sellers earning between one and two 'minimum salaries' increased from 36 per cent in 1990 to 43 per cent in 2000, while the percentage of street sellers earning up to one minimum salary dropped nine percentage points in that time frame. However, earnings for women street sellers are lower than those for men in street trade. In terms of hours of work, from 1990 to 2000 the percentage of vendors who worked only part-time, that is, between nine and 24 hours a week, rose from 13 per cent in 1990 to 18 per cent in 2000, while the proportion working a full work-week fell (Williams 2006: 16).

## Legal Issues

Cross (1998: 91–101) identifies two broad categories of street vendors in Mexico City: vendors who are 'tolerated' according to government policies, and vendors 'without tolerance' from the authorities. Among the first category are four sub-groups: concentrations of vendors in residential areas that provide the same services as a public market; '*tianguis*', or weekly rotating street markets; markets on wheels, which are similar to tianguis except that they were set up by a federal government agency and in general are better run and better supervised; and ambulatory vendors with fixed or semi-fixed stalls. Of these groups, according to Cross, the first is the most stable, as they are tolerated by government officials because they are generally in the process of moving off the streets. Those 'without tolerance' include independent neighbourhood vendors; *toreros*, or vendors who dodge the authorities by vending from plastic tarps on the pavement that are easily removable; and metro vendors.

The evolution of street commerce in Mexico City's Historic Center illustrates the difficulty of governing street commerce even in a country in which vendors have been long recognised as a legitimate political constituency. A 1993 programme launched under Manuel Camacho Solis called the Popular Commerce Improvement Programme (Programa de Mejoramiento del Comercio Popular) prohibited street vending in the Historic Center and prompted the relocation of thousands of vendors to off-street commercial centres. However, vendors were relocated to commercial centres in the Historic Center and quite close to their previous markets, and when their sales dropped these vendors simply moved back into the streets (Stamm 2006: 6). Vending organisations continued negotiating with the authorities over the years, and high concentrations of vendors were slowly displaced toward the east of the Historic Center, a popular-class zone. Two other programmes followed: the Street Commerce Reorganization Programme (Programa de Reordenamiento del Comercio en la Via Publica) in 1998, and the Commercial Plaza Programme for the Relocation of Street Commerce (Programa de Plazas Comerciales para la Reubicacion del Comercio en la Via Publica) in 2003 (Stamm 2006: 4). Notwithstanding the development of these programmes and both sides' willingness to engage in negotiations, familiar problems with the governance of street commerce persist in the Mexican capital.

## Organisation

According to Pena (1999), street vending organisations in Mexico City perform two central functions. The first is an intermediary role: vending organisations negotiate with the authorities on behalf of individual vendors, so that a primary incentive for joining an organisation is to get help overcoming red tape and navigating complex bureaucratic procedures. The second is a managerial role; vending organisations manage conflicts among members and mediate access to informal markets. Pena's (1999) study of vending organisations in Mexico City produced similar results to Aliaga Linares's (2002) study of vending organisations in Lima, in that both revealed the importance of social networks and social capital for the day-to-day functioning of street markets.

The vast majority of regular street vendors in Mexico City belong to associations, which range in size from a few dozen to 7,000 members (Cross 1998: 120). In 1993, Mexico City's Historic Center featured 60 street vending organisations with a total of 10,000 members (Guillen 1994, cited in Stamm 2006). The high level of association membership among Mexico City's street vendors is, according to Cross (1998: 120), 'a direct result of administrative procedures requiring individuals to form part of a "recognized association" before being allowed to sell in the street'.

Cross further argues that the development of street vending organisations in Mexico is closely tied to party politics, and in particular, the strategies of the PRI, the dominant party in Mexico for 70 years. Though vendors themselves 'appear little concerned about the political allegiance of the street vendor association they belong to' (Cross 1998: 123), organisations affiliated with the PRI have been shown favouritism by the political system, and the PRI has likewise benefited by organising vendors. Thus, vendors were, at least through the early 1990s, part of a mutually beneficial system of clientelism with the dominant party. This relationship between vending organisations and a single political party is an important contrast with other countries, above all, in terms of the longevity of that relationship.

## Santiago, Chile

Of the countries included in this study, Chile has been the most politically and economically stable for the past quarter century. Though poverty remains an important problem, its small population and advanced level of economic development have helped it avoid some of the problems of overpopulation and unemployment experienced in other countries, and as a result the Chilean informal economy is the smallest in the region (see Table 9.2). Equally importantly, the rule of law in Chile is more institutionalised than in other countries of the region, and property rights are well-protected. These conditions have combined to make the governance of informal street traders relatively stable.

Street markets in Santiago are for the most part planned and regulated by the government. According to Salazar (2003), the Municipality of Santiago created the city's first planned street market (feria libre) in 1915, following the formation of private markets in the two preceding decades.

Street markets were granted formal institutional status, including the formally recognised right to operate in public space, in 1938 as part of the leftist Frente Popular's political strategy to appeal to the urban poor (Aliaga Linares 2004: 4). By mid-century, street vending in Santiago had achieved full recognition as a legitimate economic activity, and vendors had become a permanent fixture in the city (Salazar 2003: 76–84). This achievement of recognition for street vendors relatively early in the century precluded the sort of large-scale invasions of streets that have characterised other cities in the region.

## Demographics and Working Conditions

The number of legal street markets in Santiago grew rapidly in the second half of the twentieth century. The 1938 law legalised four street markets, and by 1955 the number of legal markets in the metropolitan region had grown to 87. Fifty years later, in 2005, the total number of street markets in Chile had reached 657, of which 401 were located in Metropolitan Santiago.[19] According to the Chilean Association of Organisations of Street Markets (Asociacion Chilena de Organizaciones de Ferias Libres, ASOF), Santiago is home to about 40,000 market vendors, of a total of roughly 80,000 in the country.

Ferias libres originally developed around the distribution of agricultural products and consequently housed mostly food vendors, although vendors of household products, arts and crafts, electronics, and other goods can also be found. According to ASOF's president, ferias libres sustain 300,000 small farmers who distribute their produce via street markets; the same leader estimated that street vendors currently control 80 per cent of sales in fruits and vegetables (Aliaga Linares 2006: 60). The predominance of food vendors in Chile also reflects the country's broader position as one of the region's leading agricultural producers.

Working conditions in Santiago's street markets are relatively good in that the use of public space for vending is officially sanctioned and, relatively speaking, effectively regulated. This means that security of workspace, the most important problem for vendors in other countries, is a less pressing issue for Santiago's vendors; although public authorities have the ultimate say in whether a street market may continue to operate, vendors generally are not subject to the type of arbitrary expulsions that occur in other countries. Nonetheless, there are vendors in Santiago who are unable to secure a market stall and a license, and their only option is often to gather around the periphery of the established markets and dodge the authorities as vendors in other countries do.

## Legal Issues

Street vending in Santiago is regulated by local governments. Metropolitan Santiago consists of 32 political-administrative units called *comunas*, which are governed by mayors and are equivalent to local municipalities in other capital cities in the region. Local officials in the comunas primarily regulate two aspects of street commerce: first, the place and time in which street markets are authorised to operate; and second, the issuance of licenses which authorise individual vendors to occupy market space. In terms of the first aspect, most markets are open from 8 a.m. to 3 p.m., so that investments in lighting and security for nighttime vending are unnecessary. Though vending associations and residential associations are given input into the public space allocated for official street markets, local officials ultimately determine market regulations (Aliaga Linares 2005: 11).

In terms of the second issue, local officials attempt to control access to vending space in Santiago's ferias libres by issuing a limited number of licenses. By limiting the quantity of licenses available, local authorities attempt to diminish the negative effects of street markets, such as noise, congestion and the accumulation of garbage in public space. Nonetheless, limitations on the number of licenses issued in low-income areas where formal employment is scarce have led to increases in unlicensed vendors, or *coleros*. Although local authorities have developed a transparent process for licensing applications, that process is sometimes circumvented by vendors who have privileged connections in the area.[20]

## Organisation

Vendors who hold licenses and work in Santiago's ferias libres are organised into base-level associations, which in turn belong to the Chilean Association of Organisations of Street Markets. The ASOF was formed in 2001 in response to the growing threat posed by multinational supermarket chains and the generalised opinion that street markets were destined to become extinct as an outmoded commercial model.

Chile's street vending organisations play two primary roles. First, they serve as gatekeepers to officially sanctioned market spaces; for example, a newcomer to a market must have a letter from that market's organisation sanctioning their application for a license to vend in one of the market's spaces. In this way, vending organisations provide a method of internal governance that helps promote order within each feria libre. Second, these associations promote the interests of vendors in the political system. One of the major activities of vending organisations at present, for example, is to promote a new law of street markets that gives vendors more rights and brings more order to established markets. According to ASOF, the new law is currently under review in the National Commission for Small and Micro Enterprises.

## Sao Paulo, Brazil

Brazil is both the largest and most unequal country in the Latin American region. Despite some macroeconomic and political instability in the past two decades, it has not experienced the sort of political crises that drove large numbers of the unemployed into other urban centres (such as Lima and Bogota) in the 1990s. Nonetheless, street vending is a common occupation in urban areas. Brazil's largest city, Sao Paulo, is host to more than 18 million people—nearly 10 per cent of the country's population (United Nations 2006)—and street vendors represent about 11 per cent of its economically active population. (See also Chapter 11 in this book for a graphic description of street vending and its patterns.)

### Demographics and Working Conditions

According to Itikawa (2006a), 54.9 per cent of the Brazilian workforce is in the informal sector, and within that sector, roughly 7 per cent work as street vendors. Not surprisingly, as the continent's largest country, Brazil is also host to the largest total population of documented street vendors, at 711,825. In the metropolitan region of Sao Paulo, the largest city in Brazil and one of the largest in the world, approximately 42 per cent of workers are in the informal economy, and according to a 2001 estimate the city was home to approximately 73,000 street vendors.[21] In three of the five largest cities in Brazil—Sao Paulo, Rio de Janeiro and Puerto Alegre—street vendors represent more than 7 per cent of the economically active population (11.0 per cent, 8.6 per cent, and 7.1 per cent , respectively).

According to Pamplona (2004) nearly three-fourths (73.3 per cent) of Sao Paulo's street vendors are women, and more than half (52 per cent) are heads of household.[22] Compared to the city's overall labour force, in which 56 per cent are women and 46 per cent are heads of household, these figures reflect the importance of street vending as a means of generating household income. Many women traders work for 12–14 hours a day, and the lack of day care facilities means that those with children often must bring their children with them to their posts in the streets. Sao Paulo's street vending population appears to be racially mixed (58 per cent white, 7 per cent black, 32 per cent *pardo* [mixed], and 3 per cent Asian), but predominantly composed of people from either the country's north-east or south-east regions. Only 2.5 per cent of the city's vendors are from outside the country. In the downtown area, the ratio of men to women was the reverse of the city-wide rate, with nearly three-fourths men and one-fourth women. That trend is likely a consequence of the dangerous working conditions downtown (Itikawa 2006a).

In terms of working conditions, Sao Paulo's vendors face a wide variety of circumstances, as is the case in other urban centres in the region. Income levels and stability among traders vary from one street to the next (for a detailed description see Luciana Itikawa [2006b] partly reported in Chapter 11 in this book).

## Legal Issues

Though there is no national legislation on street vending in Brazil, legislation related to street commerce in Sao Paulo dates back three centuries (Itikawa 2004). However, as in Lima, the accumulation of legislation over time has done little to produce an effective governance regime for street commerce (see Chapter 11 in this book).

The last legal decision regarding street trade, sanctioned by City Hall in 2002, established controls over street vending near certain public assets, such as schools, hospitals and railway stations. According to Itikawa, only those vendors who are able to negotiate favours with the authorities are granted access to these restricted zones, which tend to be more profitable because of their high levels of pedestrian traffic. Those who cannot secure licenses must pay bribes in order to enjoy the commercial advantages of these locations. Relocation efforts, such as those of mayor Celso Pitta (1996–2000), established off-street centres for vendors, but many were located away from pedestrian traffic, offering few opportunities for vendors to maintain incomes earned on the street. As in other cases, the off-street locations were eventually used for storage or abandoned.

## Organisation

Sao Paulo is host to 770 associations of street vendors (Horn 2004). Most of these organisations lack democratic leadership practices, as is the case in many other Latin American countries. However, the electoral success of the country's political left has generated new interest in organising informal workers among trade union federations, in particular the CUT. According to StreetNet (2005), SINTEIN-CUT is the only central union of workers with its headquarters in Sao Paulo where the informal economy has experienced rapid growth in recent years.

# Conclusion

The case studies in this chapter have highlighted both the empirical importance of street vending as a major issue in Latin American urban governance and the need for more systematic research on the topic across the region. Available studies differ in their geographic scope, methodological approaches and analytic foci, making it difficult to draw broader inferences about the street vending population as a whole. The need for cross-nationally comparable, longitudinal data on the sector is clear; without good descriptive data on street traders, policy towards them will remain inadequate.

Nonetheless, the case studies do suggest some commonalities across a broad range of political, economic and social conditions. Where the legal status of street vendors is clearly addressed in national law, and where high courts can provide rulings that resolve jurisdictional disputes and prioritise among conflicting rights and responsibilities, local governments can more effectively govern the sector. Support for street vending organisations to aggregate interests in the sector through democratic, representative procedures is also more likely to produce good policy, as long as those interests are incorporated into the policy-making process. Relocation projects are a common strategy for coping with overcrowded street markets, and these can provide more workplace security and better working conditions for some vendors. However, they must also provide income security in order to prevent a return to the streets. Producing good descriptive data on vendors, clearly stating their rights and responsibilities in legislation, and assuring that the input of some of the most vulnerable vendors—including women, heads of household and those without entrepreneurial training—is incorporated into the policy process can help overcome some of the sector's most pressing problems.

## Notes

1. ILO Press Release, 2 May 2006 (available at http://www.ilo.org/public/english/bureau/inf/pr/2006/14.htm, accessed 23 May 2006).
2. I am especially grateful for the contributions of Luciana Itikawa (University of Sao Paulo, Brazil); Maria Fernanda Garcia (University of Cambridge, UK); Lissette Aliaga Linares (University of Texas at Austin, USA); and Caroline Stamm (Universite Marne-La-Vallee, France), who helped compile data and secondary sources for this report. It should be noted that information on each theme is incomplete from country to country, as published academic research on the subject of street trade in Latin America remains relatively scarce despite the phenomenon's empirical importance in the region.

3. Data collected in April–June 2005 (www.dane.gov.co).

4. These vendors are likely to have mobile stands, such as push carts, tents or tarps. They are thus distinguished from fixed-post vendors who have permanent stands (such as kiosks or other types of fixed structures) and ambulatory vendors, who carry their merchandise as they walk through the streets.

5. Law 388 reinforces this principle; see FVP (2001b: 3). The relative clarity of Colombian law with regard to street commerce has given vendors there a measure of security that does not exist in other countries where vending rights are less explicit. One example of a Constitutional Court ruling that explicitly recognises the needs of street traders subject to relocation illustrates this point. It reads:

> Although the general interest in preserving public space outweighs the particular interest of stationary and ambulatory vendors, it is necessary, according to jurisprudence, to reconcile appropriately and harmoniously the rights and responsibilities in conflict. Therefore, expulsions from public space are constitutionally permitted only when there exists a judicial process that authorizes it, in compliance with the rules established prior to the expulsion, and when policies that guarantee that the occupants will not be neglected are enacted.

The ruling also states that measures such as training for vendors and improved access to credit are permissible alternatives to relocation. The Court thus plays a critical role in calling on local authorities to consider the needs of vendors, rather than treating them as a public nuisance.

6. The Urban Reform Law of 1989 and Presidential Decree 1421 of 1993 form an important part of this legal framework.

7. Martin Kaste, 'Latin American Cities: Caracas', aired 24 March 2004, National Public Radio (http://www.npr.org/templates/story/story. php?storyId=1787749, accessed 31 May 2006).

8. My translation.

9. The term of Ellner and Myers (2002).

10. INEI (2006: 58–60). The INEI does not publish estimates of the size of the informal sector from its employment surveys, but rather publishes estimates of the size of the economically active population in small and micro-enterprises. Though some small and micro-enterprises are undoubtedly registered, we can assume that a significant percentage of those working in micro-enterprises would be considered 'informal' by standard definitions.

11 See Chavez and de la Flor (1998) and de Soto (1989).

12. Caqueta is a 'commercial conglomerate' located in the heart of Lima where the country's principal north–south and east–west highways intersect.

13. These are Decreto Legislativo 705 (Law of Micro and Small Enterprise Promotion, 1991); Ley 27268/Decreto Supremo 030-2000-MITINCI (General Law of Small and Micro Enterprises, 2000); and Ley 28015/Decreto Supremo 009-2003-TR (Law of Micro and Small Enterprise Promotion and Formalization, 2003).

14. Lima also lacks a single agency to govern street commerce, as the FVP does in Bogota, and it has not undergone a similar experience of fiscal decentralisation, so local mayors are left with few resources to deal with the problem effectively.

15. See Stamm (2006) for a comparison of the Historic Centers in Lima and Mexico City.

16. This figure does not include street vendors who live outside the Federal District. See Williams (2006: 1).

17. An analysis of definitions and available statistics in Mexico is presented in Williams (2006).

18. See Williams (2006: 12).

19. These figures are presented as part of the Information System for Street Markets (Sistema de Informacion Feria Libre, SIFL), created by the NGO Espacio y Fomento and presented on the ASOF website (http://www.feriaslibresdechile.cl).

20. For example, local governments typically require an application, proof of residence, payment of a tax, and a letter from the relevant street vending organisation designating a particular space to the applicant in order for a license to be issued. However, applicants sometimes circumvent these rules by borrowing the address of a relative or using a connection in the organisation to get the letter (see Aliaga 2006).

21. The source of this estimate is the Sao Paulo Province Data Research Agency and Foundation (Itikawa 2006b). The informal sector wing of one of the country's major trade union confederations, SINTEIN-CUT (Sindicato dos Trabalhadores na Economia Informal-CUT) produced an estimate of about 100,000 street vendors in the city of Sao Paulo in 2006.

22. Cited in Itikawa (2006b).

## References

Aliaga Linares, Lissette. 2002. *Sumas y Restas: El Capital Social como Recurso en la Informalidad*. Lima: Alternativa.

———. 2004. 'The Economic and Spatial Behavior of Street Markets: Santiago de Chile in a Context of Commercial Modernization'. Manuscript, Population Research Center, Department of Sociology, University of Texas at Austin.

———. 2005. 'Public Space and Street Markets in Modern Santiago'. Unpublished manuscript, Department of Sociology, University of Texas at Austin.

Aliaga Linares, Lissette. 2006. 'Street Markets in Santiago de Chile: An Assessment of their Locational and Regulation Policy'. Masters Thesis, Department of Sociology, University of Texas at Austin.

Chavez, Eliana and Ricardo de la Flor. 1998. 'Nuevo Rostro de la Vieja Urbe: Comercio Ambulatorio y Recuperación del Centro Histórico de Lima', in Eliana Chavez et al. (eds), *Perú: El Sector Informal Frente al Reto de la Modernización*, Lima: Oficina Internacional del Trabajo.

Cross, John C. 1998. *Informal Politics: Street Vendors and the State in Mexico City*, Stanford: Stanford University Press.

de Soto, Hernando. 2002 (1989). *The Other Path: The Economic Answer to Terrorism*, New York: Basic Books.

Donovan, Michael G. 2002. 'Space Wars in Bogotá: The Recovery of Public Space and its Impact on Street Vendors'. Masters Thesis, Department of Urban Studies and Planning, Massachusetts Institute of Technology.

Ellner, Steve and David J. Myers. 2002. 'Caracas: Incomplete Empowerment Amid Geopoliticacl Feudalism', Chapter 4 in David J. Myers and Henry Dietz (eds), *Capital City Politics in Latin America: Democratization and Empowerment*, Boulder: Lynne Rienner.

Fondo de Ventas Populares (FVP). 2001a. 'Reporte del Fondo de Ventas Populares Entregado a la Controlaría Distrital', available at http://univerciudad. redbogota.com/ediciones/indice010.htm, accessed on 19 May 2006.

————. 2001b. *Bogotá Para Vivir: Reflexiones Sobree las Ventas Ambulantes y Estacionarias y la Afectación del Espacio Públic,*. Alcaldía Mayor de Bogotá, D.C., Secretaria de Gobierno Distrital.

Garcia Rincon, Maria Fernanda. 2006a. 'A Short Assessment of the Situation of Street Vendors in Caracas, Venezuela'. Unpublished manuscript, University of Cambridge (UK).

————. 2006b. 'Appropriation of Public Space: The Politics of Exchange and Market Transactions in Caracas, Venezuela'. Paper presented at the Annual Conference of the Society of Latin American Studies (SLAS), Nottingham, UK, 31 March–2 April.

Hernandez, Patricia, Alfredo Zettna, Medardo Tapia, Claudia Ortiz, and Irma Coria Soto. 1996. 'Childcare Needs of Female Street Vendors in Mexico City', *Health and Policy Planning*, 11(2): 169–78.

Horn, Patricia. 2004. 'Building Alliances in Latin America', StreetNet News No. 4 (November 2004), available at http://www.streetnet.org.za/English/ Stnetnews6.htm, accessed on 6 October 2006.

International Labor Organization. 2002. 'STAT Working Paper No. 1-2002: ILO Compendium of Official Statistics on Employment in the Informal Sector', available at http://www.ilo.org/public/english/bureau/stat/papers/ comp.htm.

Instituto Nacional de Estadistica e Informatica (INEI). 2006. 'Situación del Mercado Laboral en Lima Metropolitana, Junio 2006', Informe Tecnico, 7, July.

Itikawa, Luciana. 2004. 'Clandestine Geometries: Informal Labor in São Paulo's Downtown Public Spaces', Translation of Luciana Itikawa, 'Geometrias da Clandestinidade', in *Caminhos para o Centro: Estrategias de Desenvolvimento para a Regiao Central de São Paulo*, São Paulo: PMSP/CEBRAP/CEM.

————. 2006a. 'World Class Cities and the Urban Informal Economy: Inclusive Planning for the Working Poor'. Powerpoint presentation prepared for the WIEGO Urban Policies Colloquium, Durban, South Africa, 24–25 April 2006.

————. 2006b. 'Street Vending in Downtown São Paulo'. Unpublished manuscript, School of Architecture and Urbanism, University of São Paulo.

Kaste, Martin. 2004. 'Latin American Cities: Caracas', National Public Radio, 24 March 2004. Broadcast available at http://www.npr.org/templates/story/story.php?storyId=1787749, accessed on 31 May 2006.

Olea Suarez, Doris Marlene and Gonzalo Huertas Laverde. 1996. 'Mercados Callejeros en Bogotá: Soluciones Integrales del Impacto Socioeconómico'. Unpublished Document, Lima: International Labor Organization.

Pamplona, J. B. 2004. 'A atividade informal do comércio de rua e a Região Central da Cidade de São Paulo', in A. Comin (ed.), *Caminhos para o centro: Estratégias de desenvolvimento para a região central de São Paulo*, pp. 307–38, Sao Paulo: CEM/CEBRA/EMURB.

Pena, Sergio. 1999. 'Informal Markets: Street Vendors in Mexico City', *Habitat International*, 23(3) (September): 363–72.

Roever, Sally. 2003. '2003 Microbusiness Survey', May–June.

————. 2005. 'Negotiating Formality: Informal Sector, Market, and State in Peru'. Ph.D. Dissertation, Department of Political Science, University of California-Berkeley.

————. 2006. 'Enforcement and Compliance in Lima's Street Markets: The Origins and Consequences of Policy Incoherence towards Informal Traders', Chapter 14 in Basudeb Guha-Khasnobis, Ravi Kanbur and Elinor Ostrom (eds), *Linking the Formal and Informal Economy: Concepts and Policies*, New York: Oxford University Press.

Salazar, Gabriel. 2003. *Ferias Libres: Espacio Residual de Soberanía Ciudadana*, Santiago: Ediciones Sur.

Stamm, Caroline. 2006. 'Comercio Ambulante, Políticas Públicas y Centro Histórico: Estudio de los Casos de México y Lima'. Paper presented at the Annual Conference of the Society of Latin American Studies (SLAS), Nottingham, UK, 31 March–2 April.

StreetNet. 2005. 'Street Vendors Confront Military Police in São Paulo'. *StreetNet News*, 6, September 2005, available at http://www.streetnet.org.za/English/Stnetnews6.htm, accessed on 6 October 2006.

Sulmont Haak, David. 1999. 'Del "Jirón" al "Boulevard Gamarra": Estrategies políticas y gobierno local en La Victoria-Lima', in Martin Tanaka (ed.), *El Poder Visto Desde Abajo: Democracia, Educación y Ciudadanía en Espacios Locales*, Lima: Instituto de Estudios Peruanos.

Tokman, Victor E. 2001. 'De la Informalidad a la Modernidad', Chapter 1 in Victor E. Tokman et al. (eds), *De La Informalidad a la Modernidad*, Geneva: International Labor Organization.

UN HABITAT. 2006. *Innovative Policies for the Urban Informal Economy*, Nairobi: UN-HABITAT.

United Nations. 2006. 'World Urbanization Prospects: The 2005 Revision Population Database', available at http://esa.un.org/unup/.

Williams, Mary. 2006. *Street Sellers in Mexico City: Characteristics and Statistical Analysis, 1990–2000*, Centro de la Vivienda y Estudios Urbanos, Mexico, D.F.

World Bank. 2001. 'Colombia Poverty Report, Volume II', available at http://wbln0018.worldbank.org/LAC/lacinfoclient.nsf/By+Country/3A36A511B2 3F3B0385256AF60073D1C6?OpenDocument.

———. 2006. World Development Indicators, available at http://web.worldbank.org/WBSITE/EXTERNAL/DATASTATISTICS/0,content MDK:20899413 ~pagePK:64133150~piPK:64133175~theSitePK:239419,00.html, accessed on 21 May 2006.

Zanoni Lopez, Wladimir. 2005. *Buhoneros en Caracas: Un Estudio Exploratorio y Algunas Propuestas de Políticas Públicas*, Caracas: Centro de Divulgacion del Conocimiento Economico (CEDICE).

# 10

# Governance of Street Trade in Caracas, Venezuela

## Maria Fernanda Garcia Rincon

This chapter examines the legal issues concerning the governance of street vending in Venezuela's vibrant capital. It includes an analysis of the laws, ordinances and general practices in Caracas that regulate the activity of street vending, as well as an examination of the struggle between the constitutional right of non-dependent workers to work and local regulations that limit street trading. This chapter also briefly discusses the lack of clear 'rules of the game' related to the city's governance of street trade.

Street vendors in Caracas defend their occupation of public space as an extension of their constitutional right to work. The municipal authority in Caracas is therefore challenged and caught between the choices of tolerating street trading, attempting to regulate public space and enforcing the regulations, or using force to clear the streets completely of vendors. Involved in all of these choices is a struggle between the law and rights at different institutional levels. This reality is further complicated by statements made by President Hugo Chavez in support of vendors in the city. As Roever (in this volume) suggests, the 'resulting interplay between vendors and governments has made street trade a major issue in Latin American urban governance'.

The underlying issue, I suggest, is a constitutional-legal one. How does the state address the contradiction between different definitions of rights in a country where employment continues to fall and the right to work and the right to property are considered in similar terms, and compete for the same privileges? How does one relate the official legal system to the existence of informal rules and popular mechanisms for self-help (Fernandes and Varley 1998)? Street vendors seek to legitimise their right to work as one that is constitutionally given, but largely ignored in practice, while simultaneously confronting a complete lack of 'recognised' rights over the space where they work.

The data presented in this chapter was collected between September 2004 and May 2005.[1] Through this effort, 366 garment traders in Caracas's most critical areas of street vending—Sabana Grande, El Cementerio, El Centro and Catia in the municipality El Libertador—were surveyed.[2] The data considered here is further complemented by the testimonies gathered from more than 30 street vendors individually interviewed. Interviews with public authorities and an analysis of legal documents and newspaper articles since 1985 are also included amongst the relevant data.

## Street Vending in Caracas

Charmes (2002) calculated that in 1997 there were 318,598 street vendors in Venezuela, representing 4 per cent of the non-agricultural labour force. The Organizacion Internacional de Trabajo (OIT) (2003) estimates that 30.3 per cent (or approximately 1.5 million people) of the informal workforce in Venezuela is dedicated to vending. Zanoni (2005: 42) estimates that there are 18,000 street vendors in Caracas. However, the national census calculates that metropolitan Caracas has 48,675 people working in the streets, 38,458 of which work in the municipality El Libertador (Instituto Nacional de Estadistica [INE] 2001; Metropolitan Mayor's Office [MMO] 2004).

The lack of productive employment is the main cause for the growing figures in the informal economy in Venezuela (Espana 2006). The permanence of street vendors in Caracas has stemmed in large part from weak state integration (Cross 1998), poor economic growth/performance, loss of jobs in the formal sector (Zanoni 2005), lack of coordination among authorities, and political clientelism (Febres et al. 1995).[3]

The ILO has recently argued that the right to vend, within reasonable limits, should be considered a basic economic right (International Labour Organisation [ILO] 2002: 50).[4] With this argument in mind, the Federation of Non-Dependent Workers of Venezuela (FUTRAND), an organisation that groups non-dependent workers at the national level, began to lobby at the National Constituent Assembly in 1998–99 to recognise non-dependent workers as legitimate actors in the 1999 Constitution. Preceding a series of presidential statements, the 1999 Constitution gave non-dependent workers, including street vendors, a formal and constitutional right to work. Although this is an important recognition, street vendors are still victims of harassment, bribes and manipulation

(Llerena 2005) because they lack legal status or the formal right to sell (ILO 2002: 49–50) at the local or municipal level.

## Right to Work on the Streets

Over time, street vendors have gained symbolic recognition and solidarity for their right—as any other citizen—to seek employment. Fifty-one per cent of inhabitants of El Libertador municipality agree that street vendors have a right to work in the street (CEDICE 2005).[5] Citizens are divided on the subject of whether street vendors should be relocated from the streets. For example, only 23 per cent strongly agreed that they should be relocated, while 37 per cent thought they should be able to work on the street (ibid.). However, these same individuals recognised that they are a problem for city management and/or planning and 60 per cent strongly agreed that street vendors obstruct day-to-day traffic (ibid.). This has been taken by organised groups as the platform from which to demand state recognition for their activity.

The law is a central determinant of the form and operation of urban social, economic and political processes. Legal studies preserve the tradition of exploring the law-as-domination, determining and regulating exclusion (McAuslan 1998: 47). Thus, it is important to discuss the legal instruments that frame the structure in which street vendors carry out their activities and struggle to legitimise their right to work. When discussing the legal framework that affects the workers of the informal economy, we must address two distinct 'layers'. First, at the constitutional and national level we have legislatures that discuss non-dependent workers' right to work, organise and protest. Second, at the municipal level we have a series of ordinances, decrees and regulations regarding the use of public space.

The state has the monopoly to legislate, regulate and control public space. The legal normative established by municipal authorities is to solve a problem of public order by prohibiting street vending (Marquez undated).[6] Such a legal normative ignores the conceptual basis and socio-economic conditions of this structural problem. In the case of the decree of El Libertador municipality (Libertador's Mayor's Office [LMO] 2004), it specifically articulates the need to hold in balance informal traders' right to work and the right of citizens to use public space. Yet, the ordinance, legally above the decree, largely prohibits this activity.

Paradoxically, ordinances and decrees are both simple and ambiguous. Implementing ordinances and decrees is difficult, given the contradiction with the national Constitution and national laws. This has led to confusion, illegality and arbitrary solutions. I will now explore each of the instruments—the national Constitution, the Organic Labour Law, and the ordinance and decree of El Libertador municipality—as well as what they imply.

## The Constitution

The Venezuelan Constitution (1999) recognises and specifically mentions the right to work of non-dependent or self-employed workers.[7] In the previous Constitution (1961), these individuals were not specially mentioned as a group with legitimate rights to organise and make claims for labour rights. As Article 87 of the 1999 Constitution states:

> All persons have the right and duty to work. The state guarantees the adoption of the necessary measures so that every person shall be able to obtain productive work providing him or her with a dignified and decorous living and guaranteeing him or her full exercise of this right. It is an objective of the state to promote employment. Measures tending to guarantee the exercise of the labour rights of self-employed [non-dependant] persons shall be adopted by law. Freedom to work shall be subject only to such restrictions as may be established by law.

This has been taken by organised groups as a platform from which to demand state recognition for their activity. In conversations with Yolanda Wundeheiler, a labour union leader, for example, I was reminded several times that for workers of the informal economy the Constitution guaranteed the right to work, and as such they are merely exercising that right (Garcia Rincon 2007). However, the majority of street vendors (65 per cent) did not agree with such a statement and only 33 per cent agree that the Constitution gives them a right to work on the street (CEDICE 2004).

> Interviewer: Look, do you think that you have a right to use the street to work?
> Carlos: The street belongs to the people, as Chavez says.
> Interviewer: And you consider that as a right?
> Carlos: We all have a right to the street, all of us. (Interview, 8 April 2005)

Those that cite a constitutional right to work on the street give citizenship and labour exclusion arguments, often referring to President Chavez's statements 'that the street belongs to the people' or that street vendors are 'not to be touched' by the municipal authority. Over the years, vendors had made appeals to the courts over the alleged unconstitutional nature of the ordinances and decrees, yet they were never successful.

## Labour Law

Furthermore, the Organic Labour Law had previously (1997) defined non-dependent workers in Article 40:[8]

> It is understood that non-dependant workers are the persons who habitually make a living by his/her work without being in a situation of dependence with respect to one or various patrons.

The Labour Law also states that non-dependent workers have the right to organise labour unions, according to the requirements established in the Law, and that 'they will be progressively incorporated into the system of social security and other norms of protection of workers, when possible'. Access to social security by non-dependent workers is also cited in the Constitution. In practice, however, such access has not materialised.

The recognition of the street vendors' right to organise came as a result of many years of struggle. Yet, only approximately 37 per cent of vendors participate in street vending organisations (CEDICE 2004).

So, although according to the Constitution and the Labour Law non-dependent workers are recognised as legitimate actors, public space is regulated by municipal regulations in accordance with national law (Zanoni 2005). Public space is regulated through a series of ordinances, decrees and regulations by the local municipality, which is contradictory, confusing and often inapplicable. The ordinance, a higher legal instrument, prohibits trading in areas such as boulevards, street corners, metro exits, and near public offices and historical buildings. Yet, those are precisely the areas with the higher concentration of street vendors: Sabana Grande, El Cementerio, El Centro and Catia. The instrument in practice regulating the activity, however, is the decree of 2004. It is this instrument that the mayor, the media and some organisations refer to when discussing the issue of public space usage.

## Ordinance

The municipality of El Libertador currently regulates the usage of public space through Ordinance 1789-3, published on 9 September 1998, establishing the norms through which natural persons may trade articles on public space. This ordinance allows only persons who are Venezuelan, over 18 years of age, who live in El Libertador municipality and who carry out trade on the street as their only source of income. Although nationality was not included in our study, a government census states that 73 per cent of street vendors are Venezuelan (17 per cent foreign nationals, the remainder nationalised), and none are under 18 years of age.[9] However, only 85 per cent live in El Libertador.

Only three structures are involved in normal, day-to-day trade: kiosks, or fixed structures that generally sell newspapers and flowers and that are fairly well regulated; stands, which are dismantled at the end of the day but have a fixed location and where vendors work according to a pre-established schedule and are the 'problematic' bit of informal commerce; and ambulant sales, such as mobile structures, without a fixed location.

The areas permitted for trading or informal commerce are determined by the individual municipality and published as an agreement (which currently does not exist, although the decree is published as a negotiated instrument). Areas that allow vending are those that do not create an obstacle or obstruct the traffic of transients. Areas of maximum restriction to trading include: (a) public areas of rapid circulation, (b) walkways, boulevards, plazas and parks, etc.[10] It is important to note that the four areas we are discussing in this chapter are, according to this ordinance, areas of maximum restriction: boulevards (Sabana Grande and Catia), areas that surround historical buildings and governmental offices (Centro), and areas for vehicular transit (Cementerio). Handicapped individuals, senior citizens (over age 55 for women and 60 for men), and artisans and painters of popular art will be allocated space exclusively for their own use.

According to the ordinance, only certain activities will be given permits for using public spaces.[11] Although dry goods are included amongst the permitted products, in practice, there is day-to-day discussion between the authorities and the street vendors' leaders/representatives with regard to this. Most of the other products allowed are sold through kiosks, while goods such as food products use mobile structures. The problematic traders are those with dry goods, such as clothing sold in removable stands, and those that sell pirated CDs, DVDs and fireworks in December.

To be able to sell commodities in a public space, a permit or license is needed. This permit is given by the municipal office.[12] However, less than 1 per cent of street vendors have a permit (CEDICE 2004). Additionally, the ordinance clarifies that civil servants cannot give a concession for the usage of public space, although it fails to acknowledge which department gives the permit or what the procedure followed actually is. This allows space for 'bureaucratic charisma' to underline decisions, or the 'turning of a blind eye'. In other words, elected officials may allow vendors to work on the street through an 'informal ok' in exchange for political support. Lack of clarity in the law allows for the legal instrument to be negotiated. The majority do not have formal licences or permits but rather informal approval to work on the street by diverse institutions and/or persons (see Garcia Rincon 2007). There is no unified unit for regulating street vending, so competing interests of different authorities lack one coherent policy. As a result, state integration becomes increasingly weak.

An issue for protest is the established maximum size of the stands at 0.75 m × 1.5 m. Most street vendors exceed this size, particularly during December, when informal sales reach their peak. The space allowed for free transit is at least 1.2 m, which again is disregarded, since part of the marketing strategy is to create a tunnel through which pedestrians must walk, thereby requiring them to pass each stand and making purchases along the way.

## Decree

In practice, the instrument used for regulating street vending in El Libertador has been Decree No. 2463-B (published 19 January 2004). Through this agreement with representatives of the informal economy, the Decree suggests that informal commerce requires a new legal normative that conciliates efficiently and effectively the right to work of the informal traders with the right of the rest of the citizens to use and enjoy the public areas of El Libertador municipality.

As Ana Esparragosa, a labour union leader, puts it: 'We disagree with the Decree. One ordinance throws out another [ordinance], not a decree'.[13] Esparragosa calls for formality in using legal instruments, since with the current negotiated conditions, street vendors remain vulnerable to political manipulation.

Essentially, the Decree establishes that 'assemblies of citizens' (*asambleas de ciudadanos*) of the informal economy should be held by geographical sector. The decree also states that informal traders in El Libertador should work between 8 a.m. and 8 p.m., and that there should be one day per week when they do not work.[14] Space should be kept clean and trash disposed. Cars are not to be used to sell merchandise, and metro exits, bus stops and street corners should remain clear. Fixed structures are prohibited, and for cultural reasons historic locations are to remain free of street vending. A series of studies, commissions and actions are to be undertaken to seek solutions to the problem of street vending. El Libertador municipality commits itself to providing security through its own police force (*Policia de Caracas*).

In practice, conflict between street vendors and municipal authorities arises over the details of the Decree and over the fact that it attempts to hold in balance the right to work and the right to the use of public space;

the police, the governmental authorities and the street vendors are all accused of disrespecting the agreement. Everyday resistance includes the pleading of ignorance with regards to this instrument, since it was reached in consensus with street vending leaders but not through general participation of the sector.

Of the 366 vendors interviewed, 34 per cent thought that the law that regulates street vending is badly defined; 39 per cent, meanwhile, thought that it was not applicable and 47 per cent argued that the ordinances and decrees that regulate public space and their activity went against their right to work (CEDICE 2004).[15] Street vendors at large ignore and evade such legislation. They enter into processes of 'negotiation of the law' with the public authority in charge of enforcing such law(s) or regulation. Many years of resistance have narrowed the policy options available and have legitimised vendors as visible city actors.

## The Executive and the Law

The policies adopted and carried out by the executive branch can add to the confusion of the multi-layered interpretation and practice of the law. Public statements incite the development of informal activity, often in a confusing, contradictory way. For example, there have been several cases in which President Chavez has declared, 'Don't mess with the street vendors [*buhoneros*]'. Street vendors have interpreted this statement as a show of direct support. In a system of 'personalistic politics', informal statements and political discourse are taken to be equal or even higher than the law. For this reason, although the law is the starting point for this discussion, it is the actions and discourse of street vendors, the president and administrative state officials that determine the working reality that allow for the exchange and appropriation of public space. The president's support of vendors has resulted in the municipal authority 'turning a blind eye' to trading activities. As a result, enforcement of the ordinance and decree is now lower. The monopoly that the state has over public space is now managed, in many cases, by local street vending organisations (see Garcia Rincon 2007).

## Space, Rights and the State

Soja (1989) has argued for the need for space to be incorporated together and complementary to the social and historical spheres in understanding social change. Thus, space should not be seen as a background to other processes but central to it. The street vendors' entire livelihood depends on access to space (Brown 2006a). Inequality is embedded in space, and such struggles, manifested through protests and everyday acts of resistance (Scott 1985), are also played out in space (Soja 1989).

From an institutional perspective, the issue of property rights is also important. As Brown (2006b: 31) argues, 'access to public space is controlled by a complex system of rights'. The exercise of rights depends on the formal legal norms and the political culture that transforms rules into action. This chapter mainly refers to rights to access and usage of public space. Although access to public space is permitted, the right to use it for trading is prohibited. As Harvey (1973) argues, urban public space is an imperfect common good, as it may be freely available but not equally accessible to all individuals. How the state controls access and enforces its regulations is central to this discussion.

The politics of space, as a change in the use of space, is central to understanding struggle. Constitutional rights are contested by the local authority and re-contested by vendors. Statements by the president therefore add further conflict to local regulations. As a result, the law is contested through everyday practices of negotiation, resistance and protest.

LaCabana (1993: 198) has argued that the quasi-legal logic of informality in Caracas overtakes formal legality. LaCabana explains that vendors invade and privatise public space, thereby altering the formal organisational logic of the city according to the 'survival logic' of vendors. The state responds to these changes by using both repression and tolerance as strategies. The state represses vendors to solve the problem of public order, while it is also tolerant of street sales because therein lies potential for clientelism and political legitimacy (also, see Portes et al. 1989: 37). The negotiation of regulations is therefore the result of the authority turning a 'blind eye' because of the political gains to be obtained. As Cross (1998) argues in the case of Mexico, this occurs because state officials better serve personal political interests by gaining the support of street vendor organisations than by applying the law aimed at limiting the growth of the informal sector. Supporting the street vendor provides both political and monetary support to patrons within the political party and government while weakening state institutions and their integration.

## Governance of Sabana Grande: A Case Study

As Roever (Chapter 9) explains in this volume, legal frameworks that are not clearly defined and enforced or that have overlapping jurisdictional mandates produce confusion and conflict between vendors and the state, which result in low levels of compliance with the written law. One of the main problems related to the governance of Caracas is the lack of coordination and conflicting mandates of the Metropolitan Mayor's Office and the other municipal offices, that is, El Libertador's Mayor's Office. Although LMO is responsible for the urban planning of its municipality, after the creation of the MMO in 1999 some aspects of urban planning became the jurisdiction of MMO. One of those areas of overlapping jurisdictional mandates was the Sabana Grande Boulevard, where between 1,500 and 3,000 street vendors work.

**Illustration 10.1**
**Sabana Grande Boulevard**

The protection and management of Sabana Grande Boulevard had historically been the jurisdiction of LMO, but in 2002 it was declared a 'Metropolitan Public Space' to be regulated by MMO. This change in management was declared directly by the MMO. It was the product of a revision of ordinances and ordinance proposals between 1980 and 1992. However, the change in management was not reached through consensus with LMO or with any other state authority.

Hoping to promote a package of public policies in Sabana Grande, the MMO organised nine months of meetings between key actors (local residents, formal sector representatives, informal sector representatives, government representatives and NGOs). These actors sought a consensus agreement over the public policies to implement oriented to provide effective solutions in the short, medium and long term for the re-ordering and re-vitalising of the metropolitan public space. This was to be done through the implementation of a 'Social, Economic, Cultural and Architectonic Action Plan' directed to recovering and improving public spaces.

The day this agreement was to be signed, all the actors attended the appointment, except the LMO. The latter office backed away from the agreement, partially because signing it would have meant that they would renounce their jurisdiction over that area, and partly because they were not promoting the initiative, thus they would not receive credit for it. Now, who did this space belong to legally? The MMO claimed responsibility for it, but had no legitimacy to manage it, since it was still under LMO jurisdiction. The area became a 'no man's land', and street vending organisations and their leaders began to manage the space, creating a market for trading space. Workers of the Boulevard also began to take advantage of the political conflict between the two authorities. If one authority prohibited an activity, the other authority would allow it, making governance of the area difficult. It is important to note that both the MMO and LMO also have their own police forces and municipal councils that make independent decisions.

In Sabana Grande, 69 per cent of vendors surveyed claimed that they had a right to work there. Of these, 34 per cent stated that LMO had given them permission, a further 10 per cent had received permission from MMO, while 39 per cent had an 'ok' from the street vending organisation (CEDICE 2004). For that right to be respected, the most important factor was not the municipal legislation but rather how long the vendor had been working there. Overlapping jurisdictional mandates and the lack of a clear legal framework lowers enforcement and compliance of the written law (Roever in this volume; Zanoni 2005). Thus, vendors initially take advantage of such an institutional weakness to negotiate informal 'rights' over the space. When a problem arises with LMO or MMO, vendors may even head to the Presidential Palace to have the problem directly managed by President Chavez. However, such practices may lead to political clientelism, making their job security very vulnerable.

One of the positive aspects of the attempt of the MMO to regulate the area was that for the first time two antagonistic sectors—street vendors and shop owners—were able to sit down and negotiate issues that affected them. Amongst the leading issues that they discussed were insecurity, health, and safety and maintenance of the area. Street vendors were pleased to see that they could agree with the business sector on many issues, yet it was largely the lack of political will that limited the results of improving the livelihood of those who worked on the Boulevard and the recuperation of such space.

In early 2007 (and after several presidential elections), the El Libertador mayor stated that the political timing was right to clear vendors from Sabana Grande in an effort to recover the Boulevard and return it to the city's inhabitants. On 5 January 2007 the LMO suspended vendors' permits to work on the Boulevard. The ensuing proposals included: (a) having vendors from Sabana Grande provisionally relocated to a nearby lot, where 1,280 stands were being built while a permanent solution was sought; (b) a pension was allocated to 62 people over 65 years old; (c) scholarships were given to 145 university graduates who worked as vendors; (d) 400 vendors took advantage of technical vocational training; and (e) a building on the Boulevard was being bought and renovated by the LMO with the purpose of building a shopping centre to relocate vendors permanently (Diaz 2007). After a period of both the MMD and the LMO being governed by the ruling period, the vendors of Sabana Grande were cleared and relocated to an open air market near the boulevard.

## Conclusion

This chapter provides a general overview of how lack of clarity in the formulation and enforcement of legal instruments that regulate street vending and public space result in arbitrary solutions and problems in the governance of Caracas. Two levels of legislation enter into conflict because non-dependent workers at the national level are seen to have a legitimate right to work, organise and defend their rights. However, at the municipal level the activity of street vending is prohibited by an ordinance and then partially regulated by a negotiated instrument identified as a decree. This contradiction allows for vendors to take advantage of weak state integration (Cross 1998) and to plot state actors against each other, in many cases approaching different authorities for permission.

In analysing the complex activity of street vending in Caracas, this chapter surveys relevant parts of the written law at the national and local levels. In doing so, it underscores the ambiguity and contradictions at the various levels of the formal law. In turn, this ambiguity and contradiction create spaces for street vendors to negotiate the law's enforcement, leading to an unsuccessful governance of street trade.

# Notes

1. In collaboration with the Centre for the Dissemination of Economic Know-ledge (CEDICE). I thank CEDICE for allowing me to work with them in gathering and using the survey information presented here and for the oppor-tunity to exchange ideas on the informal sector in Venezuela. In particular, I thank Rocio Guijarro, Wladimir Zanoni and Marcos Rodriguez. An earlier draft of this chapter was presented at the LASA 2006 Conference, held in San Juan, Puerto Rico, 15–18 March 2006.
2. El Libertador is the largest municipality in Caracas, and is the place where street vending is more evident and problematic.
3. This concept rests on the idea that state officials better serve personal political interests by gaining the support of street vendor organisations than by applying the law aimed at limiting the growth of the informal sector. Supporting the street vendor provides both political and monetary support to patrons within the political party and government. This is an issue Macharia (1997) explores when developing the notion of an 'unwritten bureaucracy'.
4. See Bellagio International Declaration of Street Vendors (1995). This declaration identifies common problems of street vendors, such as *(1)* lack of legal status that constrains the right to vend; *(2)* lack of space or poor location; *(3)* restrictions of licensing; *(4)* harassment, eviction, bribes; *(5)* lack of services/infrastructure; *(6)* lack of representation or voice.
5. Research included asking, through an opinion poll in March 2005, a series of questions related to street vendors, amounting to 230 people over 18 years of age who were voters. This is a non-probabilistic, random sample, which represented 0.2 per cent of the population of El Libertador municipality. Fifty-four per cent of those interviewed had also bought at least one article from a street vendor in the last three months.
6. For example, Ordinance 1789–3 (9 September 1998); Decree 105–1 (29 January 2004).
7. The Constitution states that 'non-dependent workers' can be taken to refer to self-employed or non-dependent workers.
8. Published as part of the *Gaceta Oficial N° 5.152 Extraordinary* of 19 June 1997.
9. Census carried out by *Alcaldia Mayor*, collected November–December 2002 and February–March 2003.
10. ...(c) sidewalks within 20 m from a curb; (d) bridges, tunnels and areas for vehicular transit; (e) areas that surround governmental agencies, metro secur-ity areas and exits, churches, historic monuments, educational institutions, embassies, financial institutions, hospitals, military and police installations, installations of political parties, museums and libraries, and other buildings determined by the municipality.
11. These activities include selling (a) newspapers and other periodicals; (b) books and school material; (c) cards and paper supply; (d) flowers, bases, baskets;

(e) scissors and wire for flowers; (f) plants and treated dirt; (g) authorised lottery tickets; (h) horse race tickets; (i) metro tickets; (j) telephone cards; (k) condoms; (l) cleaning and shining of shoes; (m) packaged candies, refreshments in cans and glasses; (n) traditional sweets, locally known as *dulces criollos*; (o) hamburgers and hot dogs; (p) ice-cream and *chicha criolla*; (q) Venezuelan art, crafts and artistic activities; (r) dry goods such as clothing; (s) orange juice, *papelon con limon*. Products not included in this list are prohibited from being sold.

12. The permit includes the following conditions: (a) the duration of the permit, which shall never exceed one year but can be renewed; (b) the amount the trader will pay the municipality to be able to occupy space; (c) a guarantee by the trader to insure compliance with obligations; (d) the way in which the municipality will supervise the usage of space in concession; (e) the right of the municipality to relocate or remove the kiosk, stand or ambulant trade before the expiration of the concession. The license must be visible at all times.

13. 'Buhoneros en desacuerdo con normas de Bernal'. *Ultimas Noticias*. 31 January 2004, p. 3.

14. Wednesday for Catia, Sunday for Sabana Grande, City Centre and Candelaria, not including El Cementerio.

15. 49 per cent said that they did not go against the right to work and 4 per cent did not know.

# References

Aliaga, L. 2006. *Street Markets in Santiago de Chile: An Assessment of their Locational and Regulation Policy*. M.A. thesis, University of Texas at Austin.

Brown, A. 2006a. 'Challenging Street Livelihoods', in A. Brown (ed.), *Contested Space: Street Trading, Public Space, and Livelihoods in Developing Cities*, Rugby: ITDG Publishing.

———. 2006b. 'Urban Public Space in the Developing World—A Resource for the Poor', in A. Brown (ed.), *Contested Space: Street Trading, Public Space, and Livelihoods in Developing Cities*, Rugby: ITDG Publishing.

CEDICE. 2004. Research project 'Building Consensus to Reduce Poverty', Financed by Center for Private Initiative (CIPE). Unpublished Data Base of Survey results.

———. 2005. 'Opinion Poll of Voters of Libertador Municipality'. Unpublished Database.

Charmes, J. 2002. 'Is Asking for "Place of Work" a Pertinet and Efficient Way to Better Measure and Understand the Category of Homeworkers, and More Generally, Outworkers in the Labour Force?' in ILO (ed.), *Measuring Place of Work*, Geneva: ILO.

Cross, J. C. 1998. *Informal Politics: Street Vendors and the State in Mexico City*, Stanford: Stanford University Press.

Diaz, P. 2007. 'Buhoneros estrenan puestos', *El Universal*, 9 March 2007, Caracas.

Espana, L. P. 2006. 'Politicas Para La Construccion De Oportunidades Sociales y reducir la desigualdad', in Acuerdo Social (ed.), *Un acuerdo social para alcanzar el desarrollo*, Caracas: UCAB.

Febres, C., Vilma Hernandez and Ghilaine Murzi. 1995. *Aproximacion al Sector Informal Urbano en el area metropolitana de Caracas*, Caracas, FEGS.

Fernandes, E. and A. Varley. 1998. *Illegal Cities: Law and Urban Change in Developing Countries*, London: Zed Books.

Garcia Rincon, M. F. 2007. 'Redefining Rules: A Market for Public Space in Caracas, Venezuela', in J. Cross and A. Morales (eds), *Street Entrepreneurs: People, Place and Politics in Local and Global Perspective*, London: Routledge.

Harvey, D. 1973. *Social Justice and the City*, London: Edward Arnold.

ILO. 2002. *Women and Men in the Informal Economy: A Statistical Picture*, Geneva: ILO.

INE. 2001. 'Censo nacional ', Caracas, Venezuela: INE.

LaCabana, M. 1993. 'La calle como puesto de trabajo: reflexiones acerca de la relacion estado-sector informal urbano', *Cuadernos Cendes* 10(22): 195–210.

Llerena, B. 2005. 'Venezuela: Experiencia en la representacion de los trabajadores no dependientes', in G. Castillo and A. Orsatti (eds), *Trabajo informal y sindicalismo en American Latina y el Caribe: Buenas practicas formativas y organizativas*, Montevideo: CONTERFOR/OIT.

LMO. 2004. 'Decreto No 105–1', *Gaceta Municipal*, 29 January.

Macharia, K. 1997. *Social and Political Dynamics of the Informal Economy in African Cities : Nairobi and Harare*, Lanham, MD: University Press of America.

Marquez, P. undated. *Trabajo informal y comercio informal en Venezuela*, Caracas: Instituto Municipal de Publicaciones.

McAuslan, P. 1998. 'Urbanization, Law and Development', in Ann Varley and Edesio Fernandez (eds), *Illegal Cities: Law and Urban Change in Developing Countries*, London: Zed Books Ltd.

MMO. 2004. *Censo de comerciantes informales*, Caracas: Alcaldia Mayor.

OIT. 2003. 'Los sindicatos y el trabajo decente en la era de la globalización en América Latina'. Paper presented at Seminario Nacional 'Economía Informal y Trabajo Decente en Venezuela: experiencias, perspectivas y alianzas estratégicas',11–12 November, Caracas.

Portes, A., Manuel Castells and Lauren Benton. 1989. *The Informal Economy: Studies in Advanced and Less Developed Countries*, London: Johns Hopkins University Press.

Scott, J. C. 1985. *Weapons of the Weak: Everyday Forms of Peasant Resistance*, London: Yale University Press.

Soja, E. W. 1989. *Postmodern Geographies: The Reassertion of Space in Critical Social Theory*, London: Verso.

Zanoni, W. 2005. *Buhoneros en Caracas: Un estudio exploratorio y algunas propuestas de políticas públicas*, Caracas: CEDICE.

# 11

# Clandestine Geometries: Mapping Street Vending in Downtown Sao Paulo

Luciana Itikawa

The controversial use of public spaces by street vendors hides sharp geometries that are far from chaotic. These geometries are designed by urban, social, economic, and institutional affairs.

A clandestine inhabitant or street vendor that lives without legal land permission, that is, land ownership or a street vending permit, creates business, spatial and institutional strategies. Spatially speaking, this depends on links to urban activities and transport systems. Besides, other strategies also provide some kind of stability through state or business subordination. Some of them—for example, connection with mass consumption and public transportation—are obvious. Others like patronage and corruption, however, are a misrepresentation of what we understand as democratic access of public assets.

This is a graphic chapter that maps street vending in the city of Sao Paulo to discover its complex operations and the dynamics of street vending. Such mapping reveals the geometries of street vending with a clarity that is hard to achieve through other methods. It then goes on to discuss the findings in terms of policy suggestions.

## Introduction

Historically, the Sao Paulo city government changes back and forth between absolute intolerance and permissiveness with regard to street vendors. There has been no clear and efficient street vending regulation and management. Therefore, policy has never affected more than half of the reality on the streets, and it has always produced a body of normative procedures on a fictitious scene. Regulation covers only a small minority.

The ineffectiveness of law is itself an instrument of segregation because it allows clandestine street vendors to be vulnerable to corruption or patronage. There are reasons why, even after three centuries of Sao Paulo's street vending regulation, little has actually been done to counter the perverse logic of the political exploitation of street vendors. However, the forms of repression as a result of ineffective management have never been seriously questioned. Rule-challenging and alliance-making abilities with one another and with public authorities have turned street clandestinity into a supreme art of escaping, evading and skirting.

If there is an employment and income deficit in the city of Sao Paulo, there is also a legitimate space deficit for street vending, mainly in the downtown public spaces. The limited number of street vendor permits issued by City Hall result in a great mass of clandestine street vendors.

The emergence of clandestine housing as a rule, not as an exception, is embedded in the clear contradiction in Sao Paulo: on the one hand, vast unoccupied areas in rich districts, and on the other, a great concentration of precarious settlements in the peripheral zones. Due to clandestine street vending, this segregation is also seen in the concentration of vacant buildings in downtown Sao Paulo, side-by-side with plenty of street vendors selling their wares in public spaces.

This is not to say that vacant and underused private lands are the reason why street vendors concentrate in some downtown streets. First, downtown vacant lots result from inherent real estate dynamics. Second, there is not only competition between formal and informal business, but there is also mutual supply and subordination between private and public land activities.

Consequently, clandestine street vending is related not only to lack of space, strictly speaking, but also to legitimate access to it. In other words, it would be possible to set up policies that regulate use of private land in order to turn it into more useful, permeable and heterogeneously usable space. This approach should be based on the Brazilian law known as the Statute of the City.[1]

Is this only a matter of location? Will displacement from public to private land unravel segregation and undemocratic access to urban infrastructure? Investigating spatiality and micro-economics inherent to street vending, together with its institutional links may generate powerful subsidies for more efficient and inclusive urban policy.

## Clandestine Geometries

The great mass of street vendors, not included in City Hall–allowed permits (only 10 to 20 per cent, according to different perimeters in the downtown area) remain clandestine on the streets, and occupy public spaces according to a very specific logic. The downtown Sao Paulo street vending atlas consists not only of whatever is visible within local urban dynamics, but also of economic and political synergies throughout the territory:[2] regional routes through which smuggled goods travel, metropolitan and even international tradeways and clandestine retail distribution centres, etc. The maps in this chapter belong to a more comprehensive research which analyses links among street vending and economic activities and sectors, together with the mass transport system. This text is focused only on the contradiction between regulation and street-based reality and draws some policy proposals.

The street vending occupation pattern in downtown Sao Paulo does not show a linear or normal geometry. This activity changes quickly through space and time. As a result, the time factor is indeed an important research guiding principle to account for the changing pace (see Map 11.8).

Downtown Sao Paulo streets are set apart in terms of different areas of influence under different leaders. Each leader heads a number of components that share common business or political interests. Street leadership is built through steady permanence in a proper place, goods supply, bargaining ability with authorities, street profitability, etc. Leadership also does not always match the official permit. In other words, a permit neither makes its owner favourable to a local political leadership nor does it ensure the vendor's trade.

Besides, a permit has been frequently distorted from an official permission to a profitable informal currency. As an example, some permit-holder street vendors rent a trading spot to a third party, and in some cases increase the official permit's value 10 times.

These seemingly 'invisible' leadership borders drawn by different street vending groups demonstrate that influential areas do not follow the same possession logic of private land; it is, above all, a political reference. Hence, they are fluid geometries whose limits are settled through frequently built informal agreements and treaties with public officials in charge of surveillance.

Competition on the streets is part of downtown street vending complexity and specialisation. Both are responses to the concentration of street vendors' consumers. There are at least three spatial features that explain downtown street vending concentration.

The first one is related to mass public transportation. In downtown areas, this matter gains a more expressive contour once there is a strong concentration of transportation lines along the central area. A macro- and micro-accessibility combination of both collective and individual transport turns downtown streets into an overflowing commuting open-air terminal that connects pedestrian ways with subways, bus stations and cars.

The second feature specific to downtown areas is the traffic imputable to municipal, state and federal administration buildings. Public administration created most of the jobs (36 per cent) in downtown Sao Paulo in 2004, followed by corporation services (7.1 per cent), textile, clothing and shoe industries (7 per cent), and financial and banking services (6.8 per cent) (COMIN 2004). Numerous government agencies, including public services, contribute to the great mass of pedestrians that demand a different street vendor profile—the one who helps passers-by looking for information about government offices and processes: the sale of government jobs, evaluation manuals, ID cards' pictures, form filling, etc. There is a great demand for this type of help for public services users who typically find it difficult to grasp bureaucratic procedures, negotiate through the red tape and the general sluggishness.

The third feature refers to a tight interchange between specialised trade streets and street vending. Even though retail trading contributes only 4.5 per cent of downtown jobs, a huge consumer mass comes from metropolitan areas, other parts of the country and even from abroad. Therefore, street vending could be regarded as a dynamic indicator of formal retail business on a given street satisfying an outstanding consumer demand.

## Map 11.1: Brazilian Clandestine Routes—Permeable and Hidden Inland Boundaries

This map shows the main countries supplying smuggled goods to Latin America—China, Taiwan, Malaysia, and Singapore. It also shows the main Brazilian permeable smuggling boundaries, whereby key frontier-cities are smuggling passageways; different merchandise passes illegally through each border. Hence, this map demonstrates that there are smuggling 'zones' in Brazilian frontiers.

It also shows an important clandestine geometry designed for smuggling routes in order to avoid Brazilian customs. Smuggled goods deriving from those supplying countries first arrive in Santos port. Next, goods go to Paraguay, and then enter Sao Paulo city, completing a triangle drawn for clandestine trade.

There is another hidden supply route within the Brazilian inland. Highways between Manaus (an Amazonian city) and Sao Paulo city are vulnerable to robbery, resulting in recurring interruptions on ordinary freight routes. Manaus is well-known as a tax-free zone ('Zona Franca') where the majority of electronic goods are made. Throughout these highway routes, freight trucks are often robbed. The stolen goods find their way to downtown streets, as field surveys showed.

## Map 11.2: Number of Permit-holder Street Vendors per Sao Paulo City Districts

This map of the entire city of Sao Paulo and its administrative districts exhibits varying concentrations of permit-holder street vendors. It also shows that the largest concentration is in the downtown area, followed by the south-east and the outer limits of the East Zone districts. There are at least two street vending occupation patterns in Sao Paulo: one is of the highest concentration in downtown; the other is towards the concentration of consumers in popular markets and mass transport stations in border areas, that is, the main entry points from neighbouring cities.

## Map 11.3: Links between Public Transport, Pedestrians' Routes and Street Vending Occupation

This map demonstrates links among mass public transportation lines, pedestrian routes and the street vending occupation. Sao Paulo's mass public transportation is highly centralised. The majority of subway and bus lines cross through the downtown area. Only a proportion of ordinary inhabitants travel downtown from residential to job-intensive areas. Others, however, need to arrive in downtown streets in order to commute. This centralised transportation system, therefore, turns downtown streets into an immense open-air commuter overflow terminal, and consequently, results in a high concentration of street vendors' consumers: the pedestrians.

## Map 11.4: Contradiction between City Hall's Planning and Reality

The survey shows that the number of legal trading spots in this specific perimeter is only around 10 per cent of all downtown street vending spots. Legal spots have not been located by City Hall in order to answer different pedestrian volumes, street capacity, links to existing urban activities, etc. Lack of street vending planning leads to increasing urban struggles.

## Map 11.1
### Brazilian Smuggling Routes — Permeable and Hidden Inland Boundaries

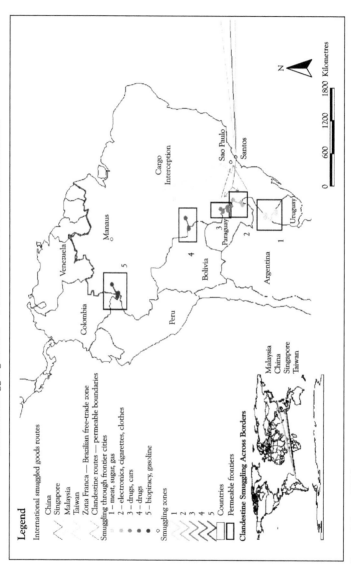

*Source:* Irikawa (2006).

**Map 11.2**

**Number of Permit-holding Street Vendors (by district) in Sao Paulo**

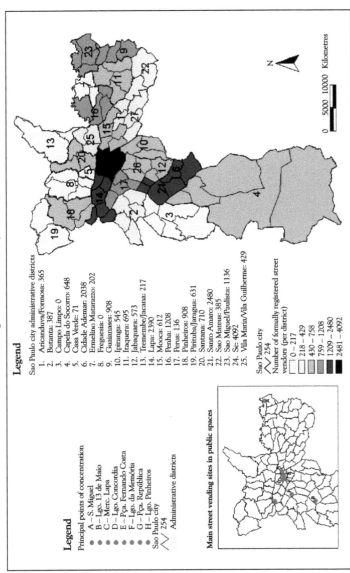

**Legend**

Principal points of concentration

- A – S. Miguel
- B – Lgo. 13 de Maio
- C – Merc. Lapa
- D – Lgo. Concordia
- E – Pça. Fernando Costa
- F – Lgo. da Memória
- G – Pça. Republica
- H – Lgo. Pinheiros

Sao Paulo city

∿ 254

Administrative districts

**Legend**

Sao Paulo city administrative districts

1. Aricanduva/Formosa: 365
2. Butantã: 387
3. Campo Limpo: 0
4. Capela do Socorro: 648
5. Casa Verde: 71
6. Cidade Ademar: 2038
7. Ermelino Matarazzo: 202
8. Freguesia: 0
9. Guaianases: 908
10. Ipiranga: 545
11. Itaquera: 695
12. Jabaquara: 573
13. Tremembé/Jacana: 217
14. Lapa: 2390
15. Mooca: 612
16. Penha: 1208
17. Perus: 136
18. Pinheiros: 908
19. Pirituba/Jaragua: 631
20. Santana: 710
21. Santo Amaro: 2480
22. Sao Mateus: 385
23. Sao Miguel/Paulista: 1136
24. Se: 4092
25. Vila Maria/Vila Guilherme: 429

Sao Paulo city

∿ 254

Number of formally registered street
vendors (per district)

- ☐ 0 – 217
- ☐ 218 – 429
- ☐ 430 – 758
- ▨ 759 – 1208
- ▩ 1209 – 2480
- ■ 2481 – 4092

**Main street vending sites in public spaces**

N

0    5000   10000   Kilometres

*Source:* Itikawa (2006).

## Map 11.3
### Links between Public Transports, Pedestrian Routes and Street-vending

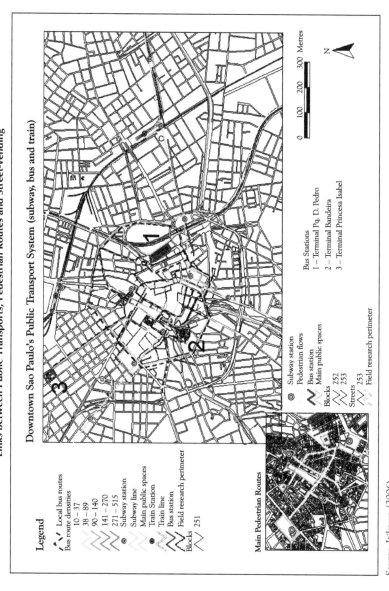

**Downtown Sao Paulo's Public Transport System (subway, bus and train)**

**Legend**

Local bus routes

Bus route densities
10 – 37
38 – 89
90 – 140
141 – 270
271 – 515

Subway station
Subway line
Main public spaces
Train Station
Train line
Bus station
Field research perimeter

Blocks
251

Subway station
Pedestrian flows
Bus station
Main public spaces

Blocks
252
253

Streets
253

Field research perimeter

Bus Stations
1 – Terminal Pq. D. Pedro
2 – Terminal Bandeira
3 – Terminal Princesa Isabel

0   100   200   300  Metres

N

**Main Pedestrian Routes**

*Source*: Itikawa (2006).

**Map 11.4**

**Contradiction between the City Hall's Plans and Reality**

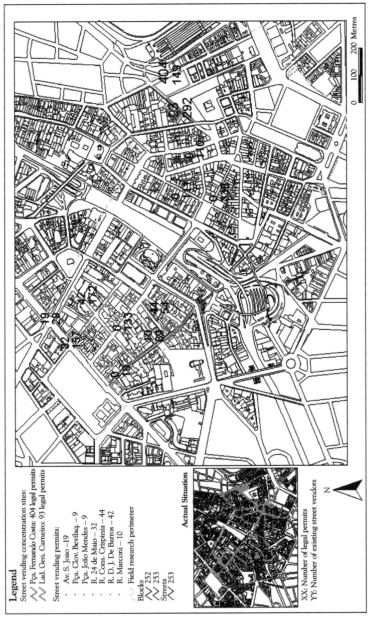

**Legend**

Street vending concentration sites:
~ Pça. Fernando Costa: 404 legal permits
~ Lad. Gen. Carneiro: 93 legal permits

Street vending permits:
· Av. S. Joao – 19
· Pça. Clov. Bevilaq. – 9
· Pça. João Mendes – 9
· R. 24 de Maio – 32
· R. Cons. Crispinia – 44
· R. D. J. De Barros – 42
· R. Marconi – 10
/ Field research perimeter

Blocks
~ 252
~ 253
Streets
~ 253

**Actual Situation**

XX: Number of legal permits
YY: Number of existing street vendors

N

0    100    200 Metres

*Source:* Itikawa (2006).

Map 11.5

Itinerant Street Vendors' Displacement Routes and Work Stops

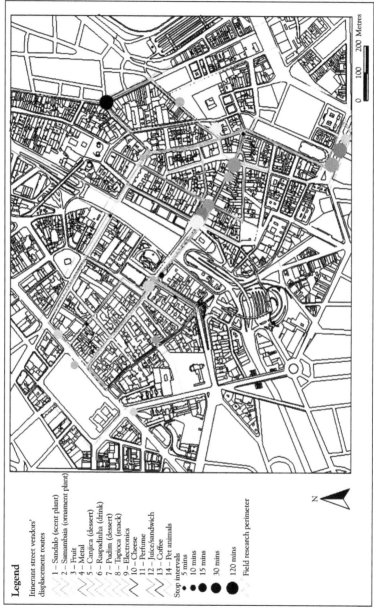

Legend

Itinerant street vendors'
displacement routes

1 – Sandalo (scent plant)
2 – Samambaia (ornament plant)
3 – Fruit
4 – Metal
5 – Canjica (dessert)
6 – Raspadinha (drink)
7 – Pudim (dessert)
8 – Tapioca (snack)
9 – Electronics
10 – Cheese
11 – Perfume
12 – Juice/sandwich
13 – Coffee
14 – Pet animals

Stop intervals
5 mins
10 mins
15 mins
30 mins
120 mins

Field research perimeter

N

0   100   200 Metres

Source: Itikawa (2006).

**Map 11.6**
**Gross Monthly Income in Downtown Streets**

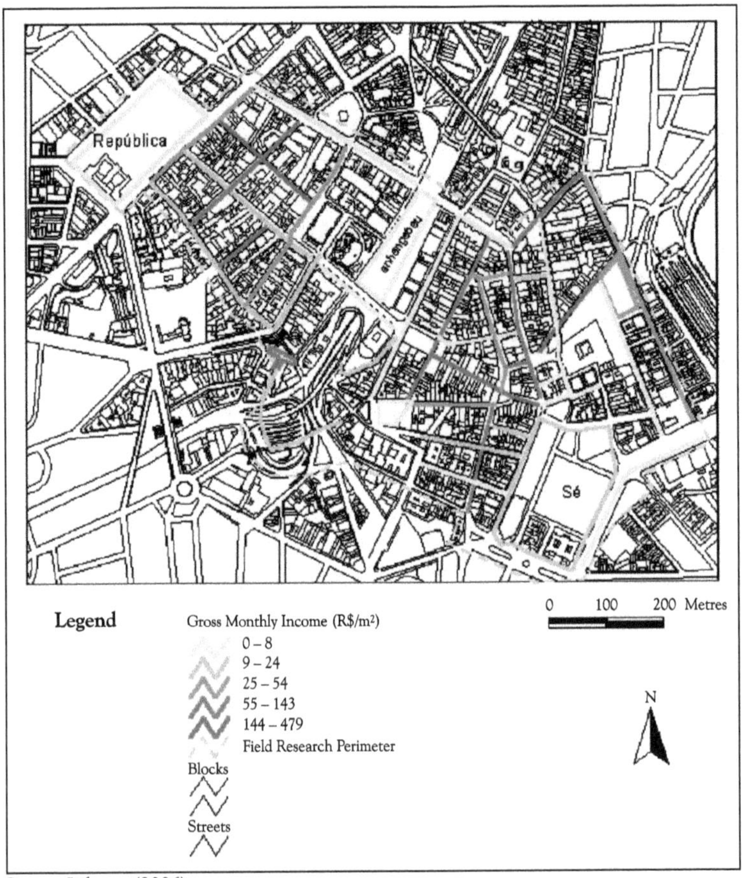
República
Sé
Legend
Gross Monthly Income (R$/m²)
0 – 8
9 – 24
25 – 54
55 – 143
144 – 479
Field Research Perimeter
Blocks
Streets
0
100
200 Metres
N

*Source*: Itikawa (2006).

## Map 11.7
## Monthly Bribes Collected from Downtown Streets

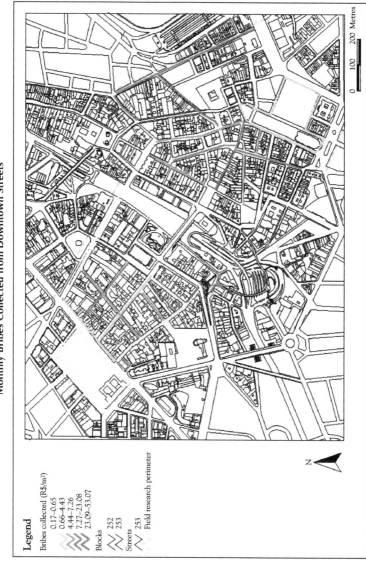

Legend

Bribes collected (R$/m²)
0.17–0.65
0.66–4.43
4.44–7.26
7.27–23.08
23.09–53.07

Blocks
252
253

Streets
253

Field research perimeter

N

0    100    200 Metres

*Source:* Itikawa (2006).

Map 11.8
Temporal Topography of Street Vendors on Downtown Streets

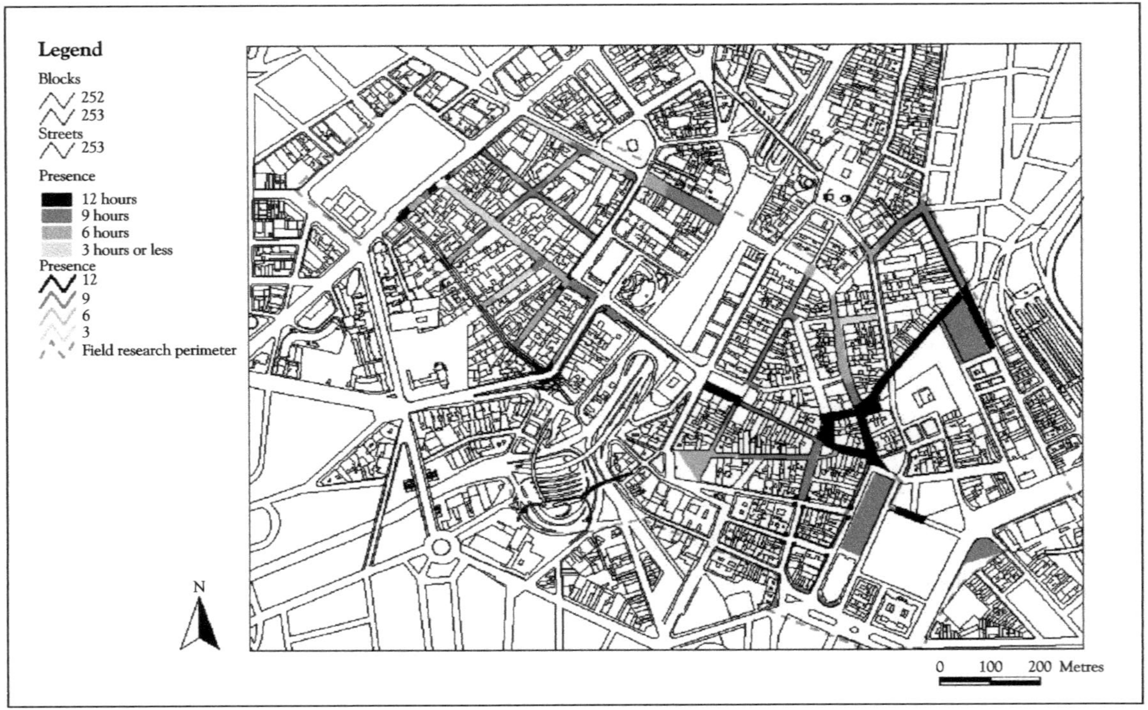

Legend

Blocks
/\/ 252
/\/ 253

Streets
/\/ 253

Presence
■ 12 hours
■ 9 hours
■ 6 hours
□ 3 hours or less

Presence
/\/ 12
/\/ 9
/\/ 6
/\/ 3
/\/ Field research perimeter

N

0    100    200 Metres

Source: Itikawa (2006).

Clandestine street vendors ignore regulation, which does not correspond to street trading dynamics and its complex logic. In the map, the number on top refers to the number of legal permits. The number below that refers to the number of existing street vendors in each street.

## Map 11.5: Itinerant Street Vendors' Displacement Routes and Work Stops

All itinerant street vendors are clandestine in order to avoid police surveillance. Their main routes coincide with high pedestrian-intense streets, so they also follow the same steady street vendors' location pattern. Itinerant vendors' work stops are often located next to public agency buildings or retail streets.

## Map 11.6: Gross Monthly Income per Square Metre on Downtown Streets

Profits vary from street to street within the downtown grid. Profitability changes according to whether a trading spot is next to dynamic urban activities or pedestrian routes. The gross monthly income among downtown street vendors is so discrepant that it is really possible to state that there is a kind of 'wealth concentration' on the streets, with the income difference being 500 times from street to street. In the first half of 2002, a field survey checked, for instance, that Comercio Street had no street vendor, while 24 de Maio Street had a business turnover of R$ 479,00 per sq m.

## Map 11.7: Bribes per Square Metre on Downtown Streets Collected Monthly

In August 2002, bribes collected in all Sao Paulo downtown districts totalled an estimated R$ 1.04 million, according to an investigation led by the City Hall's ombudsman. Map 11.7 reveals downtown bribing density, since it matches the collected amount with each street area. Certain parallels can be drawn with Map 11.6 showing incomes, but clearly bribing density is not exactly in proportion to gross monthly income per street. This subtle difference proves that location itself does not matter in street vending dynamics. The way street vendors are subordinated under a political leadership also indicates how they could be politically protected in a patronage or corruption path. The survey found that for the same value of bribe in different streets, its impact on street vendors' monthly income varies between 10.5 to 17 per cent street-wise.

## Map 11.8: Temporal Topography of Street Vendors' Occupation on Downtown Streets

This temporal topography map focuses on different street vendors' permanence patterns on downtown streets. Their permanence in public spaces is often related to the time-table of private space activities, except on streets that receive pedestrians transferring from one bus station to another or from a bus station to another subway station, which are often seen for 12 hours in a day. Wherever occupation is definitely forbidden at any time of the day, street vendors' permanence varies from three to six hours. Corners are exceptions, since escape is easier to the other streets.

## Politics and Popular Markets

According to the Sao Paulo City Hall, there were 10,000–15,000 street vendors in downtown streets in 2006. Only 944, however, obtained the Public Space Occupation Permit (TPU) early in 2005. Almost 90 per cent continue to be clandestine, and hence vulnerable to political exploitation.

Clandestine street vending exists and flourishes because it is economically and politically profitable. There has been a mutual subordination between part of the state's structure and ordinary street vendors, when the latter have privileged access to a universal right. Street vendors are vulnerable to political exploitation when they become hostages to favours bestowed through political bargaining. Patronage and corruption can emerge when work permission for an individual or a given group of vendors is conceded only through bargain with some level of the municipal administration. Two Sao Paulo City Council's Board of Investigators, in 1995 and 1999, have examined patronage and links among some City Hall or City Council officials and street vending leaders in a permit-granting and corruption mafia (CARDOZO 2000).

The last legal decision of the City Hall in 2002 establishes, among other principles, occupation interdiction near public assets—hospitals, schools, subway and railway stations, bus terminals, etc. Since they attract a high pedestrian mass, the only street vendors who may stay in forbidden places are those who submit to patronage or corruption. Map 11.7 demonstrates that some street vendors are at the mercy of inspectors who allow clandestine use of streets in exchange for bribes.[3] Nevertheless, there are a great number of vendors who have no access to decision-making channels. Those that do not choose subordination have only two alternatives: daily escaping from police repression and surveillance, or working in weak-business areas. Laws will only come closer to reality—and therefore become effective—if they are prepared with other logic. They often obey deceitful reasoning, leaving aside urban struggles, and do not represent broad civil society's opinion, and more importantly, the street vendors' needs.

Violence is the last, but jumbled initiative to control clandestine street vendors. Although repression has been stubbornly applied, it has been proved that random removal is a measure of immediate, but failed efficiency. Street vending is not always a deliberate choice of clandestine use. The government's repression demonstrates how the incrimination of street vending is authoritarian and arbitrary. Systematic confiscation of goods is but one of the cruel policies that are applied across street vendors of all origins and in all situations. Brutality has been justified in terms of public health and urban safety. Both are excuses, nevertheless, that would embarrass the most democratic experiences.

In spite of the state's repressive conduct, some Brazilian authorities believe that popular markets are enough as an alternative policy for sheltering street vendors. We investigated two different popular market experiences: one in downtown Sao Paulo in the 1990s, and another in Diadema, a neighbouring city. Each one is an exemplary example of different street vending policies.

The first one, called 'Pop Center do Bras' (Bras Popular Market), was created by the mayor of Sao Paulo, Celso Pitta, in 1999. Its failure, according to Guerreiro (2000) is related to its great distance from both the most dynamic downtown businesses, institutional activities, and the mass transport axes. Consequently, Pop Center do Bras could not spontaneously attract pedestrians. However, it was not a misunderstood policy; it was indeed a deliberate state initiative aimed at segregation.

## Pop Center do Bras

The location of 'Pop Center do Bras' was in direct opposition to street vending dynamics, since it was not based on any objective urban or economic analysis. A more serious aspect of this policy, however, was that there seems to have been a consensus by City Hall planners about poverty ghettoisation. Once street vending is removed from standard urban life, there is a deliberate attempt to criminalise it. This excluding resolution, also advocated by other city administrations in Brazil, proved to be ineffective. 'Pop Center do Bras' is but one of the failed experiences: vendors abandoned it, and returned to the streets. It became an inactive popular market, and has now turned into a warehouse.

The first measure carried out under the majority of investigated initiatives was locating popular markets as far as possible from the so-called 'renewed' centres. Guerreiro (2000), who investigated the whole 'Pop Center do Bras' design process, states that the central error was disregarding what is meant by 'urban location value'. According to him, urban location value is a business strategy based on either traditional understanding of a profitable retail place—easily accessible and next to reasonable numbers of passers-by—or even on what is known as an 'induced location'.

Some recent malls have been created on the basis of 'induced location', that is, located under an urban marketing strategy. Some enterprises 'create' locations where there is no business attraction; this is indeed a marketing engineering effort. According to Guerreiro (2000), 'Pop Center do Bras' failed due to lack of both traditional and induced location. Besides, there was no true link among all members involved in the enterprise, such as the vendors themselves (through their labour union or cooperatives), owners and businessmen, as well as the city administration itself.

Most notably, it also failed in its political evaluation, since City Hall was gradually losing its credibility due to constant political scandals involving corruption at various levels of municipal administration. In addition, there was no consensus or political leadership among street vendors, and this shortcoming limited labour union efforts and wasted many opportunities for training in cooperatives.

How can popular markets be sustainable and inclusive at the same time? Field survey has shown that the majority of street vendors do not agree to stay in such places because of the high expenses, weak-business location, or even absence of democratic representativeness, as well as lack of economic planning. In order to create sustainable enterprises, popular markets should match the vendors' profit on the streets. Not competing with streets is always hard, since they are always more profitable. Private land enterprises, on the other hand, are often safer than streets, if they do not let in vendors vulnerable to political exploitation and violence. Market sustainability is also related to street vendors' collective bargaining, that is, leaders' participation in government policy- and decision-making channels. Therefore, it is up to the state to ensure political relevance to this activity. ˙

## Diadema's Popular Market

Diadema's Popular Market is an intriguing example of a sustainable enterprise: it has four features that have sustained it since 2002. First, on the occasion of its origin, Diadema City Hall introduced a transparent selection process. Once vendors were subscribed and have been partially catalogued, a public lottery, held in the state's gymnasium, elected 241 vendors for work stations. This initiative was designed to oppose privileged access through patronage. Second, the Popular Market building was financed through a public budget, so it was clearly conceived as a social policy. Third, it is located at one of the most important busy retail streets, which is fed by mass public transport, and located on the state's property, next to urban activities. Fourth, a democratic council, composed of four government officials and four vendors' leaders, has managed Diadema's Popular Market.

To an extent, Diadema's Popular Market can be regarded as an inclusive policy, although it is limited in its range. There were more than 196 vendors on this programme as of 2006, waiting for sheltered popular markets.

## By Way of a Conclusion

The Statute of the City, a Brazilian urban regulation approved in 2001, sets up some mechanisms that make social access to land for housing purposes, for example, Special Zones for Social Use or Progressive Municipal Property Tax, among others, possible (ROLNIK 2001). An analysis is still to be done on the impact of this urban regulation on Brazilian municipalities, including struggles, to-be-detailed restrictions, etc. These mechanisms, intended to foster access to social housing, are specific to contexts where there is a wish to reverse inaccessibility to land, either related to real estate speculative reasons, or due to 'freezing' regulations. A regulation that freezes an urban grid turns land 'impermeable' and inactive. Precarious housing mainly exists in peripheral zones, where the land value is certainly more compatible with workers' wage benefits. On the other hand, clandestine street vendors are located not only in downtown areas, but also in other important retail neighbourhood cores. Nevertheless, private spaces in these areas remain expellant and impermeable.

Sao Paulo's downtown vacant land data has not been properly assessed and analysed, and there are still a few barriers between urban regulation and judicial proceedings. Second, urban regulation itself does not promote healthy urban dynamics. In Sao Paulo city, not only are real estate driving forces heading south, but also successive economic crises have inhibited investments in the downtown area. Regulation alone has no resources, which depend essentially on macroeconomic and macro-urban processes. Third, field surveys have demonstrated different street vending profiles to which urban activities have been linked and for these different programmes need to be designed.

Apart from trading and strengthening vendors' associations, Popular Markets may serve as a source of public interest information to downtown users. If those markets are designed under a broad social policy, they should provide, for instance, a task which is already customary and well spread on downtown streets: government's bureaucracy and employment information. Recent Brazilian informal economy research has demonstrated how informal enterprises lack official support. In order to embrace this activity in a productive chain, three features should be the basis of a street vending policy tripod in downtown Sao Paulo. First, technical training and legal counselling can be provided by government agencies. Second, government should support links among all members in informal chains. And third, government support can comprise or even help, for example, communication, logistics, union formation or even cooperation links.

## Notes

1. Statute of the City—Law No. 10257/2001—comprises an entire chapter on instruments for urban reform that guarantee democratic access to the land by requiring compliance with the social function of ownership. Instruments for urban reform are instruments of urban development—payment in installments, compulsory construction or use, progressive municipal property tax (IPTU) in time, and real-estate consortium.
2. Atlas of Sao Paulo downtown street vending is part of the Ph.D. developed at the University of Sao Paulo in the School of Architecture and Urban Planning, finished in 2006.
3. Map based on data from the investigation by the Internal Affairs Office of the Municipality of Sao Paulo in August 2002 and sent to Sao Paulo City Council.

## References

Cardozo, J. E. 2000. A Máfia das Propinas. Investigando a Corrupção em São Paulo, Sao Paulo: Perseu Abramo.

Comin, A. 2004. 'Diagnóstico, oportunidades e diretrizes de ação', in Empresa Municipal de Urbanizacao—Urban Planning Municipal Enterprise; Centro Brasileiro de Analise e Planejamento—Planning and Analysis Brazilian Centre; Prefeitura Municipal de Sao Paulo—Sao Paulo Municipality; Centro de Estudos da Metropole—Metropolis Research Center, Caminhos para o Centro: Estratégias de Desenvolvimento para a região Central de São Paulo, Sao Paulo.

Guerreiro, A. A. D. 2000. 'Pop Center do Brás—de comerciantes nas ruas a estabelecidos no comércio popular', Tese de Mestrado em Servico Social, PUC-SP, Sao Paulo.

Itikawa, Luciana. 2006. 'Informal Work in the Public Spaces of Downtown Sao Paulo: Thinking Public Policy Parameters', Ph.D. Dissertation, School of Architecture and Urban Planning, University of Sao Paulo.

Rolnik, R. 2001. Estatuto da Cidade—guia para implementação pelos municípios e cidadãos. Câmara dos Deputados, Comissão de Desenvolvimento Urbano e Interior, Sec. Especial de Desenvolvimento Urbano da Presidência, Caixa Econômica Federal, Instituto Pólis. Câmara dos Deputados. Centro de Documentação e Informação. Coordenação de Publicações. Brasília.

## 12

# Advocacy Coalitions Influencing Informal Sector Policy: The Case of India's National Urban Street Vendors Policy

Dolf J. H. te Lintelo

## Introduction

In urban India, public policy concerning street vending often consists of local authorities' licensing systems that regulate access to public space. As a rule, anyone wishing to sell goods or services on publicly owned land requires a license, but as these are generally parsimoniously issued, the great majority of street vendors are rendered illegal.

The National Urban Street Vendors Policy (NSVP), announced in January 2004, embodied a major break from prevalent regulatory approaches. Hailed as a 'paradigm shift' (NASVI 2004a), this first national policy for street vendors in India incorporated a more benevolent and accommodating perspective on vending. Moreover, the NSVP made part of a series of initiatives in the early 2000s illustrating the emergence of national arenas for informal sector policy making.

This chapter uses an Advocacy Coalition Framework (ACF) approach to analyse the emergence of the NSVP.[1] It argues that a detailed analysis of the cognitive preferences and ideas of key policy actors can complement traditional interest-based explanations of policy change in India. Moreover, the case study demonstrates the significant presence and influence of advocacy coalitions in the Indian policy process. Accordingly, the NSVP is shown to be the outcome of a sustained and coordinated campaign of a group of civil society and state actors espousing a clear set of normative values.

The chapter accordingly sets out the ACF theory, followed by an account of the context within which campaigns for street vendors emerged.

It assesses the key policy conflicts, and the way in which an advocacy coalition positioned itself in this respect, to successfully produce policy change, and to protect these gains from revision.

## The Advocacy Coalition Framework

The Advocacy Coalition Framework is one of the dominant contemporary theories explaining policy change and stability (McBeth et al. 2007). Whilst the ACF is deemed applicable to developing countries where a minimum level of democratic dissent is possible (Sabatier 1998), its use in these contexts has been severely limited. The ACF has not been rigorously applied in India, despite having the formal democratic credentials and institutional architecture to warrant its application. As such, an ACF analysis can complement dominant political economy analyses of public policy (e.g., Bardhan 1984; Kohli 1987; Rudolph and Rudolph-Hoeber 1987; Kohli 2007) by shifting analytical focus to the dynamics of the policy process, and highlighting the importance of ideas, cognition and normative beliefs in the Indian policy process.[2]

Paul Sabatier and Hank Jenkins-Smith developed the ACF during the 1980s and 1990s in order to make sense of the complexity, uncertainty and rationale for environmental policy change in the US. Policy change is understood as changes in legislation or government programmes, or new programmes that produce outputs or impacts at the operational level, for example, budgetary changes. The ACF posits several key concepts: policy subsystems, advocacy coalitions, belief systems, external and internal events, and stable parameters (Figure 12.1).

The ACF posits that analysis should focus on *policy subsystems*: 'the group of people and/or organisations interacting regularly over periods of a decade or more to influence policy formulation and implementation within a given policy area/domain' (Sabatier 1999: 131). Within the policy subsystem, generally one to four coalitions operate, comprising state and society actors such as interest group leaders, agency officials, legislators, researchers, journalists, etc. Coalitions can be drivers of change but also stabilisers of the status quo. They employ resources such as information, knowledge and expertise, finance, number of supporters and legal authority and various strategies to have their beliefs translated into public policies, including litigation, lobbying, commissioning research and influencing public opinion.[3] When an advocacy coalition is challenged by other competing coalitions, or when perturbations outside the policy subsystem take place, alliances realign to common positions (Sabatier and Jenkins-Smith 1993).

**Figure 12.1**
**The Advocacy Coalition Framework (Revised 2007 Version)**

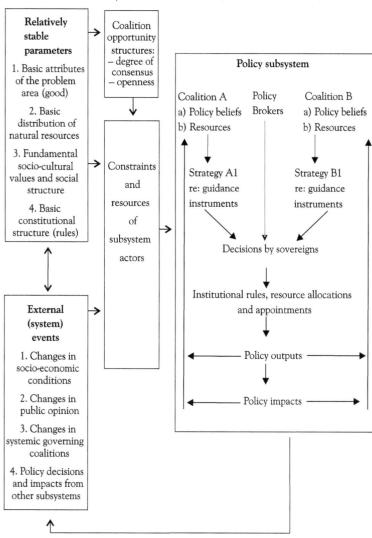

*Source:* P. A. Sabatier, ed., 2007, *Theories of the Policy Process,* Westview Press, Boulder, Colorado.

*Advocacy coalitions* are defined by coordinated action that is grounded in a shared set of normative beliefs. Actors driven by beliefs discursively shape and strategically negotiate policy ideas (P. John 1998). The ACF thus explicitly 'rejects the view that political actors are primarily motivated by their short-term self-interest', and argues that coalition formation is often 'quite constrained by ideology' (Sabatier 1993: 28). Accordingly, whilst acknowledging a limited role for interests (Sabatier 1993; Sabatier and Weible 2007) 'belief systems' are offered as the key factor explaining individual and collective action of policy actors. As such, the ACF challenges political economy models in which (policy) actors maximise utility or control over rents.

Belief systems are conceptualised as 'sets of value priorities and causal assumptions how to realise them' (Sabatier 1993: 16), at three levels of abstraction. The relationship between normative core, policy core and secondary beliefs is hierarchical. Abstract beliefs constrain less abstract ones, and are more resistant to change. *Normative core* beliefs concern basic ontological positions, such as the relative value of individual liberty versus community security, and therefore apply to all policy problems. *Policy core* beliefs concern the basic normative commitments and causal perceptions that apply across a policy subsystem. They regard fundamental value priorities, such as the relative importance of economic development versus environmental protection, the evaluation of the seriousness of a problem and its causes and desirable strategies for achieving normative core beliefs. Critically, policy core beliefs bind members into coalitions by agreement on basic value priorities and identified groups whose welfare is of concern. Finally, *secondary* policy beliefs are instrumental to implement policy core beliefs. They include most decisions concerning administrative rules, budgetary allocations, statutory interpretation, and evaluations of institutional or policy performance.

The ACF thus argues that policy change can be explained by preceding changes in belief systems held by dominant policy coalitions. Within the policy subsystem, coalitions seek to 'out-learn' each other in order to influence policy. As normative core beliefs are most and secondary beliefs the least resistant to change, negotiations about policy often concern secondary beliefs. Changes in the dominant coalition's secondary beliefs through learning translate into *minor* policy change, whereas revisions of policy core beliefs affect *major* policy change.

Major policy change often results from events external to the subsystem, such as changes in socio-economic conditions and technology, systemic governing coalitions and policy decisions and impacts from other subsystems (Sabatier and Jenkins-Smith 1993). 'Internal shocks' within the subsystem are an alternative reason for policy change, by raising public aware-ness, highlighting policy limitations and confirming policy core beliefs of minority coalitions while increasing doubt within the dominant coalition. In addition, major policy change is sometimes the outcome of negotiated agreements between coalitions that have disagreed over long periods of time, in order to overcome stalemates hurting all parties (Sabatier and Weible 2007).[4]

Having set out the key propositions of the ACF, the following sections demonstrate its relevance for understanding the process and the outcomes of India's National Urban Street Vendors Policy.

## Galvanising Street Vendor Campaigns

In the second half of the 1990s, across India, a growing number of civil society organisations engaged with street vending and the informal sector, often in direct response to drastic public policy. For instance, the Kolkata Hawkers Sangram Samiti was established following a large-scale eviction drive called 'Operation Sunshine' (1996), whilst NIDAN was founded in Patna under similar conditions. The Self Employed Women's Association (SEWA) has worked with female street vendors in Ahmedabad since the 1970s and founded a local unit in Delhi in 1999. Other organisations in Delhi concern NGO Manushi, which has been engaged with street vending issues since 1995, the Vasant Kunj Rehri Patri Vyapari Manch, founded in 2001 (Verma 2005), while the Centre for Civil Society, a classically liberal thinktank started advocating delicensing policies for street vendors and other small-scale entrepreneurs by 2001.

Such increased civil society activity related to two factors. First, in line with observations elsewhere in the world (Anon. 1995) the urban in-formal sector, and one of its component parts—street vendors—was growing rapidly (J. John 1998; Bhowmik 2002). Whilst the informal sector contributed up to 50 per cent of the labour force in cities like Calcutta, Bombay and Madras by the end of the 1980s (National Commission on Self Employed Women and Women in the Informal Sector 1988), the next decade saw massive expansion. The informal sector made up for 93 per cent of the workforce in rural and urban areas (Friedrich Ebert Stiftung 1998).

Incessant, large-scale rural–urban migration fuelled urbanisation and the supply of workers to the urban informal sector. Many also associated the growth as an outcome of economic liberalisation policies, although there was no consensus on the direction of causality. Some analysts noted that India saw an increase in the number of vendors in spite of its economic growth, globalisation and industrialisation (Centre for Civil Society 2005). Others noted that liberalisation policies facilitated layoffs in public sector enterprises and eroded labour laws, to result in a reduction of permanent and an increase in short-term employment (Singh 2000; Jhabvala and Sinha 2002). In this context, street vending was seen to provide relief for 'communities marginalized by the globalization—women, poor, formally uneducated, disabled, uprooted from agriculture, migrants from villages, lower castes, retrenched workers' (Singh 2002).

The second factor galvanising civil society activism was increasing state repression (SEWA 1998): 'during the decade of economic reforms in India, the state machinery had intensified its economic assaults' on street vendors (Manushi 2001: 1). 'Operation Sunshine' is often cited as the archetypal example. During a night in November 1996, an unannounced swoop by police and municipal authorities bulldozed the livelihoods of 100,000 vendors to clean up the city for a visit by the UK prime minister John Major, representing foreign direct investment (SEWA 1998; Bhowmik 2002). Moreover, the West Bengal government put up banners encouraging consumers to boycott street vendors, describing them as a nuisance and hindrance in the 'clean city drive' (SEWA 1998).

'Operation Sunshine' exemplifies a deep and ongoing conflict about the direction, purpose, and ultimately winners and losers of restructuring Indian cities. The state is a key actor in this process, as a locus of contestation, and by exercising power in the development and management of public space (Fernandes 2004). Accordingly, the state sells public land to the private sector, constructs new and wider roads, parking spaces and flyovers catering to an expanding fleet of motorised vehicles, but also demolishes slums, removes street vendors and conducts 'beautification drives'. Thus, in Delhi, slums are demolished to facilitate the prestigious Commonwealth Games in 2010 (Corbridge et al. 2005), a ban on begging and giving alms is introduced (British Council India 2007) and food-cooking vendors are banned from the roads (te Lintelo 2009).

These politics of urban restructuring are strongly associated with the emergence of a growing and increasingly vocal middle class (Baviskar 2003; Chatterjee 2004; Fernandes 2004). In a booming economy, middle-class identities are produced through new consumption practices and life-styles, reflecting global commodities and preferences (Fernandes 2004). Increasingly exposed to international media and travel, the middle classes envisage Indian cities one day emulating global cities like Tokyo, London, Singapore, and Shanghai (Chatterjee 2004). The private sector creates consumers' appetites, and tailors development to the requirements and the buoyant purchasing power of the middle classes. In the retail sector, shopping malls have mushroomed spectacularly in the last 10 years, harbouring cineplex halls, supermarkets and food courts, with the latter serving sanitised versions of street food.

Cities are hence reshaped around middle- and upper-class values that emphasise cleanliness, purity, order (Kaviraj 1997), aesthetics, leisure, (food) safety and health (Baviskar 2003). However, many places selectively cater to better-off denizens (Wyatt 2005; Voyce 2007), rendering groups such as street vendors and slum dwellers 'invisible', while implying a segregation of the middle classes from the poor and working classes (Fernandes 2004; Voyce 2007). By promoting a middle-class vision of the city (Chatterjee 2004) and conflating their interest with the public interest, the state actively co-produces a middle-class identity and reshapes the city to suit it (Fernandes 2004).

## Creating Alliances of Civil Society Organisations

The Self-Employed Women's Association took a leading role in the movement for policy change regarding street vendors. An established and well-connected organisation, SEWA counts 688,473 women, including 28,575 vendors in seven states as its members (SEWA 2005). Famous for its micro-credit schemes, SEWA is part of the labour, the cooperative and the women's movement (SEWA 2005). Its efforts regarding street vending were part of a broader advocacy focus on the unorganised/informal sector.[5] Its earliest advocacy for street vendors dates back to 1973 (SEWA 1998). In 1984 SEWA won litigation in the Supreme Court of India directing the Municipal Corporation of Ahmedabad to allocate licenses to 327 women vending vegetables (Friedrich Ebert Stiftung 1998). Its subsequent struggles resulted in the issue of hundreds of licenses to its members.

Whilst by the mid-1990s most civil society campaigns still addressed local authorities, SEWA had made two important strategic changes, inspired by a realisation that 'things were going worse and worse and worse and worse . . . and unless action changes to a totally different level, then the vendors are an absolutely lost case' (pers. comm., R. Jhabvala, national coordinator, SEWA, June 2006). First, attention shifted away from local decision-making arenas. Thus, in 1988, SEWA president Ela Bhatt headed the National Commission on Self-Employed Women and Women in the Informal Sector, and she became an independent member of the Rajya Sabha. Here, Bhatt proposed a (non-adopted) bill calling for a national policy for street vendors, entitled '*do tokri ki jagah*' ('two baskets of space') (Chatterji 2000). Bhatt also became member of India's Planning Commission (in charge of labour issues), while SEWA was increasingly represented in various national and international networks.[6]

Second, SEWA strategically moved from single organisation to group-based advocacy. Ela Bhatt considered: 'If we are able to increase our organized strength, make strategic alliances and link up with other groups like planners and academicians, we will be in a better position to dialogue with the political structures' (Chatterji 2000). Hence SEWA encouraged other organisations to work on street vending issues, using its networks to advocate for national policy. Accordingly, in 1995, it convened a meeting of 27 street vendor representatives from 11 cities on five continents, at Bellagio, Italy. The meeting founded an international alliance (StreetNet) and resulted in the Bellagio International Declaration of Street Vendors, which called upon governments to establish national street vendor policies (Anon. 1995).

The Bellagio Declaration exuded an air of international authority and impartiality, and served as a persuasive and legitimising reference in domestic policy campaigns. In India, the Declaration became a 'base' for subsequent street vendor policy discussions (pers. comm., K. R. Mohan, former under-secretary, Ministry of Urban Development, June 2006). The Bellagio Declaration's policy objectives were substantially derived from Ela Bhatt's parliamentary bill (Table 12.1).[7]

**Table 12.1**
**Continuity in Policy Objectives**

| Parliamentary Bill (1988) | Bellagio Declaration (1995) |
| --- | --- |
| a national policy for hawkers and vendors improving their standards of living; protect their existing livelihood | a national policy for hawkers and vendors protect and expand vendors' existing livelihood |
| provide legal access to the use of available space | provide legal access to the use of appropriate and available space |
| a special component of the plans for urban development | a special component of the plans for urban development |
| give them legal status by issuing licenses and providing exclusive hawking zones | give vendors legal status by issuing licenses, enacting laws and providing appropriate hawking zones |
| issue guidelines for action at local levels | issue guidelines for supportive services at local levels |

Sources: ( Anon., 1995, *The Bellagio International Declaration of Street Vendors*, 25 November , 1995, Bellagio, Italy; S. Krishnamoorthy, 1998, '"Do Tokri Ki Jagah", the resolution moved in Parliament by Ela Bhatt', *Labour File* (November 1998): 33–36, November 1998).

Advocacy claims on policy makers, however, needed to be firmly grounded in robust data, and to this effect SEWA conducted a vendor census in Ahmedabad in 1996. Moreover, it encouraged NIDAN to con-duct a similar survey in Patna, and a joint delegation led by Ela Bhatt subsequently presented its findings to Bihar's chief minister. The Self Employed Women's Association further started to train NIDAN's vendors (Friedrich Ebert Stiftung 1998).

The SEWA-organised 'National Workshop on the Legal Status of Street Vendors' (September 1998) was another important milestone in the emergence of the coalition, bringing together vendors, NGOs, labour unions, and academics from all over the country. The workshop formulated an action plan that was firmly based on the Bellagio Declaration, and accordingly advocated a national policy for street vendors. Moreover, the workshop founded the National Alliance of Street Vendors India (NASVI), to be coordinated by NIDAN's founding director, Arbind Singh (Friedrich Ebert Stiftung 1998). The National Alliance of Street Vendors India's aims and objectives are guided by the principles of the Bellagio Declaration (NASVI 1999, 2005). An umbrella organisation, NASVI supports local street vendor organisations, and represents its members at the national policy level (SEWA 1998).[8] The Self Employed Women's Association, NASVI and its member organisations are actively committed to refuse aligning with any political party to facilitate its long-term legitimacy in policy-making arenas.

Here, the contours of an advocacy coalition were emerging, and in order to keep the workshop momentum going, a follow-up meeting in December 1998 once more brought together 'a core group of sympathisers' (Bhowmik 2002). The group consisted of people from SEWA (president Ela Bhatt, national coordinator Renana Jhabvala, national secretary Mirai Chatterji, vice president Manali Shah), NASVI's Arbind Singh, Sharit Bhowmik, professor of sociology at Mumbai University; and prominent lawyers Indira Jaisingh and Rani Advani (Bhowmik 2002).[9]

This gathering once more established the need to be armed with better data. The initial surveys in Ahmedabad and Patna provided interesting, but limited comparative information on the nature of street vending and its relation to public space. The group thus commissioned a comprehensive study of street vending in seven Indian cities, conducted by professor Bhowmik (pers. comm., S. K. Bhowmik, Mumbai University, September 2005; R. Jhabvala, national coordinator, SEWA, June 2006). His benchmark study was published in 2002, and its findings provided an essential input to the campaign for national policy.[10]

## *Expanding the Coalition with State Actors*

By the end of the 1990s, revising labour laws was widely considered an unfulfilled part of India's economic reform agenda (Jenkins 2004). Processes devised to address this, such as the 35th session of the tripartite Indian Labour Conference (Ramanathan 1998) and the report of the Second National Commission on Labour (SNCL), however, also actively included discussions concerning the informal sector, signifying its growing importance in labour policy debates (Jhabvala 2005).

Several SEWA representatives chaired or participated in SNCL study groups (i.e., R. Jhabvala, M. Chatterji) whilst Ela Bhatt was appointed member (Second National Commission on Labour 2002). The Self Employed Women's Association's presence led to considerable cross-fertilisation of ideas. The report of SEWA's workshop on legal issues concerning street vendors thus included demands for improved social security and employment conditions (SEWA 1998). Conversely, the SNCL report has sections summarising regulatory issues concerning street vendors, strong references to the Bellagio Declaration, to advocate legalisation and provision of licences (SNCL 2002). Moreover, the SNCL drafted an early version of what later was redrafted as the Unorganised Sector Workers (Conditions of Work and Livelihood Promotion) Bill (2005).[11]

Another consequence of SEWA's close involvement in labour debates was the choice of the Ministry of Labour as the initial target agency for framing street vendor policy. Coalition members, however, engaged in 'venue shopping', the phenomenon that 'coalitions pursue multiple venues at multiple levels, often simultaneously' (Sabatier 1999: 152), to strategically seek to limit or expand the agencies and actors that engage in the policy process and to contain or enhance policy conflict to improve their chances of winning (Sabatier 1999; McBeth et al. 2007). The National Alliance of Street Vendors India thus targeted the Planning Commission (pers. comm., A. Singh, national coordinator, NASVI, May 2006), while SEWA also discussed policy proposals with the Ministry of Urban Development (MoUD).[12] This ministry's catalytic role in developing the NSVP was, however, somewhat serendipitous.

The Self Employed Women's Association set up a local unit in Delhi in 1999 to campaign for Gujarati vendors displaced by the Delhi Development Authority (DDA) from a market behind the Red Fort. This campaign took SEWA to minister Jagmohan of the MoUD, to whom the DDA reports.[13] Jagmohan had a reputation as a non-corrupt administrator, disciplinarian and tough law enforcer, not afraid of making cold-blooded decisions. He envisaged Indian cities to be beautified by tackling unauthorised construction and encroachment (Jha 2001).[14] His projects included removal of large slums from the banks of the Yamuna River and sanitising the Red Fort area. Whilst considered to have an 'anti-poor' attitude, meeting Jagmohan turned out to be a major breakthrough for the coalition. Discussions quickly moved from local to generic problems faced by vendors, with the minister requesting advice. The Self Employed Women's Association argued: 'right now what is happening to vendors is that they are being removed. And we want to go from removal to regulation that was what we were trying to explain to him. And you know he is "Mr. Beautification", but he is also a person who believes in the rule of law, a real bureaucrat, but not bureaucratic. So, he seemed to like that idea. You know, he was not enamoured by vendors, but he was a person in search of solutions. I think that was what attracted him' (pers. comm., R. Jhabvala, national coordinator, SEWA, June 2006). Similarly, NASVI's coordinator recalled: 'once he got the feel of the topic, he got very interested, and we saw a very different Jagmohan as has been projected. He started organising his officers, even sent his officers to our meetings, that kind of thing, and then we thought, let's have a workshop' (pers. comm., A. Singh, national coordinator, NASVI, May 2006). Accordingly, it was decided to jointly organise a national workshop on street vendors, effectively opening up a new policy-making venue.

Besides Jagmohan's support, the MoUD secretary was also 'very positive', as was the minister of state, Bangaru Dattatreya, who had personal connections with street vendors. Under-secretary K. R. Mohan also actively supported the enterprise (pers. comm., R. Jhabvala, national coordinator, SEWA, June 2006), and facilitated a level of continuity in the ministry, as he informed new senior officials following bureaucratic transfers about the efforts towards the national policy (pers. comm., A. Singh, national coordinator, NASVI, May 2006). Nevertheless, SEWA found it hard to get the workshop organised, and felt that there was a strong attempt to undermine the conference. The joint secretary, often the bureaucratic 'do-er' and therefore in a powerful position, was not interested, and it was suspected that real estate and merchant lobbies exercised some power over him (ibid.). Our study, however, did not find evidence in policy documents, media debates, or other public sources of information confirming the presence of competing coalitions.[15]

The MoUD/SEWA workshop eventually took place on 30 and 31 May 2001. Preliminary findings of the seven-city study provided essential inputs, setting out an overview of the problems, prospects and an agenda for regulatory reforms. The workshop participants agreed on the necessity to define, and developed preliminary national guidelines. Moreover, Jagmohan raised a Task Force to 'finalise broad guidelines on street vendors for circulation to the State Governments and Urban Local Bodies for regulation of street vending' (Ministry of Urban Development and Poverty Alleviation 2001). The Task Force included representatives of central, state and local governments, vendor organisations and experts, and was chaired by the minister of state. Whilst SEWA had considerable influence in its composition, political appointees swelled the Task Force's ranks to an unwieldy 18 members.

However, the Task Force was more severely threatened by two external events taking place within a very short period of time. First, the emerging (national) policy subsystem was shaken by a sudden cabinet reshuffle on the 1 September 2001, which shifted Jagmohan to the Ministry of Tourism and Culture. It was commonly argued that he was punished for acting against the interests of the construction and land mafia in the capital, and was an unpopular political asset to the ruling Bharatiya Janta Party (BJP) for the impending municipal elections (Our special correspondent 2001; Tribune News Service 2001). The successors of the minister and the MoUD secretary were, however, indifferent about street vendors, and this seriously threatened progress towards a national policy (pers. comm., R. Jhabvala, national coordinator, SEWA, June 2006). The Task Force appeared paralysed before its first meeting.

Fortunately, the second external event, also directly initiated by Prime Minister Atal Bihari Vajpayee, gave a much more positive impetus. On 28 August 2001, Vajpayee sent a letter to the lieutenant governor of Delhi, pleading for radical local policy reforms regarding street vendors and rickshaw pullers. The initiative received widespread media publicity. It was an unexpected outcome of advocacy efforts by NGO Manushi, whose public hearing on street vending in Delhi was attended by the government's chief vigilance officer. The prime minister took an interest in his report, and his reform proposal subsequently reinvigorated the MoUD's interest in street vending, to effectively rescue the Task Force from the doldrums.

The Task Force, however, remained severely hindered by its size, and to overcome this a Drafting Committee was set up 'to formulate National Policy' (Task Force on Street Vendors 2002). The Committee met weekly and completed its first draft of the National Urban Street Vendors Policy in July 2002. K. R. Mohan convened the Draft Committee, and the SEWA-coalition provided nearly half of its members (i.e., R. Jhabvala, A. Singh and S. K. Bhowmik) to draft substantial parts of the policy.[16] Bhowmik hence drafted the preamble and Jhabvala the section on social security, health facilities and micro-credit (Task Force on Street Vendors 2002).[17]

By February 2003, Mohan sent out the draft policy to chief secretaries of all states (Ministry of Urban Development and Poverty Alleviation 2003). Following three reminders, by the end of the year, 22 states had responded positively to the policy (NASVI 2004a). Next, the policy was sent to the cabinet for a final hearing, and here again, SEWA lobbied several ministers (pers. comm., R. Jhabvala, national coordinator, SEWA, June 2006). The minister of labour, Sahib Singh Verma supported its early adoption, and he 'convinced his bosses that it was better to have this policy before the [general] elections' of May 2004 (pers. comm., A. Singh, national coordinator, NASVI, May 2006).[18] Accordingly, the Cabinet cleared the NSVP on 20 January 2004.

## Translating Beliefs into Policy

Having demonstrated the strong level of coordination, and the important catalytic role of the SEWA coalition in the process towards the NSVP, this section analyses its belief system. It is argued that keeping in mind complexity, interrelatedness and variability over time, Indian policy actors and discourses strategically emphasised or downplayed distinct policy core and associated secondary beliefs on seven dimensions.[19] These are set out, followed by a detailed assessment of the beliefs harboured by the SEWA-coalition, and an evaluation of the extent to which its beliefs translated into policy.

### *Dimensions of Policy Conflict*

Our study of academic and grey literature, and discussions with key informants from government and civil society groups suggest that most of the policy conflicts concerning street vendors are played out on seven dimensions.

#### *Who Should have a Right to Use Public Space?*

As in many other countries (Pratt 2002), the entitlements of particular groups of citizens to use urban public space and infrastructure, such as pavements, roadsides and parks are a recurring subject of debate in India. Preferences regarding access entitlements, for instance, concern: pedestrians, vehicle drivers, shopkeepers, street vendors, etc. A related secondary belief concerns the extent to which vendors' freedom to use this space should be limited, for instance, by urban planning measures.

## The Relation of Street Vending with the Formal Economy

Policy discussions also centre on the relation of vending to the formal economy; for instance, one of dualist separation, or competitiveness and structural integration. Street vending can thus be presented as an opportunistic and entrepreneurial complement to the formal sector, or as an economically backward sector in need of modernisation.

## The Socio-Economic Value and Function of Street Vending in the City

Beliefs on this account tend to be fairly polarised, evaluating vending in very positive to very negative terms. [20] Such appraisals are informed by secondary beliefs concerning the social function of street vending in the city: for example, as a symbol of impoverishment or continuity with traditions and an antidote to modern cityscapes; as providing a safety net for the poor; as expressing public disorder, for example, by hindering the smooth passage of traffic; or facilitating or debilitating neighbourhood security. Secondary beliefs about the economic function of street vending stress aspects of employment generation; economic competition and growth; or as a cog in urban distribution systems. Moreover, vending is linked to economic reforms and market globalisation, with these forces perceived as a cause for, threat to, or opportunity for street vendors. Further, perspectives on the socio-economic function tend to inform discussions about a desirable (maximum) number of street vendors in the city.

## Appropriate Regulatory Mechanisms: State, Market, Society

Another key debate concerns the appropriate mix of state-, market- or society-led regulatory mechanisms for street vending. Particular beliefs in this respect, for instance, stress minimal or strong state intervention, free market liberalism and private, or citizen/vendor self-regulation. The preference for regulatory mechanisms is also informed by appraisals of the effectiveness and equity of the existing laws, policy and enforcement apparatus. Associated secondary beliefs emphasise regulatory mechanisms for specific aspects of vending, for example, regarding access to space, the quality/safety of goods on sale and the cleanliness of the vending environment.

## The Nature and Developmental Role of the Indian State

Some policy discussions differentially emphasise the extent to which the state should exercise a developmental role regarding street vending.

Contrasting perspectives emphasise active development and support (for instance, regarding occupational health insurance), or deregulation and a more limited role for the state. Positions are heavily influenced by the perspective on the potential of the Indian state as a force for good or bad. Competing perspectives thus may present the state as a benevolent, or as an intrinsically predatory actor.

## Appropriate Public Policy Instruments

Many policy debates address the nature of policy instruments to manage street vendors, emphasising, for example, coercion, inducement and/or persuasion. Secondary beliefs in this respect, for instance, concern numerical licensing, zoning, registration or laissez faire approaches managing vendors' access to urban space. Another secondary belief concerns positive or negative interpretations of vendors' legal status: freedom to vend unless not permitted or favouring general prohibition unless explicitly permitted?

## Participation in Policy-Making Processes

Finally, although not heavily debated, some parties stress the participative role of vendor representatives in urban governance and policy-making processes. Preferences in this respect, for instance, concern no participation, exclusive or inclusive representation of experts, vendor unions, NGOs, or licensed and/or unlicensed street vendors.

# The Advocacy Thrust of the SEWA-Coalition

Whereas the previous sections demonstrated the significant coordination and the catalytic role of the SEWA-coalition in the NSVP policy-making process, this section analyses its belief system. Specific beliefs are thus elaborated with reference to the seven policy dimensions.

## The Socio-Economic Function of Street Vendors

The Self Employed Women's Association approached street vending issues from a labour and social justice perspective, emphasising the oppression of vendors and the need for improving their livelihoods (Chatterji 2000).[21] As a women's trade union, SEWA aims to achieve full employment, income, food and social security, by means of organisation, unionisation and representation (SEWA 2005). The Bellagio Declaration and the 1998 national workshop report bear testimony of a concerted view of the day-to-day problems concerning street vending. The documents emphasise the rapid proliferation of vendors, 'because of poverty, unemployment and forced migration and immigration' (Anon. 1995), their undeserved negative image and the great deal of harassment vendors face from the authorities.

Whilst the coalition challenges the idea that vendors contest the modernity of Indian cities (Chatterji 2000), it does note that urban growth is accompanied by intense competition for space; increasing motorised traffic volumes, fashionable shopping malls and gated communities often act to exclude the poor (Jhabvala 2000). It emphasises the cultural continuity and Indianness of vending and praises its contribution to social cohesion by connecting the rich, middle and lower classes (ibid.). Vending, an 'integral part of our urban history and culture' (Singh 2000), is thus juxtaposed with modern forms of retail: 'Shopping and marketing, in a traditional Indian sense, has primarily been informal. Social interaction is integral to Indian markets in contrast to the mechanized and sterile concept of shopping favoured by modern market and super market (sic) structures' (Singh 2000).

However, negative perceptions of street vending are common in India; they are 'viewed as criminals, illegal encroachers and as a nuisance'. Shopkeepers resent vendors as they provide competition while the middle classes 'liked their fresh, cheap vegetables but not their sight' (Chatterji 2000). Moreover, to those who perceive vendors as a challenge to urban public order, the coalition retorts that their very presence brings safety and security to neighbourhoods. Also, where street vendors are deprived of earning a livelihood, the risk of criminal behaviour replacing it may grow (Bhowmik 2002; Task Force on Street Vendors 2002; Manushi 2005).

Government officials also tend to have negative perspectives of vending. Ela Bhatt recalled: 'it was not easy to even convince my own colleagues on the Planning Commission that vending was a legitimate activity' (Chatterji 2000). Consequently, vendors 'are either overlooked, or are looked down as something to be controlled, or as an eyesore to be removed. . . . And because of this negative attitude . . . they are bypassed' by urban planners and national policy-making bodies (SEWA 1998: 3, 28).

The SEWA-coalition accordingly realised that policy change must be rooted in a re-branded image of vendors. A strategic concern was therefore to 'link the street vendors with middle class consumers' and to achieve 'positive media exposure' (SEWA 1998: 31, 33). Accordingly, vendors are repositioned as hardworking entrepreneurs (SEWA 1998: 3; Chatterji 2000) that are an essential part of city commerce and the commodity distribution system (NASVI 1999; Jhabvala 2000). In the face of adversity, vendors are argued to support urban economies by providing cheap, reasonable quality goods and services for ordinary consumers.

## Links between the Formal and Informal Economy

The SEWA-coalition approaches the relation between the informal and the formal economy from empirical and strategic perspectives. It borrows elements from dualist and structuralist schools of thought on the informal sector (Chen 2004). It occasionally advances the dualist argument that the informal sector is the result of inadequate capacity in the formal sector to absorb surplus labour, and street vending thus provides income and a safety net for the poor (Singh 2002). Moreover, coalition partners question the ability of the formal sector to generate more employment (Chatterji 2000; Jhabvala 2000; Singh 2000; NASVI 2005) and thus argue that vendors 'are here to stay' (Chatterji 2000).

The concept of 'natural markets' was also much-used to refer to the complementary nature of vending to the formal retail sector. It argues that vending should be allowed freely in places where 'sellers and buyers tend to collect', such as railway stations, bus terminuses, hospitals, places of worship, and the regular markets (NASVI 2005). The concept first surfaced in a NASVI declaration (NASVI 1999), but soon became part of advocacy narratives of other civil society organisations (e.g., Manushi, Centre for Civil Society and SEWA).

In structuralist fashion, job reductions in the formal sector and vending are argued to be causally related: 'with conditions of recession and lay-offs in the formal sector . . . the number of the vendors was increasing significantly' (SEWA 1998: 3). Moreover, economic liberalisation and growing exposure to globalisation pressures informalise the economy. India's informal sector thus acts as shock absorber for an organised sector that shed half of its workers between 1974 and 1994 (Harriss-White 2003). Whilst liberalisation is seen to be able, at least in theory, to remove the licensing burden for vendors, in practice it is only the formal sector that has benefited (Jhabvala undated). Contrary to official discourses emphasising that the need for global competitiveness makes labour reforms imperative (Jenkins 2004), the coalition emphasises the negative implications of globalisation.[22] For instance, cineplex halls and malls increase the pressure on the urban spaces where vendors operate (Jhabvala 2000), while government forces often conspire with private interests (Chatterji 2000). The National Alliance of Street Vendors India's perspective also presents globalisation as exposing the national economy to the onslaught of external economic powers, leading to a weakening of worker organisations (Singh 2002; NASVI 2005).

Besides issues of urban space, Ela Bhatt highlights the strategic value of expanding the acceptance of the inherent linkages between the formal and informal sector. 'The present divide is artificial and unreal . . . there is a link . . . between formal and informal economic activities. The divide has to be done away with. In formulating employment policies, government will have to give special attention to those who are self-employed, those who are "casual", informal sector workers. They have to be considered part of the working population' (Chatterji 2000). The informal sector therefore needs to be actively integrated into the macro-economy (Singh 2000), such that people realise, in Bhatt's words, that 'We are part of the world of commerce and collectively we must find a place in the chambers of commerce to contribute further to the country's economy' (Chatterji 2000).

## Entitlement to Access Public Space

In 1989, the Supreme Court of India declared that vendors have a fundamental right to use public space, albeit within reasonable restrictions to be formulated by the state (Supreme Court of India 1989). It noted that 'it is for the State to designate the streets and earmark the places. . . . Inaction on the part of the State would result in negating the fundamental right of the citizens' (Supreme Court of India 1989). Despite such court directions, in practice, vendors often remain excluded from city plans allocating space, and imposing spatial order (Pratt 2002). With the exception of Delhi (Verma 2005), Indian city plans often lack provisions for the informal sector or vendors (Bhowmik 2002).

The SEWA-coalition hence believes that vendors are entitled to a 'right to space' (SEWA 1998), though not on a preferential basis, 'It is no one's case that street vendors may sit wherever they like, at all places all over the city. Rather that if we plan for and accommodate them in the city spaces, they will not obstruct other essential functions such as traffic flow. The reason that vendors now seem such a nuisance is that there is no place for them, and so any place they occupy belongs to some other function. It is therefore necessary to evolve both national and state policies on street vendors which could feed into urban plans and schemes' (Jhabvala 2000). The National Alliance of Street Vendors India also aims to ensure that 'every urban plan provides space for street vending activities' (SEWA 1998; Jhabvala 2000; NASVI 2005).

The right to space should hence be moderated by a fair regulatory mechanism and inclusive urban planning. Although the coalition argues that it 'is high time our planners realise that vendors are an integral part of city planning' (Chatterji 2000), the 'right to space' sits somewhat un-comfortably with the concept of 'natural markets'. The latter suggests that vendors fill niche markets, unoccupied by other economic actors. This can not be the case at railway stations, bus terminals, etc., and the idea of natural markets thus appears to downplay the potential competition that vendors give shopkeepers, and the friction this causes. It also appears to infringe Supreme Court jurisprudence declaring that shopkeepers' livelihoods have a right to be protected against encroaching vendors (Supreme Court of India 1993).

## Regulatory Mechanisms and the Developmental State

The coalition's rhetoric about present regulatory mechanisms is highly critical and emphasises a general sense of crisis. Urban policies are considered anti-poor (SEWA 1998; Jhabvala 2000; NASVI 2005), city planning systematically excludes vendors (Singh 2000; Ministry of Urban Development and Poverty Alleviation and SEWA 2001; Bhowmik 2002; Singh 2002), whereas 'laws regulating trade and business, licensing policy for the self-employed, law and order, are all applied to the detriment of street vendors' (SEWA 1998: 3).[23] The Indian Penal Code and the Police Act are considered a baneful colonial legacy and source of harassment (Singh 2002), even for licensed vendors (Drafting Committee of the National Policy for Street Vendors 2002). The Police Act criminalises vendors (Chatterji 2000). Consequently, 'The negative use of the laws not only destabilises the livelihood of street vendors but also expose (sic) them to exploitative forces' (SEWA 1998; Jhabvala 2000; NASVI 2005). Moreover, sections of the law are applied divergently in different parts of the country (SEWA 1998; Jhabvala 2000; NASVI 2005).

The SEWA-coalition is hence, whilst acknowledging occasional exceptions, highly critical of police and municipal authorities.[24] The Self Employed Women's Association notes the 'widespread harassment of the vendors by the police and the municipal corporation staff. They were not only fined but had to pay daily bribes. Hitting and kicking vendors was common' (Chatterji 2000). The harassment 'stems from an absence of official recognition of the rights of street selling' (Singh 2000), despite Supreme Court jurisprudence specifically acknowledging vending as a fundamental right (Supreme Court of India 1989).

Highlighting the daily injustices that vendors suffer has important rhetorical value, and serves to underline the moral requirement of policy change. However, despite such critiques, the coalition's labour roots and suspicion of global capital continue to underpin its fundamental trust in, and cooperative approach towards the developmental state. Accordingly, the coalition demands *public* policy and state involvement regarding infrastructural facilities, health insurance, social security, disaster relief, finance/credit, and skill development packages (SEWA 1998; Jhabvala 2000; NASVI 2005). Indeed, the coalition considers a regulatory role for the private sector an anathema, and likely to produce undesirable results, such as exclusion of the poor from privately run shopping malls and cineplex halls. Self-regulation was seen as a more viable option, however, only as a complement to, rather than a substitute for state regulation. The success of self-regulation would thus depend on (state-issued) permission to vend (pers. comm., S. K. Bhowmik, Mumbai University, September 2005).

## Policy Instruments

The SEWA-coalition prefers a conservative choice of policy instruments to regulate street vendors, in terms of controlling access to space and the number of beneficiaries. However, it wants the government to apply these instruments in a more generous manner. Initial efforts of SEWA during the 1980s focused on allowing larger numbers of vendors to benefit from licenses (Chatterji 2000). The National Alliance of Street Vendors India also demanded more licenses (NASVI 1999; Singh 2000), noting that limited issue breeds corruption (Singh 2000). Increasingly also, the demand for more licenses was justified by pointing out its revenue generation potential for local governments (Singh 2000; Ministry of Urban Development and Poverty Alleviation and SEWA 2001; NASVI 2004b).

Simultaneous pleas were made for an alternative policy instrument: registration. Whilst registration cards do not bestow legal rights on holders, they establish worker status and make vendors visible, enabling inclusion in policy-making processes (SEWA 2005), deterring exploitative authorities and facilitating mobilisation (Singh 2000).[25] Already in 1984, SEWA had experimented with issuing identity cards to its members (SEWA 1998), whereas NASVI considers issuing licenses and identity cards as one of its objectives (SEWA 1998; Jhabvala 2000; NASVI 2005).

The demand for regularisation through licenses was often combined with demands for planned, demarcated zones for vending. Zoning was proposed in the Bellagio Declaration and in the report of the 1998 legal workshop (Anon. 1995; SEWA 1998; NASVI 1999), while fee-based, multiple user and time-specific[26] access to allocated zones was proposed jointly with strict eviction measures for vendors operating in no-hawking zones (Ministry of Urban Development and Poverty Alleviation and SEWA 2001; Verma 2005).[27] However, local governments often struggle to create zones. Municipal authorities in Mumbai, Delhi, Calcutta, and Bangalore have all tried only to face protests from hawkers as well as resident associations (Bhowmik 2000). For instance, in the Bombay Hawkers Unions vs. Bombay Municipal Corporation (1985, 3 SCC 528), the Court directed the defendant to develop schemes for hawking and no-hawking zones, but this process has not yet been completed (Shapiro Anjaria 2006).

The coalition, however, went a step further by aiming to quantify a minimum limit to the required urban space for street vending: 'guidelines should decide number of vendors required as a percentage of population and plan the number of vendors to be accommodated accordingly' (Ministry of Urban Development and Poverty Alleviation and SEWA 2001). A figure of 2–2.5 per cent of urban populations (roughly derived from the seven-city study) was thus proposed, implying a sharp rise in the number of street vending licenses issued in most cities. Quantifying entitlements deliberately aimed to prevent local authorities from accepting national policy in name but not in spirit (pers. comm., R. Jhabvala, national coordinator, SEWA, June 2006).

## Vendor Participation

Whilst during the 1990s the Government of India embraced participatory rhetoric, 'one finds an increasing trend towards dismissal of the demands of the people whose interests clash with concerns of the elite' (Arora 1999). The informal sector faced legal barriers to unionised participation in national policy forums. Most informal sector workers are not considered workers in the labour laws, and trade unions therefore do not organise them. Besides, participation in policy fora is restricted to unions that have a minimum membership of 500,000 (Jhabvala undated). However, informal sector workers increasingly organise parallel movements that demand welfare rather than worker-oriented rights from the state, as citizens rather than as workers (Agarwala 2006).

In respect of street vendors, the Bellagio Declaration urged governments to 'Set up appropriate, participative, non-formal mechanisms with representation by street vendors and hawkers, NGOs, local authorities, the police and others' (Anon. 1995). The coalition repeated this demand in domestic arenas (NASVI 1999; Singh 2000; Ministry of Urban Development and Poverty Alleviation and SEWA 2001), and envisaged a role for vendors in the design of hawking zones (Drafting Committee of the National Policy for Street Vendors 2002). The coalition, however, realised that besides reformed institutional arrangements, effective participation required vendors to 'learn to be effective participants in the planning process' and for this 'vendors' organisations will have to develop capacities to read urban development plans and understand future implications' (Chatterji 2000). Some, however, complained that SEWA cornered undue space and voice in the policy process, implying that participation meant 'participation with SEWA' (Verma 2005).

## From Advocacy to Policy: Retracing NSVP Values

The previous section already suggests that many of the beliefs of the SEWA coalition were enduring. Moreover, a comparison of NSVP content with preceding documents such as the parliamentary bill (1988), the Bellagio Declaration (1995), and workshop reports (1998, 2001) shows the considerable extent to which its beliefs were translated into policy.

The NSVP thus plainly acknowledges that the current regulatory climate threatens the livelihoods of a growing number of street vendors. It considers that under prevailing circumstances, at least 10 million vendors 'are considered as unlawful entities and are subjected to continuous harassment by Police and civic authorities'. This violates the constitutional duty of the Indian state 'to protect the right of this segment of population to earn their livelihood' (Government of India 2004b).[28]

The NSVP further presents street vending as a traditional Indian occupation that is beneficial to society, and thus entitled to a supportive and protective state. As a 'major poverty alleviation initiative', the 'over-arching objective' of the NSVP is hence to 'provide and promote a supportive environment for earning livelihoods to the street vendors, as well as ensure absence of congestion and maintenance of hygiene in public spaces and streets' (Government of India 2004b). Other policy objectives are listed as:

- Giving vendors legal status.[29]
- Moving from numerical limits to nominal fee-based regulation of access to public spaces.
- Including vendors in urban development plans.
- Promoting self-compliance amongst vendors.
- Promoting vendor organisations.
- Setting up participatory mechanisms for orderly conduct of vending activity.
- Rehabilitating child vendors.
- Promoting social security and access to credit for vendors.
- Providing facilities for clean and hygienic use of identified space.

It is therefore clear that many of the beliefs expressed in the NSVP can be traced back to the advocacy of the SEWA-led coalition (Table 12.2). Moreover, many of the beliefs concerned secondary beliefs, although policy core beliefs receiving prominence include claims that vending makes a positive socio-economic contribution to city life, should be entitled to access public space, requires state and some additional self-regulation, and that vendors deserve participation in decision-making fora.

Perhaps the most important discontinuity in the coalition's beliefs concerns the move away from demands for more licenses to replacing licenses with a registration and identity card system. Whilst not yet considered in May 2001, it was offered as a major solution by the NSVP Drafting Committee in February 2002. This was a clear case of policy learning, following the promotion of registration in Vajpayee's policy note in August 2001.

## Negotiating New Challenges to the NSVP

The street vending policy subsystem was nascent, and hence unprecedented and unexplored policy territory for central government policy makers. The NSVP entailed an expansion of the Ministry of Urban Development's mandate, previously being the sole responsibility of state and municipal governments. Helping to establish the new mandate ensured that the SEWA coalition had a first mover advantage, creating favourable conditions for policy learning in the MoUD. Its novelty meant that competing coalitions were not yet entrenched, but were now given an incentive to play catch up at the national level.

The NSVP accordingly constituted an external event, and challenged the power of the multitude of actors engaged in localised street vending policies: 'All State governments should ensure that institutional arrangements, legislative frameworks and other necessary actions achieve conformity with the National Policy for Street Vendors' (Government of India 2004b). Accordingly, much contestation about the NSVP deferred to local (implementation) arenas. One of the immediate battlegrounds concerned a set of newly created regulatory institutions.[30] Although devised to ensure vendor participation, the new bodies were soon captured[31] by rent-seeking groups inimical to vendor interests, and the coalition's subsequent efforts to redesign its blueprint for the institutions failed.[32]

The NSVP was soon also challenged at the national level, by external events and influences from other policy subsystems. Three months after the NSVP announcement, a general election unexpectedly replaced the

**Table 12.2**

**Incorporating Beliefs of the SEWA-Coalition in the NSVP 2004**

| Belief about Street Vending (Policy) | Belief Type | Parliamentary Bill 1988 | Bellagio Declaration 1995 | 2001 Workshop | NSVP Drafting Committee 2002 | NSVP 2004 |
|---|---|---|---|---|---|---|
| Makes positive socio-economic contribution | * | ✓ | ✓ | ✓ | ✓ | ✓ |
| Is traditional occupation | ◄ | – | – | ✓ | – | ✓ |
| Livelihoods need protection | ◄ | ✓ | ✓ | ✓ | ✓ | ✓ |
| Number is growing | ◄ | ✓ | ✓ | ✓ | ✓ | ✓ |
| Women are important contributors | ◄,* | ✓ | ✓ | ✓ | ✓ | ✓ |
| Needs legal status and access to space | ◄ | ✓ | ✓ | ✓ | ✓ | ✓ |
| Needs more licenses | ◄ | – | – | – | – | – |
| Needs replacing licenses with registration | ◄ | – | – | – | ✓ | ✓ |
| Needs inclusion in urban plans | ◄,* | ✓ | – | ✓ | ✓ | ✓ |
| Requires space for a fixed % of urban populations | ◄ | – | – | – | ✓ | ✓ |
| Needs urban zoning | ◄ | ✓ | ✓ | ✓ | ✓ | ✓ |
| Needs move from numerical limits to fee-based access to space | ◄ | – | – | – | – | – |
| Suffers harassment from the state | ◄ | ✓ | ✓ | ✓ | ✓ | ✓ |
| Requires self-governance | * | – | ✓ | ✓ | ✓ | ✓ |
| Needs maintaining hygiene | ◄ | – | ✓ | ✓ | – | ✓ |
| Needs to prevent traffic obstruction | ◄ | – | – | – | ✓ | ✓ |
| Needs participative decision-making fora | * | – | ✓ | ✓ | ✓ | ✓ |
| Needs state infrastructural support | ◄ | – | ✓ | ✓ | ✓ | ✓ |
| Needs access to finance, credit | ◄ | – | ✓ | ✓ | ✓ | ✓ |
| Needs relief, rehabilitation measures | ◄ | – | ✓ | ✓ | ✓ | ✓ |
| Needs social security | ◄ | – | – | ✓ | ✓ | – |

◄ = Secondary belief; * = Policy core belief; ✓ = Expressed; – = Non-expressed

*Source:* Compiled by the author.

existing NDA (National Democratic Alliance) government, in its wake transferring an array of civil servants, such as coalition member K. R. Mohan. Moreover, the incoming United Progressive Alliance (UPA) government's commitment to the NSVP and other emerging social security initiatives for the informal sector was uncertain.

Recognising the threat, NASVI and SEWA soon lobbied the new government, to find the new minister, Kumari Shelja, and secretary of the bifurcated Ministry of Urban Employment & Poverty Alleviation expressing a level of support for the NSVP. The UPA's governing manifesto, the Common Minimum Programme (CMP), also aimed to 'ensure the welfare and well-being of all workers, particularly those in the unorganized sector. . . . Social security, health insurance and other schemes . . . will be expanded' (Government of India 2004a: 18).

In order to monitor progress towards the CMP, the government set up the National Advisory Council. Moreover, a National Commission on Enterprises in the Unorganised/Informal Sector (NCEUS) was founded to examine the economic challenges facing informal sector enterprises. This Commission reviewed and predominantly endorsed the NSVP (NCEUS 2006).[33]

However, a more substantial challenge to the legal status of the NSVP emerged when the MoUD explored creating a bill protecting street vendors. Minister of State Ajay Maken considered that in the wake of widespread resentment against forced demolitions, carried out by the Municipal Corporation of Delhi in early 2006 following Supreme Court orders, new legislation could capture the vote of street vendors.[34] The MoUD was, however, stopped in its tracks because the Ministry of Law opined that the central government could not legislate on street vending, being a constitutionally reserved responsibility of state governments (Ministry of Housing and Urban Poverty Alleviation 2006). This advice also affected the legal status of the NSVP from (binding) directive to guideline for local governments (pers. comm., S. C. Sharma, director, MoUD, May 2006).

Whilst the fact that the NSVP was reviewed within a year of its inception, and the legal-technical spanner in the wheels of legislation suggest the workings of powerful opponents, this study could not find evidence confirming that this was the case. The NSVP review was probably not instigated by detractors, as it endorsed the policy, and consultations only took place with Manushi, SEWA and NASVI (NCEUS 2006).

Moreover, the NCEUS was charged with preparing two bills with important implications for street vendors. The Unorganised Sector Workers Social Security Bill (NCEUS 2005a), prepared by the National Advisory

Council, aimed to provide informal sector workers (including vendors) with a minimum social security package comprising (a) health insurance, (b) maternity benefits, (c) life insurance, and (d) old-age pension. The Unorganised Sector Workers (Conditions of Work and Livelihood Promotion) Bill (2005) addressed labour conditions, and protection for the self-employed and their right to livelihood. It promoted (NCEUS 2005b):

- The right to share public space to engage in economic activities (iii b).
- That city and rural development plans pay adequate regard to the concerns of self-employed workers such as street vendors, and protection and promotion of their livelihood (iv).
- Associations of self-employed workers.

The close alignment of first, these objectives, and second, NCEUS recommendations for the NSVP with SEWA-coalition objectives is not coincidental.

The creation of new decision-making loci such as the NCEUS is a recurring feature of the Indian polity. It enables the accommodation of newly influential stakeholders, outflanking institutionally anchored power bases, but also creates complexity, superfluity and overlapping mandates. The coalition is well-prepared to adjust to such changing institutional environments. Its strategic presence in multiple decision-making venues ensures continuity of advocacy efforts. Accordingly, SEWA representatives had good inroads to the NCEUS. Dr K. N. Kannan, one of its two permanent members and chief architect of the bills, also sat on a task force in Madhya Pradesh that was chaired by Renana Jhabvala. Their close cooperation towards drafting social security legislation for the unorganised sector in Madhya Pradesh preceded and facilitated further communications in the NCEUS. Jhabvala also had good links with Jairam Ramesh, a Congress MP and member of the National Advisory Council, who drafted the Unorganised Sector Workers Social Security Bill (pers. comm., R. Jhabvala, national coordinator, SEWA, June 2006). The Self Employed Women's Association's expertise and collaborative reputation thus facilitates strategic venue shopping to consolidate already gained benefits, the NSVP, and other policy accommodating its beliefs.

## Conclusion

The urban informal and street vending sector saw tremendous expansion during the 1990s, fuelled by urbanisation, rural–urban migration, reform policies, and economic restructuring processes. In its wake, new policy arenas were established at the national level, shifting decision-making away from urban local authorities, and providing opportunities for progressive policies.

The case study of the National Urban Street Vendors Policy (2004) highlights how such shifts occurred, and demonstrates the relevance of an Advocacy Coalition Framework analysis for understanding the Indian policy process. The group of state and non-state actors with SEWA at its hub demonstrated the essential characteristics of advocacy coalitions: close coordination of effort, and a shared set of normative beliefs.

Coalition membership was more enduring for non-state than for state actors. Inclusion of the latter was essential, yet rather mercurial. External events, such as a general election, were of great import as these could instantiate the transfer of coalition members such as senior bureaucrats, or ministers, whose personal interest in policy change was crucial. Accordingly, support in the Ministry of Urban Development for street vendor policy change oscillated. To compensate for uncertainty in institutional environments, the coalition demonstrated substantial venue-shopping ability, and its presence in multiple decision-making venues ensured continuity of advocacy.

The study also demonstrates the virtue of a cognitive analytical approach to policy change in India. Indeed, a focus on the SEWA-coalition's beliefs, ideas and policy preferences over time accounts for much of the NSVP content. As the coalition effectively established a new policy subsystem, it benefited from a first-mover advantage, to achieve a substantial amount of policy learning in the MoUD.

However, new policy subsystems soon stabilise, becoming less amenable to change. Accordingly, when the coalition realised that its street vending institutions needed redesigning, it failed to make the necessary adjustments. Consequently, these new institutions present a formidable challenge to the achievement of many of the coalition's objectives, and may lead the coalition back to local policy-making arenas. After all, local policy decisions continue to have the most significant implications for the livelihoods of Indian street vendors.

## Notes

1. This research employed a qualitative content analysis of key policy documents on street vending, supported by 20 key informant interviews and an additional literature review. Using Nvivo 2.0 (qualitative data analysis software), text fragments of published and unpublished policy and stakeholder documents were iteratively coded for beliefs and topical items until no new categories or analytical 'nodes', i.e., coded topics arose. A total of 12 passages were coded

302 ⊹ Dolf J.H. te Lintelo

concerning normative core beliefs, 107 passages regarding policy core beliefs and 197 passages concerning secondary beliefs. Analytical searches were performed using keywords, actors and/or combinations of nodes to identify the dimensions and parameter states of policy conflict.

2. It is not assumed here that the state functions in full accordance with such formal structures. Political economy analyses lucidly point out that Indian public administration faces a tough challenge in rent-seeking bureaucrats increasingly subject to the whims of politicians (Banik 2001; Bardhan 2005), the criminalisation of politics, and its influence on law enforcement (Jenkins 1999; Bardhan 2005). Keeping these constraints in mind, analytical room for manoeuvre yet remains to understand the role of cognition and beliefs in policy-making arenas.

3. A recent typology of coalition resources includes: formal legal authority to make policy decisions; public opinion; information; mobilisable troops; financial resources and skilful leadership (Sabatier and Weible 2007).

4. Processes within a policy subsystem are also affected by relatively stable parameters; opportunity structures, and actor constraints/resources (Figure 12.1). Stable system parameters like the electoral democracy and the Constitution of India guarantee street vendors certain civil and political rights, whereas the scarcity and consequent contestation over a limited amount of urban space was also considered a given, and accordingly not subject to coalitions' advocacy. Coalition opportunity structures refer to structural features of a polity, such as the degree of consensus needed for major policy change and the openness of the political system. A higher degree of consensus incentivises coalitions to be inclusive, to seek compromise and to share information with opponents. The openness of the system refers to the number and accessibility of decision-making venues that a policy proposal needs to go through.

5. In 1995, SEWA founded the National Centre for Labour, the first Indian labour federation of unorganised sector workers (SEWA 1998).

6. For instance, Bhatt became member of the Global Commission on the Urban Future (Chatterji 2000), and the exclusive group of Elders, whose other members include Nobel Peace Prize winners Nelson Mandela, Desmond Tutu, Jimmy Carter, Kofi Annan, Aung San Suu Kyi, and Mohamed Yunus.

7. The Bellagio Declaration also raised several new policy objectives, e.g., (a) self-governance, (b) participative mechanisms for vendor representation, (c) access to credit and financial services, and other welfarist objectives relating to relief in case of disasters and rehabilitation for child/disabled vendors.

8. By 2004, NASVI represented 132 local street vendor organisations (NASVI 2004b).

9. Jaisingh won the 1983 Manek Chowk case in the Supreme Court on SEWA's behalf, free of charge (Chatterji 2000). She also successfully fought the famous Olga Tellis (1985, 3 SCC 545) and Bombay Hawkers' Union cases against the Bombay Municipal Corporation (1985, 3 SCC 525).

10. In the following years, research studies remained an important strategy for SEWA. Joint studies with, e.g., the National Council of Applied Economic Research and the Gujarat Institute of Development Research 'have helped to build a better understanding of the enormous economic contribution' of the informal sector 'and its growing size and importance. It has also led to visibility of the workers and recognition of how economically active they are' (SEWA 2005).

11. This bill was approved by the group of ministers in early 2004, but not passed by the cabinet before the elections in May (Jhabvala 2005).

12. The MoUD was later bifurcated, with the NSVP shifting to the new Ministry of Urban Employment and Poverty Alleviation, which was once more renamed in 2006 as Ministry of Housing and Urban Poverty Alleviation. In order not to confuse the reader, this chapter refers to the MoUD only.

13. Land in Delhi is administered by the central government. In other metropoles, such as Kolkata, state governments control land (Dembowski 2001).

14. Jagmohan had previously, as head of the Delhi Development Authority during the 'Emergency' (1975–77) been in charge of slum clearance and resettlement of 700,000 people in Delhi, and mass-scale forced sterilisation of the affected (Tarlo 2001).

15. However, analysis of the struggle to implement street vendor policy at a market in Delhi gave strong evidence of local politicians' and traders' animosity towards vendors, and MoUD bureaucrats doing their bidding (te Lintelo 2008).

16. The chairperson was the director of HUDCO (a publicly owned social housing and urban infrastructure enterprise), with other members including an assistant commissioner of police of Delhi, a joint director of the National Capital Region Planning Board and a director in the MoUD.

17. Coalition coordination continued following announcement of the NSVP, for instance, by sharing administrative duties in running the national and international alliances of street vendors. By 2004, members of the executive committee of NASVI included Bhowmik, as well as SEWA's national co-ordinator and vice-president. The latter also headed NASVI's membership committee. Moreover, at the World Social Forum in Mumbai in 2004, StreetNet organised an international congress which elected executive members, including Arbind Singh, in an election chaired by Bhowmik (NASVI 2004a).

18. However, the policy received little media coverage (pers. comm., A. Singh, national coordinator, NASVI, May 2006), was issued too late and the elections were lost.

19. In the case of street vending, as in other policy domains (Sabatier 1993), normative core beliefs are relatively difficult to detect, and most discussion focuses on a set of policy core and secondary beliefs.

20. One literature review notes that vending is perceived amongst other activities as a nuisance to street traffic and the environment, a danger to public health

and safety, not befitting a modern city, and a challenge to public order (Pratt 2002).

21. The normative core beliefs of SEWA reflected the Gandhian 'principles of *satya* (truth), *ahimsa* (non-violence), *sarvadharma* (integrating all faiths, all people) and *khadi* (propagation of local employment and self-reliance)' (SEWA 2005).

22. The coalition does not advance the structuralist argument that pressures are the inevitable result of capitalist development (Chen 2004). However, some fieldwork observations in Delhi suggest linkages between vending and the formal economy. For instance, roadside trolleys vending soft drinks are increasingly based on commission-based wages, where distributors of global brands like Coca Cola and Pepsi arrange licenses. Similarly, vendors selling 'seasonal' items like belts or hankies in busy consumer markets such as Lajpat Nagar Central Market appear to operate as a flexible retail force for local manufacturers.

23. Verma criticises the NSVP policy dialogue for ignoring statutory provisions for vendors in Delhi's Master Plan, which could have served as an example (Verma 2005).

24. Whilst individuals may be helpful, there is a systemic bias against vendors (Chatterji 2000).

25. Identity cards for informal sector cigarette rollers and construction workers assert membership of the working class, and legitimise demands on the state as worthy citizens (Agarwala 2006).

26. Actual timings remain open to contestation. The National Alliance of Street Vendors India, for instance, argued that for Mumbai, vending times from 7 a.m. to 10 p.m. were 'highly unreasonable' (NASVI 2005: 9).

27. By August 2001, Vajpayee's policy note also proposed setting up three types of urban zones in Delhi, in which vending would be allowed to a different extent (Vittal 2002).

28. Article 39 A of the Constitution of India sets out a citizen's right to livelihood and 39 B instructs that 'the ownership and control of the material resources of the community are so distributed as best to sub serve the common good' (Government of India 2004b).

29. The NSVP advocates amendment of the Indian Penal Code sections 283 and 431 and the Police Act section 34 (all re: causing obstruction of public way and line of navigation) by inserting a clause to exclude their applicability to street vendors. Moreover, it suggests replacing forced evictions with relocation and rehabilitation policies.

30. Town Vending Committees, with members including resident welfare/market/trader/slum associations, (local and traffic) police, the municipal authority, the land owning authority, banks and street vendors, would decide who would be allowed to vend in which zones. Approximately 25–40 per cent of the members would represent vendors from membership-based and financially accountable organisations. In addition, Ward Vending Committees

would decide on local vending conditions, register vendors, and carry out enforcement. It would be composed of representatives of hawkers, planners, police, local councillors, resident welfare associations, traders associations, and municipal functionaries.

31. Consequently, squabbling about the composition of committees effectuated deadlock. For instance, by 2006, few of Delhi's Ward Vending Committees were set up and none were running effectively (pers. comm., S. Kumar, head of licensing, MCD South Zone, July 2006). Many were found to be 'full of people that are . . . exploiters of vendors, not vendors themselves' (pers. comm., R. Jhabvala, national coordinator, SEWA, July 2006).

32. Recommendations by the NCEUS (NCEUS 2006), and a joint Action Plan for Delhi devised by SEWA and Manushi (Manushi 2006: 11–12) aimed, but failed to remove municipal councillors and representatives of trader and resident welfare associations from Vending Committees.

33. The review in all likelihood assessed the NSVP's compatibility with the Common Minimum Programme.

34. In March 2006, the MoUD notified an amendment to land use regulations in the Master Plan of Delhi 2001, and subsequently designed and rapidly steered through Parliament the Delhi Laws (Special Provisions) Act, in May 2006. This act froze MCD enforcement action and gave the government a year to devise more lenient land use regulations in the already drafted new Master Plan of Delhi 2021 and to redesign municipal street vending policy in accordance with the NSVP (Government of India 2006).

## Bibliography

Agarwala, R. 2006. 'From Work to Welfare: A New Class Movement in India', *Critical Asian Studies*, 38(4): 419–44.

Anon. 1995. *The Bellagio International Declaration of Street Vendors*, 25 November, Bellagio, Italy.

Arora, D. 1999. 'Policy Process in India: Patterns and Problems', in N. Bava (ed.), *Development Policies and Administration in India*, pp. 92–102, New Delhi: Uppal Publishing House.

Banik, D. 2001. 'The Transfer Raj: Indian Civil Servants on the Move', *European Journal of Development Research*, 13(1): 106–34.

Bardhan, P. 1984. *The Political Economy of Development in India*, Oxford: Basil Blackwell.

———. 2005. *Scarcity, Conflicts, and Cooperation: Essays in the Political and Institutional Economics of Development*, Cambridge: Massachusets Institute of Technology.

Baviskar, A. 2003. 'Between Violence and Desire: Space, Power and Identity in the Making of Metropolitan Delhi', *International Social Science Journal*, 55: 89–98.

Bhowmik, S. K. 2000. 'A Raw Deal?' *Seminar*, 491, July.

Bhowmik, S. K. 2002. *Hawkers and the Urban Informal Sector—A Study of Street Vending in Seven Cities*, May 2002, Mumbai: NASVI.

British Council India. 2007. 'Delhi Government Strives to Discourage Begging', *Legal eNews*, 28, 11 February.

Centre for Civil Society. 2005. *The Centre for Civil Society's Suggestions for the Unorganised Sector Workers' Bill 2004*, New Delhi.

Chatterjee, P. 2004. *The Politics of the Governed—Reflections on Popular Politics in Most of the World*, New York: Columbia University Press.

Chatterji, M. 2000. 'Interview with Ela R. Bhatt', *Seminar*, 491, July.

Chen, M. A. 2004. *Rethinking the Informal Economy: Linkages with the Formal Economy and the Formal Regulatory Environment*, EGDI and UNU-WIDER conference: Unlocking the Human Potential: Linking the Informal and the Formal Sectors, Helsinki (17–18 September).

Corbridge, S., G. Williams, M. Srivastava and R. Veron. 2005. *Seeing the State—Governance and Governmentality in India*, Cambridge: Cambridge University Press.

Dembowski, H. 2001. *Taking the State to Court—Public Interest Litigation and the Public Sphere in Metropolitan India*, Oxford: Oxford University Press.

Drafting Committee of the National Policy for Street Vendors. 2002. Minutes of the 2nd Meeting of the Drafting Committee of the National Policy for Street Vendors, 4 May, New Delhi: 5 pages.

Fernandes, L. 2004. 'The Politics of Forgetting: Class Politics, State Power and the Restructuring of Urban Space in India', *Urban Studies*, 41(12): 2415–430.

Friedrich Ebert Stiftung. 1998. *Street Vendors Organising Strategies*, December, Patna, Friedrich Ebert Stiftung (research by NIDAN): 44 pages.

Government of India. 2004a. *National Common Minimum Programme of the Government of India*, May, New Delhi: 24 pages.

———. 2004b. *National Policy for Urban Street Vendors*, January, New Delhi: Ministry of Urban Employment and Poverty Alleviation.

———. 2006. *The Delhi Laws (Special Provisions) Act, 2006*, 19 May, New Delhi.

Harriss-White, B. 2003. *India Working—Essays on Society and Economy*, New Delhi: Cambridge University Press.

Jenkins, R. 1999. *Democratic Politics and Economic Reform in India*, Cambridge: Cambridge University Press.

———. 2004. 'Labor Policy and the Second Generation of Economic Reforms in India', *India Review, special issue on the politics of India's next generation of economic reforms* 3(4): 333–63.

Jha, L. K. 2001. 'Jagmohan to Clean up North, South Block', *The Hindu*, 6 August.

Jhabvala, R. 2000. 'Roles and Perceptions', *Seminar*, 491, July.

———. 2005. 'Unorganised Workers Bill, In Aid of the Informal Worker', *Economic and Political Weekly*, 40(22) (28 May–4 June): 2227–231.

Jhabvala, R. undated., *Excluding the Majority: Workers, Producers and Categories of Employment*, Ahmedabad, SEWA: 8 pages, available at www.sewa.org.

Jhabvala, R. and S. Sinha. 2002. 'Liberalisation and the Woman Worker', *Economic and Political Weekly*, 37(21) (25–31 May): 2037–44.

John, J. 1998. 'Hawkers and Vendors', *Labour File*, A4 (11), November–December.

John, P. 1998. *Analysing Public Policy*, London: Pinter.

Kaviraj, S. 1997. 'Filth and the Public Sphere: Concepts and Practices about Space in Calcutta', *Public Culture*, 10(1): 83–113.

Kohli, A. 1987. *The State and Poverty in India. The Politics of Reform*, Cambridge: Cambridge University Press.

———. 2007. 'State, Business, and Economic Growth in India', *Studies in Comparative International Development*, 42(1–2, June): 87–114.

Krishnamoorthy, S. 1998. '"Do Tokri Ki Jagah", the Resolution Moved in Parliament by Ela Bhatt', *Labour File* (November 1998): 33–36.

Manushi. 2001. 'In Danger of Sabotage—Historic Intervention by the Prime Minister', *Manushi*, 125, July–August): 11–14.

———. 2005. 'A Rare Gesture by the Government', *Manushi* (135): 10–13.

———. 2006. 'Making our Cities World Class and People Friendly', *Manushi*, 153 (March–April): 11–13.

McBeth, M. K., E. A. Shanahan, R. J. Arnell and P. L. Hathaway. 2007. 'The Intersection of Narrative Policy Analysis and Policy Change Theory', *Policy Studies Journal*, 35(1): 87–107.

Ministry of Housing and Urban Poverty Alleviation. 2006. 'Thrust Areas Identified by PMO Policy Paper on HUDCO's Future Strategy, New Delhi, Ministry of Housing and Urban Poverty Alleviation, Government of India, available on http://mhupa.gov.in/, accessed on 15 January 2007.

Ministry of Urban Development and Poverty Alleviation. 2001. Order (ministerial order), 21 June, New Delhi, Ministry of Urban Development and Poverty Alleviation, Government of India.

———.2003. Comments on Draft National Policy on Street Vendors prepared by the Task Force, ministerial letter, 21 February, New Delhi, Government of India.

Ministry of Urban Development and Poverty Alleviation and SEWA. 2001. National Guidelines on Street Vendors and Hawkers, Report of the National Workshop on Street Vendors and Hawkers in India, 29/30 May 2001, New Delhi, Ministry of Urban Development and Poverty Alleviation (GoI) and SEWA: 2 pages.

NASVI. 1999. 'Bangalore Declaration, Resolution of the National Alliance of Street Vendors India', NASVI resolution, 30/31 October, Patna.

———. 2004a. 'Government Adopts the National Policy for Street Vendors', *Footpath ki Aawaz* (April 2004).

———. 2004b. 'Street Vendors in Globalising World', *Footpath ki Aawaz* (April 2004).

NASVI. 2005. Interim application in Civil Appeal Nos. 4156-4157/2002, Maharashtra Ekta Hawkers Union & Anr vs. Municipal Corporation, Greater Mumbai & Ors, interim application in Supreme Court case of Maharashtra Ekta Hawkers Union & Anr vs. Municipal Corporation, Greater Mumbai & Ors: 18, available at http://www.nasvinet.org, accessed on 21 March 2006.

NCEUS (2005a). 'National Commission for Enterprises in the Unorganised Sector Prepares Two Draft Bills for Workers in the Unorganised Sector', Press note, 20 August.

———. 2005b. *Unorganised Sector Workers (Conditions of Work and Livelihoods Promotion) Bill*, New Delhi.

———. 2006. *National Policy on Urban Street Vendors—Report and Recommendations*, May, New Delhi.

National Commission on Self Employed Women and Women in the Informal Sector. 1988. *Shramshakti—Report of the National Commission on Self Employed Women and Women in the Informal Sector*, June, New Delhi: Government of India.

Our special correspondent. 2001. 'Jagmohan Yields to Pressure', *The Hindu*, 4 September.

Pratt, N. 2002. *Public Space as an Asset for Sustainable Livelihoods: A Literature Review*, 16 December, Cardiff, University of Birmingham: 21 pages.

Ramanathan, U. 1998. 'Changes in Labour Laws and Second NCL', *Labour File*, 1 (2), March–April.

Rudolph, L. I. and S. Rudolph-Hoeber. 1987. *In Pursuit of Lakshmi—The Political Economy of the Indian State*, Chicago: University of Chicago Press.

SEWA. 1998. National workshop on the legal status of street vendors in India, report on the workshop prepared by Prashant Ghulati, 26–27 September, Ahmedabad, SEWA: 34 pages.

———. 2005. 'SEWA Campaigns'. available at http://www.sewa.org/, accessed on 19 July.

SNCL. 2002. Report of the Second National Labour Commission, New Delhi, Second National Labour Commission, available at http://labour.nic.in/lcomm2/nlc_report.html, accessed on 22 February.

Sabatier, P. A. 1993. 'Policy Change Over a Decade or More, in P. A. Sabatier and H. C. Jenkins-Smith (eds), *Policy Change and Learning. An Advocacy Coalition Approach*, Boulder: Westview Press.

———. 1998. 'The Advocacy Coalition Framework: Revisions and Relevance for Europe', *Journal of European Public Policy*, 5(1), March: 98–130.

———. (ed.). 1999. *Theories of the Policy Process, Theoretical Lenses on Public Policy*, Boulder, Colorado: Westview Press.

———. (ed.). 2007. *Theories of the Policy Process*, Boulder, Colorado: Westview Press.

Sabatier, P. A. and H. C. Jenkins-Smith (eds). 1993. *Policy Change and Learning. An Advocacy Coalition Approach, Theoretical Lenses on Public Policy*, Boulder, Colorado: Westview Press.

Sabatier, P. A. and C. M. Weible. 2007. 'The Advocacy Coalition Framework: Innovations and Clarifications', in P. A. Sabatier (ed.), *Theories of the Policy Process*, pp. 189–220, Boulder, Colorado: Westview Press.

Second National Commission on Labour. 2002. *Report of the National Commission on Labour*, New Delhi: Government of India,

Shapiro Anjaria, J. 2006. 'Street Hawkers and Public Space in Mumbai', *Economic and Political Weekly* 41(21): 2140–146.

Singh, A. 2000. 'Organizing Street Vendors', *Seminar*, 491, July.

———. 2002. Cities for All—A Note on Globalisation and the Women Street Vendors, Paper Presented at Workshop on Globalization and its Impact on Women Workers in the Informal Eonomy Organised by SEWA Bharat, UNIFEM, Global Network Asia, 4 and 5 December, New Delhi.

Supreme Court of India. 1989. Sodan Singh and Others vs. NDMC and Others, 1989, 4 SCC 155, 30 August, New Delhi.

———. 1993. Gainda Ram and Others vs MCD Town Hall and Others, 1993, 3 SCC 178, 12 May, New Delhi, available at www.courtnic.gov.in, accessed on 10 October 2006.

Tarlo, E. 2001. 'Paper Truths: The Emergency and Slum Clearance through Forgotten Files', in C. J. Fuller and V. Benei, *The Everyday State and Society in Modern India*, pp. 68–90, London: Hurst & Co.

Task Force on Street Vendors. 2002. Minutes of the Second Meeting of the Task Force on Street Vendors held on 19 February, Ahmedabad: 4 pages.

te Lintelo, D. J. H. 2008. 'Beyond Interests? Advocacy Coalitions in the Indian Policy Process Regarding Food Safety and Informal Sector Retailing', unpublished Ph.D. thesis, School of Development Studies, University of East Anglia, Norwich.

———. 2009. 'The Spatial Politics of Food Hygiene: Regulating Small-scale Retail in Delhi', *European Journal of Development Research*, 21(1): 63–80.

Tribune News Service. 2001. 'Jagmohan Placated, to Assume Charge Today', *The Tribune*, 4 September.

Verma, G. D. 2005. 'Hawking Hawkers (chronicle), A Collection of Online Comments', from February 2002–2005, February 2002–January 2005, New Delhi, available at http://plan.architexturez.net/site/mpisg/c/020212/index_html/view?searchterm, accessed on 10 August.

Vittal, N. 2002. 'Impact of Infrastructure on Valuation', Address at the Valuers Association Seminar, Anna University on 22 January at Chennai, available at http://cvc.nic.in/vscvc/cvcspeeches/sp18jan02.pdf, accessed on 10 December 2006.

Voyce, M. 2007. 'Shopping Malls in India—New Social "Dividing Practices"', *Economic & Political Weekly* , 42(22): 2055–62.

Wyatt, A. 2005. 'Building the Temples of Postmodern India: Economic Constructions of National Identity', *Contemporary South Asia* 14(4): 465–80.

# About the Editor

**Sharit K. Bhowmik** is Professor of Labour Studies and Dean, School of Management and Labour Studies, Tata Institute of Social Sciences, Mumbai. Prior to this he was Head of the Department of Sociology, University of Mumbai. His numerous research interests include the sociology of plantation labour, the urban informal sector, industrial labour and trade unions, problems of caste and gender among workers, and worker co-operatives and industrial democracy. The author of several books and articles, his recent published works include 'India', *Work and Occupations* 36 (2), 2009: 126–44; 'Politics of Tea in the Dooars', *Economic and Political Weekly* 44 (9), 2009: 21; 'Coping with Poverty: Ex-textile Mill Workers in Central Mumbai' (co-authored with Nitin More), *Economic and Political Weekly* 36 (52), 2002: 4822–27; 'Trade Unions and Women Workers in Tea Plantations' (co-authored with Kanchan Sarkar), *Economic and Political Weekly* 33 (52), 1998: 50–52; *Tea Plantation Labour in India* (co-authored with V. Xaxa and M. A. Kalam, 1996).

# Notes on Contributors

**Jonathan Shapiro Anjaria** is Assistant Professor of Anthropology at Bard College, New York. His research interests include the politics of public space, the state and popular culture in India. His published works include 'The Mall and the Street: Practices of Public Consumption in Mumbai', in Daniel Cook (ed.) *Lived Experiences of Public Consumption: Encounters with Value in Marketplaces in Five Continents* (2008) (co-authored with Ulka Anjaria), 'Text, Genre, Society: Hindi Popular Film and Postcolonial Desire', *Journal of South Asian Popular Culture*, November 2008 and 'Guardians of the Bourgeois City: Citizenship, Public Space and Middle Class Activism in Mumbai', *City and Community* (forthcoming).

**Shreya Dalwadi** is an urban planner with a Masters in Urban and Regional Planning. Previously a lecturer at the School of Architecture, Arvind Patel Institute of Environmental Design, Vallabh Vidyanagar, Gujarat, she is currently working as urban planning consultant with 'Planning Solutions' in Vadodara. Her research interests are physical planning and planning economics.

**Luciana Itikawa** is an architect and urban planner. She received her PhD in Urban Planning from the University of Sao Paulo, Brazil. She has been a Visiting Scholar at the University of California, Los Angeles and Columbia University, New York, and is at present Visiting Scholar at the Centre for Labour Studies, University of Campinas-Sao Paulo, Brazil.

**Sanjay Kumar** is Co-ordinator, SEWA Bharat. He received a PhD from Jawaharlal Nehru University, Delhi and has researched the impact of micro-credit organisations on poor women in India and Bangladesh. His work includes unionising and training women workers engaged in informal employment.

**Kyoko Kusakabe** is Associate Professor of Gender and Development Studies, School of Environment, Resources and Development, Asian Institute of Technology. Her research interest is women workers in the informal economy and she is currently focusing on cross-border migrant workers in the context of regional economic integration and border area development. Her published works include (co-authored with Prak Sereyvath, Ubolratana Suntornratana and Napaporn Sriputinibondh), 'Gendering Border Spaces: Impact of Open Border Policy between Cambodia-Thailand on Small-scale Women Fish Traders', *African and Asian Studies*, Vol. 7, No. 1, 2008, and (co-authored with Zin Mar Oo) 'Relational places of Burman Women Migrants in the Borderland Town of Tachilek, Myanmar', *Singapore Journal of Tropical Geography*, Vol. 28, 2007: 300–13.

**Dolf J. H. te Lintelo** received his PhD from the School of International Development, University of East Anglia. His research interests include public policy and non-state regulatory processes of informality, food and environmental health. In 2008 he was awarded the EADI Prize for Excellence in Development Research by the European Association of Development Research & Training Institutes.

**Narumol Nirathron** is Associate Professor in the Labour and Welfare Development Department, Faculty of Social Administration, Thammasat University, Bangkok. Her research interests are labour development, labour welfare and informal labour. In 2005 she received an Outstanding Research Award from the Thailand Research Fund. Her article 'The Business of Food Street Vendors in Bangkok: An Analysis of Economic Performance and Success', was published in the *Canadian Journal of Development Studies*, Vol. 26, No. 3, 2005.

**Maria Fernanda Garcia Rincon** is a Visiting Researcher at Georgetown University and a Partnership Officer at the Inter-American Development Bank. Her research interests include informal institutions, political economy and street vendors as a vehicle for exploring state-society relationships, political participation (particularly the politics of public space) and social change. In 2007 she received the Harold Blakeman Prize from the Society for Latin American Studies for her essay 'Appropriation of Public Space: Politic's of Exchange and Market Transactions in Caracas, Venezuela'.

**Sally Roever** is a Visiting Researcher in the Department of Public Administration at Leiden University. Her research interests centre on the themes of global development, work and poverty, and law and informality. Her published works include 'Informal Governance and Organizational Success: The Effects of Non-Compliance among Lima's Street Vending Organizations', in Martha Chen, Renana Jhabvala, Ravi Kanbur, and Carol Richards (eds), *MBOP: Membership Based Organizations of the Poor* (2007) and 'Enforcement and Compliance in Lima's Street Markets: The Origins and Consequences of Policy Incoherence toward Informal Traders', in B. Guha-Khasnobis, R. Kanbur and E. Ostrom (eds), *Unlocking Human Potential: Concepts and Policies for Linking the Formal and Informal Sectors* (2006).

**Caroline Skinner** is a Research Fellow in the School of Development Studies, University of KwaZulu-Natal, Durban. Her work has interrogated the nature of the informal economy in South Africa with a focus on informing better policy responses. She has published widely on the subject and has been involved in policy and advocacy work at a local, provincial, national and international level. Much of her work has been done under the auspices of the global research-policy network Women in Informal Employment: Globalising and Organising (WIEGO).

# Index

For Product Safety Concerns and Information please contact our EU
representative GPSR@taylorandfrancis.com
Taylor & Francis Verlag GmbH, Kaufingerstraße 24, 80331 München, Germany